Strategic Leadership Development

Strategic Leadership Development
Building World-Class Performance

Colin Carnall
and
Chris Roebuck

macmillan education

First published 2015 by
PALGRAVE

Palgrave in the UK is an imprint of Macmillan Publishers Limited, registered in England, company number 785998, of 4 Crinan Street, London N1 9XW

Palgrave Macmillan in the US is a division of St Martin's Press LLC, 175 Fifth Avenue, New York, NY 10010.

Palgrave is a global imprint of the above companies and is represented throughout the world.

Palgrave® and Macmillan® are registered trademarks in the United States, the United Kingdom, Europe and other countries

ISBN 978–1–137–41500–4

This book is printed on paper suitable for recycling and made from fully managed and sustained forest sources. Logging, pulping and manufacturing processes are expected to conform to the environmental regulations of the country of origin.

A catalogue record for this book is available from the British Library.

A catalog record for this book is available from the Library of Congress.

Typeset by Cambrian Typesetters, Camberley, Surrey, England, UK.

Printed in China.

Contents

List of figures

List of tables

1 Strategic leadership: a key to organisational success

1.1 Aim of the book

This book is intended to be relevant to those who occupy – or aspire to occupy – senior leadership roles in organisations. The focus is on strategic leadership. Here the concern is to understand how leaders form judgements and come to decisions about the organisation as a whole. We argue that the deployment of 'strategic leadership' can make an essential contribution to organisational success, and we suggest that strategic leadership is a particular form of decision-making and action undertaken by senior leaders. Thus while strategic leadership requires that we have recruited and developed people with particular skill sets and knowledge appropriate to senior roles, it also requires the organisation to pay serious attention to how leaders work both as individuals and as a leadership cadre. We contend that what is needed to develop strategic leadership is in important ways distinct from leadership development at other levels of the organisation or earlier in the career cycle. In this book we aim to focus primarily on what is distinctive about strategic leadership and its development.

To provide readers, be they academics, students, leadership practitioners, chief executives or leaders at all levels, with an in-depth understanding of:

- Why leadership is critical to organisational success.
- What are the current ideas on leadership relating to the improvement of organisational performance, and how they have developed.
- What are the key principles of effective leadership in organisations?
- What is going on currently in organisational leadership in the real world?
- How can leadership deliver success at both the strategic and operational levels?
- How to make it happen in your organisation.
- How leadership is not only internal to organisations but also how organisational leadership impacts on the wider community both locally and globally.

Once this is in place we hope it will help those engaged as leaders to improve their own performance, as well as that of the people they lead, and their organisations overall. In the final analysis, leadership is as much about action – making things happen and transforming lives and organisations – as it is about thinking. Throughout the book we distinguish between strategic and personal leadership development. Personal leadership development focuses on the skills and behaviour of leaders as a means of understanding effective leadership viewed in relational terms. Here we seek to understand how leaders interact with people, whether subordinates, colleagues, clients or other stakeholders, and at the impact of the nature of those interactions.

Strategic leadership focuses on the decisions, judgements and actions of senior leaders and how they came to be formed. We do not claim these to be independent factors. Thus a leader who has poor relationships with colleagues may not be adequately informed and therefore make poor decisions. However, in our view, too much attention in leadership development literature and practice focuses on personal leadership development. The purpose of this book is to seek to address that imbalance.

The book examines leaders and the development of leadership in a changing world, and in organisations good leadership can facilitate the delivery of optimum performance from individuals, teams and the whole organisation. It presents a perspective based on nearly 70 years of the authors' combined experience of working with senior leaders and organisations in both the public and private sectors, together with substantial research evidence and a number of significant case studies. It examines the latest leadership concepts and their application to the everyday world, so that readers will be able to help themselves, their teams, colleagues or organisations to perform at their best. Throughout the book we refer to relevant research-based, conceptual and theoretical material, but at some points our experience as leadership development practitioners forms a substantial underpinning of our conclusions and argument. For the purposes of clarity, this point applies in particular to Chapters 4 and 10.

We know that, without effective leadership, the level of performance for teams, organisations and nations is well below what it could potentially be. There is sufficient evidence from both history and our own experience to tell us that effective strategic leadership increases the chances of success.

Below are a few examples of data that show effective leadership can have significant benefits for individuals, teams and organisations:

- Top-tier leadership development organisations outperform their peers in total shareholder return (TSR) by 9.6 per cent over a three-year period. This means that the average organisation (£2bn market value) increases market capitalisation by approx £200m due to development and talent (Corporate Leadership Council, 2003).
- Further, low leadership quality organisations lose about 5.8 per cent on TSR and about £110m on market capitalisation (Corporate Leadership Council, 2003).
- Top quartile performing companies have a higher focus on developing leadership than the bottom quartile (Corporate Leadership Council, 2004b).
- Eighty-five per cent of top 20 performing companies out of 273 hold their leaders accountable for developing talent (Deloitte, 2007).
- Good leadership and talent systems can enable organisations to perform 10 per cent to 20 per cent better than those without (Hewitt 2005/7).
- Approximately 11 per cent of staff in most organisations are highly engaged, while roughly 76 per cent 'just do the job', and 13 per cent have a negative impact on colleagues (Corporate Leadership Council, 2004b).
- The 76 per cent who 'just do the job' could give 30 per cent more discretionary effort if they wished (Corporate Leadership Council, 2004b).
- But a good line manager who inspires and develops people can increase an individual's potential by 43 per cent, ability by 36 per cent, engagement by 42 per cent and performance by at least 30 per cent (Corporate Leadership Council, 2004c).

Good line managers can also reduce the risk of loss of talent by 87 per cent (Corporate Leadership Council, 2004c). This is a very small selection of the large volume of data showing that good leadership delivers significant performance benefits for organisations. Given this volume of evidence, the obvious question is how can we develop the leaders we need for the future to make them as effective as possible. To achieve this we need to find a new balance between the behavioural analysis of individual leaders, looking at their immediate impact on their subordinates and the future impact on their organisation, both as individuals and as a leadership group.

1.2 Leadership: the glue that holds together people, teams and organisations

The idea and practice of leadership has fascinated and impacted on human beings perhaps since time began, and certainly since humans began to hunt, work and live in groups. Almost daily, the media run stories about current political or business leaders and how their decisions are good, bad or ineffective, and the impact this has on those they lead and on wider society. These media debates often mix considerations of policy, personality and presentation.

In an organisational context, most agree that, at the very least, leaders set the tone for their organisation and therefore questions about their leadership immediately raise broader questions about the organisation, and potentially the teams that they lead being a reflection of their leadership.

Many people are fascinated by leadership, mainly because it effects our lives every day in so many ways, and that in some ways it seems to defy analysis – it just 'happens'. For many who study or write about leadership there seems to be little agreement about how to identify people with the potential to become leaders, how to develop them, or what distinguishes successful from unsuccessful leaders. But those working in the field of leadership studies agree on one point, above all: that leadership has attracted, and continues to attract, considerable attention and seemingly limitless amounts of research.

Tens of thousands of books and articles have been published, some scholarly and based on research, many personal or anecdotal, supplemented with the biographies of those seen as leaders. Many articles and television programmes have been written or made about famous leaders, leadership failures and the day-to-day practicalities of the way that leaders work. Nevertheless, our understanding of what leadership is, and our ability to predict who might make a success of leadership is unclear at best.

Despite the fact that we don't really understand how it works, we know that it does have an effect – we see the results, good or bad, around us every day. Effective leadership is in high demand – when it works well it makes significant positive differences to outcomes, be they national, military or organisational. This interest has resulted in a 'burgeoning of academic programs in leadership studies' (Northouse, 2004). There are organisations that devote considerable resources to selecting, developing, testing and promoting leaders, be they military, commercial, public sector or charitable. For example, the UK and US armed forces fall into this category, expending vast amounts of time, money and other resources on developing leaders. They do this primarily because they recognise the need for success in their operations, but also the appalling potential consequences of poor leadership within military operations for those involved and the subsequent political and reputational damage.

Despite some evidence that the impact of the investment on leadership in commercial organisations is less than was predicted, and that the complexity of these efforts is high, it cannot be denied that there is considerable interest in leadership. Further, there is a willingness among some organisations to invest heavily in developing the performance of current leaders and secure a pipeline of potential leaders with which to build a sustainable future.

Historically, many studies of leadership have focused significantly on the character of the leader rather than seeking to understand the longer-term impact that the leader has on the organisation and others through his or her decisions. Few would deny the importance of questions of basic character. For example, there is a consistent assessment that 'integrity' is a critical quality in leaders, so understanding the character aspects of the individual are clearly important. But they do not provide the full picture. Subsequent to this 'traits' approach, the most commonly studied approach to leadership is within the 'contingency models', looking at the extent to which a leader balances 'concern for the task' with 'concern for the people'. This book suggests that while leaders do need to balance these there are also other balances to consider; for example, concern for the present and concern for the future, the balance within the team and the balance with the approaches of other leaders as a cohesive leadership team for the organisation.

Above all in this book we try to understand what works in leadership in the real world, why it works and how it can be made better. This is where leadership really matters. Theoretical leadership without the ability to apply it to the real world and make a practical difference to people and organisations conflicts with every principle of what leadership is about – taking effective action and making a difference. Leadership is not about debating academic arguments.

Much of the concern about leadership has been to understand how individuals operate as leaders, how they are developed and how they interact both with the people they lead and with other leaders in the organisation. One of the key issues is that some leaders undervalue 'human factors' and seem unable to understand their subordinates, or motivate them. They thus fail to get the best performance from them, potentially resulting in poor performance for the organisation. The question is why they do this, and how can we ensure that they, and future leaders, avoid this problem.

We need to find ways to ensure that leaders are able to manage people effectively to maximise performance. Further, on a higher level, we need to understand how the interactions between many individual leaders in an organisation create a culture and holistic entity that impacts positively on everyone involved. This becomes complicated further when organisations merge. How best to understand and deal with the 'cultural consequences' of pushing two possibly different approaches to leadership together is key. We know from much research that these factors are a significant reason why up to 80 per cent of mergers and acquisitions never deliver their predicted benefits. We must ensure that these 'people issues' are taken into account in mergers and integration, to ensure that value is created rather than lost for all stakeholders.

But all is not bad, we can find many examples of leaders doing the right things, even in the most challenging circumstances. We see this in many situations, which gives us further insight into effective leadership – from those serving in situations of great danger in the military, who do their job no matter what happens, to those individuals who are caught up in disasters of some kind who manage to galvanise strangers around them to act as a cohesive team to save lives, and those individuals such as the pilot who landed his airliner in the Hudson River in New York saving the lives of many (*New York Times*, 9 June 2011). He made his decisions in the toughest of conditions with little time, and got it right. So while looking at where leadership goes wrong there is also much to be gained by looking at where it goes right. If we can learn from both our capability to lead better and our ability to develop more and better leaders should improve.

One of the issues about the study of leadership is that it is generally fixed at a specific point in time, when the leadership 'action' occurs. That also means that the requirements of leadership that drive those actions are a reflection of the society or organisation within which that leadership is being implemented at that time.

Often, the study of a leadership 'action' in the past seems to be used to justify the assertion that if it worked, or didn't, then it must have the same effect now. This is not always the case. A similar mistake is often made by untrained individuals mentoring others, where they assume that one or two similarities in a situation they experienced in the past must, by some strange logic, make it exactly the same as the situation now being experienced by the person they are mentoring. But that was a different time, a different organisation, a different person leading, a different team being led, trying to deliver different objectives. Other than that, of course, it's exactly the same situation!

Modern historical scholarship is clear that history must be read forward. So we can only make real sense of the lessons of a past event by understanding the issues and challenges the leaders faced, and with the data available to them at that time. If we don't consider these we create our own problems by trying to understand leadership backwards, ascribing success or failure on the basis of outcomes or information known now but not known at the time by the leaders who made the decisions. This is counterproductive in the effective study of leadership.

While focus on the leader as an individual is important, this book has primarily been designed to address the wider issues relating to the operation of leadership within organisations in which a number of leaders work with individuals, with their teams, with other leaders and across the organisation. The impact of these individual leaders' decision-making on their subordinates, and the aggregation of the influences of all the leaders into the management of the organisation are examined. This will enhance our understanding of how to develop new leaders for both today and tomorrow. We shall try to understand the evidence base and assumptions on which leadership decisions are based, with evidence and ideas being examined from both a theoretical and a practical perspective.

1.3 Can leadership in organisations keep up with the changing world?

The problem here is that the modern world is characterised by tension, dislocation, difference and uncertainty. Whether or not you accept Ferguson's (2007) conclusion about the pivotal role racial differences played in the twentieth century it is true that conflict was endemic at the time and continues into the present. Most of the world's problems appear to be a mass of uncertainties and often the steps we take to resolve them are themselves the origins of subsequent unintended consequences' giving rise either to new problems or to pressures that make the problems we sought to solve worse rather than better. The concept of the 'ripples on a pond' effect applies – an action in one place causing effects elsewhere. So the 'solutions' implemented by one generation of leaders can often actually create problems for the next. For example, the division of the Middle East in the nineteenth century into nations where the borders did not consider the locations or movements of communities went on to become a problem in the early twentieth century and led to significant problems later in that century and into the twenty-first.

Technology, demography, globalisation and social change are also all leading to environmental changes, none of which are new. We are now in a world where activity is determined less by hierarchical relationships of power and control, whether these are feudal, or based on corporatist principles, and more where market-driven outcomes prevail. While the most developed version of this argument is deployed by Bobbitt (2002) in his concept of 'the market state', it is clear from Williamson's original approach (1983) that in both the private and the public sector there has been an accelerating tendency to rely on market solutions to deliver objectives and change.

The argument is that the rewards and punishments of the market create a dynamic for change arising from competitive pressure. This is hard to achieve within a hierarchical organisation not subject to such pressures unless a crisis threatens. Thus 'the market decides' becomes a mantra for many seeking to lead change. That in turn means that outcomes are determined by the millions of choices people make within the market, creating the dynamism we referred to above that encourages innovation via social movement. But it also removes many of the certainties created by the checks and balances of a more 'command and control' approach to the problem of how to organise for agriculture, commerce, education, health care or war, some of which are unlikely to operate effectively within a market. While the market does not dominate all aspects of human activity, market forces are relied on increasingly by politicians and business executives in certain cultures and regions, and there is a trend for this to continue. Despite the financial crisis of 2006–10, which put into sharp focus the negative effects of a free market and led to a subsequent increase in state control via regulation over the financial markets, the general trend towards market predominance is clear.

Thus the future for the organisation and its environment are both increasingly dynamic and uncertain. For Clark and Clegg (1998) this has led to 'a transformation of management knowledge'. For these authors, 'successful management in the future must be based on intelligence and creativity and the capacity to question and learn'. Moreover, there is a constant need to seek an appropriate balance between continually confronting uncertainty, paradox and trade-offs and the need for balance, direction and motivation. Put more simply, executives must learn how to combine continual change with the ability to sustain 'business as usual'.

What was a logical and acceptable course of action in the past might now be seen as illogical and unacceptable, bearing in mind present knowledge. An example of this is in leadership style, where there has been movement away from a command and control approach to a more consultative one over the past 50 years. Some leadership styles effective in the 1930s and accepted by people then would now be highly ineffective if not counterproductive, because of prevailing practices within society in the twenty-first century. So the decisions made by leaders in the 1930s on how to lead were the optimal solution then but might well not be valid or appropriate now.

In addition, it is critical for leaders to take a forward-looking perspective. Good leaders try to forecast events and then to influence them by their actions and decisions, so any analysis must also look to where they expect the world to be in the future as much as where it is currently. What one focuses on when thinking about the present may be very different from what is thought about when looking at the needs for an organisation in the future, particularly in a fast-changing world. While the people working in the organisation today may not welcome change, the decisions and choices leaders make now will often have significant consequences for the organisation in the longer term. The actions of today's leaders create the reality of the future – and its success or failure. Nothing stands still – change is a constant feature of life, as all leaders learn.

It is not difficult to find examples of once great companies that have failed this 'test' of expectation. In February 2006 an article in *Fortune* magazine analysed the position of the US automobile giant, General Motors (GM) (Loomis, 2006). Having once been a defining organisation for US-based global capitalism, and having been the major force in the US market for new cars, with 45 per cent of that market in the 1980s, by 2006 it only had 27 per cent and falling. With an under-performing automobile business and other substantial liabilities, the GM share price by December 2005 had fallen below US$19, the lowest level since 1982. This is a business challenged by customer expectations regarding product design and price. External factors such as the desire and economics of moving towards 'greener' energy use are also likely to speed this. When such dramatic examples are considered, some of the partial approaches above are unlikely to be effective in transforming a whole complex organisation at a critical point in time.

1.4 What is happening in organisations now?

At present, the behaviourist approach represents the majority view of leadership development within organisations. Huge investment has been made in developing competence models which sit at the core of the design of leadership activities, be they appraisal, selection or development. This is an indication of the view taken that leadership can be analysed, broken into components, and then those components interpreted so as to allow a common approach to leadership to be taken. Yet both authors of this book, who have between them over 70 years of experience in the field, are aware that one common critique of the competency approach, and in particular where it is used to develop leaders, is a perceived lack of relevance and transfer back to the real day-to-day activities of the organisation of those competency frameworks. In many cases these are viewed by those outside the HR function in organisations as being only partially relevant to the organisations' real needs.

In the case of learning and development, many programme designs seek to tackle this issue, often with success. Most commonly this is through an action learning project which looks at a current organisational issue. But in reality this often ceases to use the competency framework and instead uses action learning related to the real issues of the day.

One key purpose of this book is to enable the reader to understand that leadership and leadership development in not reliant on competence models alone, and that these models, which the HR profession seems sometimes to view as the answer, are in reality only a partial view. The limitation of the competence approach is that at best it is only a static model providing a description of competence strengths and gaps at a particular point in time and at a particular level, whereas the task of leadership is dynamic: to respond to events, to meet new challenges, and to create a new future for an organisation. In practice, many of these critical leadership activities are not covered by a competency approach. A proper understanding of leadership and leadership development must therefore go beyond understanding today's behavioural competencies into understanding how leaders think about those events and challenges, and build for the future. This ranges from the systematic approach to how they decide on ambitious plans requiring organisation changes before the can be executed, to the inspirational challenges of changing minds, their own and others, about what is achievable.

The competence approach can help potential and current leaders to understand their own strengths and weaknesses as leaders, based on the optimum outcomes when the framework was developed. But it is clear that these can become out of date as time passes, and the 'optimum' leadership approach will change with time, location and other factors. One consistent factor is the relationship between the leader and his/her subordinates. Survey after survey shows that the way that leaders relate to their subordinates is critical. But this is not the only factor. Currently concern for the leader's impact on people is in the foreground of our view of leadership development, and in some cases a counterpoint to concern for the task. But both must be considered to align the leader's impact on people with what is required to deliver the task effectively and maintain the team.

This presents challenges, as those within the development community focus on the development of individual leadership to help leaders relate better to their subordinates, but the senior management of organisations want leaders to get the job done and work as a team. Ultimately, any leader's ability to 'relate to their people' is clearly important. But this does not define their ability as a leader. For example, Prime Minister Winston Churchill's behaviour towards his political and military colleagues during the Second World War created tensions in his relationships with them. Had it been a normal environment some of these might have resigned. But these tensions were transcended by a belief in a higher cause that was common to all, namely winning the war. Thus even if the relationship between leaders and followers is not as good as it might be, provided a common goal is in place then the leader's style is not critical. But if people have no cause worth pursuing then relationships become everything and the style of the leader looms large.

Thus it is that looking at behaviour is to focus largely on the present or the past – be it actions of today or those of yesterday. Looking at the mind of the leader as he or she grapples with the future is to look beyond today – here the real challenges arise as this leads into dealing with uncertainty, complexity and change. But both are important for our understanding of leadership and its development in practice.

At the simplest level one can distinguish two general themes in the study of leadership. These overlap in some of the concepts and categories used at different points but each is distinctive in terms of its starting point and reasoning approaches. These are:

(i) **Personal leadership**

In which the focus is on the characteristics of individuals that led them to be identified as, and to become, leaders. These include their background, education, experiences and attitude. This also focuses on their impact on others, whether this is their team, their peers or other stakeholders. It is important to understand how they influence people, and how they are able to establish the conditions for 'followership'. The latter was expressed in a 2005 article in *Harvard Business Review* by Goffee and Jones, who argue that the answer to the question 'Why should anyone be led by you?' lies in the idea of 'authentic behaviour'. Authenticity is not a new idea. It is a historically represented theme from the distant past of human history – the Peer Gynt notion 'To thine own self be true'. This occurs often in legend, fable and within some of the medieval concepts of chivalry. Goffee and Jones suggest that the source of the impact leaders have on others lies deep within the leader themselves.

(ii) **Strategic leadership**

Here one needs to examine the decisions and choices leaders make on a wider impact level, and in particular those that senior leaders make that have the most impact on their organisation. This is also related to the operation of the individual leaders together as a 'leadership team' or structure that as a group implements, controls and monitors the delivery of organisational strategy. They need to make the right choices to deliver success, not only as individuals, but also as a group.

One of the key debates relates to whether leadership and management are different. Here Kotter (1990) argues that leadership is different from management; indeed, the military often structure their officer training into these components – the basics of effective management is put in place first, which then allows the 'space' for inspirational leadership to be delivered on top. The military works on the principle that effective management minimises fire-fighting, which distracts effort from delivering the objective.

In time terms, 'management' action is often focused on current plans and their delivery, and 'leadership' deals with change, adaptability and the future. Evidently these overlap with personal leadership. The characteristics considered under personal leadership are relevant to the question of whether a leader can inspire people in order to encourage the successful implementation of decisions. So what is the real difference? At root it is about the real time horizon of both management and leadership. Personal leadership helps us to understand how well a leader is doing now, while strategic leadership focuses more on the future. Irrespective of an ability to inspire others, only if the right decisions and choices are made will a leader have an impact on the future. The ability to inspire will, however, make the chances of delivering success greater.

But it is worth noting that, even at the strategic level, operational leadership occurs day to day. The chief executive officer (CEO) manages the other executive officers as an operational leader as well as working with them on corporate-wide strategic and leadership initiatives. Thus the CEO is a strategic leader to the organisation and an operational leader to the executive team. They therefore need the capability to carry out both roles well. This is where many CEOs are challenged – they can do one or the other, but doing both well is difficult.

1.5   Women and leadership in senior executive and board appointments

Following an extensive focus on the intersecting issues of leadership development, the make up of boards in relation to gender and other factors, not least race, it remains the case that board composition and performance, as the body responsible for providing strategic leadership, is now more under scrutiny and challenge than ever before. The role of the board has not changed fundamentally and remains focused on:

- Establishing vision, mission and values.
- Setting strategy and structure.
- Exercising accountability to shareholders and being responsible to relevant stakeholders.
- Delegating to management and monitoring performance.

However, the challenge in delivering this role has increased and continues to do so because of environmental changes that make for a more demanding, complex, diverse and sometimes contradictory set of expectations. These result from the diversity and changing nature of the stakeholders' demands and interests; for example, globalisation, capital structures, regulators, trade politics, consumer expectations/trends/fashions, scientific discovery, societal demand around ecology, health and wellbeing and so on.

This challenge is further compounded for boards because of the increasing demands for transparency regarding not only individual board members in terms of probity and so on, but also their ability to represent the totality of stakeholder requirements/issues effectively beyond merely satisfying 'the City'. However, there have been significant moves in term of process, including the use of external agents to aid in recruitment and selection decisions.

In spite of these moves creating boards that are 'fit for purpose' in dealing effectively with an increasingly diverse agenda and set of demands, remains a challenge as a result of the imbalance in the supply/demand for women in the boardroom. Diversity with regard to internationalisation has been addressed more successfully, with most international companies having a significant representation from the areas in which they trade. However, when it comes to gender, the trend seems to be moving in the wrong direction.

We have long known that few women are given board level appointments. However, in the developed world women have become key to facing up to the challenges of an ageing workforce, falling birth rates and skill shortages, including those on boards, and to all sorts of trends in consumption and society, so that they are are now also key to the supply side. In the European Union (EU) since 2000 women have filled 75 per cent of the 8 million new jobs, but one survey found that more than 50 per cent of companies registered in 2007 had no female director.

Yet the demands on leaders seem to play to the strengths of women, not least with regard to collaborative working, creativity and intuition (softer skills). This is particularly true on boards, where the members not only have to be working in a collaborative way to deliver this challenging and diverse agenda but also to be 'seen' to be doing so. Women represent more than half of the population of Britain and are a huge 'talent pool'. One study indicates that if the skills of the female population were fully harnessed the British economy would gain £23 billion each year! A study published by Saatchi & Saatchi in 2007 concluded that consumer electronics businesses missed out on £600 million of revenues in 2007 because they did not connect properly with female customers.

There is a growing body of opinion and increasingly available evidence to suggest that appointing women to senior executive and board positions is the right thing to do, for many reasons. Currently we also think that appointing the number of women needed to boards today would be a real challenge because of the shortage of women on the supply-side – that is, both willing and prepared.

We think there are strategies that might be adopted to enable more women to position themselves more effectively and to prepare themselves to play an effective role in senior appointments on a board. We also think that support can and should be made available to those who seek to take such a step in their career; and then in ensuring their success.

Our underlying premise is that this support and preparation should not be aimed only at the areas of knowledge, skills and experience, but also at the experiential level. This way we can reduce the risk to chairmen and CEOs as they make decisions to appoint women to their boards who have not previously worked at board level, but who have experienced through training what this entails in terms of behaviour, impact, motivation and risk as well as a knowledge and understanding of processes, procedures and regulatory requirements.

In recent years a number of networks have been established to offer support to help women to position and prepare themselves for both non-executive and executive board appointments. These networks include a number of women and men currently in prominent positions working in support of members and pursue activities with two key themes:

(i)   Through **networking** to foster the recruitment of women into board appointments.

(ii) To provide **development opportunities** and **mentoring** through which members work with others who have both made the transition to board appointments and who wish to make a positive contribution in this field.

Further, the networks typically arrange activities such as mentoring, learning workshops and behavioural simulations designed to provide support for individuals engaged in the transition to senior executive roles.

1.6   Strategic management and leadership: the missing element?

A review of most leadership literature will show that relatively little interest has been shown regarding how leaders think; for example, how they come to judge a strategy as being ambitious enough to create advantage but still be achievable. The discipline of strategic management covers the implementation and execution of strategy. The term 'strategic management' was intended to represent a departure from the idea of strategy as being basically about strategic choice and dominated by economics thinking, towards a view that it must combine both strategic choice and implementation. Since around the mid-1990s, little attention has been focused on how leaders think, how they view the world and how they judge what is achievable and make it happen. This is interesting for two reasons:

(i) Most observers of organisations being led through a period of dramatic change point to the need for a change in mind set. Jack Welch of General Electric (GE) was perhaps one of the most convincing exponents: 'Adopting the Schumpeterian notion of "creative destruction", breakthrough change demands new rules, quantum leaps and a radical approach to the balance between autonomy and control – emphasising relative autonomy within a "business engine" which demands performance' (Carnall, 2007). The well-known overarching rule Welch adopted sets the tone, 'Be number one or if you are number two in your sector your business will not stay in GE'. Behind the market leadership rule lay objectives for 'well above average real returns on investments, distinct competitive advantage, leverage of value from strengths'. But at the core is the willingness to create 'new rules of the competitive game' for GE (Carnall. 2007).

(ii) Many also argue that we live in times characterised by greater competition, change, complexity, ambiguity and challenge so we would expect to see a growing concern for how best to prepare senior leaders to make sense of that environment. In one sense this is evident in that we increasingly see arguments for creativity and 'out of the box thinking' as important elements in leadership development.

Effective strategic leadership requires the solution of ever more complex puzzles in relation to finding the answer, or as near an answer as possible, to the complex and fast-moving organisational world. With often incomplete knowledge available, leaders must learn to analyse the data they have from the past and apply that to the needs of the future. Leaders must not fall into the trap of merely offering the solutions of the past, working on the premise that because they worked then they will also work now.

Leaders also often rush to implement solutions too quickly, sometimes because they find the hard work of formulating the question properly as requiring disciplined effort and time when they feel action should be immediate – with inaction being seen as 'bad' leadership. To many, this is what leadership is about: finding instant answers to problems rather than there being the inevitable delay associated with working through problems, or even worse, public recognition that at any point in time some problems may not be resolvable. The challenges faced by leaders at the start of the financial crisis of 2006–10, where each day brought new and previously unheard-of corporate collapses or problems, which led to most leaders having no idea what the world would be like a week later.

Thus often an instant response seems to be required from leaders –from their own or from other perspectives. If a company faces problems, often trade unions and politicians will demand announcements overnight, to remove uncertainty for employees and others. Our culture demands rapid answers, of both political and corporate leaders.

But getting to the right answer requires that we understand the question, explore options and so on, and this takes time. In reality, strategic leadership is often about the 'long haul'. The work of behaviourally focused leadership trainers focuses more on this immediate impact and could explain why many leaders are so preoccupied with these approaches. They can offer immediate gains and this is seen as being important. But, for more senior leaders, leadership development work needs to look at the hard choices they must make – and these take time and careful consideration because of their complexity. Long-term sustainability is increasingly important as a factor that the market considers when looking at an organisation's value.

One of Winston Churchill's maxims of leadership in war was 'Improvise and dare' (Gilbert, 2005). His leadership was underpinned by his vision of ultimate victory in the series of speeches he made. However, it is more interesting to look at his methods of work. Famous for his 'Action this day' instructions, the other important point may be the extent to which he placed himself in command of the detail of Britain's war effort so that he could challenge colleagues.

To fully understand leadership development, we need to examine both behaviour and knowledge. Not the knowledge of academic disciplines, however, but rather knowledge to enable the practical process of helping leaders to develop more effective choices. Effective leadership behaviour is important, but also how leaders come to formulate plans and goals, the information they use, and the thinking underpinning their decisions become equally relevant to leadership development activity.

Some will argue that the discipline of strategy provides much of what is needed though its analytical models, but critical observers point out the frequent failure of 'strategy thinking' to address implementation and execution until recently in the commercial world. Within the military, however, where the importance of action arising out of strategy is critical, this has naturally been addressed. The consequences for the military in terms of loss of life should mistakes be made has driven this response.

1.7   Understanding strategic leadership: the holistic picture

To better understand leadership and leadership development we therefore need to approach this based on three sets of ideas:

(i)   Understanding leader behaviour and the impact of that behaviour on others.

(ii)   Understanding the means by which leaders go about changing their own minds and those of others.

(iii)   Understanding the nature of strategic ambition and risk as leaders view it.

Added to these needs to be a focus on the ways in which current and future leadership development practices work at the various levels of leadership within organisations through applying these three ideas to understanding the outcomes.

To enable this we need to establish a clear view of the leadership challenges posed by the need for adaptability, creativity and change. Leadership is not vital within static and simple environments, so management alone should suffice there. To understand leadership in other contexts we need to explore how leaders try to understand, and then attempt to deliver, success within the changing and often ambiguous environments in which they find themselves.

Interestingly, this is where the two 'core approaches' of leadership studies we examined earlier most often collide. While the decisions that leaders make have a profound and immediate influence on the organisations over which they preside, three to five years later the impact of the leaders' actions may actually be greater as a result of the additional impact from the fact that leaders lead learning and people take up their ideas. Thus over a period of time the spread and adoption of a leader's ideas grows if the ideas have resonance.

The leading, or as a minimum, the enabling, of learning is central to change management in the current era. But organisations are not run by one person, they are run by 'leadership teams' and it does not follow that every member of a leadership team needs to play a similar role. In fact, that would be a bad thing for the organisation. Some leaders must be good at strategic leadership, developing plans for the future, while others may be more charismatic and have more impact within the organisation at the present time. Thus we need to understand both the immediate impact of leadership and its impact in the future, and how both must be present. In that way we are able to identify those with the potential to lead, and develop them to take up leadership roles, thus enabling then to be effective in both key components of leadership.

We also need to understand more fully how leaders change people's minds, not only through authentic behaviour but also through productive reasoning – acting on both the rational and emotional needs of employees. Here it could be said that we come to a clash with much behavioural-science-based practice in the field of leadership. It is commonly held that one cannot change attitudes directly, but that one must first change behaviour, and if this leads to success the positive feedback that follows will lead to attitude change – the changing of the mind. This is a simplification of learning, which often requires that people adopt a new idea sufficiently well to be willing to test it out. This confirms that we are willing to experiment with new ideas, and the ideas above suggest that leaders must play a part in creating the organisational space to encourage new ideas to be developed and implemented sufficiently to test them out. But this also has to happen within the day-to-day reality of continuing to deliver the organisation's objectives as well so the culture and 'space' to experiment must be present. This is sadly rarely the case.

No book can provide definitive answers as to exactly how leadership works. The interactions are so complex, the environments within which leadership is practised and the individuals who practise it are so varied that we can only point towards what seems to be close to an answer and work in the real world. You will see that, throughout the book, in reality it is not possible to be definitive but there are indicators of what works. For example, the exact balance between personal or operational and strategic leadership required at a given point in time does not matter so long as we enable leaders in organisations to have the capability to deliver both when they are required to make things happen. Also distinguishing between the roles, skills and capabilities of particular leaders within a leadership team is important as the team must be viewed as a whole – indeed, this is vital as it is often watched closely by those in the organisation as a whole and it should ideally act as a whole. Thus a group of individual leaders with different capabilities must, as well as acting as individuals, also act as a co-ordinated and integrated team.

The importance of interactions between leaders, other leaders and subordinates is clear in relation to the impact of the emotional element of decision-making and commitment. This allows us to recognise and work with the contribution that psychologists and social psychologists make working with leadership issues while also bringing in the rational elements of the business model, doctrine, strategy and ambition of the organisation into our analysis. This allows us to analyse the practice of leadership and its development within the real world of the organisation and its journey in a holistic way rather than being limited to the views taken by specific area of different disciplines.

The importance of the benefits of collaborative action between leaders versus the individualistic approach of the individual leader operating alone is clear. We know that achieving objectives is better delivered via the collaborative work of many rather than the solitary efforts a the few at the top of organisations.

1.8   Changing minds is key to effective strategy delivery and success

To justify significant change, leaders need to construct and articulate a compelling vision of the future, 'strategic ambition'. How can leaders make the vision compelling? How can it be made to 'resonate' for others? How can it be seen as realistic and achievable? Such a compelling vision needs to be presented together with a road map to achieve it. What changes are to be made during this journey? Are they achievable? Can new resources and capabilities be found? Can we be confident of success? Ambition without some credible means of achievement is unlikely to build the confidence required to even start the process let alone deliver success from employees.

So leadership is essentially a process of decision-making and performance management through delivery deployed over long periods of time, focusing on creating change and achieving challenging targets. Within this, 'concern for people' is important but does it play the pivotal role that some suggest? Some commentators present the 'concern for people' dimension in great depth, leaving the 'concern for the task' dimension hardly considered, while others do the reverse.

Quinn (1992) talks about 'the fundamental state of leadership'. For him, when leaders do their best work, they don't replicate the work of others, but draw upon their own values and capabilities' (ibid.). He argues that this is about creating 'the right frame of mind' (ibid.). For Quinn, the fundamental state of leadership is about being results-centred, internally directed, relying on one's own values, focused on putting the collective good first, and open to learning from the external environment. This idea is reinforced by various surveys which have tried to identify short-comings in the execution of strategy. These were often focused on 'people issues' around the relationship between leaders and their people, but other factors play a role. Mankins and Steele (2005) and Collins (2001) indicate factors such as inadequate resources, poorly communicated strategies, lack of clarity in defining what needs to be done, unclear accountabilities, organisational silos, poor performance monitoring, and a lack of 'disciplined people, disciplined thinking, disciplined action' are causes (Collins, 2001).

The conclusion that people are the problem is incorrect – and unrealistic: first, the problems are only partly behavioural; and second, in any event one cannot run an organisation without people, so no matter what problems they cause these have to be dealt with. While behaviour plays a part, shortcomings in the execution of strategy are also related to a lack of discipline and definition, a lack of accountability, no credible and clear targets, and the performance management process encouraging the wrong behaviour, alongside organisational obstacles to execution. Effective leaders are valued both because they display the capabilities of leaders and because they are capable practitioners in their own fields – the balance of the systematic approach of the manager and the inspirational skills of the leaders sums it up.

Argyris identifies two 'mindsets', which he argues dominate the world of leaders in organisations. The first is 'productive reasoning', and the second 'defensive reasoning'. Productive reasoning is used to generate valid knowledge and create informed choice, emphasising personal responsibility and based on processes aimed at clarifying needs, ideas and actions. Conversely, defensive reasoning is used to avoid transparency, to evade the valid testing of ideas, and to avoid taking personal responsibility for one's own ideas or actions. The essence of Argyris's view is that in ineffective organisations people find ways via defensive reasoning of disguising or 'covering up' what they have or have not done. The solution to defensive reasoning is to craft conversations aimed at learning; that is, to challenge ideas and actions.

1.9   Summary

The aim of this book is to set out a broad-based view on leadership in organisations, how it is practised and how best it can be developed from the organisations' perspective to deliver benefit. Successful leadership is not just about developing individual leaders or the theoretical analysis of leadership. It is about how leadership works in the real world, how individual leaders function as both individuals and as part of an organisation's leadership team, how those teams function and develop, and how through all of this the organisation achieves its aims and develops leaders for the future. While the development of individual leaders has attracted the most attention in the available literature, all of the other components are vital as they may well have more profound and long-term consequences for organisations than the former.

We live in changing times – perhaps more so at present with the issues caused by the 2006–10 financial crisis still having significant effects at individual, corporate and national levels. The seriousness of the sovereign debt crisis in the Eurozone in 2010–13 led to further fears of a near collapse of the European, if not global, financial system and the associated damage that would cause.

This all has implications for leaders, be they corporate or national. Within the corporate world senior leaders need to pay the most attention to two key strategic issues: liquidity and market valuation. These two concerns need to be allied to the development of more effective risk management and governance, with a further focus on cost efficiency, innovation, improving employee performance and customer service to maximise the bottom line. Construction companies heavily exposed to the private-house-building sector have found themselves to be targets for acquisition as with many financial services businesses. Losses, provisions and falling revenues have impacted corporate liquidity and that, plus a pessimistic market outlook, have hit valuations. These are circumstances within which some of the iconic brand names of finance have fallen, such as Lehman Brothers. There can be no better illustration of the point that the decisions and judgements that leaders make have medium- and long-term consequences, so that paying attention to the bases for decision-making needs to be a part of how we think about leadership.

At the national level, the need for leaders to set aside local considerations to build a consensus on the development of a more stable global financial system is clear. This goes back to the traditional problem for leaders – whether to deal with the local interests for which you are responsible, or work collaboratively to deal with the bigger problem. So many of the challenges of leadership are often similar, whether one is a new first line manager or the president of the USA. It is just the scale and complexity that change.

Thus the ways in which leaders go about decision-making, drawing on experience and seeking to make sense of new situations, changing challenges and unclear problems by experimenting and learning from new experiences becomes a key part of understanding how leaders work. In the financial crisis of 2006–10, leaders faced a new world where previous certainties became uncertain, and what had worked before was now unlikely to work, so they needed to re-evaluate the world and change their own and others' minds about what should be done. This confirms that leadership is much more complex than merely a behavioral analysis focused on the impact that leaders have on those with whom they engage day by day.

While that is important we also need to focus on how best to deal with the former US secretary of defence, Donald Rumsfeld's 'unknown unknowns' – that unknown new world from the Johari window, which can apply just as much to the world around us as to ourselves. The Johari window is a technique created to help people better understand their relationships with others. It divides the 'self' conceptually into four categories. These encompass the part I and others see and perceive and the part others and I cannot see. It therefore acknowledges that we do not fully understand ourselves, let alone others. It is leaders who have to face this new world and rationalise it to make some sense from what they see to at least take the first tentative steps to understanding it and making decisions.

Throughout this book we shall try to consider both theoretical and practical approaches to understanding and developing leaders, and the ways that leadership is practised around key themes. We shall do so by considering relevant research and by reviewing a wide range of case studies. We hope that readers find ideas here that will help them in two ways: first, to help them think about their own personal strengths and weaknesses as leaders and potential leaders; and second, to help them understand better the roles that leaders play in organisational settings and how these contribute to being part of the 'team'.

Leaders set the tone for their teams, organisations and much more besides. Understanding what leaders do is encouraged by looking at how they do it, how they think, and why they think as they do; and how they work with other people. In this book we hope to provide a more balanced understanding across these perspectives that brings real and practical value to readers.

Questions

1   If you consider both the operational and strategic leadership you have seen in organisations, what are your views on the shortfalls you have seen and their impact on effectiveness?

2   Have you seen situations where, despite effective operational leadership, shortfalls in strategic leadership have been significant?

3 Do you think that the development of effective leadership is given sufficient priority compared to the development of functional capability?

4 Given the changes in organisations following the economic downturn, primarily reductions in headcounts, what are the implications of this for leaders?

5 The ability to change minds, or at least to encourage open minds, is critical to enable organisations to keep pace with changes happening around them. How do you think organisations of which you have experience met, or are meeting, this challenge?

2 Key themes in strategic leadership

2.1 Introduction

This chapter sets the context for the examination of strategic leadership by looking at some of the key themes and challenges in strategic leadership, which are then developed in more detail throughout the book. The view presented here is not based on a charismatic model of the strategic leader as a 'hero figure'. Nor do we argue that strategic leadership is the preserve of the CEO or the board alone. We do not assume that strategic leadership or strategic thinking come only from the boardroom. However, we do believe that the preparation of people to take up senior-level roles is different in important ways from that needed for other leadership, managerial and professional roles.

2.2 Is the age of command and control leadership over?

Command and control (top-down leadership in which senior leaders instruct others in detail about what they must do and how they must do it) is often seen as the traditional and 'failsafe' way of leading in any situation. But how much does this style of leadership still operate in organisations ? Moreover, when used, is it effective? And in which sense? In Dotlich *et al.* (2006), when discussing 'whole leadership', their view is that the problem with leaders in practice is that they are still too 'command and control'-oriented in their approach to leadership. According to them, while corporate leaders may deliver short-term results, 'they have not demonstrated the inner fortitude and courage to consistently do the right things in face of competing stake-holder needs, the constant pressure for performance, and the requirement to keep people engaged and motivated at work' (ibid.).

Command and control leadership can be effective, as illustrated by the following case study, which looks at the leadership of Ernest Shackleton during the 1907–09 British Antarctic Expedition, and in particular during the planning of the expedition. There is some evidence that he ignored the experiences of others, and in particular of the Norwegian explorer, Fridtjof Nansen, which may have been because of an element of defensive reasoning within his decisions.

Case study   **Ernest Shackleton and the 1907–09 British Antarctic Expedition**

Shackleton was a brave and inspirational explorer, with a domineering and confident personality, but the eventual failure of the project can be traced back to his decisions in planning the expedition. He had been a member of Robert Falcon Scott's first attempt to reach the South Pole in 1901–04, using dogs to pull their sleds. Through a series of questionable decisions and unfortunate events this attempt failed: for example, none of those involved had any experience of handling dog teams, the wrong breed of dogs was used, too few dogs were taken, and the dogs' diet was inadequate for the conditions. Further, during the winter period spent in Antarctica prior to the attempt, little practice with the dog teams was organised.

These failures and problems appear to have had little impact on Shackleton's thinking during the planning phase. For the 1907–09 expedition he proposed to use dogs, plus Siberian ponies and a motor car. However, neither ponies nor cars had been used before and were untested in these challenging conditions. How to move equipment and supplies was central to the successful outcome of the expedition, and the decision on what means to use to move supplies was clearly a crucial one. In the event, Shackleton relied partly on untested methods, just as Scott had been content to rely on dogs alone. In addition Shackleton's planning and preparation for expedition's logistics had a number of flaws.

He consulted the Norwegian explorer, Nansen, during the planning of the expedition. Acknowledged at the time as *the* expert on polar expeditions, Shackleton ignored his advice in two vital aspects. First, he chose to use ponies despite the experienced advice against that decision, as Nansen had proved the value of dogs, properly organised and handled. Further, this evidence was powerfully supported by the experience of Roald Amundsen, Robert Peary and the Duke of the Abruzzi. Shackleton failed to properly assess the reason for the failure of Scott's earlier expedition. He assumed it was the use of dogs that was the problem when in fact it was inadequate planning to ensure the effective use of the dogs and having sufficient numbers of them rather than the use of dogs as such.

Further, despite the evidence of his own experience of skis, gained on Scott's expedition, he decided not to use them, despite the evidence of their value. Scott and Shackleton did not get on well and this conflict continued subsequently, partly because by then they were rivals. This impacted on Shackleton's decision-making in the planning of the 1907–09 expedition. These decisions were compounded by the difficulties he experienced in ordering the required sleds, clothing and an appropriate ship. In part this was an issue of funding and in part the lack of sufficient time taken to plan before moving into the 'action' phase of the expedition. The motor car turned out to be of little use; he was unable to afford the ship he really wanted and ended up with the *Nimrod*, a schooner under-powered for the planned expedition; and he was unable to get various members of the Scott expedition to join him so he had to select men who lacked experience of Antarctica.

Ultimately, the expedition failed to reach the geographic South Pole. Nevertheless, it was an epic attempt despite being plagued by hunger, terrible weather and bad ice conditions. It fell short of its ultimate goal by just over 97 nautical miles, but achieved more than any previous expedition. Against the most challenging of odds and circumstances, with inexperienced team members and insufficient equipment, through magnificent courage and leadership he brought his party to safety. The story of this expedition is one of ambition, adventure and of a journey into the unknown. However Shackleton's decision-making was often challenged by members of his party. This led to resentment, and in one case this was still felt strongly some 40 years later.

But Shackleton's strategic leadership capability lies at the heart of the explanation of the expedition's failed outcome – or perhaps its 'glorious failure' as it has been described. Decisions made in the first half of 1907 during planning, where Shackleton failed to take on board both evidence from his own experience and expert advice impacted on that outcome well over a year later. Shackleton's personal leadership is not in question – and given the problems that occurred during the expedition it is fortunate that he was a good leader, otherwise the outcome could have been tragic. It was his lack of ability to learn from his own experience and that of others that created the potential for his own failure.

Source: Riffenburgh, 2004.

Case study commentary

It appears that Ernest Shackleton did not make full use of either the knowledge already available nor of the experience of his own team in making preparations for this expedition. It may well be that this was partly a legacy of his own experience of being a member of Scott's earlier expedition. It may also be fair to conclude that he did not relish conflict, but in saying that we ought to note that they were embarking on an expedition in which their lives were at stake. We ought therefore to accept that the cohesion of the expedition team was of central importance. Moreover, in 1907, the principal thinking underlying any concept of leadership would have been military in its origins – rank-based command and control with little or no consent or input from those lower down in the structure.

Much of the planning was undertaken while Shackleton was recruiting the members of the expedition. Thus those who ventured with him on the quest found many decisions had already been made when they joined. This is not that unrealistic in terms of organisational reality: often decisions have been made elsewhere, or our ability to make a particular choice is constrained by the decisions of others. In his case it seems likely that while there will have been misgivings – for example, about the ship being used – the commitment of his colleagues combined with his own personal leadership prevailed. In any event, the decisions were made.

What is clear is that Shackleton's leadership of the expedition, once it started, was exemplary. However, the decisions he made before it began had profound consequences for the fate of the expedition. Clearly, the objective of reaching the South Pole was ambitious, given the times. We can only understand his decisions in relation to a longitudinal assessment of how he came to make them. How did he make up his mind? That is a key question and we cannot really know the full story behind his rejection of Nansen's advice. But clearly leaders seeking change need to encourage the learning that can lead to changed minds. In the event, is it likely that Shackleton's approach to his problems at the outset of his expedition was characterised by productive or defensive reasoning? What experiences influenced his judgement? What led him to ignore the experience and views of others? We cannot tell, but the fact that challenges to his decisions from the expedition party, which he rejected, caused resentment that lasted for a long time afterwards points to defensive reasoning as an explanation. It should be noted, though, that these were men whose lives Shackleton eventually saved.

It is interesting that many commentators on leadership focus on Shackleton's behaviour during the expedition, but this alone is insufficient if we are to understand how this case can enlighten us in relation to leaders and leadership. A focus on behaviour is not sufficient to analyse leadership; we need understand the strategic ambition that led to the action and how that ambition influences decision-making both before and during 'implementation'. The level of ambition analysed in relation to the resources available and the deployment of those resources indicates whether a strategy is 'fit for purpose' – in other words, are the decisions made and plans developed likely to optimise the chances of a successful outcome? It is whether the implementation of the strategy can be judged to be achievable versus the risks.

2.3   Moving forward: implementing new strategy

Individual leadership often focuses on making the status quo better. The problem is that, in the modern world, this is not enough. Success is delivered by incremental daily change and longer-term strategic change. To be effective at this we need to understand 'the art and science of changing minds'. Gardner (2004) argues that there are seven factors that can be at work where minds are changed:

(i)   **Reason,** obviously enough rationality, appeals to evidence, logic and the use of metaphor and analogy.

(ii)   **Research,** the collection of relevant data to reinforce (i).

(iii)   **Resonance,** more complex but essentially whether an idea 'feels' right, whether derived from a reasoned basis, or intuitively, or because we feel the proponents of the idea are reliable, credible, admirable and so on.

(iv)   **Representational redesign,** essentially to do with whether an idea has application in many fields of application and endeavour. If others are using the idea successfully then so can we.

(v)   **Resources and rewards,** which may tip the balance but will be unlikely to be sufficient in the absence of the above.

(vi)   **Real world events,** such as war, disasters, terrorist attacks, recessions, law, new technology, creating challenges and opportunities.

(vii)   **Resistances,** not a facilitating factor, obviously, but needed as part of the model.

Gardner's argument is that a key task of the leader is to articulate and oversee change, that change requires learning, and learning requires that we change our minds. Change cannot be achieved with only a change in behaviour – that is, where the employees do as they are told, but do not believe in doing it the new way. This may work in the short term, or in the case of simple activities, but it is unlikely to be effective in cases of significant change, nor to release the full potential of the change because employee commitment is lacking. So the changing of minds as well as behaviour is key to successful change.

The approach to leadership proposed by Dotlich *et al.* (2006) encompasses three broad aspects of the problem, namely 'head', 'heart' and 'guts', the latter relating to intuition and instinct. They describe them as follows:

(i) **Head leadership:** rethinking business models, reframing boundaries, rethinking assumptions, developing mind sets, expanding knowledge and developing a 'point of view'.

(ii) **Heart leadership:** balancing people and business needs, creating trust, creating engagement and commitment, knowing what is important, and understanding and overcoming potential obstacles to change and improvement.

(iii) **Guts leadership:** taking risks with incomplete data, balancing risk and reward, making tough decisions, and persevering in the face of problems.

In practical terms these three aspects are interrelated, because how can leaders create trust or engage commitment if they are not seen to be credible in terms of the other two aspects? However, leaders often play down the importance of the heart side, consciously or subconsciously, as it is more difficult both to define and implement. But in practice this is counterproductive: CEB Corporate Leadership Council's research found that the decision by employees to deliver high performance is determined by 53 per cent rational influence and 43 per cent emotional, and of the emotional influence, 76 per cent relates to their immediate boss and his/her behaviour. Securing rational commitment first will enable up to a 57 per cent increase in emotional commitment, 26 per cent increase in effort and 35 per cent increase in commitment to stay in their job (Corporate Leadership Council, 2004b).

It is interesting to note that Dotlich *et al.* (2006) also do not include the concept of 'time horizon' in their analysis. With real world decisions there is always a time-related element, be it in the limits on the time taken to deliver, or the time lag between action and effect. For leaders, the key question often is 'Is it realistic to attempt this in the time we have available?' In particular, this is important in relation to the level of ambition set out in the strategies put forward by senior leaders. People respond positively to ambitious strategies which are realistic enough to be achievable and resonate with them, but they do not respond well to those that are clearly impossible to achieve in the time allowed.

Overall, then, in simple, practical terms, it is not the view of the leaders themselves presenting the core business cases or implementation plans that is important, but the view of those being asked to put them into practice. The credibility of those leaders asking for action is based on the appropriateness of the time they have allowed to achieve the desired outcome. This is then a key factor in determining the response of those being asked to do the job.

But do leaders aim for the optimum outcome, or just something that is easy to achieve? Is there is a credible 'fit' between the perceived level of ambition and the proposed means to make it happen? Human nature often means that, for some people, reaching a lower goal successfully is better than possibly failing to reach a higher one. This relates also to perspectives of risk and the risk appetites of individual leaders. In addition, for some senior leaders remuneration may also play a part in setting ambition. When developing their objectives they will want to have targets they can easily achieve to ensure they receive their full potential remuneration. This is a frequently quoted issue with board-level executive remuneration, that the targets set to achieve significant bonus payments are in reality not that challenging and are set low. This is often put down to colleagues in the organisation, even though they may be independent non-executive directors, allowing easy rather than challenging targets.

Time is also a factor. The position of the leader on his or her career path may influence the 'type' of leadership applied. Early on in their career, as people are preparing for first level and middle manager leadership roles, their ability to motivate and inspire their own teams and other colleagues is important, 'heart leadership'. But in senior leadership roles, decisions and choices between various complex options become more significant and therefore 'head' and 'guts' leadership become more important. Thus the optimum leadership mix changes with time and management level. This is one issue for the development of leaders – helping them to be effective at different levels where the approaches of the previous level may not be optimal.

The principle of command and control leadership assumes an ability to control events tightly within the leader's remit so that his or her instructions are followed precisely to produce the desired outcome. However, as we know from reality, even in the simpler medieval world, the control that leaders exerted was not total and events themselves often took over control. For example, in battles, the fact that one leader lost and one leader won means that the loser must have lost control of events. So we know that command and control breaks down and this, even in pre-industrial times, led to the idea that perhaps there was a fundamental weakness in this approach to leadership. If on the battlefield those in charge of sub-elements of the various forces were not told of the overall plan as well as their own objectives, if things went wrong they could not adapt to the changing circumstances to support the overall plan. So ever since early times there has been some suggestion that using command and control has drawbacks. Certainly, more recent experience and research now shows that command and control removes the ability to respond rapidly to changing circumstances if the leader is not 'on the spot', and it also discourages the questioning of potential flaws in planning, and blocks innovation, learning and creativity.

As we shall see in later chapters, in the work of Vroom and others, and in the training of military leaders, there may be circumstances where the command and control approach is the best option; for example, where sudden life or death decisions have to be made both locally and instantly. But it is clear that circumstances affect only a very small percentage of all decisions made, and that command and control is increasingly a style of leadership that is potentially ineffective, inappropriate, and even counterproductive in most situations in the fast-changing modern world. In particular this applies where the leader or decision-maker is not present when the original plan requires changes because of the effect of events. If the leader is not present, those who are there cannot update the plan as they lack the knowledge or authority to do so.

2.4 Developing effective strategy: data from the past, new ideas for the future, or both?

Piore and Sable (1984) argued that only decentralised firms have the necessary flexibility, skills and commitment to respond to sudden market or environmental shifts. A number of theorists have developed ideas relating to this, which are often labelled as 'postmodernism'. Modernism was the emergence of rational, objective science combined with an underlying belief in human progress. Historians refer to the 'Enlightenment', which comprised the evolution of laws and knowledge to advance human progress, and the development of that progress through the application of science to the study of human problems. Postmodernism is said to have replaced modernism by adopting a more 'realist' perspective.

Within postmodernism, 'critical' theory relates not to criticism of prior theory but focuses attention on the idea that through rationality and science it is possible to understand definitively the human condition, given its complexity and the continuing reality of complex change. The idea that management is a neutral, technocratic discipline is rejected (Willmott, 1984). Relying on the work of Habermas (1974), 'critical' theory seeks to understand how knowledge is derived, identifying two knowledge domains, one from human interpersonal interaction, and the other from our capacity for reflection. The idea of this is that organisational problems cannot be solved by scientific methods alone, as these problems (or the actions organisations wish to undertake) are socially constructed and can only be dealt with socially.

Most thinking about strategy is based on a commitment to positivist thinking; that is, on the idea that all will be well if only we have enough data. This holds true whether we examine Kay (1993), Mintzberg (1990) or Whittington (2001) or Mansfield (1986), even though these authors start from very different positions in terms of discipline and perspective. Alternatively, Darwinist principles of adaptation are presented by (Porter, 1985) or, more specifically, Hannan and Freeman (1983), looking at the popular ecologist idea of selection via 'survival of the fittest'. More recently Hamel and Prahalad (1994) have examined organisations achieving rapid strategic change in terms of 'strategic fit' or of the evolution of new 'strategic competencies'. In principle all of these approaches are based, to some degree, on the assumption of an objective reality which, once understood and analysed, can then be exploited by organisations.

Critical theorists view the strategy discipline as having been dominated by a positivist logic (see Stacey, 1993; Alvesson and Willmott,1992). However, it seems obvious that knowledge is socially constructed and transferred. Therefore, if decisions about the way forward for organisations, 'strategy talk', is dominated by senior executives it may not necessarily reflect wider interests nor deal with questions and concerns of others in the organisation, which is vital to ensure its successful operation.

This leads to a potential challenge to the legitimacy of leaders. However, this challenge need not arise and if it does there are ways of responding. To prevent such problems, effective two-way communication and appropriate consultation is key. This is set out in the general principles of stakeholder theory, which suggests that the modern organisation must respond to the concerns of its various stakeholders and operate within the social and legal framework established by the modern state. Thus there is a response to both internal and external requirements. In the context of the emerging 'market state', assuming we accept that the view of Milton Friedman (1972) holds true, that the modern business organisation, in pursuit of profit maximisation and operating within the law, it would benefit shareholders, employees and the society of which it is a part.

However, the developments in 'ethical' management, sustainability and social responsibility would suggest that reliance on the unfettered pursuit of profit does not always produce the most beneficial results for staff, society or even shareholders. We know from a number of examples that short-term financial results in organisations can be manipulated to the detriment of long-term performance; for example, by using money to boost profits that should be invested in new plant or the maintenance of existing equipment and buildings. So the profit motive is questionable in practice. Hence measures that reflect the return on 'inputs' are more likely to be of value.

It is clear that the concerns raised in critical theory are not only the concerns of those who support the theory – many others see that the existing organisational paradigm does not always work effectively. For example, Argyris and Schön (1978) clearly distinguish between 'espoused theory' and 'theory in use' – the age-old difference between theory and the real world. They show that decision-making in organisations is not as simple or as deterministic as many suppose. Senge (1990) also argues that a reflective personal style and dialogue enable people in organisations to explore issues and assumptions more freely. Why would that be needed in a purely positivist world? In such an environment, spending time and money to enable leaders to discuss and explore thinking together would be unnecessary. But in reality we know there is much evidence that, via learning, leaders can and do undertake a fuller exploration of their thoughts and experiences that enables the possibility of developing or improving current views and ideas.

Fraher (2004) has presented an even tougher challenge to critical theory via a history of group study and the 'psychodynamic organisation' through a study of the origins and development of the Tavistock Institute of Human Relations and the A. K. Rice Institute. Using the ideas of Sigmund Freud, Carl Jung, Melanie Klein and Wilfred Bion, these institutions developed approaches to the study of groups and organisations. The initial impetus to this was the problem of expanding the UK armed forces rapidly early in the Second World War, giving rise to the need to establish an effective Officer Selection Board process. The emerging ideas and practices were subsequently discussed at conferences of practitioners interested in issues of authority and leadership in groups and organisations. Viewing organisations as 'idea organisations', Fraher (2004) showed that they achieved transformation through reflection, the willingness to experiment, and by openness to new ideas and groups, but they did not ignore the past thoughtlessly. To achieve transformation, organisations 'must find ways to acknowledge and then mitigate inter-group rivalry that inevitably arises when competing ideas are engaged' (ibid.).

Does this study provide a challenge to critical theory? The idea that the development of knowledge and 'strategy talk' may disadvantage those without power is significant even though in practice it may be an inevitable consequence of various stages of the development of society. The resistance by those in power to the spread of knowledge, or worse the requirement to consult others, to wider groups than their own is well documented. History is littered with examples that often resulted in dramatic and sometimes violent change. But similar principles continue to affect organisations and societies today. The Arab Spring in 2010–11 and the violence in Syria beginning in 2012 shows its presence in societies but is also a theme in organisations. Once you have power you don't want to give it up.

The whole apparatus of organisational development as described by French and Bell (1995), Kotter (1996) and Kanter (1983) may at best be a process based on collusion with power-holders, or at worst 'brain-washing' of staff. However, it is unlikely that such a simplistic critique can be the reality of events during a period of rapid change or throughout a population of organisations as diverse as the Tavistock Institute of Human Relations, public bodies of varying kinds, professional organisations, hospitals, colleges and others.

In summary, critical theory raises real and important questions, and seeks to replace 'positivist' thinking. The question is the extent to which critical theory raises queries not already posed by existing organisational and social analysis. In one sense, critical theory contains the important idea that human history is not always best judged as a process of continued progress – that there is not always a solution to the dilemma being faced, and possibly there may be no way forward.

2.5   Identifying the optimum future state: the group as catalyst

Societies and organisations are not locked into the status quo and we need to understand the complexity of human activity in organisations and how to cope with, and manage, such complexity. Throughout history each generation has assumed that the times within which they lived were complex. In relative terms, to the preceding generation they probably were more complex, but each generation had to learn to manage the new complexity that the thought leaders of that generation were creating by advancing understanding to reveal new ways of doing things. The rest of the society had to face the challenge of how to 'catch up', much as those in organisations experiencing change change today, with thought leaders developing new ways of working and everyone else trying to keep up with them. There has therefore been an emerging body of 'complexity theory' to respond to these challenges.

Darwin *et al.* (2002) provide a convincing survey of the emergence of complexity theory within the organisational behaviour literature. The fundamental idea underlying the work on this theory is based on a complex adaptive system defined as:

(i)   It is a network of change 'agents ' acting in parallel, often interconnected, ways, but with no 'command and control' framework.

(ii)   These agents are 'adaptively intelligent', constantly seeking and making sense of patterns, testing ideas, evolving and learning.

(iii)   Change is achieved through learning, evolution and adaptation.

(iv)   Control of the system is dispersed throughout the system.

(v)   Coherence within the system arises out of competition and co-operation among the agents as they see advantages in alliances and other arrangements for mutual support.

In effect, this is based on the idea of 'self-organisation' by a group of individuals. Harré (1984) and Wheatley (1992) consider how ideas and practices can emerge from groups which transcend the ideas of the individual members of the group. As people take action new issues will arise, including, as a result of 'unintended consequences', as will new possibilities – for example, the discovery of penicillin.

Capra (1996) traces the emergence of the concept of self-organisation from the early years of 'cybernetics'. Darwin *et al.* (2002) suggest that the interest in complexity theory within management studies has come from the attempt to understand problems in planning systems which appear not to be able to predict the future effectively. This is reflected in any systems we see around us everything from weather forecasters trying to predict natural events, be they short-term or long-term, such as global warming, to those in financial institutions trying to predict market movements or assess risk. The failure of the latter was a major factor in the global financial crisis that began in 2008, so these predictions are of significant importance.

The question of how to develop, agree and implement public policy or corporate strategy in the context of high levels of uncertainty is not new, but it has become increasingly important as our global political–legal–economic activities have begun to be both more complex and more interconnected. This could be seen as building a global 'house of cards' that is so interrelated and dependent that a problem in one place has impacts in many others. The financial crisis of 2006–10 is again an example of financial problems spreading across the world from their start in the US mortgage market. In some ways the lack of connectivity for previous generations, while being seen as barrier to trade and economic development, did offer some protection from contagion.

On the micro level, Fraher (2004) and Pascale (1990) both seek to show how organisations adapt, not by valuing consensus above all, but by stimulating innovation through emphasising tension, contention, conflict and debate. Emery (2004) goes well beyond this position in presenting an analysis of open systems-theory-based action research as an enabler of learning and change. Both emphasise the role of leaders in this process. In particular, Fraher's (2004) analysis places the thinking and ideas of successive leaders of the Tavistock Institute of Human Relations in moving the organisation forward through successive stages in its development as a key driver.

2.6   Reaching the future state: delivering change as a leadership group, not just as individuals

Much of the change management literature positions leadership as the key source of the driver or 'energy for change', essential to build the level of commitment to achieve change. However, it is not as simple as it sounds – in reality, where leaders are positioned in the organisation and what are they doing to deliver change is key. In the real world a single leader, even a CEO, will only have an impact on a limited part of the holistic process by which change is delivered. Thus in any large organisation, be it single-site, multi-site, regional or global, where change is successful, leadership for change must come from leaders at all levels and not just from the top. Thus there is clearly a need for leadership at various levels of the organisation, not only the top, and for varying leadership 'roles' to be undertaken to achieve the successful delivery of objectives or change.

During the process of delivering successful change, two key populations have to be engaged – the leaders and the followers. The leaders give 'signals' that changes are needed, can describe those changes, 'pathways' to change can be set out, and plans, resources and support for implementation provided. The leaders' role is to obtain buy-in and engagement for change because without 'followers' no change is possible; the leaders cannot do everything themselves. The practical problem is that, for reasons we discuss later, not all 'followers' will embrace change (but neither will all 'followers' resist it). Borrowing an idea from innovation theory, we can identify a 'change vanguard' and 'early adopters'. These are the groups upon whose support successful implementation is based. They carry forward the change ideas and practices within the organisation. As we shall see, success in change management is based to some extent on identifying and supporting people so that they become 'leaders' of change even if they are not defined as such in the sense of formal roles.

Clearly therefore, within this context, 'leaders of change' do not always have to be in 'leadership roles'. Those individuals who have the capability to influence others – be it peers, subordinates or other stakeholders, can also be 'leaders of change'. It is not just about reporting lines but the ability of the individual to encourage others to accept the need for change and make it happen. Thus while those in leadership roles have the main responsibility to make change happen, to make it happen more effectively requires that 'leaders of change' also have to be engaged.

Effective change leaders must also provide 'management' as well as leadership – resources, facilities, training, time for staff to implement the change, day-to-day activities and 'organisational cover' so staff do not neglect key organisational deliverables. Early on in the process of change implementation, plans will potentially go wrong, take longer than expected and be misunderstood or misinterpreted. In such circumstances those initiating the change and early adopters have to experiment, problemsolve and build others into the process of change in order to get things back on track or schedule. To be effective this must happen at both the individual and the organisational level. But with any change there will be detractors. These have to be brought on board over time, or if they will not embrace the change, meaning that it never fully embeds, they should possibly leave the organisation.

At the individual level, leaders must articulate change ideas effectively using 'frame resonance' based on the concepts used in 'social movements', in which leaders align others to 'acceptable' ideas regarding the organisation's desired 'direction of travel'. This is achieved using words and phrases which stakeholders and others see as meaningful in relation to the organisation's overall purpose and their own situation.

For example, an environmental organisation might focus attention on 'polluted beaches' as a theme, hoping that this will resonate with current and potential supporters, encouraging them to action, just as the phrases 'save the planet' and 'feed the world' have had a similar impact. The same use of themes applies in the commercial world. Colt Telecom used to describe itself as 'building rings around cities' at once symbolising to its customers that it intended to service companies in financial centres and that it offered the certainty of access to them. This approach is put forward in the idea of 'resonance' in Howard Gardner's book, *Changing Minds* (2004). But during change, leaders must also provide for 'quick wins' and 'demonstration projects', showing that progress is being made and to help keep up motivation and momentum. This demonstrates that achieving the 'objective' or 'vision' in the future is possible. In other words, milestones along the way show progress towards a credible end destination.

The ideas that underpin any particular change initiative need to have an impact throughout the organisation, not just in parts. We know that adults learn best from direct experience, so new ideas are assessed in relation to the problems we want to solve or things we want to achieve. We test them in practice. Thus we learn from the experience of success or failure how to resolve more effectively similar problems in the future. The feedback generated then creates the learning that leads to the change being more likely to succeed as people become aware and more confident that the change is relevant to their own situation.

It is possible that using 'social influence' or 'contagion models' could be a basis for assessing progress, from initial concept of change through early adoption to the achievement of critical mass to support full implementation. This idea is drawn from both innovation literature (Rogers, 1986) and work on 'social movements'. In this environment, ideas such as the 'tipping point' then become relevant. Is there a point where the accumulating evidence from experience across an organisation is such that change becomes irreversible? The wider social influence model depends on the extent to which people's judgements about what they should do are affected by their perceived view of the likely reactions of the groups with which they are associated in some way – for example, peers, subordinates, leaders or others in the organisation. Hence 'peer pressure' or the idea of building 'critical mass' to get others to join their colleagues in making change happen is a real factor in organisations.

Where this 'social influence' is used it raises questions about leadership and the impact of leaders on this process. Which leaders, and positioned where in the organisational system, are likely to be the most influential? If one accepts the idea that social factors play a part in enabling change there must also be a question about whether social factors can equally be a 'blocker' as well as an 'enabler' of change. Even in a relatively simple organisation where small changes occur we know that in any change existing power bases often become challenged, or need to be challenged.

However, the key point bought out was that traditional sources of authority are not always sufficient to ensure that things the top leaders wanted to happen did actually happen. In simple terms, command and control will not work in complex situations; that is, with large spans of control, multiple management levels, multiple locations, and multiple cultural or social groups. This is the classic situation, where staff at lower levels think their lack of visibility means that they can ignore change and carry on as before with impunity, in effect blocking change. Add to this the demands of external factors often forcing organisations into almost continuous change, then the challenges to effective leadership this presents are often underestimated and must be assessed realistically for leaders to stand any chance of success.

If social influence and collaborative models are important in a period of change we need to see if there is any longitudinal evidence to indicate how such approaches to leadership might operate in a change setting. It is interesting to note that even the military, with its strong historical and practical allegiance to command and control, have generally now ceased to use it in its formal sense and adopted a more open structure that takes in ideas and data from different viewpoints before setting a direction. Further, this new flexible process only sets a 'general' direction and objectives, and does not specify the steps needed to deliver those objectives, as command and control does – in organisational phraseology 'empowerment'.

An interesting longitudinal study of change and of the role of leaders in change was undertaken in the US Department of Defense. Kelman (2005) published a study of changes to procurement policy and practice in the US government which uses innovation theory to examine the way that positive feedback can create a self-reinforcing process which consolidates change. For Kelman, the 'change effort' can feed on itself. In effect his claim implies that a 'tipping point' can be reached, beyond which change is irreversible. However, this idea is presented rather simplistically. For example he argues,

In this view simply launching the change effort and continuing it over time generates forces building support for change. Thus launching and persisting in a change effort itself increases the likelihood the effort will succeed. What is amazing about this is that it occurs automatically, with no further intervention on the part of change leaders other than to launch and persist with the effort.

Many observers might add that, given the positioning of his own office in the Clinton White House, he was appointed to lead the process of procurement reform, the importance attached by the Clinton administration to that reform programme, the interest to the Budget Office and others in government, and in Congress, means that success was probably a result of the support for change from all key stakeholders. We may reasonably conclude that the support for these changes is rather more extensive than Kelman is suggesting, but his core idea has value. It is based on 'diffusion of innovation' work. The expectation is that there is likely to be a slow start but eventually the pace of change will grow and irreversible change will result, with the 'tipping point' having been reached.

While his contribution relating to the importance of 'positive feedback' as a source of reinforcement for change efforts is clear, his phrase 'persist with the effort' needs clarification. It is interesting that, in Kelman's study, while senior executive and middle manager efforts in support of change had a positive impact on employees overall, their 'most respected co-workers' also had a positive and significant impact. Indeed, the data suggest the impact of the 'most respected co-workers' was substantially more important than that of the leaders. So there is a suggestion that the influence of respected peers maybe more significant than that of management. In practice, this implies that one part of an effective strategy for change implementation uses 'champions' across the organisation:

(i)   Identify people in teams who are respected members of those teams.

(ii)   Convince them of the value of the intended changes.

(iii)   Train them in the new methods and in change facilitation.

(iv)   Encourage them to support other members of their own team through informal or on-the-job training.

(v)   Invest some of the training effort in the sharing of best practice across the teams.

(vi)   Ensure that supervisors and others support and provide 'organisational cover' for the efforts of those 'most respected co-workers'.

(vii)   Senior executives to secure the 'space' for this to take place – for example, in relation to performance management processes.

This is supported by a concurrent action by leaders to 'deepen' the impact of change by persisting with the changes, not moving on to other initiatives but rather constantly reinforcing existing efforts. This is signalled by the way that leaders prioritise and categorise those efforts, the words they choose to describe change, and by the effort they continue to maintain on what some will try to label 'yesterday's solution'!

Adapting the change process during implementation is perfectly acceptable, if not expected. Processes, communications and delivery will change. For example, there is a difference between 'better value' and 'best value'. Early on, leaders might call for the former and then, following early successes, change the message to the latter – this is a change that will be noticed by staff and various conclusions drawn. At the very least leaders need to be aware that their individual words and behaviour are important 'signals' in the change process that will be observed by staff. This was a critical success factor in the investment banking company UBS (see the case study in Chapter 4), where the specific phrases to describe change were consistent in all communications to staff, verbal as well as written. This encouraged clarity and transparency, which are vital in effective change.

Clearly, in this case, the role, style and decisions of senior leaders are under examination. While 'personal leadership' issues are in play here it is also clear that credibility, track record and business impact are at the core of the analysis leading to this change in senior leadership. The organisation is not simply looking at finding a 'hands-on' leader. The change goes beyond personal leadership dimensions into looking for a senior leader who can be expected to both understand and embrace the decisions and choices that must be made to implement and lead significant change to ensure the organisation's longer-term viability.

2.7   Moving from status quo to future state: the learning organisation – the logical path

Emery (2004) has long been seen as one of the founders of the application of 'systems thinking' to organisational problems. His starting point is that learning is essential to sustainable change. Further, he argues, to achieve sustainable change organisational development practitioners must work with people at all levels of the organisation – from senior executives to customer-facing staff. Moreover, all levels and functional areas must be involved in a process within which they can engage with this learning, which will vary in form in different places and for different levels of staff.

This creates problems for some practitioners, who may, for example, be members of an 'elite' with their own 'language', frameworks and meaning systems. This effect is often seen operating within organisations where the HR function responsible for developing the change process uses an approach and language that is often not used by either senior leaders or employees. HR's failure to use the language or approach of these groups often leads to the failure of change initiatives, not because they were essentially flawed but because they were not communicated in an understandable way to key stakeholders. This relates to both the content of the messages and how they are presented; that is, the content may be relevant and of value to the listener but it may be presented in a confusing way and be full of technical language to which they cannot relate, or the content maybe explained clearly but not be positioned in a way that listeners can see that they will gain any potential benefit.

This goes back to the issue of a small, 'disconnected' group trying to make change happen. In this case, rather than being a small group of leaders it is a small group of Human Resources specialists or external consultants. Any lack of relevance and transferability of their message to day-to-day activities reduces significantly the chances of learning happening and change being successful.

In reality it can be hard work to operate collaboratively, at least in the perception of the often thousands of employees who are involved and will be impacted by a set of intended changes, whatever the intentions of those involved. For sustainable change to be achieved, every step of the process must lead to learning that engages and energises action; see Strebel (2000) and Collins (2001). Even if communication is effective, people learn at different rates and through different learning styles. Also, and inevitably, employees positioned differently in any large organisation have very different learning opportunities depending on many factors – for example, the nature of their roles, variable access to information, their experience, and the time they have available to learn.

The crews of the early space missions organised by the National Aeronautics and Space Administration (NASA) developed knowledge and experience that others could not access in the same way. It was similar with the early heart transplant surgeons. Clearly, in both cases they were supported by teams and worked within an evidence-based system designed to capture and codify the data gained from experience so that they could be shared. The British bomb disposal officers of the Royal Engineers in the Second World War also had a similar issue, as the Germans developed more complex and dangerous anti-handling devices to try to stop them defusing the bombs. If things went wrong in this case, the data gained regarding the mechanics of the device could be lost if the bomb exploded and killed the disposal officer.

This is important, but in the midst of complexity and uncertainty when we try to engage people in learning to take forward change this has to be done in a range of ways and at differing stages of the process, because knowledge and experience are variably distributed across the organisation. This returns to the key question in terms of employee engagement in many activities – to do what with whom, why, when and in which ways. Complexity of whatever type. be it cultural, locational, structural or environmental, makes this more difficult as complexity increases.

Certainly from the perspective of one of the authors who has led change in both complex global organisations and smaller, less complex organisations, the increase in complexity has a significant effect on the difficulty in making successful change or spreading learning, the time it takes to achieve, and the effort that has to be put into implementing it and managing the risk of failure. The addition of complexity in practice means that more stakeholders need to be persuaded to buy into the change. The more systems it effects, the more parts of the organisation are involved – each new element of complexity will add more time to the delivery of change, increase the level of learning required and increase the risk of things going wrong.

For Emery, however, the key idea is 'diffusive learning'. Diffusive learning is the form of learning that motivates the learner to re-create the learning environment for others. This is particularly interesting, because it links powerfully to a study by Kelman (2005), who uses the diffusion of innovation literature and in particular the seminal work of Rogers (1986), noting that this literature takes seriously differences of opinion about innovation. Rather than label people as 'resistant to change', Rogers views people as ranging from enthusiasts to critics. Some are 'early adopters' and Kelman refers to these as the 'change vanguard'. This is very important in practice, when he combines this notion with the identification of people as 'opinion leaders' within organisations.

Interestingly, Rogers noted that the 'early adopters' were not likely to be 'opinion leaders in an organisation'. More oriented towards external or new ideas (that is, external to their own social group), they were more likely to be viewed as 'deviant' and be perceived as having 'low credibility'. In his study (of procurement reform in the US government) Kelman (2005) found that the 'early adopters' were likely to be opinion leaders. Kelman does not really explain the reason for this difference between the two cases. The most likely explanation is that senior managers, working through their own line managers, have identified 'opinion leaders' at the local level. Kelman refers to them as 'most respected co-workers'. Significant efforts are then made to engage them in the change process, including training in the relevant skills and knowledge, and involving them in working groups, task forces and so on. By going through this learning and the change-related activities, these employees become knowledgeable and skilled in the new procurement systems and ways of working. No doubt these people also derived satisfaction and even status from this engagement, but it is interesting to note the process involved.

These 'most respected co-workers' were being provided with a 'psychologically safe environment' within which to learn. Senior executives present the case for change and then create the 'learning space' for it to happen, which in effect creates 'organisational cover' for the learning. Sponsorship from the senior team creates legitimacy for the activity. Traditionally in organisation behaviour literature this is known as 'organisational slack'. Burns and Stalker (1961), in an early study of innovation within organisations, note that innovation requires that there be some slack or unused resource in an organisation to provide for experimentation with new ideas. Of course, this is a task for leaders – providing the 'learning space', creating sufficient slack and sponsoring particular individuals may be seen as part of what the idea of the 'leader as coach' is all about. This idea is increasingly put forward as being essential by organisational theorists and is certainly beginning to be influential within at least the HR community in large organisations. Certainly one of the key reasons put forward by Miles (2010) for the failure or stalling of organisational change is the lack of slack that allows employees to both do the 'day-to-day' job as well as to develop the change and make it happen. Thus this 'learning space' is vital to successful change.

Emery is very clear on the point that organisations do not 'learn' in the sense that people do, because they do not have a single brain. His best definition of a 'learning organisation' is one that is structured in ways which encourages learning continuously. He also questions the idea of 'organisational memory', because in periods of rapid turnover organisations often find that the memory leaves with the individuals. However it is possible to observe organisations codifying learning in many ways – for example, new working and business models that are then passed on, spread and become permanent as changes are achieved. Certainly the challenge for organisations is to make sure that the 'intellectual capital' held by the employees does not leave the organisation when they do. Taking Emery's own research, it suggests that action research is the basis for learning and change within organisations.

Based on the sources we have reviewed and our personal experience, it is clear that change and learning require those involved to share and exchange views on the organisation, the environment in which it operates, how well it is doing, and how best to change it for the better. Consistent with the ideas of critical theory, in particular the work of Weick (1979, 1995) on dialogue and conversations about strategic change, is significant, and Argyris's (2004) concept of double-loop learning, which may well be essential to the achievement of sustainable change, at least in some circumstances. Such circumstances might be where the leadership of an organisation has become dysfunctional and leadership behaviour is characterised by the 'organisational defensive routines' identified by Argyris. These comprise actions and behaviour that, while apparently rational, serve to distort or deflect the discussion of real problems, with those involved often colluding in doing so; that is, typical avoidance or denial of the reality and need for change. This is another significant factor in the failure of change initiatives.

This seems to imply the need for 'equilibrium' so that learning can be facilitated by the provision of support and space, 'organisation cover' by senior leaders, as has been suggested. Lack of balance can be a basis for learning and change (de Caluwe and Vermaak, 2004) their argument is that lack of balance or 'bounded instability' requires organisations, and thus leaders, to choose between competing options, goals, structures, technologies and so on. It is not lack of choice that is the problem, but the unwillingness to decide, and the absence of ambition, that leads to disruptive levels of performance, chaos and the possibility of failure.

Are these not the very conditions for failure of the learning organisation, creating the 'confused' and 'demotivated' organisation? Change initiatives cascading in ever-increasing numbers, with few being properly explained, neither the business nor the personal benefit presented, the lack of an inspiring vision or the way forward agreed, codified, described or understood. This will sound familiar to many readers who are leaders in organisations.

In these circumstances, as the conditions for interactive and diffusive learning are not satisfied and additional pressure has been created inside the organisation as there is now both change and normal work to do, it could be argued that such change, rather than being of benefit actually increases risk. All too often that is the reality of today's organisations. Indeed, one central and practical conclusion of all of this thinking is that the best and most effective strategy for senior leaders is to make only a few key changes and to ensure that these are sustained and embedded by investing in learning in order to consolidate them throughout the organisation before undertaking more change.

2.8   Engaging everyone with the future state: social movement and large-scale change – the inspirational path

When we discuss strategic leadership in terms of taking forward an organisation and a group of people with ambition, inspiration, clear decisions and choice, then change driven by leaders through a social movements approach needs to be considered. For example, the anti-apartheid movement in South Africa led by many, but most obviously by Nelson Mandela, might be worth examining. 'Social movements' are about achieving large-scale change within significant groups of people. Be it civil rights, the Ban the Bomb campaign, or the anti-smoking campaign, it is clear that social movements may have something to tell us about how to engage people in large-scale change. Clear direction, ambition and inspiration is something one would associate with campaigns of this sort – and all of these are also what the organisation needs to achieve successful change.

Paul Bate and his colleagues (Bate *et al.*, 2004) consider the differences between a management approach to achieving change and a social movements approach (see Chapter 3). The main difference is that social movements engage people at a 'deep' or even emotional level. The change is essentially self-directing and follows a near-absolute commitment to the cause, and ultimately 'social movements' are voluntary. Linking this to recent research from the Corporate Leadership Council, as mentioned earlier, suggests that 47 per cent of an employee's decision to give high performance to the organisation is emotional and not rational, suggesting that perhaps social movements can teach organisational change practitioners something, and that to ensure success there is a need for leaders to address the emotional needs of employees as well as their rational minds.

Management models of leadership do not always work on crude 'What's in it for me?' assumptions about people (see the Collins (2001) 'Good to Great' model as an example). However, certainly at the practical level, the 'What's in it for me?' question does have impact in the commercial world – in that this is the very core of the relationship between the organisation and the individual – a commercial value exchange: 'my work for your money'. Social movements often inspire courageous choices where significant cost, danger or hardship maybe involved for those deciding to follow the course. Here, the relationship is not about an exchange of effort for some return, a rational decision – but an emotional decision based on what is seen to be the 'right' thing to do.

While we can characterise traditional organisational change models as emphasising questions such as 'What is this programme of change seeking to achieve, and what evidence is there that it will have the desired effect?' it is simplistic to contrast that with a social movements' emphasis on 'Who supports this objective, how were they mobilised, and how much influence can they deploy?' But it is clear that, through social movements, change is inspired, released, channelled and enabled. Corporate leaders seek to mobilise organisational processes rather than engender specific programmes of social change, but elements of social movements exist in organisations. The strategy literature provides for this through the idea of emergent change (Mintzberg, 1990) and concepts such as 'whistle-blowing' have some of the characteristics of social movements, and organisation seek to harness internal social movements to drive employee engagement.

Some social movements can lead to transformational change, but many social movements may be more modest in their success. It seems to be that the greater the challenge the greater the risk, but also the greater the success if the social movement works. Traditional approaches to organisation change and social movements share some characteristics; the latter involving collective action by people who have come together voluntarily as an informal network around a common cause, typically, though not always, involving radical action and having spontaneous beginnings driven by emotional needs as much as rational ones. Organisational changes often have less spontaneous beginnings and are more typically a process of learning, carried out systematically with a logical business-driven objective. However, if one looks at successful modern social movements, after an initial phase of ad hoc activity some of the successful ones seem to take on board a systematic approach to subsequent change that one would expect within organisations. At the same time, organisations are searching for that emotional and inspirational driver within social movements that engages people around action that the systematic and purely rational approach often fails to deliver.

2.9   Summary

Ultimately, what is different is that to be effective in strategic leadership those in senior roles must both inspire transformational changes and be ready to take the ultimate responsibility. They must change minds, convince others and generate confidence among key stakeholder groups. They are the 'agents of change'. Whether we view this as a matter of 'head' leadership, or a challenge of 'changing minds', or a question of being the ultimate arbiter of risk and reward (noting, of course, that the final arbiter is the market, other stakeholders and clients) does not really matter. What matters is that to meet new challenges we need a new way of practising strategic leadership.

Crucial, then, is a focus on senior leaders as a cadre of people going about the practice of 'strategic leadership'. Strategic leadership is an emergent practice. It is what leaders do. Working together to enhance the understanding of and learning about our complex and changing world. Or not doing so. Open to ideas from wherever they may come. Or not. At the last, able to take decisions and bear the responsibility to deliver transformational change. Or not. Willing and able to lead change. Or not. These are the challenges senior leaders face in seeking to develop an appropriate form of strategic leadership, and it is these challenges we shall continue to explore as we develop the arguments in this book.

Questions

1   Appealing to both the head and heart of people as a leader is key, but how well do you see this being done? What do you think is required to do both?

2   In planning for an organisation or a team, to what extent should the experience of the past dictate the end, or new and untried ideas be the key factor?

3   As there are clearly 'group' mindsets in organisations as well as individual ones, how can both be changed; and from your experience does the individual change the group or vice versa?

3 Development of leadership theory

3.1 Introduction

Given the wide range of studies into leadership since the 1960s, it is important to understand how we arrived at where we are now. We need to review the approaches that have been developed, not least to set out the 'domain' of leadership studies and the chronology of the principles we adopt today. Looking back, we can identify a series of approaches to the study of leadership, each of which succeeded its predecessor chronologically and to some degree built on previous knowledge and integrated that knowledge. The approaches are listed below:

(i) The 'trait' approaches: in which leadership capacity and practice/success is deemed to be a consequence of the personal qualities and characteristics of the individual; for example, intelligence or height.

(ii) Behavioural/style approaches: in which leadership success is deemed to be a consequence of leader behaviour and style of leadership, on so far as it can be observed from day to day – for example, how the leader balances 'concern for the task' with 'concern for people'.

(iii) Contingency approaches: in which leadership success depends on the situation/context within which the leader operates – that is, factors external to the leader.

(iv) Transformational leadership ideas: within which it is argued that leadership success is largely a matter of the leader's concern for future vision and the achievement of radical change.

(v) 'New' leadership models: in which leaders are seen as 'sense makers' and builders of capacity and capability within organisations, rather than 'charismatic' leaders of change.

The differences between contingency approaches and behavioural/style approaches are differences of emphasis only. Interestingly, recent work on 'authenticity' (Goffee and Jones, 2005), 'resonance' in leadership (Goleman *et al.*, 2002) and on emotional intelligence and leadership (Goleman *et al.*, 2002; Higgs and Dulewicz, 2003) bring us back to some extent to earlier 'trait' theory approaches. However, in fairness, these later approaches represent attempts to integrate previous work, and to achieve much needed development in terms of concepts, frameworks and applications. We should also note an emerging interest in the field in relation to narcissism and leadership, with attempts to understand ineffective leadership either in terms of narcissistic behaviour and/or in relation to ideas about 'authentic' leadership (Higgs, 2009; Kets de Vries, 1993; Maccoby, 2004; Padilla *et al.*, 2007).

Fascinating though this latter approach may be, it remains speculative at best and in any event rather prompts the question of how leaders come to make ineffective strategic judgements and decisions. For some it may be comforting to conclude that poor decisions must derive from 'bad leadership', but our contention here is that leaders who are trying their best to do the right things and engage their employees may still do the wrong things. Our main intent in this chapter is to consider the various leadership theories in relation to our understanding of leadership but also how the theories help us to understand leadership, its development and its application within organisations to deliver optimum performance in the real world.

3.2   Trait theory

What characteristics or capacity within individuals predispose them to behave as, and be perceived by others as, leaders? There are three broad types of factors that many have considered to be important: namely physical differences such as height, age or appearance; capacity differences such as intelligence, scholarship, knowledge, and communication skills; and finally, personality aspects such as self-confidence, emotional control, the need for achievement, the need for power, or interpersonal sensitivity.

Trait studies are based on the search for an explanation of leadership success related to the qualities of the leader as a person, sometimes known as the 'great man' theory of leadership. In reality, however, while many studies have been undertaken to identify common personality, physical intellectual or other personal characteristics to distinguish 'good' leaders, little in the way of an agreed list of traits has ever emerged. Thus the research remained inconclusive (Fielder, 1964) but it has now re-emerged, albeit in work seeking to combine trait theory and behavioural approaches; see, for example, Hogan and Hogan, 2001.

Trait theory work produced long and often contradictory lists of traits. Moreover, it was evident that there was substantial subjectivity in the judgements of success in much of the research. In any event, even where judgements of success appeared to be more objective it was also apparent that other factors were also at work – at least where success measures were based on economic performance. Ralph Stogdill (1948) noted early on that no consistent set of traits differentiated leaders from others across a range of situations, nor did this approach encompass the reality that individuals might take a lead in some situations but not in others.

The most comprehensive surveys of this research are those of Stogdill (1948, 1974). By the time of the second survey, Stogdill was accepting that leadership success may well be a combination of traits and other situational factors, or factors relating to behaviour and skill. Traits associated with successful leadership included:

(i)   Drive for responsibility and task completion.

(ii)   Persistence goal – driving behaviour/activity.

(iii)   Originality/creativity/flexibility in problem solving.

(iv)   Willingness to be creative – to be 'different' – in social settings.

(v)   Sense of identity, self-esteem and self-confidence.

(vi)   Willingness to take responsibility for one's own actions.

(vii)   Ability to absorb stress.

(viii)   Response to frustration.

(ix)   The capacity for social influence.

(x)   The ability to focus people on tasks, objectives and purposes.

Later research does indicate some level of association between personal/personality characteristics and leadership success. Kirkpatrick and Locke (1991) identify six traits: drive; motivation; integrity; confidence; cognitive ability; and task knowledge. Traits such as 'authenticity' of behaviour, 'resonance' and emotional intelligence have a positive effect, but we should add the idea of 'level five' leadership, as presented by Collins (2001). The five levels are:

1   **Highly capable individual**: Makes productive contributions through talent, knowledge, skills and good work habits.

2   **Contributing team member**: Contributes to the achievement of group objectives; works effectively with others in a group setting.

3   **Competent manager**: Organises people and resources towards the effective and efficient pursuit of predetermined objectives.

4   **Effective leader**: Catalyses commitment to and vigorous pursuit of a clear and compelling vision; stimulates the group to high performance standards.

5   **Executive leader**: Builds enduring greatness through a paradoxical combination of personal humility plus professional will.

Northouse (2004) has produced a convincing summary. He asks 'what, then, can be said about trait theory research'. For him, the answer is that it does at least identify lists of traits which might be used either by aspirant leaders or by those seeking to select people with leadership potential. These include intelligence, self-confidence, determination, integrity and sociability. Of course, this is something many have long believed, but rarely does the evidence support such an approach.

The trait approach is based on leaders and their individual attributes. The suggestion is that having a leader, or leaders, with a certain set of traits is important for the leadership to be successful. Two questions follow: (i) Does this mean that a person with certain traits who has succeeded as a leader in one situation will succeed in other situations? Clearly this is not always the case, but we cannot be definite on this point because there is little real evidence available to allow a judgement to be made. We can identify people who have been successful in one role but have failed in others, and can certainly point to senior executives who have moved from company to company, some of whom have been successful and some have not, even in roles identical to the ones they had had before. But was that only because of the possession of traits, or the lack of traits, or other factors? It must logically be other factors, as traits are unlikely to change when a person changes jobs.

Most large organisations have multiple leadership roles. Does each role require the same set of traits? This seems unlikely. For example, take NASA. Would one argue that identical traits are observed among leaders in the varying leadership roles in that organisation? Do all the astronauts share traits that distinguish them uniquely from others? And that raises questions about individuals over time during a career going through various leadership roles. Further, over a career do traits change? Are they the same at age 55 as they were at age 20? Do we seriously imagine that success in a leadership career is solely a result of the possession of certain traits? This also links to the repeated discussion about the entrepreneur leader being different from the corporate leader, with each being needed at a different point in an organisation's life cycle.

All of this accepted, the value of the trait approach ought to be stated. The approach is based on a foundation of personality testing which, in turn, has been the basis of leadership selection in many organisational settings over 60 or more years, not least for the selection for military officer training since the Second World War. It also provides a foundation for personal awareness and development work. Obviously, we cannot make ourselves taller than we are, but we can use trait assessment to judge how far along a given career path we might move – but noting that this is effected by social stereotyping. In areas where they feel themselves to be lacking, leaders might seek to take steps to increase the impact of the traits they do possess.

Following Northouse (2004), the trait approach is intuitively appealing. In the modern world 'image' is important and the possession of traits is clearly relevant here. The approach has been researched extensively. While it is true to note that the research is inconsistent in terms of findings, nevertheless it is hard to argue that traits play no part in leadership. Finally, personality assessment tools can offer valuable data to individuals, helping them to make judgements about themselves, about others and about career moves. It is worth noting that many leadership development programmes and activities include a range of psychometric tests as the basis for self-reflection and feedback, and that these tools are also used in other developmental activities.

The important point here may be to question how fixed are these traits within leaders and potential leaders? Clearly some are fixed. As noted earlier, people cannot change their physical attributes, but some other traits could be adapted, not all perhaps, and in any event there is the question of whether, if an individual cannot change a trait, whether he or she can find a way to fine-tune it. The real problem with too strong a dependence on traits is that the approach to leadership can become fixed and therefore limited in scope. Further, the central weakness of the trait approach is that it ignores the leadership situation. The re-emergence of trait theory firmly linked to situational analysis represents an influential recent departure in the leadership field.

Perhaps it is also worth noting at this point that certain traits, while positive at one level of application, can be negative at another, so the 'level' of the trait must match the situation. This is the basis for 'derailers', as put forward by Robert Hogan in his Hogan Development Survey Tool (2003) where, for example, it is possible for self-confidence to be seen as or become arrogance, and attention to detail become perfectionism.

3.3 Behavioural and leadership style approaches

The trait approach focused on the person of the leader. The behavioural and leadership styles approach looked at what leaders do, at how they operate, typically in relation to the task and the people with whom they relate. Thus it focuses on leader behaviour and leader actions and priorities.

Task	Team	Individual
Task	**Team**	**Individual**
Need to achieve:	Sustain the team:	Focus on people:
■ Setting tasks	■ Building morale	■ Giving recognition
■ Defining outcomes	■ Team cohesiveness	■ Respecting needs
■ Success criteria	■ Team dynamics	■ Resolving conflicts

Leader role to be aware and to respond

Fig 3.1 Leader role in team setting

Adair (1973) developed what became a most influential model under the title 'action-centred' leadership. This model was developed at the Royal Military Academy at Sandhurst, UK, where the British Army develops the leadership capability of its potential officers. Thus the model was designed to be simple, practical and easily adopted. Here the success of a leader was viewed as determined by the extent to which that leader meets three areas of need within the work setting: the need to achieve the task, the need for team maintenance and the individual needs of the people with whom they work (see Figure 3.1).

Task functions include achieving objectives, setting tasks, defining the work to be carried out, allocating resources, work organisation, setting standards, reviewing performance and obtaining data. Team functions include maintaining morale, team spirit and group cohesiveness, training the group, maintaining momentum, pace and communications within the group. Individual functions include giving feedback, reconciling conflicts, dealing with individual issues. Actions by the leader in each area will affect the other areas. In particular, Adair suggests that leaders need to be *aware* of what is going on in the group and *understand* what the implications are for the three functions of any particular set of group behaviours. It is important to note that Adair here refers to leadership skills with regard to the balance between these three needs. That is, he seeks to develop leaders with the ability to 'read' group behaviour and judge which of the three sets of needs is requiring attention.

In the Ohio State Leadership Studies (undertaken at Ohio State University, USA), Fleishmann (1953) identified two dimensions of leadership behaviour:

(i) **Consideration**, being the extent to which the leader establishes trust, mutual respect and rapport with the group, and demonstrates warmth, concern, support and consideration for subordinates.

(ii) **Structure**, being the extent to which the leader defines and structures group efforts in relation to goal attainment, organising activities to that end.

These clearly relate to the three functions of Adair (see above) but also have much in common with McGregor's (1960) Theory X and Theory Y assumptions about people and the employee-centred versus production-centred supervision identified through studies at the University of Michigan studies, as reported by Likert (1961), and in the

Blake and Mouton Leadership Grid, which identifies and contrasts concern for people and concern for production.

So far we have considered research that has focused on what leaders should consider as part of their leadership focus. There has been a considerable amount of work done on leadership skills, culminating in the leadership competency approach emerging in the 1980s, which is examined in Chapter 4. There is a need to take into account various studies of the balance of needs at different levels of leadership; for example, first-line leaders or supervisors, middle management and top management, with regard to the three sets of skills: technical, human and conceptual. Technical skills are those related to the tasks of the organisation, some specific (such as, product and customer knowledge, knowledge of company capabilities, resources and history), and some more general (for example, accounting skills, information management skills and so on). Human skills relate to 'people skills' – and clearly are those identified by Adair regarding team maintenance and individual needs. Finally, conceptual skills relate to planning, organising, problem-solving and related skills.

The balance between technical and conceptual is obvious enough. Lower-level leaders work in technical disciplines and therefore these skills predominate, while higher-level leadership focuses more on the future of the business and on planning, organising and change, so conceptual skills predominate. As to human skills, these are required at all levels – but the higher in the organisation they are, the more leaders are dealing with and seeking to influence people/stakeholders external to the organisation as well as internally. Further, their internal influence has to be delivered indirectly through other leaders, not directly face to face as with operational leaders.

Mumford *et al.* (2000) propose a skills-based model of leadership, which they describe as a capability model. From their work it emerges that desired leadership outcomes (for example, effective problem solving and performance) derives from individual attributes (general and crystallised cognitive ability, motivation, personality) and competencies (problem solving skills, social judgement skills, knowledge). Along similar lines, Yukl (2002), building on Likert's (1961) work (see above) proposed a three-factor structure:

(i)   Task orientation.

(ii)   Relations orientation.

(iii)   Change orientation.

In item (iii) the leader is concerned with focusing on activities aimed at improving strategic decisions, achieving adaptive responses in the organisation and gaining commitment to change.

This work on behaviour, style and skills makes a positive contribution to the field of leadership studies. First, it represents a shift of focus from the characteristics of leaders as individuals on to what they do, how they do it, and the priorities on which they focus. As with the trait approach, a huge number of studies have supported these approaches (Yukl, 2002, Blake and McCause, 1991, Boyatsis *et al.* 2000).

Of course, there is one obvious and certainly questionable assumption here: that there is a single best style of leadership applicable to all situations. However, this assumption must suffer from the issues referred to in relation to the trait approach, as discussed above.

3.4   Contingency theories

The limitation of the skills/styles approach led to the emergence of contingency models. These add a further factor to the mix: what it is in the context that requires the leader to do certain things, in certain ways? The best-known formulation of this approach, known as contingency or situational theory, is that of Hersey and Blanchard (1969, 1993). These scholars argued that it is not leadership style that is important, but rather the leaders' ability to adapt their style to the needs of followers and the situations in which they are working.

If there were a range of leadership skills, behaviours and styles through which leaders at different levels of the organisation lead differently, deploying the skills and styles in differing combinations, then surely there must be variations in the context within which they are working? Further, the expectations of followers regarding leaders vary depending on the level of leader being considered and the roles they play. Thus the expectations that executive directors hold with regard to the CEO may be very different from those held by employees at lower levels of the organisation with regard to their immediate managers.

Tannenbaum and Schmidt (1973), building on McGregor's Theory X and Theory Y, propose a continuum representing a range of leadership actions related to the level of authority used by the leader and the degree of freedom to act allowed to subordinates. Simply put, this moves from Tells to Sells, to Consults and to Joins in. In the latter, joining in, the leader specifies the problem and the parameters within which solutions must be delivered to be judged successful, but then joins the group as a member, as the group works on the problem.

For Tannenbaum and Schmidt (ibid.), there are three factors that enable judgement on which is the most appropriate leadership approach: forces in the manager; forces in the subordinates; and forces in the situation. Taking each in turn:

(i)   Forces in the manager are consequential or in personality, life history, knowledge and experience, including:

   ■ personal values
   ■ confidence in subordinates
   ■ leadership preferences
   ■ confidence

(ii)   Forces in the subordinates, again, are a result of personality and expectations, including:

   ■ need for independence
   ■ willingness to take responsibility
   ■ level of tolerance for ambiguity
   ■ commitment to resolving the problem, including perceived importance
   ■ knowledge and experience

(iii)   Forces in the situation, including:

   ■ type of organisation
   ■ work group effectiveness
   ■ nature of the problem
   ■ pressure of time
   ■ prominence of the issue

Overall, then, leader behaviour involves the deployment of a repertoire of behaviours to suit a range of circumstances, some internal and some external to the organisation concerned.

The need to understand the impact of the situation is evident in a competitive environment. There are other factors that can impact or influence behaviour in addition to competitive pressures and organisations of all types, and their leaders need to be able to respond appropriately. This was recognised in 1942 by Mary Parker Follett, who was concerned to avoid two extremes: authoritarian leadership with tight control; or laissez faire leadership characterised by little or no direction. For her, the answer was 'the law of the situation'. Each leadership or management problem can be understood in terms of its underlying 'law', and then actions become obvious. Perhaps a rather idealised view and rather simplistic, not least because to adopt it one must assume a shared rationality applying to all situations, whereas we know that rationality is 'in the eye of the beholder' depending on the position from which the situation is being viewed. In a pluralist society this is by definition a cause of 'contending rationalities' (Weick, 1973). Thus a series of contingency theories of leadership have developed, focusing on key aspects of the leadership situation, as follows:

■ By analysing the leadership situation – Fiedler, 1967.

■ Quality and acceptance of the leaders' decision –Vroom and Yetton, 1973, and Vroom and Jago,1988.

■ Path – goal theory – House *et al.*

■ Maturity of followers – Hersey and Blanchard, 1993.

3.5   The Fiedler model

An early example of a contingency approach, based on studies of leadership and organisational performance Fiedler (1967) developed a least-preferred co-worker scale (LPC) as a means of measuring leadership style – leaders who score highly on the scale are described as relationship motivated, while those who score low are task motivated. However, the LPC scale is completed by the leader, and thus involves the leader making an assessment of the person with whom he or she works the least well on dimensions such as friendly/unfriendly, helpful/frustrating, distant/close, co-operative/uncooperative, self-assured/hesitant and so on. It was a subjective measure, not an objective one. The less critical the scale outcome, the higher the LPC. High LPC scores are seen as being associated with high performance in the group.

Fiedler's model proceeds to identify three variables describing the leadership situation:

■ Leader – member relations: the extent to which the leader is trusted and liked by team members.

■ Task structure: the extent to which the task(s) are clearly defined and that well engineered procedures are available.

■ Position power: the position power of the leader in terms of rewards and sanctions.

These three variables were combined into eight combinations of group-task situations, linked to leadership style and propositions about effectiveness. Task-oriented leaders (low LPC score) will be more effective where the situation is either:

■ Very favourable (good leader–member relations, structured tasks, high levels of position power).

or

■ Very unfavourable (the opposite of the above).

A leader with a strong relationship approach will be more effective where the situation is:

■ Moderately favourable (with a mixed position regarding the three variables).

Thus Fiedler proposes that leader effectiveness is a function of the situation, and that the leader needs to 'fit' style to situation. One gap in the model is that it takes no account of the level in the organisation. The nature of the work is considered, but not the level – bringing with it the likelihood of variations in capabilities of both leaders and subordinates. More seriously, the LPC scale is leader self-assessed, as noted above, and so it is not obvious what mechanisms operate between the leaders' assessment of the least preferred co-worker and the assumed leadership style. The theory is also complex in its application. Nevertheless, Fiedler's data do support the theory as far as leader LPC and group performance are concerned.

3.6   The Vroom and Yetton model

In their book *Leadership and Decision Making* (Vroom and Yetton, 1973) the authors analyse two aspects of leaders' decisions, namely quality and acceptance, as follows:

■ Decision quality – how important is it to come up with the 'right' solution? The higher the quality of the decision needed, the more should other people be involved in the decision.

■ Subordinate commitment – how important is it that your team and others buy into the decision? When team-mates need to embrace the decision participation levels should be increased.

■ Time constraints – how much time is available to make the decision? The more time available, the more there can be the luxury of including others, and of using the decision as an opportunity for team-building.

In addition, the model includes the true dimension and identifies five principal management styles, as set out below.

Vroom and Yetton go on to identify a number of decision rules (see Figure 3.2), relating either to the quality of the decision (are there sufficient data; is the problem structured; is there likely to be one best outcome?) or the acceptance of decisions (is commitment to implementation important: are there shared goals, would the preferred solution lead to conflict, are subordinates likely to accept the preferred solution?):

■ Autocratic: A1   leader decides alone
               A2   leader obtains information from the group and then decides

The model comprises a number of decision steps set out in decision-tree form, as follows:

(i)   Quality of decision:
       How important?

(ii)   Team commitment:
       Is that important in relation to the decision?

(iii) Information available:
       Do you have the required information?

(iv)   Structure of the problem:
       Is the problem well defined?

(v)   Team support:
       Would the decision-maker get support from the team?

(vi)   Goal commitment:
       Does the team feel committed to organisational goals?

Fig 3.2   Structure of the Vroom–Yetton–Jago decision model

- Consultative: C1   leader shares the problem with others, individually, and then decides alone
                   C2   leader shares the problem with the group but then decides alone
- Group: G2   leader shares the problem with the group, acting as a chair person, not an advocate.

In general, the model suggests that a consultative or collaborative style is most appropriate when:

- The leader needs information from others to solve a problem.
- The problem definition is not clear.
- Team members buying into the decision is important.
- The leaders has enough time to manage a group decision.

An autocratic style is most efficient when:

- The leaders has more expertise in the subject than others.
- The leader is confident about acting alone.
- The team will accept his/her decision.
- There is little time available.

Ironically, it is possible to object to this model either because it is too complex or not complex enough. Regarding the former, we would note that two (or three if you include time) main factors, five styles and seven decision rules creates a complex model to research. Of course, were you to accept the model then it does possess the advantage of being focused on providing guidance to the leader as to the optimum course of action in any given situation. Thus it could be a useful developmental tool, potentially to give those with no leadership decision-making experience 'a starter for 10'.

If you are the chief executive, which is the group you consider: The board, the executive team or your direct reports alone? Indeed, this is a problem with the whole situational/contingency field. The models may work well when used to predict leader performance in the context of the immediate group or team (and most studies look only at this). However, senior leadership performance impacts not only on the immediate group but success also depends on the effective working of multiple levels and many groups, perhaps in many locations, through other leaders. Are these models robust enough to stand up in such a situation and form a valid basis for understanding, let alone prediction? However, some will argue that this is a test no currently available model would survive!

In fairness, Vroom and Jago (1988) subsequently revised the original model, retaining the five original decision styles but adding 12 contingency variables including geographical dispersion. Inevitably, the outcome is even more complex decision trees to guide managers but it still does not really deal with the objection set out above. Nevertheless, it does provide a useful basis for thinking about leadership in the context of decision-making.

There remains a further 'ghost at the feast' when one looks at decision-making. The model takes no account of the decision-making problem as a problem-solving or learning issue. Thus no attention is devoted to the underlying assumptions or 'mindset' the leader brings to the process. Nor is any attention directed on to how issues are 'surfaced' to require decisions. Yet we know that the issues that are not brought forward for decision may be vital as a means of understanding how leaders come to dominate policy and practice in an organisation (Schattschneider, 1960).

3.6　The Path–Goal theory

This theory brings expectations into the analysis. If people expect/predict that increased effort will lead to increased performance, which will lead in turn to valued outcomes such as reward, then this will enhance their motivation. The extent to which a leader satisfies subordinates' expectations is predicted to impact on their performance. (This is based on the expectancy theory of motivation; see Vroom, 1964; Porter and Lawler, 1968; Lawler, 1978.)

In the Path–Goal theory (House, 1971) it is predicted that subordinates will respond to a leader in a situation where:

- The satisfaction of their needs is linked to performance.
- Leaders provide appropriate support, direction guidance, resources and training.

House identifies four leader behaviours:

- **Directive leadership** – similar to 'initiating structure', where the leader directs and subordinates are expected to work with clear directions, objectives and rules.
- **Supportive leadership** – leaders are approachable and show real concern for subordinates' needs – 'consideration'.
- **Participative leadership**, where leaders involve subordinates before making decisions.
- **Achievement-orientated leadership**, where leaders set challenging goals, seeking improvement and showing confidence in employees.

House (1971) argues that leaders can exhibit these different behaviours according to the situation, and the model takes changes of situation, performance improvement and the level of challenge in goal-setting into account.

3.8   The Hersey–Blanchard situational leadership model

This model considers two basic dimensions in leadership style: direction and support. The effective leader must vary the balance between direction and support according to the situation. In truth, and indeed in reality, the main factor in the situation is the 'readiness' of subordinates – essentially a measure of whether they possess the skills, ability and motivation to accomplish specific tasks to particular standards of performance and quality.

In the model, four levels of readiness are set out:

- R1: low, where people are unable or unwilling, lack motivation and commitment, or feel insecure.
- R2: low to moderate, where people are lacking the needed skills and ability to complete tasks but are otherwise willing to try.
- R3: moderate to high, where people are able to achieve tasks but are either unwilling to do so or feel insecure.
- R4: high, where people are able, willing and confident of the future.

Known as four levels of maturity, the appropriate leader style is a combination of task behaviour (directive) and relationship behaviour (supportive), and the model proposes four leadership styles:

- S1: telling
- S2: selling
- S3: participating
- S4: delegating

Each is linked to readiness, as follows:

$$S1 \text{ links to } R1 \qquad S3 \text{ links to } R3$$
$$S2 \text{ links to } R2 \qquad S4 \text{ links to } R4$$

The model proceeds to work through to development and this provides real value to leadership development practitioners. Here the focus is on capability (skill and ability) and motivation (willingness), with the argument that the role of the leader is not simply to accept the situation as 'defined' by employee 'readiness', but to work to improve it through development. Hersey and Blanchard (2000) report that the model has been used in training programmes of more than 400 of the Fortune 500 companies. From the authors' own experience it remains a credible and convincing model in wide use in company training and within business schools and other providers.

Certainly it is the experience of one of the co-authors who has used a slight adaptation (using more memorable descriptors for easy learning) of the core Hersey and Blanchard model for many years when developing leaders that it does set out a simple range of leadership style options for day-to-day use by line managers. In particular, it provides those with little or no previous leadership experience with a guide that will allow them to deliver a competent leadership outcome for most situations and to develop their skills going forward. In the worst case it is likely to, as a minimum, prevent the wrong approach being taken by inexperienced leaders – which is in itself a good thing. So in this sense it also acts as a risk mitigation system.

The Hersey and Blanchard model can therefore provide a basis for leadership development work in organisations using role-play exercises with video and feedback. Working in groups of three, 'learners' can each act out the leader, follower and observer roles in respect of a series of situations and a range of leader-style options. It also allows a focus on the immediate context of leader behaviour. Thus a young army officer accompanied on a field exercise by an experienced non-commissioned officer may feel the need to pay attention to the advice the non-commissioned officer offers because it is based on hard-won experience.

Thus we can practise the effects achieved by leadership-style choices. We can look at supportive versus directive leadership behaviour in varying leader contexts (e.g. with well-developed as compared with less well-developed followers) and in different situations. The situational leadership model turns out to be robust and soundly based in contingency thinking and is readily capable of being given operational form in a training setting. The one clear limitation is that to compare leader styles properly the role player needs to both understand and play out the differences accurately. However, the model is a workable basis for feedback and the focus is at least on observable behaviour. Of course, it is less effective where the leadership issues are more complex because multiple variables are likely to be involved. However, in the authors' experience, at all levels of leadership training and development, the model offers the basis for constructive discussion of alternative leadership styles.

3.9   Transformational leadership

Transformational, as opposed to transactional, leadership (see explanation below) has attracted considerable attention (Bass, 1985). This approach positions the leadership of change as a central feature of the leadership role (see Kotter, 1990; Kouzes and Posner, 1987; Bass and Avolio, 2004).

The model emerged as the changes resulting from globalisation, competitiveness and new technology have increasingly led senior executives to seek to renew or revitalise their organisations. Since Burns' (1978) original formulation there has developed a distinction between two forms of leadership: transactional and transformational.

Transactional leadership is based on accepting the status quo, working within existing ideas and expectations, and is focused on ensuring that leaders maximise current performance through the process of setting goals, work organisation, rewards, training and so on.

Transformational leadership involves the recognition that fundamental change is needed to adapt organisations to the changes that the world forces upon them, be they political, technological, economic or social. To meet these challenges, leaders thus need to rethink their vision, values and purpose in order to 'reset the clock', as it were. In a transformational situation the task is to move the organisation forward to entirely different levels of performance or into new areas of activity or approaches to the organisation's role, purpose and directions with stakeholders. The link between transformational leadership and charismatic leadership has been identified by observers such as Hunt (1991).

Following Bass (1985), the transformational leader seeks to engage subordinates to perform at new levels of performance. Bass proposed that transformational leaders seek to do so by generating a greater awareness of the organisational purpose, by emphasising that a more challenging environment requires renewed emphasis on an organisation's requirements and through activating higher-level needs. It comprises four essential components:

(i)   Idealised influence, charismatic leadership respected and admired by followers.

(ii)   Inspirational motivation, the provision of meaning and challenge in work.

(iii) Intellectual stimulation, including creative problem-solving, creating re-engineered solutions to old problems and constraints.

(iv)   Individualised consideration, the willingness to listen and respond to people's concerns and need for growth and development.

Certainly, as we shall see later, from a number of studies, there is clear evidence that the factors identified above, if acted upon, will improve individual, team and organisational performance.

Bass and Avolio (1994) contrast this to the main characteristics of transactional leadership, being contingent on reward and management by exception. Their research shows evidence to support the importance of transformational leadership, studies of which have shown to have a significantly greater impact than transactional leadership across a range of indicators including corporate financial performances.

Case study   **Television news**

Charles had been a successful television journalist working in the industry for some 15 years. Over that time he had progressed rapidly, eventually becoming African correspondent and Washington correspondent, and being seen regularly on prime time news. After that he was promoted into a key news management role, working for the network's Director of News and Current Affairs.

While he entered his new job with clear expectations about how his former colleagues would relate to him, he also experienced serious anxiety. He was moving from a glamorous role, through which he had gained some celebrity status, into a role with no external profile and therefore much less celebrity and with lower total rewards – for example, he would no longer qualify for various allowances paid to those who operate outside the UK.

Second, he felt he had received very little training or preparation for his new role. He had very little understanding of the financial and operational systems with which he would now have to work. At the same time the network was seeking to make budget cuts of 10 per cent to15 per cent in expenditure on news.

Charles said:

> My former colleagues are going to see me as not possessing the skills set to be in management and directly involved in the budget cuts. Where is my credibility in that situation? I feel like an impostor. At the same time, I listen to my new colleagues in management. I do not understand the jargon. To some extent I feel lost among them. Their priorities feel foreign to me. I was told I was being promoted to bring fresh perspectives but there seems to be little interest in my contributions. I am afraid to ask colleagues or my boss about this because that would display weakness. To tell the truth, I am afraid I will fail, but in trying to avoid this I am cutting myself off from others.
>
> In my present situation I feel that everyone is watching me. I feel isolated. Colleagues clearly do not trust my judgement and because I fear making that too obvious I find myself taking too long to make decisions. Yet news is a fast-moving culture. People are used to making quick decisions. I am losing my previous skills.

Source: Interviews undertaken by author in 2004 in a UK broadcasting organisation.

Case study questions (1)

1 What would you define as the key challenges of this first step into a management role?

2 How should the individual prepare for it and what can/should the organisation do?

3 How best can Charles deal with and change the sense of isolation to which he refers?

4 What strategy would you suggest for building credibility in this new role?

Many people describe this as 'transition anxiety'. One study indicates that not only do more than half of managers view promotion as a challenge but also that many see promotion as being risky. Kets de Vries (1980) has identified eight management 'types': strategist, change catalyst, transactor, innovator, processor, coach, communicator and deal-maker). He suggests that an effective leader needs to be a balance of all these types, but it is unlikely that any individual has the capability to do all of these equally well. This demonstrates the criticality of the leaders in an organisation working as a team, not just as individuals, and that the building of effective teams needs to ensure that all of the key roles set out above are present. This enables the 'leadership team' to be more effective than the individuals – a key purpose or organisational leadership.

Case study questions (2)

5 Can leadership development be a means of supporting the promotion process? Should selection for promotion be based on performance in a previous role or potential for the future, or both?

6 Should people be selected for promotion with more emphasis on the outputs they must deliver rather than on the traits they may possess?

7 What is the role of the divisional head appointing Charles into his new position? What should the Director of News and Current Affairs be thinking about to ensure that Charles can work effectively in his new role?

3.10   The social identity approach

Here the key question to be asked is how are the tasks of leadership achieved? So rather than pointing to characteristics of the leader, his or her style and the situation in which he/she is operating, the social identity approach involves looking more at what leaders do. The approach sees leadership as relational – creating a relationship between leader and followers.

This is not unique, but what is different is the idea that leaders represent and define social identity (Haslam, 2004). The approach says that leaders are 'categorised' by others and it is this perception of them as leaders that is important; and the extent to which they meet the expectations of others that is the determinant of success in the role. This appears obvious enough but Haslam argues that this 'social categorisation' approach is of limited value in aiding an understanding of leadership. Indeed, he argues that the evidence supporting the idea of transformational leadership ought to be combined with this approach, thus bringing into play a framework for examining leadership within the ongoing dynamic of the group acting in a changing environment – changing relationships and perspectives in a changing environment.

There is certainly value in this focus on the 'relational' dimension, supported by significant data that these relationships impact on performance and retention.

It could be suggested that while this idea may be effective at lower levels of leadership where a leader is working with a single and definable group, it may have less to contribute when looking at senior leadership where leaders relate to many groups. Certainly in terms of impacts, the 'direct' leader – that is, the individual's line manager – has a significantly greater impact on performance than have 'indirect' leaders such as senior management. That said, the approach certainly enables us to consider the social dynamics of the process within which leaders operate.

Aligned to this, Haslam (2004) quotes Kanter (1983) as arguing that senior executives must not merely 'fit in' with peers. Rather, they need to convince stakeholders, including other people in their organisation, that they are promoting a common interest – obviously vital to the creation of an organisation's common vision and values.

Groups develop an identity through the perspectives and emotions of members, and these then operate as a system of mutual feedback within the group. This creates a sense of unity and stability for the group, thereby leading to a shared social identity. The leader is likely to be central to this process.

3.11   New leadership

Describing an 'emerging perspective on leadership', Higgs (2003) notes that the frustration felt about the perceived lack of coherence of leadership research is based on a paradigm which 'suggests that there is a fundamental truth which is yet to be discovered'. Following Weick (1995) employing the notion of 'sense making', he notes that new insights might be gained by rethinking leadership studies, moving away from the idea that the purpose is to discover something new, but rather to develop a newer understanding of ways to rethink what has already been developed to meet current conditions. This must be the best tactic as previous approaches to leadership have not been found to be wrong – it is just that they do not seem to provide an answer giving a complete explanation of how leadership works.

Higgs argues that emerging work on leadership focuses on the leader's behaviour and the impact of that leader on the followers, in contrast to the leader's selection of style to 'fit' the situation, which includes aspects of the characteristics of the followers.

Kouzes and Posner (1987) view effective leadership, seen from the follower perspective, as including the following actions:

- Leaders challenging the process and allowing their own role to be challenged.
- Leaders inspiring a shared vision.
- Enabling others to act.
- Modelling the way.
- Encouraging the heart.

Goffee and Jones (2005), on the other hand, refer to 'authenticity' of leadership as deriving from approachability, vulnerability, intuitive responses to 'soft' data, tough empathy: that is, being concerned to understand people but at the same time being realistic and having the ability to reveal, explore and work within differences. Here there is much more in common with the Collins (2001) concept of Level 5 leadership, which sees successful CEOs as combining high levels of willpower with humility, in particular the absence of arrogance.

Higgs (2003) therefore sets out a model of effective leadership combining skills/competencies and personal attributes, arguing that leaders need both to act effectively and to know themselves. He then adds emotional intelligence (EI) to this model, but many would take that as being within the 'personal attribute' category.

Conversely, Goleman *et al.* (2002) introduce the concept of 'resonant' and 'dissonant' leadership styles, and the notion of 'formal leadership'. The argument is simply set out, at the start of their book, as 'Great leaders move us' suggests that leaders ignite our passion and inspire the best in us. When we try to explain why they are so effective, we speak of strategy, vision or powerful ideas. But the reality is much more primal: great leadership works through the emotions (Goleman *et al.*, 2002). Primal leadership refers to the emotional role of a leader as someone to whom the group can turn for reassurance and clarity when facing uncertainty and threat. But, in particular, primal leadership is positive and emotionally supportive. It pushes people to do a good job *and* leaves them feeling a part of a living and worthwhile community.

Resonance derives from primal leadership. When leaders bring out the best of people and create a shared sense of purpose, they create resonance, but when they rely on negative emotions or fear, they create dissonance. Similarly, Gardner (2004) refers to the importance of 'resonance' when looking at 'changing minds'; clearly something that a leader must achieve in a changing world. However, from the author's perspective there must also be a 'morality and ethic' behind this resonance that makes people act to do the 'right thing'. Some might view one of the greatest creators in modern times of resonance among people was Adolf Hitler, so it prompts the question as to whether resonance or primal leadership is always a force for good.

Goleman *et al.* go on, while noting that the tasks of a leader include generating enthusiasm, engagement, passion and so on, to demonstrate how EI enables this to be accomplished, by showing how the four domains of EI – self-awareness, self-management, social awareness, and relationship management – enable leaders to create resonant leadership. The core idea here is that of 'rules of engagement'. These develop out of the personal and social competence of leaders as they relate to others. In outline:

I	Discovery	■ respect the group's values
		■ sustain the organisation's integrity
		■ slow down in order to speed up
		■ lead from the top, build from the bottom
II	Vision	■ look inside
		■ don't align: attune
		■ people first, then strategy
III	Sustain change	■ create action
		■ create systems to support resonance
		■ manage the myths of leadership

Interestingly, this model becomes internally focused, looking at how leaders behave in achieving success. But in practice the model makes one key assumption that, when faced with challenges, the answer must lie within the organisation and not outside. However, as we know from both case studies and experience, that if an organisation is forced to transform itself into something new it seems very unlikely that the solution for doing so is always within. The importance of 'resonant leadership' is that it provides a means of linking together the ideas of 'trait' theory, situations and contingency models, and transformational leadership. This represents an important contribution to a divergent field of thought to bring some valuable consolidation to the divergent models.

It is important in one other sense. Under 'Rules of Engagement' and within the category of 'Sustain Change', Goleman *et al.* (2002) list 'manage the myths of leadership'. Here they talk about stories and symbols supporting the development of 'resonance'. Wills (1991) argues that, in the Gettysburg address, Lincoln elevated quality to a position of paramount importance. In effect, Lincoln was reinterpreting and reworking the Constitution in the minds of those he addressed. The identity of America was being defined around his famous words:

Four score and seven years ago our fathers brought forth on this continent a new nation, conceived in Liberty, and dedicated to the proposition that all men are created equal.

The point here is that effective leadership works via tacit means through 'shared identity'. This is reinforced by stories and symbols, but the foundation is shared identity and by the desire to use that as a driver of change. The challenge is that, in a rapidly changing world, leaders must articulate ideas which 'resonate' with the people they seek to influence but this means that they cannot just simply conform to current group ideas. To mobilise people for the future they must shape the ideas and build a compelling vision. Leaders need to create credibility by building resonance around current ideas then working through into new resonances via social identities as a means of helping people to make sense of the new realities with which they must engage.

There is an opportunity here to build on an emerging 'social movements' literature. This is interesting because 'social movements' are about achieving large-scale change. Whether we are looking at US civil rights, the UK's 'Ban the Bomb' campaign or the South African anti-apartheid campaign it is clear that social movements may well have something to tell us about how to engage people with large-scale change. Lack of ambition is not something one would associate with campaigns of this sort, whether they are ultimately successful or not.

Bate *et al.* (2004) offer a survey of the social movements approach. Social movements are mainly about engaging people at a 'deep' or even an emotional level. Change is essentially self-directing and follows an absolute, some might say messianic, commitment to the cause. Ultimately 'social movements' are voluntary. However, can we really argue that 'social movements' have no leader? Martin Luther King? Nelson Mandela? While the comparison may not stand up to detailed scrutiny, there is something to be said for it. Martin Luther King was a civil rights leader who captured world attention, but how much progress would he have made without someone like Rosa Parks making her own stand? Nelson Mandela was in prison for decades until the fall of the apartheid regime and thus was unable to act as an effective operational leader. Here the role of the 'inspirational figurehead' needs to be balanced with the function of 'leadership'. In the cases of both Mandela and King there were a number of less well-known leaders working on strategy and operational tactics while leaving the 'figurehead' role to the high-profile individuals.

Nevertheless it is right to note that social movements often inspire courageous choices, where personal cost, danger or hardship may be, and sometimes is, involved for those making choices. Taking this further, what is the role of the leader in creating a movement to address what is seen as morally wrong, and is it necessary for a leader to be present to encourage individuals to take risks to right that wrong?

The significant changes in the Arab world in early 2010–11, often called 'The Arab Spring' have an interesting dynamic here in relation to leadership, and it answers that question. If there is enough of a common grievance that gets to the point where people lose their fear of authority, punishment or even death, then those people will spontaneously rise up. The common repeated view from those on the street was that they would rather be dead than continue to live under such circumstances. This meant that the popular uprisings that swept the long-standing leaders of Tunisia and Egypt away in just a few weeks had no leaders to speak of, similarly the uprisings in

Yemen, Libya, Syria and Bahrain were also 'leaderless' initially, but that caused problems. It appears that unless the uprising can depose the leader in a few weeks and the rebels have direction, focus and co-ordination through leadership, the uprising loses momentum in the face of organised resistance from the existing regime where the leaders have the capability to hold on to power or at least retain some element of support. So it was in Libya and Syria, where the regimes had time to regroup and fight back, resulting in significant loss of life and the persecution of anyone seen to be potential leaders of the uprising, to the degree of mass arrests, detention, torture and the shooting of large numbers of protesters.

Another example is that if the number of individuals is considered who volunteered to take part in the work of the British Special Operations Executive (SOE) in the Second World War and work behind enemy lines at significant risk of torture or death, one cannot identify any specific leader encouraging them directly to be involved in such high-risk action. While Winston Churchill was seen as the overall war leader in the UK, there was no direct relationship between him and the thousands who volunteered for such operations. Why did many do this, knowing that death was a strong possibility, without a specific leader encouraging them to do so? Perhaps because there comes a point at which some individuals take it upon themselves to challenge what they see as wrong no matter what the personal cost based on a self-actualising calculation and not as a result of there being a leader. No one who has seen the historical films covering these events, *Carve Her Name With Pride*, about SOE operations, or *Cry Freedom* – about the anti-apartheid movement, cannot fail to be convinced of the power of individual and social action.

Returning to the organisational world, while it may be reasonable to characterise traditional organisational models as emphasising questions such as 'What is this action seeking to achieve, and what evidence is there that it will have the desired effect?', it is simplistic to contrast that with a social movements emphasis on 'Who supports the idea, how were they mobilised and how much influence can they deploy?' Following Kelman (2005) it is clear that such questions could and would be asked by the organisation practitioner and theorist. However, it may be reasonable to argue that within the context of 'social movements' change is 'released, liberated, channelled and enabled'. Within the organisational world, strategic leaders seem to mobilise logical processes of change that people accept and support rather than create inspirational drivers of change that mobilise individuals to take action and initiative. Perhaps if they did more of the latter greater numbers of changes in organisations would be successful? This goes back to the Corporate Leadership Council's finding that the employees' decision to supply high performance is 57 per cent rational and 43 per cent emotional. Failure to use the emotional element to gain buy-in by leaders must reduce the chances of success.

To summarise, social movements can lead to transformational change on a national or international level, albeit that the achievement of many social movements may be more modest. Traditional approaches to organisation change and social movement principles share some characteristics, particularly if one is contrasting the idea of emergent change with social movement ideas. The latter involve collective action by people who have come together voluntarily around a common cause, typically (though not always) have spontaneous beginnings and involving radical action and protest. Interestingly enough, organisation changes often have less spontaneous beginnings and are more typically a process of learning, carried out systematically.

Conversely, social movements are often informal networks, based on shared beliefs and the mobilised perception of 'wrongs needing to be righted', often through the frequent use of protest.

As we have indicated, the consideration of followers is important to much recent work in leadership. The links Goleman *et al.* make between EI and leadership behaviour look to have value and this is being supported by an increasing body of empirical evidence. Dionne *et al.* (2004) for example, collected data from 50,000 employees and over 50 organisations in their survey of the top 300 drivers of employee engagement. They found that 73 per cent of the emotional commitment by an individual to deliver discretionary effort was linked to his or her manager's behaviour.

3.12   Competency models for leadership development

These models became influential from the 1980s onwards. They typically seek to link objectives and outcomes to leadership behaviours (Boyatsis, 1982). Crucially, this whole field takes as its most basic assumption the idea that individuals with high levels of leadership competence are likely to be more successful in leadership roles.

If relationships are the primary means through which leadership is practised, then these interpersonal competencies are certainly going to be important for success. The evidence linking these behavioural competencies to success may be less than comprehensive but House (1996) and Yukl (2002) examined the links between leader behaviour and success. House noted that supportive behaviour, directive behaviour, participative behaviour and achievement orientation are all important in the prediction of successful leadership, while the work of Yukl (2002) examined the interaction effects between leader behaviour, other factors and work group performance. However, Yukl noted six intervening variables as affecting performance: subordinate effort; role clarity and task skills; work organisation; cohesiveness and co-operation; resources; and support. Other factors he called 'neutralisers'. One of these was 'interesting and challenging work', which can produce high levels of effort irrespective of leader behaviour. Where neutralisers are low, leader behaviour becomes important for performance. Note, however, that this work relates to lower levels of leadership in terms of organisational level. Higher-level leadership effectiveness is likely to depend more on the ability to work through other leaders than on interpersonal behaviour.

It is argued that the key weakness of this whole field relates to the difficulties of integrating the many studies because each is uncommon in important respects. Each uses its own definitions of success and predictors of success, and each looks at particular settings. Typically, these studies work with the following themes:

(i)   Balancing performance, concern for people and the need for change.

(ii)   Deploying intra- and interpersonal competence.

(iii) Engaging in transformational and charismatic behaviours.

(iv)   Thinking and acting in more complex ways.

(v)   Overcoming limitations in pursuit of success.

(vi)   Seeking a wider variety of leadership performances.

Certainly many of the behaviours considered above are not specific to leadership. For example, self-awareness is important in most fields of human endeavour, as is relationship building. Moreover, no single leader will possess all these behaviours to the same degree. Indeed it is worth noting that high levels of some will mitigate against others. Finally, it is not obvious what is meant in all cases. What do we mean by balancing task, concern for people and concern for change? Back to Adair's (1973) principles again to some degree. In theory it is obvious enough – that is, we need to deliver today's business to continue to generate resource streams. We need to change to guarantee tomorrow's business in a changing environment. If all employees wish for stability, then the former may satisfy that need but not the latter – at least in the short term. But sooner or later this may not be true.

It is easy enough to argue generically but how can we measure, assess or evaluate this balance in the present and in a particular situation? In practice this is unlikely to be achieved other than by asking participants for their views. And if we do is this appropriate without the reference point of being able to assess data independently of participants? This returns us to the problem of the theory of leadership versus its day-to-day practice in the real world – where leaders have to make their own decisions guided by overarching principles set against the situations they are in, driven by time pressure and incomplete information, rather than by applying the complexity of a precise theoretical model with all the time in the world available.

Regardless of these issues, competency models have emerged and found widespread application. These comprise a definition of the leadership capacity and capability needed by any leader – viewed in terms of behavioural competencies. Combined with selection and assessment tools and leadership development 'pathways' these models often form the basis of leadership development in modern organisations (see Chapter 4). Three interconnected questions need to be resolved as part of developing a competence framework, as follows:

(i)   Do you wish to restrict development to certain key roles, or develop a generic set applying to leadership roles throughout the organisation?

(ii) Do you wish to focus on today's requirements or future requirements, or both?

(iii) How can you ensure that the framework is credible throughout the organisation?

Given the effects of the 2006–10 financial crisis, point (ii) is of particular interest. Here, many competency frameworks developed prior to this event were modelled on the behaviours of leaders in an environment characterised by rising and expanding markets, confidence, some degree of certainty, easy credit and good corporate performance. After the crisis, organisations faced reductions in markets, restricted credit, lack of confidence, uncertainty about what was going to happen and diving corporate performance, all suggesting that new leader behaviours were required to be effective.

More fundamentally, there is one underlying issue associated with the competency approach that needs to be recognised. In a global economy where knowledge and professionalism increasingly form the basis of competitive advantage, it is hard to define in detail what leaders and professionals need to know and to do. Their work goes beyond discrete tasks governed by simple, clear 'operating rules' or job descriptions and must increasingly address uncertainty and complexity through experience, intuition and judgement, the latter involving weighing 'gut feeling'. Leadership tasks and challenges now are increasingly complex and there are often multiple ways of achieving the end result.

All of this mitigates against the concept of a competency framework, at least to some degree as a practical tool. There is nothing wrong in principle with developing a competency framework or model. Competency maps can provide a useful starting point for both individuals and organisations. to examine what leadership development is needed and how best to organise access to it. We shall return to this issue in Chapter 4. However, we have already noted the increasing interest devoted to the 'strengths based' approach (Buckingham, 2005).

Competency based approaches tend for some people to focus on 'gaps' and therefore on weaknesses rather than on strengths, which may make it harder to base effective leadership development on the analysis derived from such a model. But, more importantly, a competency model focuses attention on the leader, rather than on the basis for 'leaders' and 'followers' to relate to each other in an effective way. Including interpersonal skills in competency models may hope to mitigate the problem in practice but does not completely deal with this difficulty because it ignores the followers. What is needed is a focus on the leader–follower relationship as a process of two–way exchange rather than one way, along the lines of the situational models.

Competency models can be a means of improving policy and practice for leadership development. This naturally leads into the ideas relating leader effectiveness and effective leadership development. Both clearly interrelate, but just as clearly there are differences. What will lead to the development of effective leadership development in practice is more than an analysis of the quality of leadership currently in place. It is the motivation and capability of leaders to learn and change, and the associated learning and development mindsets, that are important.

Sadly, in the real organisational world the competency model has fallen prey to the HR professionals' own desire to make it as accurate and effective as possible by including all the possible factors that have an impact on leadership performance. This has resulted in more and more factors being included, which has increased the complexity of the framework to the point at which it can only be a theoretical exercise. In many cases no line manager has the time to measure his or her subordinates against such complex frameworks, given the other tasks that have to be completed.

On many occasions, talking to corporate executives, their view has been that competency frameworks are often too impractical and they will avoid completing them if at all possible. One senior HR leader in a UK public sector organisation proudly told one of the co-authors that they had reduced the number of competencies leaders are assessed against from 27 to only 15! The authors' experience suggests that anything more than eight was unlikely to be used effectively by the majority of line managers. However, the senior executives in organisations with more complex competency frameworks are often provided with a pack by the HR function including forms, explanations and definitions of each competency, indicating how they apply at each level of responsibility and functional activity. These executives have assured the authors that these texts form excellent door stops or paperweights rather than a means of assessing leadership capability. One UK public sector organisation even had two different competency frameworks for different groups and a conversion guide to use at the interface that, in itself, exceeded 130 pages. This gives rise to the question of whether a competency framework is an intellectual exercise for the HR function or a real tool that makes a difference day-to-day in the organisation in developing leaders?

3.13   What next?

The fallout from the financial crisis of 2006–10 suggests that while good leadership principles have not themselves changed in what is perceived to be a more uncertain and tougher world, the delivery of good leadership is reliant on a different style of delivery of those core principles.

There appears to be a greater acceptance of the emotional content of leadership than was previously admitted by some theorists. Perhaps because the relationship between the leader and those who are led is much more difficult to define and quantify using what might be perceived as objective tools. It is likely that this area is going to be subject to greater scrutiny than previously.

The data are already building up, for example the Corporate Leadership Council (2006) took data from around 50,000 employees in 50 organisations in 27 countries. One of the key findings was that, to improve performance, 57 per cent are delivered by rational performance enablers – for example, information and experience – and 43 per cent by emotional factors. Of this 43 per cent, the line manager is responsible for 73 per cent; that is, about 33 per cent of total commitment is through the emotional influence of the leader. So this is saying that 33 per cent of all performance improvement comes from an area of leadership that has had little detailed investigation. The strange thing is, however, that we already know what it is going to say! From personal experience we all know what motivates us to go that extra mile for an individual – and we don't really need research to tell us as individuals what we know personally – but the research should summarise what we all think, and many of those thoughts are common across society. So perhaps this and new seemingly more complex area of leadership is actually simpler than we think.

There are some interesting ideas developing that have been carried over from psychology and behavioural economics regarding the behaviour of individuals and teams. The common assumption is made that leaders make the right decisions, that groups of leaders make even better decisions, and that these decisions are ethical. Sadly, this assumption that underpins our belief in leadership may not always be right. Campbell *et al.* (2009, pp. 60–6) argue that leaders make the wrong decisions because of inappropriate self-interest, distorting attachments – emotional links to people or places and misleading memories, and assuming that the current situation matches the past when it doesn't. They quote the US Army officer who left the control centre in New Orleans on the night of the overwhelming of the defences by Hurricane Katrina in 2008. Despite reports that some defences had been breached he rationalised them as being inaccurate and ignored them, with disastrous results.

Behavioural economics argues that human beings are essentially irrational more than rational, and often motivated by unconscious cognitive biases. Could this explain why a logical case for organisational change, why the logical requests of a leader or the right thing to do does not seem to persuade the individual or group? In an article, Dan Ariely (2009, pp. 78–84) suggested even more worryingly that human beings are motivated to 'cheat' a little and rationalising that cheating on this level is not really cheating. Even more worrying is Ariely's finding that the team, rather than reduce the effect of cheating, can actually amplify it. When one considers the behaviour of senior leaders in some of the corporate scandals or disasters of the later 2000s, maybe there are factors in leadership behaviour that we haven't yet touched on. And what does this say in respect or organisational values? There is still much for those who study leadership to find out.

3.14   Summary

In this chapter we have sought to describe and assess the principal theories of leadership developed to date. The long history of research into leadership has often been controversial but has always been viewed as a starting point for subsequently developing tools and techniques for assessing, reviewing and developing leaders in practice. Leadership development is the logical output as if we accept that high-quality leadership is a good thing for society and organisations, then we should seek to develop more good leaders. To do this we need to understand how leadership works, and the development of theories is the only way to achieve that. Linked to this it is natural to look at how leadership has been defined and how the concepts developed have influenced leadership development more generally. In an organisation this is not a linear process but rather a circle which comprises theories and the means of development for one generation of leaders, which in turn creates the next generation (see Figure 3.3).

However, over the years the number of theories has grown so much that we need some consolidation and integration, and this is now beginning to emerge. In general the transformational leadership concept as it has been developed has been consolidated with situational and contingency models and with competence models. This work has also led to an extensive treatment of how to link leadership theory to the

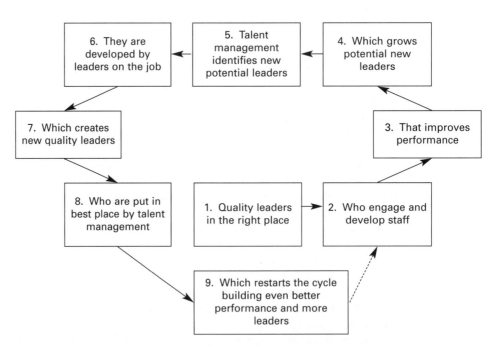

Fig 3.3   Building sustainable leadership for the future as well as delivering in the present

development of effective leadership and successful organisations. Here the work of Bass (1985), Bennis and Nanus (1985), Kouzes and Posner (1987), Kotter and Hesketh (1992) and Conger and Kanugo (1998) ought to be mentioned, alongside the contribution of Goleman *et al.* (2002).

The links between these leadership models and organisational success is less clear, given the number of factors impacting on that success – for example, economic cycles – but that said some is emerging when using effective benchmarking against peers within industries or sectors. But this is not to say these theories are irrelevant. As already discussed, the difficulties of undertaking leadership research in what is inevitably a complex, multivariable environment make this an aspiration.

One question that those engaged in the development of leadership theory must ask is why they are doing this? There seems to be a divergence of opinion. Some say they are seeking a model of leadership that effectively finds the answer to the question 'How does leadership work?' and thus identifies all the factors involved in making this happen; and others say they want to help to make leadership work in organisations better than it does now. The problem is that at the start of the development of leadership theory the two objectives seemed to be mutually supportive – see, for example, John Adair (1973) – but now we have to accept that they aren't. The ultimate theory that gives us the academic and theoretical answer we want is unlikely to be something that organisations can use on a daily basis to deliver operational leadership. The challenge for leadership experts is now to find a way to do both, not just one of them, or our relevance to the real world will decline. It is also to find out more about the emotional side of leadership, which leads to either admirable behaviour or appalling behaviour that we know so little about.

Case study   Qualco

Qualco is a (fictional) manufacturer of weapons systems hardware. Over some years there has been considerable evidence of both leadership ineffectiveness and the need for specific changes. Top management did not understand the causes of this ineffectiveness, or how to tackle it. The CEO, who had held the post for some years, adopted an autocratic management style. After an early period of profit growth the company had stagnated, with profits remaining at the same level despite growth in sales. Consultants had been used to review systems and procedures, and to help with the introduction of techniques such as enterprise resource planning (ERP) systems.

The finance director had played a major role in the various changes. Qualco is a mid-market company and the finance director also covers the HR function. In this case study, using his own assessment, he reviews the approach he had adopted with individual managers, linking this to the specific changes made and to how he has used approaches similar to those discussed in this book to learn from the experience. From the many examples, two will suffice.

Tony, the Company Accountant

Tony is the Company Accountant and reports directly to me. He is a qualified accountant who joined the company late in 1986 and is experienced. He is very competent, particularly in the field of computers and systems, where his knowledge exceeds mine, and is also highly self-motivated. I have therefore used a delegating style with him and have gone out of my way to let him do things his way. Consequently, he has been able to make a substantial number of changes and introduce many new systems, in many cases replacing systems I installed when I was doing his job. This leadership style appears to have been effective with him, and he has achieved a great deal in terms of systems development.

Despite a high level of achievement on Tony's part, however, problems do occur. Deadlines are frequently missed. On several occasions he has found himself with a problem by devoting a substantial amount of time to new work, such as developing the computer system, while being over-optimistic regarding the amount of time necessary for the routine work. It appears that he had not placed a high enough priority on current work, such as having the monthly accounts prepared on time.

Missing these goals has been very personal and very difficult for Tony. He has been embarrassed by people such as the auditors, the Group Chief Accountant, Mike, and myself waiting for his work, and has had to explain on many occasions that he is unable to deliver. I have therefore reverted as quickly as possible to a participating style in as low key a manner as possible. I have discussed with him future priorities such as accounting deadlines. I have shown as much sympathy as possible with his problems and avoided criticism, but have not avoided the subject of missed deadlines. I have initiated a two-way discussion on how we can meet deadlines in the future 'now that you have developed a computer system that is so much better than before'. I try to emphasise 'our' difficulties and 'our' failures while referring to 'your' successes. I have made particular efforts to engage in active listening and to try to accept all of his suggestions while avoiding my own suggestions except when he has not had any of his own. My general objective is to motivate him to organise things in his own way but to slightly increase the emphasis on the company's objectives so that the company's and his own are as closely matched as possible.

Recently I have noticed some improvement, which seems to be sustained. I am gradually reducing my involvement but keeping some pressure on him, requiring regular updates on progress and future plans.

John, the Production Director

I noticed there was a problem with John, the Production Director, in relation to enabling change. Following an investigation by a consultant, a number of significant changes were to be introduced in the production department. These changes included the introduction of just-in-time techniques, Enterprise Resource Planning (ERP) systems, total quality concepts and changes in the method of organising technicians and production managers. John had shown continued opposition to these measures, though they eventually proved to be popular with the rest of the management. In view of John's intransigence towards change, the consultants had recommended that he be dismissed, but at the last moment he agreed voluntarily to support the changes. At the suggestion of the consultants he agreed to use me as a supporter/counsellor. I was unavoidably absent from this meeting, and shortly afterwards I was away for two months for business reasons.

On my return, in view of the long delay and the fact that I was not present at the original meeting, I thought it inappropriate to broach the question of ongoing collaboration between John and me. I felt that John was suffering from the dilemma of having problems in his department that he was unable to solve, particularly those that required some degree of interpersonal skills. In the long term I think John needs training to help him improve his interpersonal skills but in the short term I thought it would be helpful if I were to try to ease some problem areas for him.

Improving the performance of John's production managers in dealing with disciplinary problems seemed to be the most obviously profitable area. I therefore asked him if he would be happy with me trying to sort out some ongoing personnel problems by direct contact with his staff. As I cover HR and am closely involved in general management, this could be done in a reasonably natural way. For some time there had clearly been disciplinary problems with the shop floor and these had not been properly addressed by management. Absenteeism was running at a very high rate, and a number of people were taking 20–40 days off per annum on a regular basis; and there were complaints from the production managers that some people, notably on the nightshift, were very difficult to supervise.

For some reason, the production managers had been unable to get to grips with discipline on the shop floor. A fair amount of aggression had been used by them but no improvement had been seen and shop floor morale was low. There had been claims from the production managers in the past that these problems would be solved 'if the managers got enough support from the directors', but it was never entirely clear what was meant by this statement. However, I agreed with John that I would try to sort out whatever personnel problems there were, and keep him generally informed about what I was doing. We agreed that he would let me know if he thought I was interfering over much. I determined to talk to each relevant manager and to discuss their problems with them.

Initially their reaction was as it had always been in the past: they said that if they were left to get on with their jobs, take whatever decisions were necessary and dismiss whichever people they felt deserved this, there would be no problems. They said that the personnel department had restricted management action on discipline in the past. I said that what I wanted to do was to examine each individual case and follow it through to its conclusion – which I hoped would be an improved performance on the part of the employee.

My initial approach was to examine each employee's file to see who had been issued with written warnings that could be followed up. When I produced a list of the employees who needed to be spoken to or written to again, two of the production managers admitted that they had each had a number of written warnings for their department on such things as unexplained absence, excessive sickness and bad discipline, and that they had failed to hand them out. They each said that they had forgotten to do so. This seemed extremely unlikely, and on further discussion it transpired that none of the production managers was sure what to do in any given disciplinary situation.

One of the managers had developed an extremely aggressive personal style over the years and tended to shout at people when they did something wrong. He did not really know how to follow up this approach, especially when the employee concerned seemed willing to enter into a reasoned discussion. The other two confessed that they found it very difficult to enforce discipline and were not sure how to go about it. With these admissions in the open, it was a relatively straightforward business from then on to tackle the situation.

We decided to start from scratch. I saw each of the worst offenders personally with one of the production managers present, explained the situation and said that their performance had to improve. Some employees commented that a large contributory factor was the attitude of management and that they did not respect them. My response was to say that we are aware of shortcomings throughout the company, and that all managers, including directors, would be receiving training, but that I expected an immediately improved performance from the employees as well. Also, the company was looking for a situation in which genuine problems could be discussed between management and employees. However, failure to meet a satisfactory standard would not be tolerated in the future. In other words, we wanted a frank and open atmosphere in which problems were discussable but we did not intent to be soft.

Most employees seemed to warm to this attitude, though over the course of the months it was necessary to dismiss several whose behaviour did not improve. After a fairly short time I found that the production managers were becoming enthusiastic and coming to me with progress reports. They also seemed to be happier in what they were doing once they had some direction.

During those months I rewrote and substantially expanded the Company Handbook, a publication I introduced only last year. I took the opportunity to call a meeting of all production managers and supervisors to ask their opinion of the section relating to disciplinary procedures. This was an excuse to discuss how to act in different situations, and quite a lengthy discussion ensued. It was surprising how many people were pleased that they had the opportunity to ask how to act in various situations. Having a set of rules to discuss removed some of the embarrassment of them admitting that they did not know how to act – they were able to ask what was expected of them in enforcing each rule.

All this indicates that frank and open discussion of problems helps to motivate staff. The managers and supervisors referred to above were very grateful to be treated in the 'telling' and 'selling' styles, and had previously found themselves uncomfortable with John's delegating style because they lacked the maturity to deal with the situation in which they found themselves. It must be remembered, of course, that John had delegated by default, not because of a conscious opinion of the proper way to react to his subordinates. Though I do not envisage a situation in which I will continue to instruct managers and supervisors in this manner, I believe that they have been given more confidence to work under John with his delegation style.

A further example of increasing motivation by increased communication is the training course that many of our managers and supervisors attended several months ago. This was agreed with the consultants although Mike, who is very cynical about training, agreed that it could be run partly because the consultants supported it and partly because it was included in their original fee. It was a fairly short course at a local hotel and covered basic aspects of supervision and work planning, but I felt that the biggest benefit was the opportunity it created for managers and supervisors to talk together about their work. While there was little discussion afterwards regarding the individual topics dealt with on the course, on their return there was a noticeable increase in esprit de corps. It also created an expectation of further change and support, and there has been substantial agitation from the managers for the board to attend a broadly similar course, and this has now been agreed.

Simultaneously, there was a change in the work pattern of the production managers. There was previously one nightshift manager with two dayshift managers splitting their duties but without the two shifts overlapping. Problems occurred in both areas on days and there had been severe disciplinary problems on the nightshift for years. With the three managers working rotating shifts and covering the whole 24 hours, there was substantial opportunity for improvement. For example, whereas the nightshift manager could previously hide from his problems at night, it was now necessary for him to discuss them openly with the manager who was about to take over from him, and problems had to be faced because they would be noticed by the next person working on that shift. This enhanced the atmosphere of having to address problems frankly and openly. It was interesting to note that whereas previously managers had failed to hand out warnings, there have recently been cases where they have gained such confidence and enthusiasm that they have been competing to be the one to hand out the warning. One manager even insisted on coming in from holiday to see a particularly difficult employee who had worked exclusively for him before the rotating shift system had been introduced.

By working hard to create an atmosphere in which managers could take on the task of changing their approach without fear of reprimand, it was possible to encourage behavioural change. This was enhanced by ensuring that frank admissions (for example, regarding the written warnings) were not 'punished' but at the same time it was necessary to ensure that the proper approach was discussed.

Commentary

It is not difficult to conclude that the problems here are a consequence of a combination of factors. The autocratic style of the CEO may well have combined with a need to push through a series of changes quickly to create a situation in which managers felt 'out of control' and, fearing punishment from the top level and conflict from those they managed, they reverted to a 'laissez-faire' management style within which performance management could not develop. Problems were ignored and there was a real need to move to a situation where problems can be faced openly and in an evidence-based way.

Trait theory could be used as a means of thinking about the way that the individuals described tackle their leadership roles. In reality, however, analysing the problems requires that they are viewed in context. This leads to examining the situational and contingency models, but each looks too narrow. Both the transformational leadership model and the resonant leadership model can provide a basis for analysing these problems and the finance director's response to them.

Questions

1 Does the phrase 'born leader' make sense to you, or demonstrate the level of misunderstanding about leadership that exists?

2 Of the many leadership models that have been developed over the years, which seems to you to be the most effective?

3 Do you think that the models you have learnt about are viable for use in the real world?

4 If you were to make up your own leadership model, what would the key elements be?

4 Can leadership be developed, and if so how best to do it?

4.1 Introduction

The age-old question of why some people become leaders and some don't makes us to look back to the past to try to find solutions for the future. We know that great leaders guide us through difficult times, inspire us to achieve more than we thought possible, give us a clear direction amid the fog of life. The mystique of leadership from the great heroes of history confuses the issue, and means that we make assumptions about the difficulty of developing leaders that we would not apply to the development of anyone else. We need to have more and better leaders at all levels in both society and our organisations. To do this we need to find a structured and successful way to develop leaders.

This chapter is designed to take a critical but practice-based view of the mystique of leadership, to show that it can be developed to a level of competence viable for day-to-day organisational activity; that most people have some leadership potential; and that organisations can therefore control the supply of leaders to match their needs if they have a competent strategy to do so. We discuss leadership in its different guises: the direct, hands-on operational leadership of the front line: the indirect leadership in the complex and long-term environment of the strategic leader; and the development of good senior leaders from operational to strategic.

We recognise that leadership and development is not just the focus of an HR initiative; it is the glue that holds the organisation together and makes action and delivery possible. It is an enabler of corporate success, not merely a by-product of success, though success can help to develop leadership further. We argue that leadership development must deliver what the organisation as well as the individual needs, and it must enable the creation of leadership teams as well as individual leaders. Some elements of leadership can be systematised successfully, but others defy this systematisation. Because leadership is to some degree about character and process, simplicity and complexity, it follows that to create a rounded leader is really a much more difficult task than many think, but yet it can be done, and in ways that drive organisational as well as individual performance.

Can leadership be taught? Clearly, this is an important and often controversial question which is important to address in any discussion of leadership and its application to people, organisations and society. Some people argue that because we cannot agree a comprehensive definition of leadership, we surely cannot teach leadership. This may seem obvious from a theoretical sense, but from a practical point of view that is like saying we shouldn't drive cars unless we fully understand all the engineering of the vehicles. We know the end result is that we want to travel from A to B. If we can achieve this, does it matter if we don't fully understand how the engine works, or if some people use a Ford and some an Aston Martin?

For example, is there an agreed definition of other roles that capture public attention? Of an international footballer, a television interviewer or a movie director, perhaps? No agreed definition exists, of course. But does that mean that we make no attempt to identify people with the potential to play such roles, or give up on creating opportunities for such people to develop because we can't define the role to everyone's satisfaction? Clearly not, as it is results we are looking for, the ability to deliver the output: well-directed films, good football or entertaining television interviews. So we might not be able to define leadership but we know it when we see it, especially if we experience it directly from those leaders. Some of the greatest leaders, when asked to analyse what they did and how they did it, cannot find a clear answer.

In the simplest terms, as suggested in Chapter 1, we want leaders to be able to draw out the best possible performance from the people they influence. Remembering that this may include some who are not directly led by them but who their influence will affect. This performance could be focused on a number of outcomes, whether corporate, social or creative. In achieving the best possible performance it implies that the individual is engaged by the leader in the delivery of the outcome and thus is likely to be giving a higher level of discretionary effort than without the leader's influence. Perhaps that is the overall objective of leadership: maximising discretionary effort to achieve the objective.

If leadership cannot be taught, then there is a problem. It means we are reliant on some mystical process by which an individual becomes a leader, and over which neither they nor others have any influence. It means that we have to wait for leaders to appear and then cannot develop their capability further. It calls into question everything we believe about the ability of the human race to learn from experience, transfer knowledge from generation to generation and understand how to work with our fellow human beings to create a better world. Our pragmatic response must therefore be to argue:

(i)   We must assume that we can teach leadership to some degree, on the basis that becoming a leader is not a mystical experience or a revelation, and must involve practical learning and/or the transfer of knowledge.

(ii)   Therefore we should seek to understand the basis for our current approach, because that will help us to understand what is possible, even if ultimately not receiving a conclusive answer to the age-old question 'Are leaders born or made?'

(iii) In understanding what is possible that gives us an indication of the best way to develop leadership to meet organisational, individual and social needs in an optimum way using limited resources.

This chapter will consider the important aspects around these issues.

There is little dispute from history that some individuals have leadership capability, and become leaders: Alexander the Great, Horatio Nelson, Abraham Lincoln, Winston Churchill and Nelson Mandela are examples. The more critical question is whether everyone has leadership potential of some kind; can it be taught and developed; or is it possible with only a few? If it is just a few, then how do we find them – and what about everyone else? Do they have no leadership capability? If this is so, given the organisational structure that underpins modern society we have a very big problem, the number of 'natural' leaders being much lower than the number of leaders needed.

In reality, however, while we can name many examples of leadership at the highest level of capability there are even more examples of unnamed leadership capability being shown at lower levels by any number of people throughout history. So clearly, leadership capability is a variable, not just a 'yes, you have it' or 'no, you don't' question. Many people have it and some people are better at it than others, and leadership comes at different levels of capability, as with anything else.

It is sometimes argued that major leaders from history were effective leaders by virtue of their position or birth alone. This does not stand up to close examination, as there are a significant number of examples of those in leadership positions for these reasons who failed rather than succeeded and, equally, there were many who were adequate but not exemplary. In addition there are many who did not have the head start of accident of birth but still succeeded – for example, Horatio Nelson. However, it is likely that those who were exemplary could have been helped by virtue of position or birth by having the opportunity and support to develop their skills more effectively than others.

As to the question whether leadership can be learnt, if we work on the assumption that any process of trial and error is a learning experience, then leadership can be learnt. After the third repeat of the same action that results in failure, even the most stupid leader can work out that it might be time for a change of plan. Kolb (1984) and others have shown that experience produces learning. And at the most basic and practical level, research shows that even animals are capable of learning by experience, so we must assume that humans can do the same! So, as a minimum, leadership can be leant by trial and error.

But can it be taught? If we then take the human capability to transfer knowledge from one individual to another, then clearly leadership has the potential to be learnt from others to some degree. 'Don't do it that way, as when I tried it the whole thing failed' is effectively a transfer of experience that teaches one individual about the knowledge of another. This is confirmed by the whole panoply of work around learning, coaching and mentoring, where knowledge is transferred successfully between individuals to improve performance.

In simple, practical terms, if leadership can't be taught why are establishments such as the Royal Military Academy Sandhurst in the UK and West Point in the USA and their respective governments spending vast amounts of money on leadership development courses for military officers? There must be something in it.

In some ways these link to providing some of the answer to the question of whether leaders are born or made. The answer is both, and over time the prevailing views of commentators move between each as more research is completed. Strangely, many of us who review our experience of life come to the same answer as the research – we have seen people who are brilliant leaders and some who are terrible, and people who over time have learnt to become more effective. We know that some people are naturally adept at sport, art or music, and others who aren't so good. So why should leadership be any different? The suggestion is that most people can, with teaching, achieve a level of basic effectiveness in these things but will never be great unless they have an underlying natural capability that is probably influenced by genetics and upbringing. Research on leadership would suggest that the same applies.

This concept of different levels of leadership capability is critical as it links directly to the organisation's need to balance allocation of resources in an efficient way. Leadership needs to be developed and taught to the level of capability that the organisation requires for different levels and roles within it. If the leaders are not developed enough the organisation won't perform to its potential, but if attempts are made to develop them too much resources are effectively wasted at that point; for example, it is not necessary to develop the leadership of a group of commercial managers to the level required by army officers, as they will never need that level of capability for the roles they undertake.

So we could say that leadership falls into one of three simple categories: competent; good; and great. The test of which of these applies relates to the basic criteria of leadership – to be able to inspire and enable people to deliver objectives – as the environment becomes more and more challenging and the complexity of the task increases, then the greater the level of leadership required to be effective. Thus a competent leader in a situation requiring great leadership will fail, but will succeed in situations requiring only competent leadership. Luckily for us, few situations demand great leadership but many demand competent leadership, and some require good leadership. But this also impacts on:

(i)   The leaders we require to match the challenge.
(ii) The way and degree to which they are, or can be, taught to improve.

The great leaders are people who have a significant impact on organisations, and sometimes on society as a whole. They have the capability of inspiring the masses and move forward against the challenges of the most difficult environments where others seem unable to cope. They create in us something that is greater than we ourselves thought possible. In day-to-day life we really do not need to have too many of these, and nor do they occur that often. However, it is these leaders who create the mystique surrounding leadership. This is because we cannot understand how they did what they did when we know we could not have achieved the same results.

Leaders leading their people in a way that adds value to both the individuals and the organisation in which they work, taking on the challenges that day-to-day life throws up. Earning the admiration of colleagues and others may be identified, but how many such leaders would any of us recognise in our own experience of organisations? They are not viewed as the same as the rest of us, but as something a little special.

The more interesting group might be characterised as the competent leaders – those we see around us in everyday roles, doing a reasonable job getting things done and keeping their people motivated. Often they do not see themselves as leaders, nor do others; they are often viewed mainly as managers. This group has the potential to become good leaders with simple development as they already 'get it' with respect to engaging people and delivering objectives. They just need a little development to provide the extra skills and knowledge to become good leaders. These are the individuals we need to develop to lead day-to-day in key roles in our organisations.

And everyone else? Can they possibly become competent? The answer is, very simply, yes. Provided they have the basic values of leadership in terms of integrity, a genuine interest in others and a desire to make a difference for the benefit of both themselves and others, then becoming competent is not difficult. One could argue that the Vroom–Yetton–Jago decision 'tree' (see Chapter 3) provides a basis for those with no knowledge to be given a systematised solution that ensures a level of basic effectiveness, and would help them to develop basic knowledge. Certainly there are simple 'flow chart' approaches that can provide those new to leadership with a first step which also provides base-level assurance for the organisation. This is inherently the point at which the military academies start the development journey for those entering training as potential military leaders.

Moving from good to great is something that largely relies on elements of personality that probably cannot be taught: a level of belief in oneself, the ability to influence, to create an inspirational vision, integrity and natural presence. This is where all the experience and knowledge of the good leader is topped with something special. Moving from competent to good is done through increasing knowledge and experience, learning what works and what doesn't, being able to be flexible in style to match leadership to more situations. So logically this can be taught through theory and practice, but mainly through guided practice. Moving from no experience to becoming competent is more of a process, learning the mechanics of the management process first and then the mechanics of leadership. To reach the competence level, leadership can be systematised, as military training demonstrates.

So, from the organisation's perspective it becomes an input/output equation – how many great leaders do we need, how many good ones, and how many merely competent? In reality one probably cannot say great leadership is needed in an organisational context nor can it be developed, but good and competent leaders are certainly need, and they can be developed. However, there are certain key elements of leadership that cannot be taught that have to be present in all leaders. If they are not it is not even worth trying to teach such individuals to be leaders. But, luckily, most people have these elements, but sadly there are some who don't. Integrity, respect for others, a genuine belief in what they do, the ability to think of others first are examples of these innate abilities.

In addition, 'leadership' (as discussed in Chapter 1) is not just one thing. The effective exercise of leadership requires a number of key sub-components to be delivered successfully. The ability to communicate clearly and in an inspiring way is very important to effective leadership. However, the ability to build a logical and appropriate course of action in any situation is also vital. Having both is good, but missing one of them could significantly reduce the chances of success. So, within the 'leadership' recipe there are some key ingredients that are critical and others less so, and within these are some that can be taught simply as a matter of process and others that relate very much to character and ability to influence, as discussed above.

For example, it is possible to learn a logical system with which to analyse problems and produce a potentially viable plan, but it is not possible to learn how to summon up the courage to confront really difficult situations rather than ignoring them and hoping they will go away. That is why, when leaders fail, it is often not the process side of leadership that lets them down but the character side that comes under increasing pressure as the environment becomes more difficult: the great, good and competent issue.

All we can do is to give the individual the best tools for the job and hope that those tools, plus his or her own ability, wins out over the challenges that the environment throws up. That is why, as we shall see in Chapter 11, the military spends much time giving its leaders the best tools so that the 'process' side of leadership is under control, thus allowing the motivational and inspirational to flourish.

As leadership is practised in the real world and not in a vacuum, the leader must take into account his/her followers, their interrelationships, peers, superiors and other stakeholders. No two followers are the same, and no two situations are the same. While past decisions, both individual and organisational, will be part of the context and may give some ideas, leaders must have the ability to innovate, creating new solutions for new situations, and have the confidence to make the solutions work.

There is another issue about 'teaching' leadership. What does 'teaching' mean? If it is to mean anything of value it must not just be the imparting of information to people, but the imparting plus the transfer of the information to be implemented so that it delivers performance improvement. Otherwise it is just an academic exercise. Therefore the transmission of the information is just the start of the journey. The 'teaching' process must then follow through to implementation into the real world, another reflection on the fact that leadership is delivered in the workplace and not the classroom.

The other critical issue for the teaching of leadership is that it must be reflective of changes in wider society, and thus as they change it must constantly change. The optimum style of leadership is very different these days from what it was 100, 50 or even 25 years ago. This is because the leader has to operate within the norms and expectations of society, as we shall examine in more detail later. So, as society changes what it expects and needs from its leaders changes. You could say that since the 1950s leadership development has gone through thinking, first, that the best leaders were 'the born leader', then in the late 1980s, 'the great man/hero', and the in the 2000s the 'interactive/consultative leader' ... so what next? All are different in the application of leadership but appropriate for their environment and time. Even within the same time the optimum style must adapt to the situation – if the building is burning down, is a consultative or authoritarian approach better – hold a meeting to debate if you should leave or stay, or just tell people to get out?

So it is not just about learning the theory; it is also about the application of those principles to constantly changing environments. This leads to two areas that are often confused in both research and practice. These are:

(i)   Generic leader development – the development of the general leadership capability of individuals.

(ii) Organisational leader development – the development of leadership as it is practised in organisations, including the definition and codification of leadership methods, ideas, modes of thinking, 'language' and 'discourse'.

The former is concerned with individuals and their growth into leaders, while the latter relates to bodies of knowledge and practice, the effective utilisation of leaders by organisations, and the development of aligned leadership effort to deliver organisational objectives. The two are linked, and interact, but should not be confused with one another.

Often missed is a third component:

(iii) Organisational enabling – the enabling of other key organisational objectives via leadership development. Many organisations consider leadership development to be a stand alone HR initiative like any other, when in fact it is an enabler of everything else that the organisation wants to achieve. Here, a combination of having good individual leaders who also act as an effective team of leaders it critical.

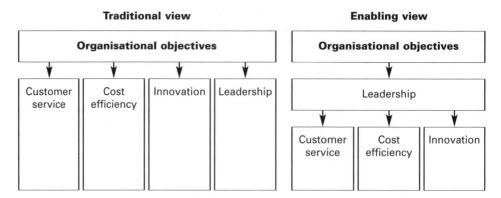

Fig 4.1 Alternative views of organisational leadership

Leadership is the tool by which everything else is enabled, so it must be viewed as a precursor to delivering anything and everything else to world class standards. This is critical to enable the individual leaders to operate as an integrated team. Having great individual leaders is not enough in itself; they must work as a team to maximise the potential of the whole organisation (see Figure 4.1).

4.2 How best to develop individual leadership?

There has been much debate about the best way to develop individual leadership. If we take the general principles set out previously, the knowledge or skills transferred must be (a) relevant to the individuals roles and the organisation's needs; (b) transferable to the current environment; and (c) have sufficient flexibility of operation to be applicable to potential future situations.

As suggested earlier, there is a number of different leadership components that must be covered, and that the mix and prioritisation of these will vary with the level of operation of both organisation and individual. Obviously this must be a match between organisation and individual; teaching graduate managers organisational strategy formulation will not help the organisation as much as teaching them how to brief a team. This is a reflection of the changing proportion of operational versus strategic role content as individuals move up the organisation (see Figure 4.2).

Figure 4.2 sets out a concept of the balance between the operational and strategic leadership required by leaders at different levels in organisations. There is no strategic leadership for junior managers as their job does not require it, but there is still a small amount of operational leadership activity at even the most senior level, where the CEO acts as a line manager to the executive team in a traditional operational way.

Figure 4.2 sets out the content of leadership and not the ability of the individual – therefore junior leaders can be both competent or good, as can senior leaders. One would hope that the senior leaders were more towards good than competent, to maximise organisational performance. So leadership development is in high demand as organisations seek to face performance and other challenges, but it is important to

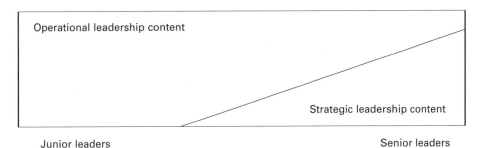

Operational leadership content

Strategic leadership content

Junior leaders   Senior leaders

Fig 4.2   The changing proportion of operational versus strategic role content

position leadership development in its specific organisational context, linked to the individual on which it is focused.

The leadership development content will change as the individual moves up the leadership chain. As the content becomes more strategic, increasing complexity enters the decision-making processes of leaders as the number of variables increases in comparison to lower-level leadership; for example, there are multiple internal and external stakeholders. This has the effect of increasing the number of factors to be considered in any decision, which leads to more potential options for action.

With some leaders this causes delays in action as a result of them seeking 'the right answer' when in fact there is no such thing, just a range of answers that are positive in some ways but negative in others. Waiting for the right answer to appear is a risk in itself; in a dynamic environment the 'right answer' for the original problem may not appear before the dynamics have changed the problem itself. Equally, 'doing nothing' is a leadership action, one that may be the best option in many situations but one that many leaders shy away from as there is often a mindset among some leaders that one must always be doing something to be a leader, and doing nothing is not leading. But, as many great military and indeed commercial leaders know, waiting for the right moment to act is critical, and thus doing nothing can be perfectly valid.

The more senior the 'target audience' for leadership development, the more important the context becomes in addition to the 'process' side, and the move from competent to good also applies. It follows that, at senior level, leadership development needs to include a decision and choice perspective. Moreover, at this level it is important that the development process is integrated effectively within the ongoing concerns and challenges of the organisation. It is not just 'going through the process' as operational leadership can sometimes be, but dealing with an often confused process, in uncertain situations and with fewer guarantees of a specific action producing a specific and predictable outcome.

Given all of the above, then, how best to develop leadership? And this also leads on to the question of where is best? Do we use internal or external resources or a combination of both? In the majority of cases the logic of ensuring that the content of development is relevant to the organisation one would encourage delivery to be internal. However, for many reasons – for example, resources and internal capability – it may be better delivered by outside providers, or a combination of internal and external resources. However, that should be the last decision rather than the first.

Before debating this we need to look at what kind of process is needed to meet our criteria of relevance, transferability and future flexibility. The process must be designed by a partnership between business managers and development experts, be they internal HR experts or external advisers, or a combination of the two.

Two differing areas of practical leadership thus emerge from the above model: operational and strategic. These tend to operate in slightly different ways, which makes teaching them also slightly different. Operational leadership is essentially direct, face-to-face leadership of a group of people (i.e. those reporting directly to the leader and others involved in operational delivery). Strategic leadership is essentially leadership exercised through others and involving the longer-term delivery of the organisation's wider strategic objectives.

4.3   Individual operational leadership development

Operational leadership can, to some degree, be systematised so that it can by taught by giving the individual a step-by-step process map. This approach is adopted by many military academies around the world. It focuses on giving simple checklists to ensure effectiveness in areas such as:

- Identification of problems or objectives.
- Consideration of viable options.
- Identification of the optimal solution.
- Creating a simple plan.
- Briefing a team on the plan in an effective way.
- Monitoring performance.
- Conducting a feedback exercise to identify possible improvements.

All of the above can be systematised to enable even inexperienced leaders a reasonable chance of a successful outcome. These are often described as 'management' skills, and there is a debate as to whether they are part of leadership or something different. This is another distraction about semantics, though, as in reality a leader must be able to do all of these things well whatever they are labelled.

It is only with these in place that the leader has the time to think about and apply the influencing, inspirational and character skills they have. The ability to do the 'management' elements well then gives the individual the confidence to add inspiration to process.

4.4   Individual strategic leadership development

Strategic leadership is more difficult to teach, and it is indirect delivery of leadership, in most cases, and operating in areas with substantially more variables and stakeholders, and with greater unpredictability of outcome than operational leadership. The same core components apply but the delivery has to be achieve indirectly.

Effective strategic leadership is the solution to ever more complex puzzles. With incomplete knowledge, leaders must learn how to analyse the data they do have and hold back from merely offering the solutions of the past. But getting to answers requires that the question is understood, options are explored and so on, and this takes both time and data. In reality, strategic leadership is often about the 'long haul', delayed gratification balanced, but also accepting that you can never get the perfect data or answer. Thus often two natural groups of leaders appear at the strategic level:

(i) **The action heroes**: they often rush to implement solutions because they find that formulating the question properly about the real issue requires disciplined effort and time. Yet the company wants a clear answer, and preferably quickly. To many this is what leadership is about – finding instant answers to problems rather than the inevitable delay associated with working through problems – or even worse, admitting to public recognition that at any point in time some problems may not have a clear answer. Our culture demands answers from both political and corporate leaders. This goes to the heart of the concept and self-image of the 'hero leader' that many still aspire to, but by doing so condemn themselves to inevitable stress and at some point being forced to admit that they don't know everything, nor can they solve every problem.

(ii) **The perfectionists**: here the leader delays making a decision until there are sufficient data to ensure that the answer is correct. While negating the risks associated with the hero leader, the perfectionist leader runs the risk of events overtaking him or her. The complexity of strategic decision-making related to the greater number of factors outside the leader's control and the greater unpredictability of each of these that the operational leader faces means it often takes longer to obtain any viable data let alone enough to make a decision with a high chance of success.

So a balance needs to be struck between action and thought – and that needs to be reflected more in the development of senior leaders. Martin Gilbert's book looking at Churchill's wartime leadership with the title *Continue to Pester, Nag and Bite* shows the balance struck by a 'great' leader (Gilbert, 2005). One of Churchill's maxims of leadership in war was 'Improvise and dare'. And one cannot understand his leadership without looking at the series of speeches through which he articulated his vision of ultimate victory. However, it is more interesting to look at his methods of working. Famous for his 'Action this day' instructions, the other important point may be the extent to which he placed himself in command of the detail of Britain's war effort so that he could challenge colleagues. He read reports on production, technical developments, manpower, training, resources and copies of all messages between the three service ministries and all commanders-in-chief in the field. With this he was in a position to 'pester, nag and bite' – and identify where immediate action was required. Improvise and dare was based on the recognition that risk cannot be planned out of war. Sometimes opportunity is short-lived and any attempt to eliminate risk through more extensive planning might entail acting too late. In such circumstances waiting may entail the greater risk. Decision-making may be driven by a 'calculus' of utility, cost, benefits and strategic advantage, but in real life, decisions are often needed before all the data are available.

The ability to asses the best course of action is a key requirement of all leaders, but at the strategic level the complexity and time horizons required in planning organisational strategy make this much more difficult than at the hands-on operational level. The secret is to balance the possible with the impossible, the challenging yet attainable organisational objective. Relatively little interest has been shown in how leaders think they come to judge a strategy as ambitious enough to create advantage but yet still be achievable. While strategic management theory covers this ground on implementation and execution of strategy since the 1990s, little attention has been focused on how leaders think, how they view the world, and how they come to judge what is achievable. What is realistically achievable is the key to organisational success – too little and the organisation doesn't achieve the potential possible; to much and it fails.

This effect is compounded by change; most observers of organisations being led through a period of dramatic change point to the need for change in mindset. Jack Welch of General Electric (GE) was perhaps one of the most convincing exponents of this (see Collins, 2001). Adopting the Schumpeterian notion of 'creative destruction', breakthrough change demands new rules, quantum leaps and a radical approach to the balance between autonomy and control, emphasising relative autonomy within a 'business engine' geared up to focus on performance. The well-known overarching rule Welch adopted sets the tone: 'Be number one or number two in your sector or you will not stay in GE.' Behind this Market Leadership Rule lay objectives for 'well above average real returns on investments, distinct competitive advantage, and leverage value from strengths'. But at the core is the willingness to create 'new rules of the competitive game' for GE.

These more complex issues are rarely discussed in the development of senior leaders. To make the problem even greater, the 2006–10 banking crisis also introduced the concept that, contrary to previous belief leadership does not know or control everything. Where the leader cannot provide all the answers and, like everyone else, they are human, and sometimes things happen that no one can control.

We live in times characterised by greater competition, change, complexity, ambiguity, challenge to sources of authority, anxiety and so on. So we must prepare senior leaders to make sense of that complexity.

4.5 The individual in relation to the organisation and team

It is clear that there are another two key parts to the development of leadership – the individual and the organisation – so we need to consider both, and the means to optimise them while understanding that they may not always be optimised in the same way, or that it may not be possible to optimise both and thus a compromise will be required. However, both must be taken into account and the linkage between them used. Here, however, it is important not to lose sight of the reality that for the individual it is also a career choice of what to do in the organisation, or even whether to stay or go.

4.5.1 Leadership skills must develop with age and role

Individuals change over time. A study by the Centre for Creative Leadership shows differing behaviours and focus for leaders at different stages of their careers. Thus at 30, to be successful, leaders generally need to demonstrate the following:

- Independence.
- Ability to control short-term results.

- Creativity.
- Ambition and high standards.
- Strength in speciality/professional discipline.
- Willingness to take a stand, to challenge.

Whereas at the ages of 40 to 50, leaders need to demonstrate the following:

- Team player.
- Strategic vision.
- Managing innovation/creativity.
- Self-esteem.
- General management skills.
- Creating unity and cohesion.

While some of the difference here clearly relate to job level (that is, at 40/50), as the leader who was effective at 30 will now more than likely be in a more senior position, but partly it relates to the individual career and life cycle.

The nature of the meaning that individuals attach to work, both in terms of career and in a broader sense, clearly changes over the length of a career. It seems unlikely that a 30-year-old and a 50-year-old in the same appointment will experience the role in a similar way – or at least, it would be simplistic to assume that they would. Over and above individual difference, however, we refer here to the differences that may flow from the position in the career and life cycle.

It is obvious that it is possible to identify stages in a life and career. For example, Bloisi *et al.* (2007) identify six, as follows:

1 Early childhood.
2 Exploration and initial jobs.
3 Trial work period – aged 25 to 34.
4 Establishment – 35 to 44.
5 Stability and maintenance.
6 Post-retirement.

During Stage 3 (typically ages 25 to 34), people are testing themselves and possible direction in the work setting, beginning to feel confident and successful or confused and frustrated.

At the next stage (35 to 44 years), people are accepting roles and career paths and either seeking advancement, or finding satisfaction in a role or acceptance, or trying different paths. The point here is that sense-making, behaviour or attitudes and experience will differ across these situations.

It is clear from a substantial number of studies that the way that leaders relate to their subordinates is a key issue in the sense of delivering both individual and organisational performance. However, the majority of research effort is focused on the leader's impact on people as a necessary counterpoint to concern for the task. Thus the main focus of development activity is on helping individual leaders rather than creating systems that align leadership as a group to delivery of organisational tasks or objectives.

The simplest approach to the key elements of leadership set out by John Adair (1973) working at the Royal Military Academy, Sandhurst, close to London set out three key elements, focusing on the individual, the task and the team. These are detailed in Chapter 11. Given that attention must be paid to all three elements to deliver success in general terms, leadership development tends to focus much more on the relationship between the leader and individuals rather than on the team and the wider task. The reduced analysis of the latter does have an impact on our understanding of what leadership is about and thus its effective teaching.

In many cases the focus on the individual leader often also neglects the linkage to the organisational delivery needs other than in a cursory way. Significant time is often spent either by using psychometric tests, 360° feedback tools (almost without exception based on 'behaviourally anchored' scales within a competency framework) or personal development exercises. The enabling of the application of the new leadership capability is not often given a similar depth of analysis. Occasionally, this is covered, possibly via an action-learning project.

So many current leadership development interventions lack a balance between the development of the individual's leadership and the application of the capability to deliver organisational objectives or to be an effective part of a cohesive corporate leadership team. This links to the issues around strategic planning of leadership pipelines in organisations, and questions such as 'How many leaders of each type will we need in the next two years?'

Leaders must be concerned about the impact of their behaviour on others. Ultimately, any leader's ability 'to get things done through people' is clearly important. But this does not totally define their ability as a leader. As noted earlier, we know that Winston Churchill's behaviour towards his political and military colleagues during the Second World War created tensions in his relationships with them. However, as these tensions were transcended by a mutual belief in a higher cause, they did not have a negative impact on performance. Some would argue that they might actually have enhanced it. So even poor relationships may be transcended via a mutual vision or challenge.

If people have no cause or vision worth achieving, then relationships become all-important, and the style of the leader has a much more significant impact. There are two key elements to this: looking at behaviour means focusing largely on the present; while looking at the mind of the leader as he or she grapples with the future is looking beyond today. Both are important for our understanding of leadership and its development in practice.

The need to separate the individual and organisational aspects can become confused. Universities such as Oxford and Cambridge play a crucial role in what is called leadership development through what some would call 'elite formation'. Graduates of these two universities often take up leadership roles across the UK and abroad. Many people would not view this as leadership development, yet the process of elite formation by creating cadres of people believing in themselves, and being perceived by others to be leaders of the future, is historically central to leader development. This creation of self-belief feeds into the trait approach through the need for leaders to have self-confidence and the perception from others that they must be leaders by virtue of the fact they have attended such institutions, though such attendance in no way builds leadership skills or knowledge.

But educational attainment is a key factor in the appointment of people to roles in which leadership is likely to be a growing part of what they have to do, regardless of other characteristics they may also require. Correlli Barnett, a British historian, seeks to identify as one of the causes of *The Collapse of British Power* (Barnett, 2002) in the twentieth century the point that the British elite, progressing through the fee-paying public school system and on to university encountered a curriculum preparing them for roles in everything but industry. This, he argued, had fateful consequences for the performance of the British economy. The essence here is that their development in some elements of generic leadership had been completed, but their ability to exercise it within the specific context of industry was extremely limited. This has had profound consequences for the workplace and indeed for the performance of the economy.

The development of the theory and practice of leadership is itself often confused by similar issues. Books on leadership focus on individual and organisational theories of leadership but rarely on the content of leadership, a point we made at the start of this book. The development of the theory and practice of leadership as it is undertaken in real-world settings must focus on what leaders do; how they do it; the assumptions they make; the ideas, variables and priorities that impact on what they do and so on.

We are also concerned with how leaders come to agree on what to do. The language and discourse of leadership becomes an important focus because it creates the dialogue through which leaders and others make sense of their situation, share ideas about it and then decide on courses of action.

Historically this has led to the emergence of the disciplinary fields of management, for so long the preserve of business schools and management consulting firms. But here there has also been an emerging recognition that leadership in particular is not a discipline-bound activity. Leadership involves decisions, but decisions can rarely be made within the framework of a particular discipline; thus the need for integration. Whether one calls the decision process interdisciplinary or multidisciplinary really does not matter here. Real decisions are rarely informed by more than a single discipline. This is not to argue against the importance of disciplines. Rather, we note the advantages from both a developmental and a professional point of view.

Clearly, both aspects are linked. But leader development is different from the development of leadership practice. Leader development also provides for succession and growth, drawing our attention to the future well-being and performance of the organisation and of leaders at all levels within it.

4.6   How can we design a good individual leadership development process?

If we take the core principles of relevance, transferability and future flexibility that we require, and the basic principles of learning by transfer of knowledge and experience, then the solution to some degree presents itself. We need maximum relevance, maximum transferability and maximum flexibility that focus on both organisational and individual need that is deeply embedded to deliver behavioural change. This ultimate solution is, however, more elusive that many think, and indeed to deliver it effectively is very costly in terms of resources.

Taking the principle that it is experience of application rather than delivery of knowledge that makes theory become reality, then the more the knowledge is applied to the real world with support, the greater the chances of success. This drives us to conclude that the effective teaching of leadership must be an experience, and not a one-off development programme. Thus, while the traditional development programme has its place, it is not a stand-alone solution. To embed good leadership teaching, other vehicles must be used.

The work of behaviourally-focused trainers centres on the more immediate impact – the 'action hero' approach, which is why we are so preoccupied with these approaches. This is what the organisation expects – a rapid return on investment, and this approach seems to offer immediate gains, which is important, and it can be effective for operational leaders. For more senior leaders, however, leadership development work needs to look at the hard choices they must make. In truth, the more complex the problem and the more uncertainty is associated with it – for example, the issue of predicting the likely responses of competitors to actions we may take, and so the more we are forced to take an experimental approach. We make adjustments to our strategy, business model, operating model and other elements in an attempt to learn what will work. Our development interventions need to reflect this.

We also need to understand who are the key stakeholders in the teaching of leadership. This point is often confused and neglected. What role does the HR function play? What does the line manager do? How does top management contribute, if at all? One of the key reasons for the failure of leadership development to be effective in many organisations is that everyone assumes it is someone else's responsibility and then it doesn't get delivered. Much greater clarity of role and responsibility is required in this.

4.7   Gender and leadership development

As a practitioners of leadership development, we have often observed that the inclusion of women leaders in learning groups makes a difference. This is a little-researched area but is one on which many have opinions. Grint (2005) presents some evidence. He relates his own experience of running leadership development programmes in the UK's Royal Air Force. He described a learning exercise called 'Low Ropes', a team-based exercise involving a set of ropes slung between trees. As is typically the case in real life, team success in the exercise required balance, teamwork and leadership. He described a team, including two women, undertaking the exercise. In this case it was readily agreed that the two women should be placed in the middle, where their lesser physical strength would have less of an impact on the team's performance. The debrief after the exercise is interesting. The team were asked to explain how they felt when the group appeared to be making no progress. From the middle positions the women appeared to be in control of the exercise. What would have happened if had there been men in that position? Would the rest of the team shout at them? And if that made no difference, what would happen? Would they have merely shouted louder! Did the women ask to be placed in the middle? Where did they end up? Leading the team? Why was that? Was it because of the starting position or because of gender differences in relation to leadership style?

Following Haslam (2004), we can argue that a sense of shared social identity is a vital link between the actions of leaders and those of followers. Clearly, all participants in this case were in the Royal Air Force, which created a strong sense of shared identity. In this case is the behavioural response to the team becoming stuck a leadership response, because within that shared identity the team has accepted difference and found ways of coping with it while respecting all contributions? Thus the response is not merely to shout at each other but rather to accept responsibility and follow a lead. As one commented 'Now I could have just stood there and done nothing … but what good would that have been?'

Eagly and Carli (2004) compared the leadership styles of men and women. In experimental situations gender-stereotypic differences in leadership style were observed. Women tended to be more focused on interpersonal considerations and men to be more task-focused. In field studies in organisations these differences do not appear to the same extent. Some differences are observable but in a narrower range of leadership behaviours. Women's styles tend to be more participative and men's more directive. Women leaders tend to adopt a rather more transformational style. In contrast, men focus more on failures to meet standards but even so tended to avoid performance problems until they become acute.

The evidence is as yet not complete but it does appear that the leadership style preferences favoured by women are those more likely to cope with complex and changing situations and are thus more suited to effective leadership development work in the twenty-first century. But is this a gender difference alone, or is it that women leaders are now being appointed at the point where it is becoming increasingly clear that traditional leadership styles will not work. They may be less affected by the socialisation of existing leadership cadres by virtue of the reality that hitherto men have been dominant. Younger male leaders may also adapt? Evidence does suggest that this is happening, as 'macho' leadership is increasingly being viewed as a problem. We cannot tell on the evidence available to date, but at this stage it would be wise both to value the different styles women leaders bring, and value women as leaders simply on ethical and egalitarian grounds – and because this represents a better use of resources. Clearly, similar arguments can be used for other groups in society whatever the basis of diversity and difference.

4.8 Who are the key stakeholders in developing individual leaders?

For the teaching of leadership to be effective, all of the following stakeholders must be engaged in the process:

- **The individual.** The individual must want to be developed. Too many organisations waste money on trying to develop people into being things they do not want to be, or to do things they do not want to do. While people often have to do things they do not enjoy in organisations, making large numbers of people undertake leadership training is not likely to maximise performance. It is better to try to ensure that some process is put in place through which individuals are matched to roles or tasks they want to do. Some commentators would suggest that 70 per cent or more of the success in developing an individual and his or her performance is the person's own desire to do so. However, we know that the next stakeholder in the list can influence this significantly.

- **Individuals' line managers.** Given that individuals spend most of their time with their line managers, often spending more waking hours together than they do with their families, this person is critical. It is the line manager who, according to research data, has the greatest impact on the performance and development of both the individual and the team.

- **Internal consultants.** These are often HR department personnel, either the target group's business partners or specialist experts. They will either design and deliver the programme with business management or act as the 'middleman' with external providers. Their role is to ensure that the development meets both organisational and individual needs and is delivered in such a way that it is relevant and transferable to the real world. This requires them to work closely with those for whom the leaders are being developed in the organisation.

- **Business top management.** The top management sets out its vision for the future and the current strategic objectives that have to be delivered. This makes clear to the organisation where it is going and, via the values, the rules by which it must go there. Senior management's example sets the tone for everyone else. They must be the champions of both strategy and execution, and set an example of the desired behaviours. They must communicate clearly and simply what is required and take time out to develop not only their own teams but also other leaders.

- **External consultants.** These provide the expertise and experience often not available inside the organisation. Over a period of years they will have gained experience in the development of leaders in a wide variety of situations, they should know what works and what doesn't, and they should have developed simple tools to enable the organisation to move more quickly and effectively than if it were to try to develop its own solution by trial and error.

4.8.1 Vehicles for leadership development

We need to remember here that when we talk about development we mean all activities that will develop the individual for the benefit of the organisation. This is not just about development programmes. This includes all on- and off-the-job development. Here are some of the frequently used processes:

- On-the-job leadership development:
  - coaching of individual
  - coaching of others by individual
  - challenging assignments
  - secondments
- Off-the-job leadership development:
  - development programmes – internal
  - development programmes – external
  - mentoring
  - personal study and research

It is unlikely that any of the above on its own will produce a good level of embedded leadership capability. As we said in earlier chapters, effective learning comes via both information and experience. Thus often a combination of these will be required in an integrated development approach. Building a world class leadership development system must look at the practical implementation of delivering information and building experience. The key areas that any leadership development strategy should consider are:

- Clarity – what exactly do we want our leaders to do, both in terms of the organisation and its personnel?
- Capability – what capability will they need as a result: competent, good or great?
- Culture – how do we make sure our leaders reflect and embed our culture?
- CEO – will our CEO and top management champion set examples for the development of our leaders?
- Character – what basic values are critical for our leader to possess – for example, integrity, respect for others?
- Customers – how does all of the above add value to our customers, and how can we make it align to deliver what our customers want?

Case study   **Leaders developing leaders – UBS strategic mentoring**

The global financial services company UBS was created from a series of mergers and acquisitions in the late 1990s and early 2000s. Given the many cultures and groups in the bank by 2002, the corporate objective was clear – to enable the seamless delivery of a full range of world class services to customers globally while maximising profit. The existing development landscape was made up of a patchwork of unaligned legacy initiatives created mainly by reactive delivery of HR product driven by ad hoc requests different business areas or individuals. To create 'One UBS' the top 500 leaders of the bank had to be aligned to the new organisational strategy, to make their own business area world class and to build a new local high performance culture. They would then work in partnership with colleagues to do the same for the whole group. In reality this potential could not be achieved without aligned world class talent and leadership activity. All of the initiatives had to be acceptable to all the different business divisions who, driven by their differing business models, adopted substantially varied approaches to development and decision-making. The ability to tailor to local needs yet retain a consistent global approach would be critical.

The core Leadership Institute/Academy team was established in 2002 reporting directly to the CEO.

Having considered a range of options for the strategy and implementation with the CEO the most effective was likely to be a combination of development, assessment and support to key groups plus unusually, for an HR team, targeted communication activity to support and embed the implementation. This would all be publicly led by example by the Group Executive Board (GEB) headed by the CEO and then facilitated by The Leadership Academy.

The 'One UBS' business model was designed to create a single integrated and networked leadership team across business divisions boundaries, together with a new business strategy, culture and brand. In addition, to make this effective it was vital to improve the performance of individual leaders, their teams and thus the wider organisation. There was much discussion about how to achieve such objectives. The obvious choice of development programme activity was rejected as there would be a significant lead time to deliver this, some of the key individuals would not be available to attend, the individual focus on such programmes was not high enough to deliver the required support, and it meant time away from the job for some critical individuals.

The decision was taken to meet the objectives via a mentoring programme that focused on organisational delivery as well as individual benefit. The mentoring relationships would operate across business divisions and would, unusually for mentoring, be between individuals of nearly similar experience and rank. The relationships would be designed to operate between individuals where there was an opportunity for business development as well as individual learning. Thus the Strategic Mentoring Programme was born – a hybrid of mentoring, coaching, peer review, networking and business development.

The matching of the mentors and mentees was complex – given the 200 participants, the global spread of individuals, and the concentrations of different business divisions in different geographies. Individuals' frequent travel movements were mapped to make cross-border and cross-regional matches viable. Training had to be delivered in under half a day to gain buy-in from such senior participants. The training was designed to be delivered to both mentors and mentees using the same content, thus mentees would also have information on what the mentors should be doing for them. This enabled effective benchmarking and positioned the mentees to become mentors in the next phase of the programme.

The training was aimed to take between two and three hours in total and was delivered in a simple and practical way that gave participants a structure and set of steps to ensure a base level of competence. Mentors and mentees were in the training together where possible, so the workshop effectively became the first meeting – thus by the end of it a rapport had been established, draft objectives agreed, key challenges identified, and an ongoing meeting schedule agreed. In other words, the relationships were up and running.

Initially the twelve-member group executive board (12) mentored some of the Group Managing Board (60) and around nine months later these in turn mentored the bank's key position holders (150), mainly senior managing directors. Feedback from participants indicated that within four months of starting the programme, the vast majority of mentees said the programme met their expectations and 65 per cent identified a specific personal or business benefit that had resulted directly from the programme. Significant business benefit was delivered via a number of business efficiencies or new business opportunities identified through the mentoring relationships.

A year later, some of the key position holders were asked to mentor the newly identified 'high potential pool' group, thus cascading the benefits further down the organisation to four levels below the group executive board. This mentoring was a key component in the development of performance in the 'high potentials'. Subsequently this group was then encouraged to mentor others within their own business division mentoring programmes.

The benefits of this strategic initiative led to the development of new mentoring programmes across the organisation for diversity, for professional skills and other business or personal development reasons. By 2006, it was accepted in UBS that mentoring was part of the role of all leaders, and as a result a culture of development and, in particular, the principle of leaders developing other leaders was embedded.

The strategy worked to deliver improved capability and change line managers' 'costs benefit' analysis of spending time becoming good leaders and developing others. This again reinforced the internal use of the external branding 'You and Us' - as applied to You the employee and Us the rest of UBS. The results from feedback continued to show that the programme had delivered significant benefit to the mentors and mentees involved, and specific examples of organisational benefit via new business, more efficient process and leverage of good practice across the globe.

4.9   Competency models

As noted in Chapter 3, leadership theories have been looking at competency models for a number of years – and thus it is logical for leadership development to follow this trend. Huge investment has been made in developing competence models, which sit at the core of the design of many leadership development activities. However, this is often a distraction from the real issues that leaders need to address. As practitioners with 70 or more years of experience in the field, the authors know that one common critique of development programmes relates to a perceived lack of relevance and transfer back into the organisation of the learning for participants. Of course, many programme designs seek to tackle this issue, often with some success. Most commonly this is accomplished via an action-learning project, which looks at a current organisational issue. There is no doubt that value can be generated in this way, but in practice this is achieved effectively by focusing on outputs that the organisation needs and leaving the competency model out of the development.

The limitation of the competency approach is that at best it is a static one, providing a description of competence strengths and gaps at a particular point in time, normally the past, whereas the task of leadership is to find solutions to current issues and create the future of an organisation. Further, as the competencies used were developed at a fixed point in time, they can fall into the trap of reflecting the organisation, its culture and management, and the external environment at that point in time, and not what is relevant for the present or what will be required in the future.

A good example this relates to leadership reflected after the sudden change of organisational environment brought about by the 2006–10 financial crisis. Within a few months, this moved all organisations from operating in a booming market to the worst downturn in 60 years. Thus the requirements of leaders changed dramatically, from leading in an environment of confidence, with ease of doing business, plentiful resources and good compensation to one of uncertainty, sharply contracting markets and customer expenditure, reduced resources and redundancies. This environment required a very different leadership approach to enable organisations be effective.

Many organisations have found that the key competencies of leaders that they required prior to the credit crisis are not those they needed afterwards. A proper understanding of leadership and leadership development must therefore go beyond understanding merely today's behavioural competencies into understanding how leaders think about the future, how they come to decide on plans requiring organisation changes before their execution, how challenging those plans can be, how they respond to the external and internal variables that affect those plans, and how they seek to change minds – their own and others – about what is achievable.

Such an approach would certainly incorporate competence principles, because we do need to help potential and current leaders to understand their own strengths and weaknesses, not least in the area of their impact on people – a common issue; however, the competence approach is not the only route to leadership development.

4.10   The 'strengths-based approach'

During the development of this book, one of the authors chaired a conference focused on the role of coaching in leadership development. During this event one of the speakers asked the audience made up of senior human resources and leadership development practitioners, 'How many of you have competence models?' Almost all raised their hands. 'Well, you might just as well use them as spare paper for your children to draw on for all the good they do. The future is "strengths"' (see Linley *et al.*, 2010). The speaker continued, explaining that it is better to 'value people for who they are, celebrating what they do best, rather than lamenting what they don't do well, and matching people to roles, rather than expecting people to change'.

As an example, in a large UK general insurance business a culture change programme was put in place that included a process for switching from a competency based to a strengths-based approach. One example relates to the key role of claims adviser, who advises customers who are making a claim on how to complete the process. The firm employed 2,500 claims advisers. The approach was to recognise that 'high performing claims advisers' would be in a good position to promote customer loyalty. These individuals would need attributes such as sensitivity, empathy and tact, because when the customer initiates a contact, it is a result of an immediate 'loss' of some kind – such as a car accident, a robbery, a fire and so on. Thus the situation is, by definition, stressful. But to add value for the customer, the claims adviser needs to be fully aware of the technical aspects of the job, understand the claims process, the nature of the insurance cover, arrangements for recovery or repair, and for replacements. The firm sought to recruit people who were 'made for the job' rather than who were 'able to be trained to do the job'. Recruitment used a strengths-based approach, which it was claimed halved turnover among claims advisers.

Ironically, the 'strengths-based' approach represents a return to the thinking of Kurt Lewin (1948). In the context of change management, Lewin is famous for the idea of a 'force field'. In this model the strength of forces for and against change in any setting determine whether the change will be effective. To deliver change, the organisation must build up the forces for change (strengths) so they are greater than the forces against change (weaknesses). The same can be applied to people. A focus on an individual's weaknesses brings the risk of conflict, anxiety and reduced self-esteem for those involved, and therefore the risk of resistance. Focusing on the individual's strengths, however, like the forces for change, in effect 'goes with the grain' of the organisation and its culture and the individual's capabilities. Not all weaknesses are acceptable and can be ignored. It is taken as read that organisations must manage risk, so weaknesses that are thought to have a significant risk for the organisation must be minimised or reduced to an acceptable level. However, once this has been achieved, then concentrating on enhancing strengths has a greater benefit than trying to remove weaknesses that do not present a critical risk and are often deeply embedded.

In this context, a 'weakness' is something that the individual is not as good as doing as hid or her 'strengths', thus it does not mean that it presents a risk to the organisation. Merely that for the individual concerned they are not as good at doing this thing as they are at other things.

More interestingly, however, is the observation in the example discussed above, that the claims adviser role is one in which the employee relates to a 'client' who is experiencing stressful circumstances. Dealing with clients and others in stressful situations is likely to be more pivotal for the formation of loyalty and commitment from those clients by delivering high-quality support. Dealing effectively with inherently difficult situations appears to be more likely to be remembered positively by clients, and positive client perception is the acid test' for any organisation. Creating it certainly represents a challenge for organisational leadership. Developing such an emotional linkage could be seen as leadership more than management. Leadership relates to coping with uncertainty, strategy, and avoiding or dealing with failures and change, while management handles 'business as usual', running the 'system' in a 'steady state', securing effective performance and incremental 'continuous improvement', for example.

4.11   The importance of senior management involvement

The link between leadership and managing uncertainty, developing performance and creating a new world is clear. Thus it is important that senior-level executives are fully involved in the design and delivery of the development effort. Leadership development needs to find ways of helping leaders to work on the choices and decisions they make, the ideas underpinning those choices, and the business models in use. Moreover, they need to judge the impact and implications flowing from those choices. Certainly at the strategic level, if not at all levels, creative thinking is needed increasingly, and this must be reflected in the intervention design that is planned to develop such a capability.

Fundamentally, if a choice/decision-making emphasis is used then it is possible to pay more attention to existing and possible alternative business models using simulation/gaming methodologies. This is best achieved when working with senior executives jointly to design and deliver these solutions. Realism must become a central requirement of development, so working with senior executives in design and delivery is a necessary condition of success, and the deployment technology is often the other prime facilitator of the success of these interventions. Leadership development, driven by leaders developing other leaders based on real current need itself becomes a key intervention in the process of leading the organisation and improving its performance.

It follows that leadership development focused on changing how leadership is practised *must* be future-focused. It must be integrated with the organisation focusing on real issues and must also be co-designed and co-developed where an internal or other provider is involved with current leaders. The key point here is that this form of leadership development can be successful with the full and active engagement of senior leaders.

In these terms, leadership development means much more than putting leaders through assessment centres and development pathways, including MBA programmes and the like. It is also much more than the creation and delivery of a customised programme. It is more about creating a leadership experience in the organisation that transforms behaviour and performance by replicating the current reality in a safe environment where options, choices and innovations can be tested. The 'programme' element is only part of the experience. Thus to make leadership development there must be a partnership between current leaders and development experts, not just putting into practice the ideas of a few HR and external trainers.

4.12   Using customised leadership development design

Organisations can learn significant lessons from the development of customised programmes delivered over a number of years by major business schools in partnership with major corporate clients. This process or partnership has led to the creation and implementation of some of the most effective leadership development to date.

The process by which these programmes are designed is a template for organisations to follow to deliver high-quality outputs. However, these cannot just be copied and implemented, as the specific nature of the tailoring to specific organisations at specific times makes this ineffective. They do, however, demonstrate some general principles that all organisations should observe when designing any development intervention.

One of the authors was working for Henley Management College in the UK when Henley launched a Tailored Programmes Division in 1977. This division, under different names since then, has designed and delivered programmes for executive and leadership development to a range of UK and European corporate organisations, both public- and private sector, as have many other European schools, most notably INSEAD, IMD, London Business School, Ashridge Management College, Cranfield School of Management and Warwick Business School. The European business schools entered this market earlier than did those in the USA, but US, European and Asia Pacific business schools are all active today. The earliest record of a corporate programme tailored by Henley goes back to the launch of a programme designed and delivered to the then National Iranian Oil Company as early as 1969. So by now organisations, in conjunction with business schools, should be getting the development of leadership more right than wrong, but sadly this often is not the case.

These tailored programmes have differ from open programmes; that is, programmes of a generic nature open to anyone from any organisation, in two ways. First, they are typically delivered to managers from only the organisation concerned, normally with the intention of using the programme to support a wider programme of corporate change. This leads the organisation to require a consistent delivery across the 'target group' of managers, and to require that often large numbers of managers go through the programme in a defined period of time to support the delivery of organisational objectives within the specified timeline.

Clearly, an organisation will therefore opt for a tailored programme as it is more likely to meet the relevance, transferability and future flexibility criteria than would an open programme. Using open programmes will not serve these objectives, not least because only a small number of managers from any one firm can enrol on a particular programme. However, business schools or other providers still offer open programmes a number of times a year as there is a requirement from organisations that do not have the size or funding to run a tailored programme to have their managers undergo training; SMEs (small and medium-sized enterprises) are a case in point.

Even if the design of an open programme was relevant to a large organisation, it might need to use that programme over many years to put a cohort of 200–300 managers through that learning experience, and with 'churn' as managers leave, move jobs and new managers join it could be much longer. Using different schools or providers in parallel would speed progress but could also lead to issues of consistency.

Moreover, it is unlikely that a generic design focused on providing appropriate development for a wide range of participants (in terms of organisation, sector, jobs, nationality and other differences) would be as effective as a tailored approach.

On tailored programmes, the developer (HR function/external adviser) and the client (the organisation) work together in designing a programme to meet the organisation's needs. Typically, the expertise of the provider is deployed against 'statements of requirement' from the client. Increasingly, these 'statements of requirement' are set out via competence models and supported by interviews with key client executives. Good practice would include the setting up of joint client and provider design terms, and a clear process of co-design and 'sign-off' by one or more internal 'client sponsors', followed by pilot programmes, reviews, a final sign-off and then full implementation. Ensuring that our three key criteria – relevance, transferability and future flexibility – are met often requires that the senior business leaders involved in programme development also take part in its delivery. This is also often critical in positioning the programme to maximise credibility with both the participants and the wider organisation.

Most fundamentally, co-design and co-delivery with business management, while not often achieved, is of central importance to the effective development of leadership as it is practised in the organisation. That key objective often cannot be achieved by external providers alone even where the external provider obtains inputs from client executives. Certainly a programme whose core design is managed solely by an external provider will not achieve this. This is true even where active learning is part of the solution being deployed. Only the active engagement of senior executives in the core design and delivery is likely to ensure that the engagement needed occurs. This is because the intervention needs to embrace leadership as it is practised currently within the organisation itself for effective leadership development to result.

As one progresses through the approaches to tailored development activity, there is an increased focus on transforming the learning experience. The transformation is caused by the pressure to build an active learning experience, and thus active learners (Kolb, 1984). It is also from an input and academic discipline oriented model to a solutions oriented learning model. But ultimately the intervention itself is part of the solution. Because, as the two case studies illustrate, the active engagement of senior executives in the leadership development process changes the way that development is undertaken. Thus the intervention becomes the solution.

To achieve this end, organisationally specific leadership development solutions are characterised, as follows:

(i)   Integration, with the business.

(ii)   Convergence, where the intervention itself becomes a 'living version' of the solution.

(iii)   Joint design and delivery, central to this convergence being achieved.

(iv)   Design of outcomes to focus leadership on current organisational needs.

Looking in more detail at the design of customised programmes, there are three key elements: the delivery system, the learning cycle, and the organisation itself. Examining these three in order to examine the relationship between each, we consider the delivery system and the learning cycle first (see Figure 4.3).

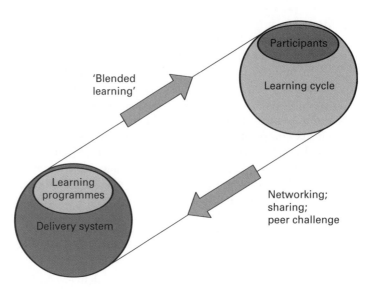

Fig 4.3   Leadership development: delivery system, part 1

The delivery system comprises learning programmes that combine appropriate learning activities, processes, curriculum, tools and people (either delivering the development or receiving it) creating a 'blended learning' process for the participants. People are engaged in learning via the adult learning cycle, which includes processes of networking and knowledge sharing based in the processes of peer challenge. The delivery system delivers learning materials and opportunities. Learners engage with the delivery system both individually and as a group, share ideas, learning and their own experience. The process is interactive because often the delivery system is impacted by the outputs of the learning participants using feedback loops and thus develops itself as the process moves forward.

Case study   **Leadership in action – leaders developing leaders – delivering development at UBS**

One of the new elements injected into the development programmes at UBS (see Case Study above) between 2002 and 2006 that was very successful was the development of leaders by leaders. This principle of leaders developing leaders is fundamental to effective leadership development work, as we shall see as the UBS case study unfolds below.

The design team had personally experienced a number of programmes in other organisations where development programmes had failed to deliver on the key 'relevant' and 'transferable' criteria for learning. Further, many had been delivered by external faculty, often without sufficient tailoring to ensure that either the criteria were met or the audience was energised sufficiently to execute the transfer. This is still a significant problem, even when there is a joint development between business schools and organisations.

It was decided that, in general terms, the external input on the programmes would be minimised to maximise the business relevance and increase the likelihood of transfer and participant buy-in. However, for these objectives to be delivered successfully to participants, gravitas on the part of the internal faculty was required. Given the participants' positions as senior managing directors this meant that the faculty had to be at least at group managing board level (top 60 in the bank) or at group executive board level (top 12 in the bank). Obviously, there are a number of significant issues here in terms of a group that senior personally facilitating development. These revolved around:

■ Time free from business demands to act as faculty.

■ Personal motivation to do so.

■ Personal capability to facilitate learning.

■ Meeting the logistical needs of both individuals and the programme.

However, it was determined with the CEO that the involvement of senior management was critical to get the key messages across and to have credibility among the participants to drive forward the ideas developed in the organisation.

Some element of external faculty was included in the programmes but this revolved around delivering the general leading-edge knowledge of specific subjects necessary for the programme not held internally – for example, future developments in global financial markets or leadership delivery. Thus, in general terms, internal faculty delivered about 75 per cent of content on average.

The response of senior management to their new developmental role varied from enthusiasm to shock and horror. There was very careful selection and briefing of those selected to deliver the first few programmes. As the initial success became known, more of the senior management group became willing to develop their own skills as facilitators and the role had significant benefits for both participants and facilitators. A good number of senior management staff discovered hidden talents as teachers and facilitators and subsequently began to expand this role in their own business areas. This also had significant benefits for the level of respect for them within the bank as a result of their newly demonstrated skills.

In most cases the format of delivery was simple. A presentation by the faculty on their business is not unusual for such programmes, but, the GLE, as the programme was known, went a stage further, requiring them to cover their current strategy, challenges they faced, and things that had gone right or wrong. Then they would have to run a discussion session with the audience for at least 30 minutes, looking at how the audience could help them to get more from their business, or how they could help the audience with their business needs. Open and frank discussions were held that added new ideas, solved problems and developed new networks. This would not have happened with a standard presentation and a few questions.

Further, at every GLE 1, the CEO, Peter Wuffli, personally attended for an afternoon, both to view the other discussions and to run his own workshop setting out his view of progress together with at least an hour of free-flow discussions and debate, which again resolved issues and developed new ideas for business initiatives.

Thus the programmes were not just about the faculty of internal leaders developing the audience leaders, it was also about the audience developing the faculty in their skills and understanding, and both groups developing the performance of UBS.

To drive debate and deliver insight, organisational reviews or audits can be effective. The presentation of data to participants based on audit data from a sample of managers from their own organisation can be reviewed to examine the 'change readiness' of the organisation. Further, then each cohort of participants can also be

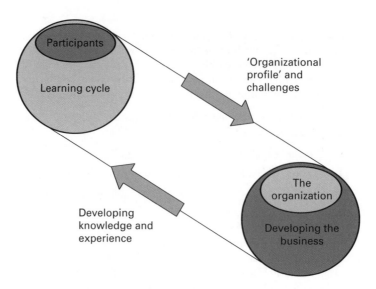

Fig 4.4   Leadership development: delivery system, part 2

debriefed on their views, which adds to the reviews undertaken by all previous cohorts. Thus as the process went through successive cohorts a fuller 'picture' of the organisational audit was built up that reflected changes in attitude and progress over time.

Figure 4.4 depicts the process of developing the organisation and the learning cycle. Here the focus is on the participants and the organisation. In a customised programme the organisational profile and challenges, and how to respond to them, become the focus of learning, with developing the effectiveness of the organisation and improving the way that leadership is practised as a key planned outcome. By doing so, participants develop 'grounded' knowledge and experience 'embedded' in the organisation's current needs and build relationships and networks with the senior executives co-delivering the intervention.

Here the programme becomes an intervention within an ongoing process of developing the individual leader and leadership practice within the business, including the concept of a 'leadership team'. As we saw in the UBS case, learning takes on a natural position in the organisational development 'life cycle', with dialogue about problems, issues and possible solutions engaging participants, key faculty and senior executives, working together to find and implement solutions. While this may be achieved rarely in practice and is certainly not the only mechanism for learning, it can present an effective and convergent opportunity for leader and leadership development.

On the relationship between the delivery system and the organisation, in Figure 4.5 the co-design and co-tutoring of participants responds to the issues facing the organisation. It represents a key driver building relationships combined with the learning outputs and feedback available from the interaction between participants, senior executives and faculty, as this brings together curriculum material to help people focus on the issues to be addressed. Senior executives bring data and perspectives on these of which the participants are unlikely to be aware.

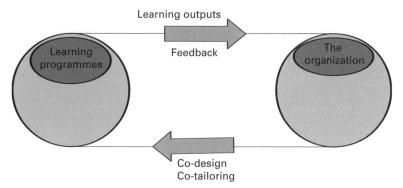

Fig 4.5   Leadership development: delivery system, part 3

However, external academic faculty members do add significant value when used effectively by the organisation. They add value by bringing academic work to these issues, not least relevant research data and case examples from elsewhere that appear to be relevant. This deals with the issue of organisations tending to look inwards and to think they are operating effectively as they have no external benchmark. This mix of internal practice and external best practice is most effective in a problem-oriented dialogue that involves all in devising new ideas and solutions. But where academic faculty are left to determine too much of the structure and delivery, the content tends to become too academic and less relevant or transferable than when they are guided by executives.

Case study   **Leadership in action – UBS: aligning development to critical deliverables**

The design of the development programmes at UBS was focused on dealing with the problem that large organisations have, where a large suite of development programmes have built up that do not align to current organisational objectives or needs but provide only generic skills development. Further, the presence of a large number of programmes also suggests that not all of them may provide a real return on investment to the organisation or to the individual. Such interventions may be intellectually interesting but their value in adding to the bottom line is questionable.

At the outset it was decided to minimise rather than maximise the number of programmes. They had to be focused on supporting the delivery of key business outcomes as much as possible rather than on the generic content. The aim was to develop and improve business performance as well as individual performance, not merely to provide intellectual stimulation.

In line with the overall corporate objective of developing 'One UBS' that would seamlessly support the delivery of all the bank's services across the client base, the programmes would focus on the key elements of that strategy:

■ Understanding and leveraging the whole bank.

■ Providing best client service.

■ Delivery through great leadership.

Further, each programme would be aimed at providing a significant personal experience that participants would remember for many years together with the networks they built at the event. The programmes were therefore named 'Global Leadership Experiences' and known by the initials GLE followed by the programme number. There were three programmes, each taking 3.5 days and each focused on one of the key elements above. That was all that was needed to achieve the objectives. Any additional programmes would only complicate and potentially confuse the critical messages that had to be disseminated detailing what was required of leaders. Participants, drawn from across all business areas and geographies to provide as wide a mix as possible, were invited to attend by nomination from the CEO of their business division and then formally invited by the Group CEO to ensure that attendance was seen as a reward and something to aspire to.

GLE 1 – Leveraging the whole bank: this was designed to enable the participants to understand how the bank as a whole functioned, the strategies and challenges of the different business divisions, and to seek ways to leverage the knowledge and client base across the bank more effectively. Part of this was to identify areas where the business could be made more effective or new business developed by working across boundaries. Several significant business initiatives that added substantial amounts to the bottom line were developed in this way.

GLE 2 – Providing the best client service: this focused on creating effective value chains within the organisation to maximise the quality of service to clients across the bank, and where possible find cost efficiencies. This included people working in the support functions as well as those in client-facing roles.

GLE 3 – Delivery through great leadership: this was the only programme that focused significantly on the development of the individual. In this case, both prior to, during and after the programme participants were given diagnostic support and feedback on their own individual performance as leaders. This was provided by a full range of instruments based on real life performance –for example, 360° feedback. The group worked together and as individuals with personal coaches to identify areas where they could improve their own performance and that of their teams for the benefit of the bank.

The success of these programmes led to this model of simple, practical and business-focused development being adopted across the bank for other development programmes. A new assessment system to identify future leaders was a key element in cascading the development strategy down the bank. Those identified and prioritised by their business as having potential were classified into two groups based on experience. The most experienced, the Advanced Career Group, were then developed via a new single global High Potential programme, (Accelerated Leadership Experience – ALE), which reflected the key GLE themes: understanding the organisation, excellent client service and excellent leadership. They were supported by pre-course self-assessment activity and the delivery of a business focussed project that solved a real business issue. Post-course support was by line manager coaching and a senior mentor from another part of the business.

The ALE programme was replicated within different business divisions for their own high potentials; (for example, in the bank's High Potential Future Leaders ASCENT programme). 50% of those on the programme were promoted or took on additional responsibilities within 6 months.

The critical success factor of the UBS programmes was that they not only developed individual capability but also the performance of the organisation to a measureable degree. Something most development programmes fail to do.

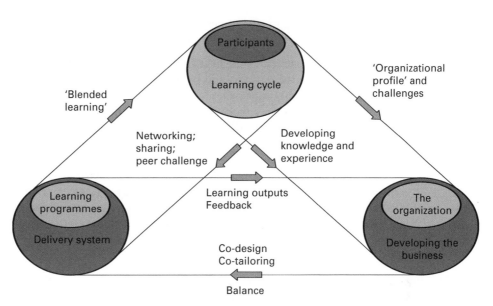

Networking;
sharing;
peer challenge

Developing
knowledge and
experience

Learning outputs
Feedback

Co-design
Co-tailoring

Balance

Leadership development: delivery system, an integrated framework

Bringing all the elements together in Figure 4.6, the key point to make is that there must be an effective balance between these three relationships. While bringing all of this together and creating an appropriate 'blend' can be expensive, it is likely to deliver the optimum output. It is unlikely that most organisations, other than those at the leading edge of global excellence, would have the expertise in house to design such solutions.

The demand from corporate clients is for solutions, and such solutions require good data and good technology. Business schools need to become more effective in the design and delivery of client-focused solutions incorporating technology in ways that build on the strengths of the technology that is related principally to remote access, speed of delivery, consistency and the capability to capture and manipulate data. 'Soft systems decision tools' and 'groupware' are particularly useful in this context, alongside simulations and scenario models, in developing leaders and leadership teams. This also allows for the ability of leaders to test ideas and strategies in a 'safe' environment.

Traditionally, optimum solutions for leadership development, developed in business schools, have emphasised three themes:

(i)   Discipline-based learning via instruction-led sessions on strategy, marketing, and operations/service management and organisational behaviour using devices such as case studies, role plays, simulations and projects. Typically 50 per cent or more of the time is devoted to the instructional element with the balance being participative.

(ii) Feedback-based learning using psychometric tests, diagnostic exercises and 360° feedback sessions, with a focus on reflective learning for the individual or group.

(iii)   Action learning, sometimes combined with 'three-way' reviews, involving participant, line manager and faculty.

These basic approaches, as illustrated by the UBS case, can be extended by working more closely with the business and by deploying technology in relevant ways. This is of fundamental importance: the development of leaders cannot and should not be outsourced. The less the involvement of the organisation, the more likely the development will fail to meet the three key criteria and become irrelevant, non-transferable and fixed in time. Ultimately, leadership development cannot be wholly outsourced as this is too much of a risk for the organisation, especially at the strategic level. External providers can play an important role by engaging participants as individuals and groups, and by using experience from a range of external settings and best practice combined with world class development tools and techniques, but ultimately leadership development is also about securing the future of the organisation and thus top leaders must be fully engaged in the process and not just marginally so.

4.13   Senior leader development

4.13.1   The importance of holding up the mirror

To fully understand senior leadership development, we need to deal with both behaviour and knowledge. Not the knowledge of leadership as an academic discipline, but in helping leaders to develop more effective choices and approaches. Appropriate patterns of behaviour are important. But how senior leaders come to formulate plans and goals, the information they use and the thinking underpinning their decisions is a relevant subject of leadership development activity. A recent survey of leadership throws up an interesting and balanced set of findings on leadership effectiveness set in the context of this argument. The findings are summarised as follows:

(i)   Leaders think the ability to deliver 'the numbers' is the most respected leadership quality.

(ii)   Roughly a third of internally sourced and promoted leaders fail, usually because of poor people skills or interpersonal qualities.

(iii)   Thirty per cent of leaders fail to demonstrate the key qualities necessary for effective leadership.

(iv)   Twenty-five per cent of organisational plans and strategies fail because they are not executed properly.

(v)   'Strong' leadership can enhance the successful execution of plans by 20 per cent or more.

The first result is no surprise, but in rank order of importance the leaders surveyed saw 'deliver the numbers', the ability to take 'tough decisions' and 'the ability to create a strategy for success' as the top three, with interpersonal skills only in fourth position. Moreover, looking at the third finding, it is interesting to note that many of these 'key qualities' relate more to the ability to cope with ambiguity than with the impact on people, with the ability to learn, handle feedback, cope with complexity and think broadly using multiple perspectives being very much in evidence. Finally, turning to 'the execution of business plans', the issues identified in the survey are focused almost entirely on the analytical and on the performance agenda ;that is, as we saw earlier, Churchill's 'pester, nag and bite'. If there is an interest in dealing with people here it looks at how to call people to account, not how to engage with them.

4.14 Key points on optimising development programmes

To further enhance leadership development, there are some key points to note:

(i) The more leadership development is undertaken in a genuinely integrated way, the more effective it will be; thus delivery should include senior executives actively involved in tutorial work – that is, going substantially beyond checking the design, positioning the programme at the outset, and attending a dinner.

(ii) We must continuously seek fresh and innovative ways of communicating learning in a simple, effective and delivery-focused way.

(iii) Leadership development can be particularly effective where development programmes are designed as part of wider programmes of change and development, as in the UBS case. In that sense, leadership development is part of a broader intervention strategy focused on the future of the organisation.

4.15 Deciding between internal and external resources

The landscape of leadership development has evolved, fragmented and become more complex. In addition to organisations themselves developing leaders internally, increasingly organisations are becoming involved in this field. These include business schools, e-learning providers, consulting firms, training providers, conference organisers, professional bodies and many more.

4.16 Using external providers

If the decision has been taken to use external providers in some way there are a number of aspects to be considered.

4.16.1 The 'value proposition'

What, then, is the potential value offered by leadership development providers? At one level this can be determined by looking at the characteristics of the provider. Here we examine the key features:

(i) **Reputation:** this is linked to brand, but also to 'track record', not least based on similar interventions and/or in the same sector.

(ii) **Range of capabilities:** can the potential provider offer the knowledge, skills and experience needed for the planned intervention?

(iii) **Depth of intervention:** to what extent will this provider genuinely tailor content and learning style, and move forward with a co-design and co-delivery philosophy?

(iv) **Client management:** how actively does the provider seek to build and sustain constructive relationships with the client, both short- and long-term?

In truth, though, the tailored market covers a wide range of interventions in terms of style, price and depth. This is shown in Figure 4.7. The figure differentiates value and premium customers. Value customers tend to seek limited/minimal tailoring because they have a well-conceived need for an identified target audience and seek a competent solution at a value price. This may be because they do not have sufficient financial resources or they have taken a cost/benefit decision about the resources they will allocate to the development of leaders at different levels – for example, senior, middle and junior. The common analysis is that senior leaders need more tailoring and a better quality faculty on their development interventions then do junior ones.

Lowest price generally involves the delivery of the 'mini-MBA', where the faculty use standard MBA materials, albeit where the overall design will respond to client need to some degree. No attempt is made to take leader development very far in this context, at least not beyond ensuring a basic level of briefing about relevant business issues and management disciplines.

Mid-range programmes tend to have some additional features, allowing for a degree of customisation. These may often comprise a practical project or some use of psychometric tests and 360° feedback to allow for either application of learning or some personal development. But nevertheless the focus remains on standard MBA-style material with some additional features.

Looking now at premium customers and prices, here we see two types of solution: programme plus and customer specific. In the former, a serious attempt is made to tailor from existing material using what might be called a 'plug and play' approach. Thus they define client needs and then offer a design to meet it with a day of this, a half day of that, and a day of something else taken 'off the shelf'. Sophisticated

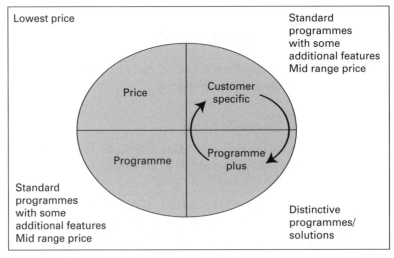

Fig 4.7   Leadership development: customer value proposition

versions of this approach will include projects, personal development work, coaching and a tutor in place to 'weave' a coherent 'path' through the programme for participants. These programmes can be delivered to meet the needs of leader development for people likely or soon to be promoted, or for people engaged in the implementation of an otherwise pretty clear and formalised change plan. Designs like this can be deployed quickly and rolled out to large numbers of managers. They have a significant place in leader development as they deliver appropriate benefit at acceptable cost.

But if we are looking at a requirement for developing new leadership in practice as well as leader development, in particular where an organisation is moving into 'unknown' territory, then the organisation-specific solution comes into its own. The starting point is to focus on the outcomes desired in terms of strategic and cultural change, and the way that leadership is currently deployed in the organisation. Here joint design and delivery becomes a vital part of the solution – not merely a 'nice-to-have feature'.

To summarise, each of the four approaches is characterised by distinctive features:

(i)   Price: standard, volumes, focus on teams, process focus, conformance, 'one size fits all'.

(ii) Programme: add-ons, service upgrades, adaptable.

(iii) Programme-plus: distinctive, branded, breakthrough innovative, school lead, future focus, 'thinking outside the box'.

(iv) Customer-specific: integrated, resolves client's broader problems, client relationship focus, solutions orientated, enabling, teams form around clients and change.

4.17   Issues for executive education providers

Increasingly, good providers rely on 'storyboarding techniques' developed for film and TV to tell the 'story' of how the development will work with the participants. This 'experience' concept engages participants and inspires them to go back and implement what they have learnt in their day-to-day work is key and was a central theme of the UBS Global Leadership Experience programmes. These were still talked about by participants referring to things they had done and discussed at the event even three years after it had taken place.

To achieve this takes ever more planning time, and needs to be reflected in how business schools and so on build their bids and prices to clients, but also how they develop their faculty. Some academics are not always keen to adapt their academic content to executive use, so business schools must seek out trainers with the necessary skills, experience and interest. There is a demand for faculty for executive education able and willing to work across typical discipline boundaries to reflect the realities of organisational operation. In addition, with the range of delivery required, traditional career paths will need further thought as they will not necessarily be either relevant or appropriate for the delivery of executive education. Increasingly, the answer is being found in visiting faculty, who are often former senior business executives with academic links who understand the reality of organisational operation and guide their academic colleagues and organisational executives into an effective partnership.

4.18   Final thoughts – the future

As the range of leadership development interventions becomes more complex, the process of programme design and delivery is becoming more demanding in increasing complex environments. However, as this happens, clarity about what leaders need to do and how to develop them is suffering. This represents a real challenge for those concerned with effective leadership development. We need designs that are integrated within the real world of organisation, that are as simple as possible, and aligned to what the organisation needs. Over-complexity builds in potential confusion and risk.

Complexity of leadership development approaches may seem to match the complexity of the situation, but complexity takes more time to understand and implement than does simplicity. There comes a cut-off point where, irrespective of whether the intervention is technically perfect, the complexity it creates results in so much time being taken that individuals do not bother to use it. So, for the organisation, the marginal benefit of perfect performance is outweighed by the resources used. Technical perfection of development programmes is not what real business leaders require: what they need is the capability to do the job well. These are different aims and are often confused with one another. The future of development must therefore enable the development of leadership capability to deal with increasingly complex real-world situations in a straightforward way by using simple principles that maximise the chances of a successful outcome.

The design and delivery needs of leadership development must work with the grain of other activities going on in the business, including talent management, strategic change, reward systems and processes and so on. Design and delivery must increasingly be the joint concern of both internal and external providers focused on organisational outcomes and integrating with existing systems. Thus leadership development must become a 'boundary-spanning activity' that provides solutions to fit with everything else that is happening. While there is a compelling need for more effective theory development in this field, we also need much more serious attention to focus on the practical joint and collaborative development and delivery of solutions that 'connect' leader development to the day-to-day operation and development of the organisation rather than continuing to leave it abandoned in an HR organisational silo where its contribution is lessened both for the individual and the organisation.

4.19   Summary

There is clear evidence from both research and the real world around us that leadership can be both learnt and taught. Some individuals are able to be merely competent, others are good and a very few are great at leadership. Organisations do not actually need great leaders – just enough good and competent ones to get the job done. The development of leaders has to match their roles. Operational leadership teaching can be systematised to a degree, but as leadership becomes more strategic and complex, situations for the leader move away from yes or no answers to grey areas.

In developing leadership, as with anything else, it can be badly delivered, which will cause confusion and cynicism, or it can be delivered well, which will deliver inspiration, engagement and success. Effort must be put into making the right decisions when planning how to develop leaders. Leadership is not an intellectual debate but about making thing happen in a practical environment, so the development of leadership must focus on this. As has already been said, the delivery must be both relevant and transferable to the real world of work, and to achieve this it must be kept as simple, delivery-focused and relevant as possible, and preferably should link to some ongoing learning experience back on the job.

It is a fatal flaw to think, as many organisations do, that leadership is developed only on development programmes. While development programmes, coaching and mentoring have their place, the best place for leadership to be developed is on the job, enabled by the line manager. Such development has the unique advantage of delivering organisational objectives as well as concurrently developing skills and knowledge. Thus the linkage of development on development programmes with development on the job following the programme integrates the process into a single aligned process where the benefits for both organisation and individual are likely to be much greater.

Who delivers leadership development depends on who has the capability to deliver what the target group needs to know to develop themselves and improve organisational performance. Sometimes this can be internal resources only, sometimes a mix of internal and external, and sometimes – for example, senior-level mentoring – it may be only external. In any event, the question 'How is this going to improve the way that the organisation performs? ' must be asked constantly to avoid the creation of an ever-increasing list of generic leadership programmes that add little value but divert significant staff time and costs. The concept of leaders developing leaders is critical to leadership development, building both credibility and effectiveness. It also has the benefit of enhancing organisational networks, communication and culture.

Leadership development in many organisations therefore has to go up a gear and focus firmly on delivering real value to both the individual and the organisation in an efficient way that then continues on the job. This not only delivers objectives but also builds credibility for development, otherwise leadership capability development will never be seen as being of real value and leadership capability will never be properly constructed nor good leadership delivered as it needs to be.

Leadership is the 'glue' that binds other organisational activity together and aligns effort. Thus the development of leadership is not a separate 'nice to have' initiative delivered by the HR function; it is a 'need to have' strategically vital activity that has to be driven from the top. It is the enabler that makes everything possible that the organisation wants to achieve.

Questions

1 When considering your own leadership development, do you think your leadership capability has been developed to the full?

2 Which areas do you think should have been focused on more? Are they strategic or operational?

3 How much development was on the job and how much off the job? Which did you find to be the most effective?

4 Who in organisations should be the key developers of leadership capability? Is this what happens in the real world?

5 Leading for high performance

5.1 The drive for high performance: the leader as performance enabler

Much of the early study of leadership focused on who leaders are and how they came to be in their positions, including the sources of legitimacy or credibility as leaders. Subsequently, since the 1970s there has been a continuing concern for the impact of leaders and leadership on the performance of organisations. From the early twentieth century much of this work focused on productivity and value added, focusing on leaders and the work setting within which they operate. Thus developed a concern to understand how and why leadership style ought to be matched to situations to ensure enhanced performance. In turn, much of this work focused on the team or teams of people in work settings. In particular, this has been by examining the extent to which leaders need to balance concern for the task with concern for people and relationships within the situation in which they lead, to achieve the best results.

In this chapter we look at the leader in relation to the ongoing challenge of building high-performance teams and leading change – these can be part of the responsibility of any specific leader, or combined within an organisational transformation. Much of the emphasis is on understanding how a leader enables a team or teams to generate high levels of performance. Over many years it has become increasingly clear that authoritarian leadership alone is not a basis for high performance. So the question becomes one of matching leadership style to situation, but also increasingly there is a focus on why people 'follow' leaders. Given that leadership is ultimately a relational activity, there is a clear case for studying leaders and leadership within a team setting. This is the focus of this chapter.

In terms of delivering high performance, to go to the most basic level there are some key components:

- Good leadership – comprising good engagement and alignment of effort, clarity of role/ responsibility
  +
- Good team – comprising the right people, right place, right time – talent management, leadership development
  +
- Good delivery system – comprising good cost efficiency, quality, innovation
  =
- High performance.

To maximise the outcome, each of the components has to be of good quality. The best leader in the world cannot do much with low-ability people and a poor process if that is what he or she has to deal with. Conversely, the best people will not function well without a good leader, and if the delivery process is poor, the best efforts of the leader and his/her team would be impaired. Thus high performance is not just about leadership; it is about a holistic approach to delivering the best-quality output with good components. The leader can, however, have a significant impact by creating those should he or she wish to within his/her span of control. The question then is what makes a competent team into a high-performing one? Is there a special ingredient that makes this move to high performance occur? In simple terms, our conclusion is no, all ingredients must be high quality – the leader, the team and the process – then the outcome must be of high quality.

In this chapter we shall examine the leadership component as the critical element in delivering high performance, but also examine the other key components – the people and the process. The factors that impact on the team's performance and those related to the process are covered in the relevant sections.

5.2   Leadership for high performance

5.2.1   Does leadership make a difference to performance?

If we take an overview of all the evidence around high performance in relation to both team process and culture, be it from the individuals' perspective, the development of skills and capability, the engagement of staff, or the creation of an effective structure and framework to deliver objectives, it is clear that the role of the leader is likely to be the single largest influence on the level of performance. For example, the effective engagement of the team by the leader could increase individual performance by increasing discretionary effort by up to 30 per cent, the effective focus on skills and capability development could increase those by up to 40 per cent; this is aggregated data from a large range of studies. These are the possible improvements in individual performance that can be delivered in order of size from various factors (Corporate Leadership Council, 2004c):

■ Connection between work and organisational strategy: + 27.5%

■ Manager cares about employees: + 24.4%

■ Manager demonstrates honesty and integrity: + 24.1%

■ Manager respects employees as individuals: + 24.1%

■ Accurate evaluation of performance: + 23.7%

■ Manager puts right people in roles at right time: + 23.6%

■ Feedback is fair: + 22.3%

■ Accurate evaluation of potential: + 21.1%

It should also be noted that the highest remuneration-related drivers were:

■ Internal equity of compensation: + 7.4%

■ Total compensation + 4.1%

So if we want high performance and successful performance or change, the team leader is the key player in delivering success.

When taking an organisation-wide view, we have to take into account the capabilities of all the leaders in the organisation at all levels, as it is only by mobilising all staff that the organisation can gain the real benefits of high performance or implement change effectively. Thus delivering success requires leaders at all levels of organisation to inspire employees rather than solely depending on senior executives.

5.2.2   The basics

Working on the principle that leadership can improve individual performance, then if applied to a team it can do the same for a number of individuals. To have even a base level of performance, let alone to build a high-performing team, some basic leadership capabilities must be in place. These, as set out below, must be delivered in a way that develops the performance of the team and the individuals within it while delivering the objective. These are the leader's ability to:

- Identify the problem or objective.
- Consider viable options.
- Identify an optimal solution.
- Create a simple plan – including alignment of effort.
- Brief the team on the plan in an effective way.
- Motivate the team to deliver the plan and to accept mutual responsibility for success.
- Monitor performance.
- Conduct a feedback exercise to identify possible improvements.

The optimum delivery of the team's objectives is influenced inherently by the situation, and thus the leader needs to adjust his or her leadership accordingly. This will relate to a number of factors; for example:

- Complexity of the task.
- Time to complete the task.
- Resources available.
- Capability and motivation of the team.
- Other external threats or risks.

This set of influencing factors led to the development of the models of situational leadership referred to earlier and examined by Hersey and Blanchard (1998), Vroom (1964) and others. Thus effective leadership also includes the ability to match style and content of leadership delivery to the situation. These same principles apply at both operational and strategic levels, but in the latter the complexity, span of control and other factors make delivering results much more difficult. At this level the alignment of effort of people on to key deliverables is significantly more difficult than at the operational level, where generally a smaller number of activities are taking place in a single location and with fewer people.

Since the work of Mary Parker Follett (2003) and her development of 'the law of the situation' there has been an approach to leadership based on seeking to understand what leaders actually do. Mintzberg (1973) produced a thoroughly researched study in this tradition. More substantially, Kotter (1990) produced what has been an influential study of leaders and leadership, examining the impact of the situation on the emergence of leadership in practice and over time. For Kotter, leadership style is not something that emerges instantaneously. Rather, in any given set of organisational circumstances, long-enduring patterns of leadership are likely to develop, effectively creating key elements of organisational culture.

Kotter (1988) identifies a number of the 'characteristics needed, to provide effective leadership'. From his view, to be effective, leaders need a range of knowledge of industry, business functions and the firm itself – the *strategic overview*. Also needed are a broad range of contacts and good working relationships both in the firm and in the industry – *networks and the ability to build rapport and influence*. Linked to this will be a good track record in delivering a relatively broad set of activities: – *high performance*. Kotter also refers to 'keen minds', strong interpersonal skills, high integrity, seeing value in people, and a strong desire to lead: – *intellectual capability, ability to deliver results through people, genuine concern, integrity and ambition*. Interestingly, this concept is modelled in the UBS case study (see Chapter 4), where the Leadership Academy was tasked with putting in place many of these capabilities among the top 500 leaders in the bank.

In turn, Kotter may well have influenced studies such as that by Kouzes and Posner (1987), in which effective leadership, as judged from the 'followers' perspective is determined by leader behaviour. Effectiveness is determined by the extent to which leaders exhibit these behaviours:

(i)   **Challenging the process** – a willingness to question current ideas, methods and practices, combined with themselves being open to challenge.

(ii) **Inspiring shared vision** – the ability to help people, make sense of the current position and come to believe in an alternative 'future', as well as becoming engaged in actions seeking to achieve that future state.

(iii) **Enabling others to act** – creating the conditions in which and through which others can both realise their own potential and contribute to the new organisation.

(iv) **Modelling the way** – offering leadership by example, and through leaders' own behaviour, showing others how the future can be created.

(v)   **Encouraging the heart** – recognising effort, contribution and success, but in ways that demonstrate the 'value' placed on people.

Clearly, there is a substantial overlap here with the idea of 'transformational leadership'. This is not unexpected, given that transformation and change are often used to describe the same types of activities.

Following Higgs (2003) it is clear that the study of leadership and leadership development sees combinations of personal characteristics of leaders and areas of competence as being important. Higgs refers to 'the re-emergence of personality ... as a component of effective leadership'. To what extent is the role of the leader in relation to a team that of enabling the emergence of team processes which facilitate team performance?

Collins (2001) undertook an important study of 'great companies' using a rigorous set of effectiveness criteria and examining elements of success, including leadership. The 'great companies' were defined as those that outperformed their direct competitors by a significant extent over a 20-year period. For example, taking share price, the great companies he identified outperformed competitors by a factor of between four and 15 times over the period. The rigour of the study is real enough, but it had a consequence in that only 11 companies were actually identified as 'great'.

The study included leadership, using a definition of 'level 5 leadership'. The core idea was that level 5 leadership is a key characteristic of the CEOs of the 'great' companies. In simple terms, level 5 leadership involves a combination of humility and will. Humility relates to a lack of arrogance and an acceptance of weakness – the opposite of the key thrust of the charismatic leadership model. The latter refers to persistence and determination in the pursuit of business goals, with the willingness to take any and all actions needed to see them achieved. But note the following quote from a discussion guide included on www.jimcollins.com: 'If Level 5 is about ambition, first and foremost about the cause, the company, the work – not yourself – combined with the will to make good on that ambition, then how can each of us as individuals learn to take actions consistent with being Level 5?.' This, combined with a 'set of questions for reflection' emphasising other aspects of what he refers to as the 'good to great' world, it is hard to conclude that the model is driven by rational ideas about organisation. Interestingly, Collins argues the value of a high questions-to-statements ratio from leaders when leading teams, inherently the introduction of at least the opportunity to establish clarity by team members if not the ability to question the leader.

Since the earlier work of human resources management scholars looking at the impact of various motivational and work/organisational design practices on performance (see, for example, Porter and Lawler, 1968, and Pfeffer, 1998), there has emerged a set of ideas relating to how to achieve historically high levels of performance and performance improvement. Here, the claim is that there are practices that deliver performance gains well ahead of the long-run average productivity gains common in modern economics. These authors are describing a 'high performance paradigm' which is seen to embrace a wide range of practices including job design, team-based organisation design and a range of participative activities including 'whole system events', 'town hall meetings', quality circles and similar.

We argue for a distinction between 'lean' and 'team' systems. Collins argues that the former involves a conventional supervision approach, whereas the latter 'typically entails truly autonomous teams and no just-in-time supervision'. He goes on to reinforce his view by distinguishing between 'involvement' and 'intensification' approaches. 'Involvement' is seen as achieving improvement through higher employee commitment and engagement by relying on high-commitment employment practices, whereas 'intensification' achieves gains by cost reductions and work intensification.

But the distinction is not as clear-cut in reality. In truth, in the real world, lean thinking, just-in-time approaches and business process re-engineering focus on improving delivery or the execution of performance of the system. Inevitably the focus will be on flawless operational performance, right-first-time and every time, pushing decision-making authority down as close to the customer as possible to enhance responsiveness and the elimination of excess waste or unnecessary processes, including the minimisation of repeated work caused by poor quality. Is Collins really arguing that gains from involvement will not inevitably look at such matters? Locally, in any discussion involving those delivering a process, the involvement must include a discussion of 'hard' as well as 'soft' issues. Further, if actions are agreed by a work group, is it likely that the result is no less one of intensification as well as involvement? This makes no practical sense. The real issue is to distinguish between conventional command and control approaches, and approaches that engage employees in decisions on the one hand and with the question of gain-sharing on the other.

Thus, as with many other issues around leadership, it is about practice as much as principle. So the real issue is not 'lean versus team', following Goddard, but rather looking at what works in practice, how decisions are made, and who gains, following Nohria *et al.* (2003). This study looks at the companies that outperformed their industry, concluding that, in each case, these high-performing companies excelled at four primary management practices: strategy, execution, culture, and structure, and supplemented that with a mastery of at least two of four secondary management practices: talent, innovation, leadership, and mergers and partnerships.

Further, more recently the development of the concept of the entrepreneurial leader has added to the list of capabilities required for high performance. To some degree this builds on some of the previous research which indicated that the high-performing leader does more than merely deliver the job in hand. What do entrepreneurial leaders do? As well as being good leaders they also have stronger business skills and understanding, putting profit-seeking, managing change, innovation, and looking for market disruptive processes and process improvement ideas to the forefront. Thus the normal good leader's vision, inspiring motivation of staff, understanding of the current organisation, and the desire to make it more efficient is augmented by the entrepreneur's capability not only to make the present world better but also to find a new world that's better still. Also, if the leader behaves in this way, then most of their team will do the same, a positive multiplier effect that can ripple across the organisation adding value where it is taken up.

Despite the concerns of some senior management, this more entrepreneurial attitude is not a threat to the organisation's stability, structure or safety if aligned in the right way by top management. If focused on the achievement of the organisation's vision, aligned to key deliverables and underpinned by its values, it then has the capability to improve performance both in the present and, perhaps more importantly, in the longer term. Some current leaders may not have the capability of taking on this more entrepreneurial role, but most, if already good leaders, will have. It is not a mystical revelation; it is just as much a process that can be learned as many other things. It is about helping leaders find the 'gaps' in the system, market or environment and then exploiting them. This should happen at both strategic and operational levels to really make a difference.

This all suggests that there is a team-building role that the leaders have to fulfil in addition to their 'delivery' role in purely getting things done. This is about building capability, vision and collective (as well as individual) responsibility in the team, and turning the team from a group of individuals into a team. This team-building role, as identified in Adair's (1973) model is key to building high performance in the team as we shall see.

5.3 Strategic leadership: spreading high performance

As organisations expand and grow, they become more complex. The simplicity of the smaller organisation, where it was clear to all what the critical deliverables were is

Fig 5.1   Organisational performance alignment

gone and now different departments are wrestling to deliver different things to enable the delivery chain to function. This leads to there being a lack of clarity about what is really important and what is not. Departments tend to forget the end customer and focus on the delivery of their 'product'. Confusion starts to grow around what people should be doing as the highest priority, and conflicting messages begin to be sent to staff from different sources. While the board may be clear on what the priorities are, staff lower down often are not, and they are the ones that both serve customers and receive feedback from them – both vital to organisational success. If one considers the different factors that influence staff behaviour and staff allocation of time to various deliverables, they are probably influenced by many things – some of which encourage staff to do different things; that is, what is important and what is not (see Figure 5.1).

This misalignment needs to be reversed to enable high performance to spread across the organisation. Alignment has to be done from strategic level, where top management ensures that all the key influencing factors align staff behaviour with the key deliverables for that period that underpin the delivery of the optimum end product or service to the customer. This is a simple exercise in deciding what needs to be done and then ensuring that everything points to those things from the perspective of staff. While this is designed to deliver strategic benefit, it will also inherently support individual leaders across the organisation, as long at they themselves are aligned with the strategic agenda, so that the other organisational influences on their teams –

cultural or process – will tend to align them to what the leader wants to deliver. Thus this approach supports high performance at team and individual as well as strategic level.

The basics set out above to enable high performance through leadership should be the guiding drivers for all leaders in the organisation, led by focused top management who ensure proactively that this happens at all levels. High performance will not occur across the organisation by chance, and pockets of high performance will not spread by osmosis. There has to be a strategic initiative to spread and adopt high performance for its benefits to be leveraged effectively. The many case studies in this book confirm that.

The concept of the entrepreneurial leader has significance in particular at the strategic level as it links with finding a route from the current world to a new, higher-performing world. Once a culture has been created in the organisation where this behaviour can flourish, where people take the initiative, give feedback (especially on what customers are saying), look for innovation, find cost efficiencies and seek to increase profit, and look for gaps in the market that might provide new revenue or disrupt competitors, then the company will naturally have a competitive advantage. Entrepreneurial behaviour should not be the preserve of only senior management; it is required at all levels.

5.4 High performance and the team

From the perspective of the end user, the individual, to create an environment where they will perform at their best we should be delivering what we know they want in the workplace. This has to be the starting point of effective leadership for high performance. Through a number of sources it has been known at least since the 1970s that people at work want simply to be able to:

- Deliver the best work they can.
- Grow and develop.
- Contribute to the bigger picture.
- Gain the respect of their bosses and colleagues.
- Be treated fairly, honestly and with integrity.
- Be asked for their views if they feel they could contribute.
- Be praised when the have done well.
- Be told what is going on and be able to ask questions.

The data from studies on individual performance suggest that, if leaders make the above happen, they obtain better performance through extra effort and less risk via employees doing the right thing! For example, the questions used by many engagement surveys, such as Gallup, focus on these areas. So this is the mirror image from the individuals' perspective of what they want leaders to do, which confirms the research on what successful leaders do from the organisation's perspective.

However, this will mainly impact on the individuals, but creating a group of high-performing individuals does not necessarily mean they are also part of a high-performing team. Hence the reference above and in John Adair's (1973) model to the team as well as the individual, and the individuals have to be made into a team. This is one of the major challenges that teams face when comprised of high performers; for example, in parts of investment banking. The skills and attitudes required to be successful are those that also make the creation of a team more difficult – the culture and practice of individual performance versus that of team working.

Any working group can become either a potential team or a pseudo team. The latter remains limited to individual performances, rather than becoming focused on group performance. Potential teams recognise the importance of group performance and the need to agree group objectives, but never create a sense of shared accountability as real teams do. The latter accept mutual accountability, and team members view the team's output as being 'shared'. To achieve this level, team members must make the critical choice to invest themselves in the team and its mission, overcoming obstacles along the way. Successful teams need team leaders who help to focus the team members on the key deliverables, endorse a team-based philosophy of shared accountability, and foster a climate of courage and success, but in the end the team has to do the work.

This view led many scholars to see the team as a more effective source of 'high performance'. If one cannot rely solely on the leader role to achieve high performance alternatively it can be delivered, as has been suggested, by the team itself also creating a drive for high performance. While the leader will have a significant impact on the creation and maintenance of an effective team he or she is not the only influence, as in practice the leader may simply not be present all the time, so the team has to function on its own to some degree within the framework the leader has set out. Research has long indicated that the norms and social pressures within teams are by far the most effective means governing high (or low) performance. This goes back at the well-known 'Hawthorne research' (see Sofer, 1973; Grey, 2008).

This then links into the development of teams in stages, as set out by Tuckman (1965) – the 'Forming, Storming, Norming and Performing' stages. These demonstrate the stages of development that the team must go through to move from being a group of individuals to become a team. While being facilitated by the leader, the team itself has to move willingly through each stage, so the final success or failure of this is significantly in the hands of the team itself.

Key is the fact that we have to have the right people in the team to be effective and they have to want to work together to build a high-performing team. The guidance of an appointed leader will naturally aid and speed this process if that person is skilled at team building. If he or she is, it can in practice reinforce some of the negative elements; for example, supporting cliques that agree with them in power struggles rather than trying to avoid such groups.

Katzenbach and Smith have produced an influential book on this topic, entitled *The Wisdom of Teams* (2005). Their core idea is that effective teams represent the best means of building a higher-performance organisation. The team is viewed as a group of people possessing 'complementary skills', committed to a common purpose and working within an agreed set of performance standards. The distinctive feature of a team is a synergy arising from the emergence of mutual or shared accountability. In turn, shared accountability is based on processes of social exchange within the team. This shared accountability is powered by the team and the leader agreeing on the successful delivery of objectives for which they are all responsible.

Case study   **Clive Woodward**

Clive Woodward coached the English Rugby Union team to its victory in the Rugby World Cup in 2003. Facing teams such as South Africa, France, New Zealand and Australia in a sport demanding the highest levels of physical fitness, playing intensity, strategy and team-work, no one who knows the sport in general or was aware of the build-up to the 2003 competition in Australia was unaware of the challenge the England team had to face. Woodward was the only person to date to ever have led/coached an England team to victory in the Rugby Union World Cup.

Woodward identifies seven 'winning behaviours' that he and the England team developed during the build-up to the competition; two examples are given below:

(i)   The basics – what are the fundamentals of winning a game of rugby? It took two years to agree on this, but the focus was on three basic aspects: line-outs, scrums and rucks – the three 'contact situations' in which the teams (or parts of the teams) fought for the ball.

(ii) Pressure – putting the opposition under pressure to disrupt their basic aspects.

Just as important was the concept of 'teamship'. This was basically about agreed standards of performance/behaviour which the team would 'manage'. Including ideas such as punctu-ality and dress code. The important point was that Woodward and the team took time to get them right, via an inclusive process based on consensus. Once in place, the power of peer pressure and the authority of the leader, in this case Woodward, his other coaching staff and Martin Johnson, the team captain, all playing leadership roles.

Woodward's contention is that teamship creates the space for leaders to carry out their role within a team operating under the most intensive pressure (on the field of play, in front of the world's press and media, and during preparation as players attempt to balance family life, playing for their club and playing for England. The approach creates a platform for resolving operational issues, bringing new players into the team quickly and for setting incredibly high standards.

Source: timesonline.co.uk.

Interestingly, this approach mirrors some of the content of the team building and operation approach taken by the military in their work.

Case study questions

1   Is sports coaching different, or is it a special case of leadership?

2   Is the motivation of sports stars a key difference, or would it be dangerous to assume that motivation will always lead to success?

3   Consider a recent game in which your own national side under-performed. What does that tell you about leadership?

Katzenbach and Smith (2005) then identify the 'team performance curve' to show how to create winning teams. This is a trajectory from a new team to a 'potential team' and onwards to a 'real team'. At the heart of this is the role of the leader. It is unlikely that the team will naturally create itself unless it has been operating as a team previously or is presented with an external threat that forces mutual co-operation. Normally, someone emerges as a deputy leader to make this happen if the formal leader is not present.

On this basis, teams can become critical building blocks to organisational success. Provided a strong performance ethic and vision-driven leadership are set at the top of the organisation and by the immediate leader, teams can work together collectively to contribute the skills, energy and performance to build success, customer loyalty, shareholder value and so on.

This assumes three essential steps to high performance:

(i)   **Engaging,** requiring a sense of purpose, commitment and trust.

(ii)   **Enabling,** requiring capability and accountability.

(iii) **Energising,** with creativity, client and colleague responsiveness, empathy and recognition.

5.5   Roles within teams: high performance through the right team 'mix'

There has been significant work carried out over the years on individual personality types, going right back to McGregor's (1960) Theory X and Theory Y, and through analysis by assessments such as Myers–Briggs Type Indicator (MBTI) and others showing that individuals do have different personality types. Also that this impacts on their capability to carry out some roles within the workplace better than others. This has extended to the work around teams and the research showing that certain 'role' types need to be present in all teams to make them effective.

Margerison and McCann (1989) focus on functions and work preferences, developing a Team Management Wheel and characteristic 'roles' including *creator-innovators*, *explorer-promoters*, *assessor-developers*, *thruster-organisers*, *concluder-producers*, *controller-inspectors*, *upholder-maintainers*, and *reporter-advisers*, rather similar to the Belbin (2010) team roles. The key is to get the right balance of these roles in any given team. Their own research indicated the relative proportion of each role mature organisations appeared to have. From roughly 25 per cent of people who prefer the *concluder-producer* and *thruster-organiser* role to just under 10 per cent each for the *creator-innovator*, *explorer-promoter* roles and *controller-inspector* roles; and 17.5 per cent preferring the *assessor-developer* role. But it will depend on various contingencies. Hewlett Packard Laboratories in California appear to have 22 per cent who have *creator-innovator* preferences, but given the effect of what the organisation is seen to do and the people who would seek to join it, this is not surprising.

Margerison and McCann (1989) also and usefully refer to a *linker* role – a skills-based rather than a preference-based role. This can focus on external linking, internal linking and informal linking. It clearly represents a leadership role or quasi-leadership role. They note that high-performing teams appear to be those where one or more people are playing the linking roles; often the leader, but not in all cases. Leadership as it relates to 'the drive for high performance' is really a two-'part' process – the people and the process – some would say engaging the heart and the head of the team. At the people level it is about engaging people and teams, because commitment and motivation are central, but also part of that is people and teams agreeing and enforcing standards, of both behaviour and performance.

The other process level is more analytical. It is related to the collection and analysis of evidence. Ideas and concepts such as those underpinning 'lean' and 'six sigma' are essentially ways of looking at the world of organisation. Focused on the horizontal flow of value across the organisation's structure – the value chain – they represent a coherent set of ideas upon which performance improvement can be based.

Neither 'part' is sufficient in itself as a means of understanding how organisations seek performance improvement today: both 'parts' need to be engaged. Therefore, thinking and practice in leadership development must embrace both if it is to have impact in an organisational setting. One might argue that this follows from the distinction made here between leader development and the development of leadership practice, but relevance and impact appear to be essential to ensure the credibility of leadership development. Whatever view one takes on this distinction, both 'process' and 'people' need to be considered. This is not least because, in practice, to deliver organisational outputs people have to action a process.

5.6   Impact of organisational cycles

Organisations are not static. No team operates in an unchanging environment – change is all around us and organisations are constantly changing and developing. This means that often a team may have to change the way it operates as the organisation changes. Kotter (1988), for example, suggests one 'syndrome' associated with the need for good and flexible leadership linked to organisational cycles. The argument is that successful organisations can carry the seeds of their own later decline, unless leaders learn to be both successful and adaptable. The syndrome comprises three key phases. These are as follows:

(i)   An **opening phase,** in which the organisation is a new one, and faces low levels of competition and/or possesses a real competitive advantage. Here there will be a heavy dependence on the leader or leadership team.

(ii)   A **maturity phase,** characterised by the problems and issues of growth that typically require the establishment of professional management posts.

(iii)   A period of **decline,** characterised typically by denial, organisational rigidity, tension and problems.

The tensions created by declining performance create further performance problems. Early in the life of the organisation, the role and importance of leaders is paramount and they are normally entrepreneurial in approach.

The model sets out the situation that a few key people in leadership roles have moved from entrepreneurial activity and created a period of corporate success, which is then followed by growing organisational complexity as the organisation expands as a consequence of that success. This complexity, if not well managed, obstructs high performance because of the creation of internal inefficiencies which can lead to declining performance – the system designed to manage delivery actually obstructing that delivery. Growing bureaucracy is an example – the focus on monitoring and data gathering becoming more important than the output itself is a common sign of this.

This decline in performance leads to a new generation of leaders being appointed to manage growth, but is focused increasingly on stopping the decline and fighting for the survival of the business. They often feel impelled to use short-term decision-making to reverse the problem, and tend to take an inward focus on the organisation rather than on looking outside to realign to the customer, thus missing the need for continuous adaptation. Once performance starts to decline in an obvious way, this can lead to a lack of credibility for the leadership combined. This then creates a 'fear of failure' throughout the organisation, where decisions that might make things worse as well as better are avoided – risk aversion takes over. This then causes those in charge often to be seen as managers rather than leaders. As a result, a cultural change starts to embed and then often seals the fate of the organisation – inward-looking to solve problems, high risk aversion to avoid mistakes, removal of decision-making powers from those lower in the organisation to reduce errors, and the centralisation of control. All these tend to accelerate and deepen the problems.

Particularly interesting is the point about 'fear of failure'; this is often described as 'the blame culture', where decision-making, innovation and new ways of working are stifled, and excess supervision, complex systems and measurement mean that in the end the organisation's systems and culture degrade the delivery of critical objectives. Going through the process becomes more important than the outcome. Often this is a problem that affects organisations within the 'public' or 'governmental' sphere, where there is an end user who has no power to punish the organisation for inefficiency or poor service by taking their business to competitors, as they are often effectively a 'monopoly' supplier.

The other issue is that these environments are counterproductive as leaders move through careers and, by thinking short-term and by not having to take risks, they do not learn from their mistakes. Nor do they learn skills as quickly, and in particular, the interpersonal skills that they need. Often they find it difficult to give effective and accurate feedback on performance to others, and sometimes even to themselves. Adequate performance becomes 'good' performance, and expectations and standards fall further. The ability to give accurate feedback is vital – according to the Corporate Leadership Council (2004b) Engagement Survey – it can improve performance by more than 25 per cent.

When under pressure by being forced repeatedly to respond to events using the same short-term approach, they often do so inadequately and possibly in a way that is counterproductive and impacts negatively on the performance of both individuals and the team. This has the immediate effect of reducing the willingness of those in the team to take any risks, to give discretionary effort, to do nothing other than the minimum possible to do their jobs. Assuming that these individuals were previously applying discretionary effort, this could result in a drop in individual performance of up to 30 per cent (Corporate Leadership Council, 2004c). This can lead to a powerful 'vicious cycle', continually reinforcing any tendency to underperform.

5.7   Process design and leadership: the other part of the answer?

As stated earlier, the key components of high performance are the leader, the team and the process. If the organisational delivery system is not effective, even well led, high-performing teams will be obstructed in their delivery. The final component in high performance is this system component.

Therefore, to obtain high performance, while work must be intrinsically meaningful and satisfying to get maximum output, it must also be efficient as a delivery process. The two are not unconnected, as the individual is likely to give more effort, up to 32.8 per cent more, if they see that the process by which they are able to deliver is effective, and that their work will contribute to the bigger picture (Corporate Leadership Council, 2004b). If it is not the case, their motivation and effectiveness reduce as the poor process obstructs the desire to deliver a good job. Within the National Health Service (NHS) in the UK there is a well-known quote dating from 2009 and reportedly by a nurse on the front line treating patients. She felt that the delivery system in place at the time made her job more, rather than less, difficult: 'I love my job but the system gets in the way.'

At the outset we indicated that the 'measurable' aspects were also important. In Chapter 6 we introduce the Toyota case study. Whilst the Toyota story comprises a number of interesting themes, it is worth noting that the company's 'system' is one of a number of connected developments that might be referred to as the 'Design' school of performance improvement.

Today there are two particularly influential 'modes of thinking' about delivering high performance that deserve mention here, namely lean thinking and Six Sigma.

(i)   **Lean thinking** is an approach that seeks to improve the flow in any value stream, whether that be a factory, an employment office, a hospital or a bank. Lean thinking developed out of a number of innovative practices including the Toyota Production System (TPS), just-in-time, lean production and lean enterprise. It requires that we 'determine the value of any given process by distinguishing the value adding steps from non-value-adding steps and eliminating waste' (Liker, 2003). While lean thinking is often viewed as solely a way of eliminating waste from 'value streams', essentially the sequential flow of activity undertaken when a customer is served in reality involves more because, properly applied, lean thinking requires that we understand value from the customer's perspective.

(ii)   **Six Sigma** emerged from efforts by Motorola in the USA in the 1980s to implement total quality management (TQM). Six Sigma comprises methodology to eliminate defects and process variation in organisations. It provides an evidence base for decisions and, properly applied, enables decision-makers and others to understand the 'root causes' of problems, quantifies benefits and savings, and therefore facilitates the prioritisation of improvement efforts.

Both systems use tools and activities as a means of approaching delivery improvement in a disciplined and evidence-based way. Thus lean thinking uses value stream mapping, *kanban* techniques, *kaizen*, whilst Six Sigma uses statistical process control, Pareto charts, capability analysis and so on (see Chapter 6 and Martin, 1995).

As remarked earlier, it is important to note that neither approach is inconsistent with a behavioural strategy enabling high performance – back to the 'process' and 'people' elements of high-performing teams. With lean thinking and Six Sigma, performance improvement flows initially from process improvement, but this in turn leads to a positive behavioural outcome if staff are fully engaged in the process leading to change. A multiplier process can therefore be created leading to more substantial gains.

This 'harder' process approach to enabling high performance through process changes is based on a series of assumptions relating to the effective measurement of performance management. Which factors impact on performance? What is performance? Which factors are most important, and can we measure them? Can we establish relevant standards of performance? What we know is that the closer the factors relate to the deployment of inputs, the easier it is to measure them and the more diagnostic validity is achieved. Thus, quality, utilisation, speed, cost and flexibility can all be measured, as can (but to a lesser extent) productivity, customer satisfaction and adaptability. Conversely, the more strategic the factors, the more difficult measurement and diagnosis become; for example, financial and market objectives, strategy or market position. This is particularly so where we seek to understand competitive position. Thus there appears to be a real possibility of a genuine improvement being achieved by using these methods. However, there are also behavioural inputs to their applicability and use, namely leadership, judgement, intuition and experience, which all play a part in decision-making.

Similar approaches have been taken by organisations outsourcing elements of the value chain that they view as low value added – for example, administration – so that they can concentrate on high-value-added elements. This is a reflection of the reality that organisations face. For example, it is estimated that transactional HR services add 18 per cent in value to organisations, whereas transformational services add 43 per cent (Quinn and Brockbank, 2006), so the former are often outsourced.

Lean thinking logically develops into approaches emphasising flexibility and customer responses. Lean thinking is based on observations that only a proportion of the tasks undertaken in any organisation really create value (Womack and Jones, 2003). The agile manufacturer can produce highly customised products at costs comparable to mass production by competitors but with shorter lead times. Agility requires flexible workforce structures, multiskilling and computer integrated manufacture. Suffice it to say here that tools, concepts and techniques including lean thinking, Six Sigma, *kaizen*, *kanban* and agile manufacturing exist and are being used to approach the issues of performance improvement in fundamental and evidence-based approaches. Some proponents of these ideas claim that organisations might double performance, thus achieving current levels of performance with the expenditure of only half of the resources.

Tooze (2007), in an economic history of Nazi Germany, shows how, under the most extensive and damaging sustained bombardment in history, the German economy continued to produce an ever-increasing output of weaponry until close to the end of the war. But this is not a relevant example; however good the data, the question here is 'at what price' this output was delivered. The increase of production irrespective of end price or consequence in war is relatively simple, and the significant use of unpaid slave labour makes high output at low cost easy. But, irrespective of the cost savings, this use of people is obviously unacceptable. We have seen from history that significant success can be achieved in delivering massive projects ordered by dictators who have no concern for either economic or human cost. This success is not achieved by an effective process but by the forced mobilisation of vast resources, against economic or human sense, for the personal gratification of one individual. Often these lead subsequently to economic crisis for the country concerned, as the inefficiency of the delivery was so great that vital resources needed elsewhere were squandered.

What we are seeking via these process changes is not greater output by greater input, but rather greater output from the same inputs by employing greater efficiency. Clearly, then, any examination of leadership must include 'concern for the task' getting beyond 'concern for the people', to use the language of one of the standard situational models, and accept a 'two-part model' of leadership. This goes to the heart of many models of leadership – the balance of the task and the team/individual – 'people' and 'process' being key to this.

Success will be delivered where there is an effective balance, and the team and individuals are engaged in the process development – it becomes *their* process as much as the organisation's. This can have a number of benefits – as well as gaining engagement it also encourages the team to update the process as and when required to maintain effectiveness, and to innovate when required. Thus behaviour becomes a key part process improvement.

5.8   The performance measurement challenge

On the strategic level there is a wider question about whether and how we can measure the 'value' being created by any organisation. In the private sector this may be 'economic value', 'shareholder value' and 'customer satisfaction'. In the public sector it may be 'value for money' or 'public value'. The measurement of value requires that derivative questions be answered, such as:

(i)   Where along the value chain is it appropriate to measure performance? (Inputs, processes, outputs or outcomes?)

(ii)   Should we measure 'customer or client satisfaction'? (If so, who are the customers and what would satisfy them?)

In effect these questions link to three sets of issues. How does the organisation justify its existence in terms of the continued support of key stakeholders? Does the organisation make efficient use of its resources? Are its values, mission and goals appropriate for both the present and the future that it must embrace? How is it perceived by society as adding value to the 'greater good'? This latter question is of increasing importance through corporate social responsibility and reputational risk.

We measure outputs because they are easy to measure and can focus attention, enable us to look at efficiencies, productivity and utilisation rates alongside benchmark data and best practice. But outputs do not necessarily measure value. Take a hospital, for example. Measures of the number of completed patient treatments is an output. But the outcome and value are more to do with patients' subsequent life chances and life quality. So an output maybe delivered but the outcome could be either good or bad – a value difference. Outcomes are clearly more difficult to measure but do focus our attention more on the question of value.

Taking all this into account, it seems clear that effective performance measures must meet the following criteria:

(i)   Meet demands for external accountability.

(ii)   Establish a basis for clear mission, strategy and goals.

(iii)   Focus a strong sense of internal accountability.

(iv)   Build reflectivity in practice; that is, the capacity to learn and to improve.

But to be effective, systems of performance measure must be designed to recognise and deal with the following issues where organisations seek to manipulate the data:

(i)   Behavioural manipulation – where the cost of the product/service is significantly increased as a result of the measures; or where people focus activity on the measurable aspects only rather than on creating value. A significant issue in organisations working to targets or just to the profit and loss statement (P&L) – we hit our targets, only our targets, and the way we do it does not matter. This is a risk time bomb waiting to blow up. This is reflected in the UK's NHS, where the meeting of output targets has reduced the quality of patient care and not improved it.

(ii)   Definitional responses – where organisations aggregate data to exaggerate or obscure performance – the data aggregation is designed to hide 'awkward' or 'embarrassing' information –a risk already exists here, denoted by the desire to hide something. Overall retention figures are examples; they mean very little – what matters is whether you have kept the people you need to keep and got rid of those you don't.

(iii)   Numerical responses – organisations double count, omit outliers (that is, observations inconsistent with other data), fake records and so on – again indicating that a risk already exists and is being hidden. The accounting procedures used by Lehman Brothers in 2007/8 to take US$50bn debt off their official balance sheet and hide it in the years prior to their collapse is a good example. Here the motive was to disguise the real debt/asset ratio from regulators, clients, employees and the market.

So the measurement of performance to see whether organisations, teams and individuals are reaching the 'high' benchmark required is often not as straightforward as was thought, and some deeper analysis of data is required.

5.9   Summary

We cannot escape the importance of all the key elements in high performance: leader, individuals, team, process and so on. Success in this endeavour is about a holistic approach that acts on all of these elements to (a) maximise the effectiveness of each; and (b) align them with key deliverables. This simple, two-step solution in principle then becomes a much more complex process when applied to an organisation in a dynamic environment. Further, as the number of stakeholders increases, the size of the organisation increases, and the geographic, cultural and business activity variation within the organisation increases, then the complexity and thus difficulty increases. This makes significant change in major organisations, in particular complex, globally spread ones with different business lines, very difficult. In reality, the chances of implementing the change fully at all levels are in reality pretty slim from the evidence, let alone getting the full potential benefit.

This failure is often not related to complex issues that cannot be addressed, but more likely to simple things that have just been missed in the complexity and rush; for example, effective communication of the future benefits of change to staff, checking the direction of change with customer feedback, or leaders having the capability to lead change. None of these is difficult, but a succession of small but important omissions leads to a loss of momentum and the change often grinds to a halt half-implemented, only to become yet another failed initiative.

What is needed is a 'road map' that ensures clarity of objective, the means to achieve it and the roles, responsibilities and actions to be undertaken along the way. This is the implementation plan for the organisation, but it is founded on the change architecture that sets out the general principles and approaches for any organisation seeking successful change.

In summary, establishing comprehensive change architecture is the first step when faced with ambitious change, then getting the immediate implementation decisions right should be the next priority. These will vary across organisations and change situations, but are likely to include the resonance, buying into, of change proposals, change accelerator decisions and some aspects of leadership (for example, the early briefing, training and engagement of 'early adopters' is capable of an immediate decision and often of local-level decision and action). Getting these 'change levers' understood and actioned can, as change gathers pace, create a positive impact on some of the longer-term leadership and culture issues.

Does such an approach guarantee success? No, of course not, but it does seek to equip those involved with a framework within which decisions can be made that will help. As a leader, I am told that to lead change successfully I must change my approach, and that guidance and feedback provided will help me increase the chances of success, and this support from the organisation will help me feel positive about change and champion it. All too often the critical components of both high performance and change as set out in this chapter are dealt with individually and in an unaligned way. This dooms any initiative to failure. Organisations and teams operate as holistic entities influenced by multiple factors. Unless all relevant factors are considered and provided for within an appropriate 'change architecture' (see Chapter 6), then the prospects for development and improvement are limited.

Questions

1   What role should leaders play in achieving high levels of performance for their organisations?

2   What do you think is more important – the people or the process – in delivering: (a) high performance; and (b) successful change? And why do you think so?

3   What are the critical elements that need to be balanced in change, and what are the risks in getting the balance wrong?

4   Examine the idea of co-creation. How relevant is this idea as a means of performance improvement?

5   Does the Clive Woodward experience illustrate leadership qualities and a leader with performance-enhancing ideas?

6   To what extent is the strategic convergence of change initiatives a necessary response to limited resources for change?

7   What are the key elements of an effective change architecture?

8   If you were running a change initiative for a major organisation, who would you see as your key stakeholders, why, and what would you ask them?

9   How would you measure the success of a change initiative in terms of:
    (a)   Changes to process.
    (b)   Changes to performance.
    (c)   Adoption and spread of change.
    (d)   Buy-in to change.
    (e)   Business impact.
    (f)   Customer impac.
    (g)   Leadership capability.

6 Leading change

6.1 Overview

This chapter reviews 'change leadership', taking as its starting point the idea that leaders are judged by the changes they instigate and the outcomes they deliver, whether these are profitability, market value, customer satisfaction, service delivery or business survival. Leadership is 'contested terrain', but this chapter suggests that the debate on this aspect of leadership has moved on. Where once the key critique of leaders was about whether they devote enough attention to 'people issues', now at least as important are ideas about organisational models. Does an organisation possess a sustainable delivery model? Do leaders possess a 'mind set' about what change is achievable and the level of ambition to pursue? Effective 'change leadership' is about engaging people, but to do so leaders need to create a realistic assessment of what can be achieved and communicate this to stakeholders in a credible way. Ideas such as 'authenticity' and 'resonance' become important as leaders, challenged by changing circumstances, need to change their own minds and those of others about what is possible and how it might be delivered.

6.2 Leading through change

For fifty or more years from the 1960s, organisational thinking and practice operated without significant thought about change. More recently, however, since the 1990s, it has been grounded in some simple ideas:

- All change is difficult, resisted and often fails.
- Management of change goes through series of stages.
- The problems are related to people.
- Effective communication is essential.

Most organisations today are very different from the way they were 20 years ago and now are more likely to face continuous change rather than change at different times. The change encountered in structures, governance, technology, customers and customer service – reputational management – is now constant and apparently speeding up. People in organisations are not heard to talk about the absence of change but rather to bemoan the cascades of change initiatives pursuing different, and sometimes conflicting, goals. Often people will complain of too many initiatives, of 'initiative fatigue'. Some would label this as 'resistance to change'. In reality, this not connected with resistance to change per se but is more to do with resistance to the constant pressure of complex, often unclear, ill-defined and occasionally conflicting initiatives thrown at them without any explanation of either organisational or personal benefit. Given this environment, is it any wonder change initiatives fail?

In Chapter 3 we discussed various theoretical approaches to understanding leadership. Among them were theories and frameworks wherein either the legitimacy of leaders (to positions of power, authority, esteem and reward, for example). No longer is 'position power', or 'intelligence', or any other particular trait or characteristic a sufficient basis for answering the question 'Why should anyone be led by you?' (Goffee and Jones, 2005). This point of view has long run through critiques of the leadership literature, but today the most powerful version of this critique relates to judgements about what leaders achieve, and to explanations of lack of achievement and the consequences that follow under-performance. Many raise this as an issue of leadership accountability.

In this context one main justification for the position of leaders relates to the issue of change. It is argued that leaders ought to play a pivotal role in energising and engaging people in necessary change. In a complex and competitive world, no one can assume that an organisation will respond automatically to new challenges or adapt to changing circumstances. Rather, organisations must be compelled to act in response to competitive and other threats. Here, then, lies a key role for leaders: change leadership. Many corporate leaders find themselves subject to criticism from shareholders and media commentators.

On his appointment in 2003, Arun Sarin, CEO of Vodafone, faced a difficult challenge. His predecessor had guided Vodafone successfully through a period of growth as the mobile telephone market grew rapidly. By 2003 it was a leading telecoms business with global operations achieved through a series of mergers and acquisitions, and was investing substantially in new generations of technology providing many potential new functionalities. Faced also with both regulatory and competitive pressure as market penetration grew in each market there was a clear need to make changes to integrate the evolving business and respond coherently to major corporate customers. Complex questions arose, such as: Where a customer seeks to do business across country borders, how should groups like Vodafone seek to build business with that client? Country by country? In a given geography? And if so, which geography? These questions are not readily answered and are inevitably linked to issues such as the motivations and rewards of key executives whose commitment the company wishes to retain. To take an example: What do you do when a corporate customer hitherto served only in Germany now extends its business globally? Do you leave it to the German business or do you serve it from an international business? What if the detailed implementation of technology or the business model is different between different countries, each of which still retains features from its pre-merger existence?

For example, product development remained at country level immediately after the series of mergers creating Vodafone Europe. There is a case for country-level provision. This is likely to lead to more effective customer knowledge being provided to support product development. It may well mean faster response times because development is organised locally. However, it also means that the group risks the duplication of development activities across countries as country-level development teams work on similar issues. More fundamentally, many corporate customers buy service on a regional basis, across the whole of Europe, or at least across several European countries. The possibility of country-level solutions being capable of effective integration for those applications was reduced significantly. This led to a need for additional development on a regional basis, which meant further duplication and delay.

This demonstrates the complexity of the leadership task. Both points of view have merit. Development should be close to the customer and to business development teams. In large markets this is a particularly convincing argument, and Germany would be an obvious example here. At the same time, the counterarguments clearly have force, and the issue is how to get the right balance.

Sarin's task was to create a coherent organisation across multiple geographies that was capable of meeting corporate and domestic customer needs both within and across those geographies. Not least, the need for coherence is essential to create a high degree of alignment across the business. We know that in complex organisations many sources of inefficiency, delay and error lie at internal interfaces. In pursuit of enhancing the flow of value to customers we often seek to engineer the business around how it creates value for its customers.

The critique of Sarin's period as CEO ranges over strategy, organisation change and financial results, both now and in terms of the likely future financial resilience of the Group and of returns to shareholders. It is clear that there is an expectation that a corporate leader will continue to make sense of the current situation and create a positive outlook for their firm by implementing any changes needed to respond to external changes and pressures. Sarin moved from a country-based approach to development to a regional one. So, from 2007, Vodafone Europe led on solutions development. People from every existing country team were appointed into the new Vodafone Europe team, each of them carrying the explicit responsibility for building effective relationships between the new regional team and executives at country level. The important point here is to recognise the pragmatic nature of this change, along with a recognition that it can only work well if regional and country-level personnel communicate and collaborate effectively in seeking effective client solutions.

Perhaps the problem of change is as much about how to end change as well as how to begin and manage it, by reaching a successful conclusion. To sustain the effort going into change such that benefits are shown to have emerged, and to measure benefits so they can be recognised. To create 'success measures', 'celebrations' and 'rites of ending' for changes so that the people involved recognise progress has been achieved and can celebrate this. All too often we move from one initiative to the next without recognising the progress we are making or bothering to give ourselves credit for our success.

Here we look at what impacts on making change happen, how it can be done successfully, and how we can construct a framework both to ensure success and to measure it.

From the organisation's perspective, what is required for successful change is, first, the capability to develop an overall strategy to deliver the required changes that should align to the overall organisational objectives; in the simplest terms, to maximise performance and minimise risk. Second, is to implement this operationally by engaging the individuals or teams involved. This is delivered within the context of an environment – whether that is inside or outside the organisation. So the environment is a key influencing factor on the strategy and its delivery. Third, it is to measure the success of the change and the benefits accrued.

The problem is that, while change is being delivered there is another factor that links both environment, strategy and operational delivery – more change. Thus, as change is being implemented, all of the above are either changing themselves or being influenced by change elsewhere. So change is a constant – it is happening all the time, and the pace of change in general terms is increasing.

No matter their role or rank, as well as delivering objectives all leaders have to manage change – whether that is small, day-to-day adjustments or significant trans-formational change. In such a situation, rather than being reactive and respond to the events that change throws up, it is better that leaders drive change and create events. So no matter what they think, every leader is a change manager; it is just that the good ones recognise this and the bad ones don't! This also means that managing change must be in the toolkit of every leader, but the reality is that this is not the case, and that is why organisations have such problems with change, even of a simple nature.

The external pressures driving towards change, combined with organisational barriers to it, plus the ambiguities, anxieties and uncertainty thereby created, all tend to make the leadership of change a characteristic of the leadership role that most observers will see as a key test for leaders. Survey data indicate that leaders often have problems handling the human aspect of change, and this is one reason why a significant proportion of mergers and acquisitions (M&A) activity does not realise its full potential. Leaders are often viewed as being unwilling to allocate a high priority to managing change, but in reality it is because they often lack clarity about what they should be doing and the capability to do it.

To make change effective we need to be able to recognise the key success factors of the processes, the culture and the implementation, and be able to measure our progress against those criteria; this creates a framework for change.

6.3   From the leaders' perspective

There is a number of factors influencing leaders' capability during times of significant change: first, the leaders themselves are under more pressure at such times because they have the same concerns as everyone else about change and the personal pressure they feel increases. Second, the individuals in their team require better leadership during periods of change, so work pressures also increase. Adding to these pressures is the fact that very few organisations have any structured formal development regarding managing change to help their leaders build capability in this area, and this mix of lack of capability and increased pressure is likely to increase the risk of fail-ure in one way or another.

As situations change and pressure builds up, leaders and leadership may emerge from within the team, not solely derived from the decisions, actions and characteris-tics of the formally appointed leaders but by leadership being demonstrated and delivered by individuals through personal credibility. This links back to situational leadership principles. In a certain situation the team needs a leader with the capabil-ity to do X. If the current leader only has the capability to do Z and not X, but within the team is an individual who can do X then who is the optimum leader for the team in that situation? It could be that the individual rather than the formal leader is better placed to lead here. However, if the current leader is an effective principal, he or she will recognise this and will use the capability of the individual to guide their own performance. This is a real day-to-day dilemma for leaders.

Modern organisations and the rise in complexity mean that no individual leader can know as much about everything as do the people in their team. People join the team to fulfil certain roles, as set out earlier, thus neither the leader nor indeed other team members will have the expert capability of everyone else. This emphasises the difference between the leader and the expert. Thus, if an individual is a good leader but not an expert on the problem facing the team, that person's leadership is still effective, more so than an expert on the problem who is a poor leader. This is why the military develop primarily leadership and subsequently add expert knowledge.

This underlies the challenge of the modern leader in change – leveraging the capability of others who know more than their leader about the task in hand without calling one's own credibility as leader into question. This goes to the heart of the role of the leader as a facilitator rather than the all-knowing superhero of old. Logically, in this case, the leader who knows little about any of the technicalities of delivery could lead a high-performing team purely by virtue of excellent influencing and facilitation skills. Looking across technical industries – for example, pharmaceutical and financial – there are many good leaders who do not know as much of the detail as their team. And this fact becomes even more important as the leader moves up the organisation to the strategic level. So the real art of the modern leader is to facilitate the building of co-operation in the team, using expertise, new models of leadership and emphasising collaboration and co-creation.

When making any change, the chances of success are determined essentially by the effectiveness of the process combined with the degree to which those involved see a benefit in changing – in other words, from their perspective there is a cost benefit of supporting the change bearing in mind all the factors. If this isn't the case then the change will eventually fail. In day to day organisational working this goes back to the 'what's the point?' and 'what in it for me?' questions. This may seem over simplistic but this is the reality of making change happen. If people don't see the point, while they might not openly object they won't implement effectively, and the result will be the same – failure. This has significant implications for leaders – people only recognise value if they are informed about it, see it for themselves and are convinced it will be delivered. Thus it is a key role of leaders to make the case for change, where possible, as a means to enable individuals, teams and the organisation to benefit.

In addition, the idea of sustainable change must be central to effective change; if a change is not sustainable, it is not really a change, particularly if there is a reversion to the status quo after the passage of time. Further, it is all very well arguing that the key contribution a leader brings to strategic change is that of creating a 'compelling vision'. But what does that mean? At one level, Kouzes and Posner (2009) provide the answer: it is a vision that others share. It is forward-looking but also engaging with others. So such a vision needs to set out what is going to be different and better, but it must also make sense to people and be credible in their eyes. In turn, what might this mean? Is it sufficient to argue that this simply means that credible visions are those that have been articulated by leaders who have listened carefully to their subordinates to the extent that they appreciate the latters' hopes and aspirations. Necessary as this is, can it be sufficient? Of course, people's hopes and aspirations are all going to be different. In truth, it appears more likely that a compelling vision can be credible if it is both understood and appears likely to be sustainable. People can then judge how and on what basis their own needs might best be met once that vision is in place. Certainly, one of the tasks of those engaged in 'change leadership' is to help people understand where and how they might contribute to the new organisation that is likely to emerge out of the new vision. Rarely is that likely to be possible when the vision is first articulated, particularly in an organisation of any complexity.

From this view, then, the 'change leadership' role becomes both important and more complex. In truth it appears likely that the 'change leader' must first convince others that he or she has a credible vision of the future likely to lead to sustainable changes that will work well for the organisation. The leader must create sufficient 'space' and 'organisational cover' to enable the vision to be given the chance to work before there are any guarantees that it will (see section 6.13 below for a discussion of the idea of 'transformational space'). One cannot possibly argue that all stake-holders need answers to the questions and concerns they might raise in connection with the vision *before* implementation begins. Some of those answers can only be created by the learning associated with implementation. In an ideal world, answers would be available before people had to decide on what to do, but in the real world that seems pretty well impossible. That is the real challenge for change leaders.

6.4   Organisational choices in change

In any change framework balances or trade-offs have to be resolved. These are likely to be in the areas of:

- Autonomy of change: centralisation versus local autonomy.
- Speed of change: rapid change implementation versus slow, organic change.
- Scale of change: ambitious large-scale change – 'big bang' – versus small, local, 'incremental' change.
- Capability for change: using current organisational capability to make change happen versus needing additional capability from elsewhere.

The logical thinking behind some of the factors above in measuring change capability and any framework to assess it may be summarised as below.

6.4.1   Autonomy of change

In planning change there is always the question of the balance between central control and local autonomy, and tension between strategy, ambition and centrally determined objectives and emergent or organic change. This debate is a key discussion at many levels and in many areas within organisations. Any framework to help drive effective change will need to take this into account. Wierdsma (2004) notes that one of the great problems facing leaders in practice is of striking a balance between different perspectives. In addition to the challenges of a complex and changing world, they face tensions over the 'right' balance – between, for example:

- Centralisation and decentralisation.
- Global versus local.
- Quality versus volume.

These are also a changing set of dilemmas that are not static, so it must be matched to the real position of the organisation concerned, as it operates in its markets and, given its strengths and weaknesses, the organisation's business model, and the need to position itself for the future.

This drives the need for variety. The question now is, how much is best? On the one hand, variety allows for alternative responses to new demands and can thus allow for learning and development of the organisation. Conversely, variety can lead to inefficiency if different client service groups respond to the same need in different ways, resulting in, perhaps, higher costs, and confusion among both clients and staff.

Further, it is also possible to distinguish between natural and artificial variation. Natural variation occurs because clients are different, while artificial variation is created by the ways in which organisations are staffed and managed. For example, if we organise into specialities, or client segments, it could create the need for clients to 'visit' or be served through more than one client service unit. This brings with it the clear risk of duplication of effort and lost information at interfaces, with the attendant need for the client to provide the same information a second time and perhaps suffer inadequate diagnosis of what he or she now needs. This is a frequent issue in large organisations who have the same clients served by more than one part of the organisation. Often the client knows more about what each part of the organisation is doing than the organisation itself! Many organisations set up co-ordination structures to ensure that this is managed effectively. For example, the Group General Client Initiative at UBS from 2003 onwards sought to co-ordinate and co-create activities with key clients to prevent duplication, and as a result managed to improve the standard of service and increase business development.

The idea of co-creation is that client-facing personnel work with clients, responding to new needs via the variety available to them and through learning via the experience of which responses work best. Thus it is that these people and others working alongside them recognise new patterns of client response via reflection on experience and learning, and these are captured in new 'rules', insights and principles. This happens at the level of the client-facing group and then at the level of the organisation, to ensure that the new 'rules, insights and principles' can be shared and adopted in other places to add value. Diffusion is essential, but so is the idea that in a changing world the purpose of 'co-creation' is the development of a 'temporary workable consensus'.

Essential to this is the idea of the organisation being on a journey into the future, that people are 'responsible actors', and that building networks and leaning are central. Leaders are challenged to create dialogue based on shared experience, enabling people to make sense of that to codify these new 'rules, insights and principles'. As was suggested earlier, by virtue of increased specialisation in teams and further confirmed here, the role of leader is more than simply to lead. As Wierdsma (2004) argues, in social settings individuals are often required to take up 'positions in the no man's land between two simultaneously present forces'. For example, where the leader acts as the facilitator when there is a need to consider both the role of a reflective insider and a committed outsider, as critical client knowledge and effective delivery require both views.

Co-creation represents a move away from the idea of 'positional organisation', where the focus is upon systems, structures and processes, towards what Wierdsma labels 'transactional organisation', where the focus is on mutuality, contribution and value-added. Organisations are viewed as organised transactions located in value chains. Here the vital point is to establish the right level of variety within the value chain. Variety is defined as the number of states the organisation can assume. The greater the variety of external demands made on the organisation, the greater the internal variety required. Variety within agreed and specified parameters allows employees to respond to changing client needs and create a culture of involvement. In turn, employees can learn about new patterns of need, thus changing the organisation's response to clients and therefore ultimately changing its 'offer'. In this context, the role of the leaders is to specify the parameters within which people are able to operate, and the appropriate level of variety.

Similarly, Gravenhorst and in't Veld (2004) offer a methodology for 'working together in change'; their starting point is very similar to what is described above. In a complex world, the use of top-down, content-driven, single-issue leadership using command and control style change is often ineffective. Their preferred alternative owes much to the ideas of Jacobs (1994) and Bunker and Alban (1996). Co-creation and 'large group methodologies' represent a new kind of social innovation for resolving organisational problems. However, their characterisation of the traditional approach to change as being 'content driven' and 'simple-issue' focused is not necessarily accurate. But it is clear that for some situations the co-creation ideas combined with large-group, conference-based approaches provide a good means of dealing with complex situations where the leader must establish or re-establish parameters – or at least it provides a method for doing so, if agreement can be found within the group. Admittedly, that poses the wider question as to whether outputs from a large group, even if they are consensual, are actually always the best answer to the problem. It is more likely that they are, but, as we have seen, 'group think' and other issues can impact upon this and deliver a consensually approved wrong answer.

Elsewhere, Carnall (2007) has developed a model for thinking about strategic change that attempts to encompass both 'parts'. In effect, the model takes as its starting point two issues rarely considered in the change management literature. First, we note the reality of multiple change initiatives. Even quite small organisations may be handling many change initiations at any one time. Organisations of the size of BP, IBM or UBS will be handling many hundreds concurrently. This must be considered as part of any coherent attempt to understand whether, and how, change management efforts can lead to higher performance. This links back to the issue of establishing clarity on critical deliverables and role responsibility. The more initiatives that are running, the greater the chance of confusion and diversion of effort.

Second, the change management literature has no means of assessing the level of ambition in relation to capability – is the objective realistic and achievable within a reasonable time, given the resources being committed? One cannot judge ambition without examining the combined effects, intentions and objectives of all changes being implemented and the resources to deliver them. Is there a sufficiently robust 'change architecture', defined as the implementation arrangement, in place to deliver the change, and the capability to do so within the organisation? Here leadership and the decisions of leaders related to change implementation will have the most impact on implementation and its success or failure.

At its heart is the difficult question of 'appropriateness', which is inherently one of judgement of fit of action to a number of questions, some of which will have a higher priority than others. Which has the highest priority in this situation? For example, cost savings delivered by a common global approach delivering economies of scale, or a localised approach which, while being more costly is likely to deliver greater revenue? This is why appropriateness is so difficult to deliver as it is the product of a number of questions, each of which also have to be agreed in terms of their own priority, almost a matrix of interrelated questions that lead to other questions before the answer even starts to emerge.

6.4.2   Speed of change

It follows that we need to consider the rate of change being attempted. Are we looking at radical or so-called 'big bang' changes, or is a more incremental approach envisaged? In reality, this forms part of the judgement about the level of ambition in change, but just as obviously radical change demands more from all stakeholders. Actually, it may be that the more important distinction is between imposed change and those developed organically within the organisation. There may well be more to do in the definition of the level of ambition in change with these distinctions in mind, but at the moment the approach seems sufficient. In any event, the leadership issue relates to making a judgement about whether the proposed changes are achievable and it is to achieve this that this model is proposed.

As we shall examine later, the change accelerator dimension derives from the quality of the design of the programme of change and relates to immediate decisions. Conversely, change leadership and change culture are rather longer-term dimensions. But they interlink in that decisions are made at the start and have an immediate impact, and getting them right will help with some of the longer-term issues. For example, getting change decisions made that have a high degree of resonance and create engagement throughout the organisation are likely to ease the management of expectations and build a perception of informed choice, which makes subsequent actions easier to implement successfully.

6.4.3   Scale of change

The more ambitious the change and the clearer the need, the more likely it is to succeed, given the operation of a robust change architecture achieving high levels of the characteristics described above. However, this is only the case if the benefits expressed as resulting are delivered via that change architecture and outweigh the costs of change, including the likely destabilisation of the organisation. Back to the basic principles of perceived cost benefits for those involved. Obviously, the establishment of robust change architecture directly provides clarity for management of the risk around such issues to be mitigated by various means, such as a compelling business and personal benefit and excellent communication.

6.4.4   Change capability

Does the organisation have the capability to make this change happen? Looking at both its normal systems and behaviour where relevant, and at the arrangements it puts in place to handle change, is it likely to succeed? As has already been said, it is one thing to have a change implementation plan in place, but quite another to operate it effectively.

Here we are looking at whether particular management processes are in place, how effectively they are deployed as part of 'business as usual', and how well they are operated in support of change. Specifically, we look at the following processes:

- **Performance management:** first, we need to know whether the change objectives have been defined and are measurable. It is impossible to measure what is unclearly defined, or indeed to know when it has been achieved. Most significant organisations have performance management systems in place. These typically comprise some mix of budgets, monthly reporting, key performance indicators (KPIs), balanced scorecards, performance appraisals and so on, but the real question is how well they are they operated. There is along list of studies showing that the answer here is not particularly positive. Often poor performance is not explored, challenged or resolved and appraisal results may be over-generous, leading to 'rating creep' over a number of years. This is not a complex problem and can be solved simply. It is often based on the inability of leaders to have open and honest conversations about performance with their teams. Thus the tools are generally effective if used properly; however, the challenge is getting that to happen. Unless the changes are seen by those implementing them as having real value in terms of the output they get from the effort they put in, that will not happen. Also, we need to look at how well integrated are the measures used to track a change programme into the performance management framework already in place.

- **Governance:** this relates to the arrangements in place regarding accountability for change. Poorly managed changes are often characterised by unclear accountabilities. This goes to the heart of one of the issues facing organisations even during 'business as usual' – a lack of clarity about who is responsible for what. Interestingly, the military go to great lengths to ensure that everything that needs to be done has someone responsible for it, to ensure that it gets done. In turn, behaviour in organisations can be observed that appears to be indifferent to the achievements of the intended change outcomes. People suggest that change is outside their control. This is a cultural and leadership issue. 'What can you do about it?' some cry. 'Resistance is inevitable,' say others. But if the change has a genuine business purpose and will deliver benefit to both individuals and organisations, then leaders can and must 'sell' the change as an opportunity. A robust governance arrangement will define board-level accountability for change and for benefits realisation, programme management structures and processes, and reporting arrangements. However, this is insufficient unless leaders at all levels know what they have to deliver and are building engagement in their teams to deliver the change.

- **Risk management:** the concern here relates to assessing risk, in terms of change outcomes but also in terms of the risk of disruption associated with implementing change. Put simply, what potential risks does the change throw up, and can the organisation both assess those risks and provide appropriate risk mitigation strategies?

- **Unintended consequences:** in effect, a special case of risk but deserving of separate treatment. Here we seek to assess whether the decision process associated with any set of change initiatives has taken a thorough look at all the possible consequences of any proposed changes. This is important. Organisations are interconnected systems and communities, an action at one point could well have an unintended effect in another place. This is particularly the case with cultural and behavioural aspects of change that are, in any event, less predictable. A group of people could easily, when they are expected to view some aspect of change in a certain way, view it in another way. And this needs to be allowed for. At the simplest level it is about preparing for a 'no' – Ernest Bevin, the respected British Labour Movement leader, once said that even if expecting a 'yes' in negotiations you should always have something to say and a plan should you unexpectedly get a 'no'!

6.5   Resonance

Moving to develop the cultural and behavioural side of change, we are building on the ideas of Gardner (2004) and Kelman (2005). In his book, 'Changing Minds', Gardner defined resonance, an attempt to change someone's mind, as relating to the affective component of the human mind. An idea, view or perspective resonates to the extent that it feels 'right' to individuals, seems to fit the situation and the prevailing need, and therefore convinces people that further consideration is not needed – action is possible. While ideas often gain resonance because there is evidence to support them and/or because the proponent of the idea is credible, nevertheless the concept is more than an idea based on rational judgement. It allows for an affective component. In the model we seek to judge resonance in the following terms:

- *Felt need*: the extent to which change proposals respond to felt needs of key stake-holders; we are interested in both the organisational level and local needs, problems and issues; a problem was perceived, and this change initiative offers an opportunity to do something about it.

- *Convergence*: the extent to which change initiatives are convergent or mutually reinforcing in terms of purpose, objectives and consequences.

- *Adaptability*: the extent to which the implementation of proposals allows sufficient scope for local level response to need or circumstances as experienced in the locality concerned.

- *Willingness to experiment*: the extent to which the implementation process is explicit regarding the need to experiment with solutions and learn from experience.

- *Customer primacy*: the extent to which the proposals will provide for needed developments in customer service/delivery.

- *Lean thinking, Six Sigma and other performance analytical methodologies*: conducive to an evidence-based approach diagnosis and change planning.

Measuring proposed change against these and ensuring they are considered is important. From the perspective of the individual we know that, from market research, 80 per cent of the decision made to choose a certain product is logical and 20 per cent emotional, but at the decision point of buying these percentages reverse. Thus people make impulse buys. Given that this impacts on on part of human behaviour it is probable that it can also impact on another – that is, the decision to agree to and support change. Resonance supports this concept and suggests, as does our own experience, that 'the heart', and thus emotion, play just as much a part in change as does logic and 'the head'.

6.6   Culture and its impact on change

Culture covers variations in national, occupational, organisational and often local belief systems regarding appropriate ways of operation, and behaviour. As such it is a complex and multifaceted dimension that influences change in many ways. For our purposes we are setting aside national, and to some extent occupational, variation, in pursuit of a simpler model to guide our analysis of change in a particular organisational setting. We note that these applied caveats present a limitation to the model.

There is no doubt that a fuller treatment of these issues would be needed to allow for a comprehensive analysis of multinational organisations. Also, we are clear that occupational aspects will need to be examined in some areas. For example, you would certainly need to have an understanding of occupational variation when looking at a hospital, for example, or at, say, regiments in the British Army, or particular departments of central government, law firms and many others. Here the culture is probably the key determinant of the approach and acceptance of change. That said, no other change model deals with these issues comprehensively and in any event, this model provides a more comprehensive treatment than do existing models. We examine change culture as follows, looking at the capability or quality of the organisation and its change plans in respect of:

- *Evidence-based leadership*. This is a development of the 'willingness to experiment' idea noted above. To what extent are leaders prepared to learn from experience, codify that learning and thereby build on it? To what extent is the organisation a 'learning organisation'?

- *Informed choice*. This relates in part to the extent to which the choices made and decisions taken are based on valid data. The degree to which there is an authentic process of decision-making in place that key stakeholders will perceive decisions as necessary, timely and appropriate, and which as a result they will support and implement.

- *Problem solving or blame orientation?* Is there a 'blame culture'? Do leaders search for a solution to a problem, or search for a scapegoat to the problem? If activity and effort are constructive and focused on finding solutions and achievement rather than failure and blame, then the quality of the change activity and time taken to implement change successfully will be better.

- *Communication and transparency*. In any organisation, the informal communication system will interpret the actions of both the organisation and the leaders, especially in times of uncertainty – for example, change. In the absence of formal communication and transparency, assumptions will be made about these actions. Often those assumptions will take on the most negative aspect and the staff will respond accordingly. Even if subsequent formal communication occurs and transparency is offered, this is unlikely totally to remove the suspicion among staff that they are not being told the truth. For example, faced with a proposal for 'downsizing', staff will conclude that those who remain will have to work harder. Even so, many will predict that others will not be affected. In the absence of hard information, employees will predict consequences, and those predictions will reflect existing stereotypes, including views about who wins and who loses. Failure to communicate effectively and be transparent breeds a lack of understanding, lack of trust, suspicion and the possibility of staff actually doing the wrong thing, thus increasing risk. There must be a formal communication plan in place for any effective change programme.

- *Management of expectations.* People respond to expectations of what they think about the change as much as to the change itself. Predictions about 'what's in it for me?' will abound, as will fears or enthusiasm about the demands and opportunities in the new ways of working created by the proposed changes. This is an important question. Too many senior teams assume that, provided there is an organisational benefit to change, then staff will embrace it. This is often misguided, though. Staff have to be shown a clear personal benefit of supporting change to counter the effort made to achieve it, the undeniable 'what's the point?' question everyone subconsciously asks before doing things. Here we are looking at the extent to which expectations are provided for and managed proactively in terms of communication about the impact of the process in which they are about to be engaged.

6.7   Leaders leading change

Leadership cannot be examined other than as an interactive process. Leaders must have 'followers', so, logically, if we are to understand change leadership we need to say something about followers. We alluded to the idea earlier in the chapter that any form of leadership, to be effective, needs to provide key benefits to individuals and thus to the team. A limitation of many models of change is that each 'stakeholder' group is treated as if it were a homogeneous group in the context of change. In this model we seek to go beyond that simplification by relying on the diffusion of innovation literature (essentially the work of Rogers, 1986), identifying four categories of responses to change within any group impacted by a given change.

Interestingly, research by Kelman (2005) shows that the 'most respected co-workers' are most influential with peers once the initial case for change has been made, when the company is seeking to consolidate and deepen change implementation. One key role for leaders during this period of implementing change is that of providing support and 'cover' to people attempting to come to terms with the changes. This encourages local-level problem-solving led by the most respected co-workers, supported by local leaders, with senior leaders focused on the overall integrity of design and the intended outcomes. Following that route offers the possibility of a sense of 'ownership'.

Moreover, the sponsorship of these 'most respected co-workers', group by group, as 'early adopters' should become a key leadership task. Not that all will immediately respond positively, but if respected group members who will embrace change can be identified and engaged early on in the change process this will provide a 'critical mass' with which to work. There are early and late adopters, to make a simple distinction. The early adopters are likely to be more venturesome, more able to cope with ambiguity, uncertainty and risk. They are also more likely to be 'well adjusted' members of the organisation.

These people can be given early briefing in the changes proposed, which may pay dividends later in terms of problem solving, ownership and desired attitude changes. Thus one key task of the 'senior leader' group is to work with 'local' leaders to identify these 'champions' and then encourage their engagement in the change process. Later it is to provide support and 'cover' to the group as it adjusts to the new situation.

This also relates to how many of the staff need to be engaged before change can start to be implemented – what is the critical mass? It would be impossible to get a 100 per cent buy-in for change as this would suggest, if achieved, it was not in fact a change, as no one would have any worries or problems about it. The suggested figure is that once you have a 20+ per cent buy-in, especially if these are the 'respected co-workers' then they will provide the critical mass for the leader to encourage the rest of the staff to move to acceptance over a period.

Setting out the change leadership criteria in detail:

- *Credibility*: the extent to which the leader has a successful track record of change management experience.

- *Visibility*: the extent to which the leader has been and is accessible to people.

- *Learning orientation*: the extent to which leaders display an orientation to be open to new ideas and to learning both for themselves and for the team.

- *Sponsoring early adopters*: the extent to which leaders sponsor and support early adopters.

- *Deadline flexibility*: the extent to which leaders allow for slack periods in the implementation timelines to allow problems to be resolved and provide employees with 'cover' as they adjust to change. This also allows time to ensure that new arrangements are adjusted to local conditions.

- *Creating a holistic approach*: the extent to which leaders use change as an opportunity for learning within their teams, partly by coaching but also by the leadership practices identified above. That is, the extent to which leaders encourage learning through change.

6.8   The accelerator effect

In a sense, this category of measurement criteria represents a recognition that we need to view change management as a special case of programme management. We need to identify whether project and programme management tools and processes are in use, and to understand whether these tools are being used effectively to focus on the particular needs of change situations, as follows:

- *Connectivity*. The extent to which change initiatives are connected explicitly to existing organisational processes, thus the degree to which they are seen to move forward from the current situation. For example, do the performance management processes measure the contribution of the individual to the change process? Are measures of success on key change deliverables included in the existing performance management system or other current initiatives?

- *Leverage*. To ensure that change initiatives are managed appropriately, particularly with regard to timing, so that those that are designed as 'platforms' on the critical path and need to be in place before others can be implemented on time; this can create impetus, energy for change, and a sense of purpose and momentum.

- *Integration.* This is the effective management of a range of initiatives as a portfolio with a common set of overall objectives. Also known as a 'solutions' approach, the degree to which the management of change takes an integrated view of common objectives and purposes is important.

- *Critical mass.* The result of high levels of connectivity, leverage and integration, but, in particular, a perception of confidence in outcomes flowing from the degree of coherence in the overall design of the change programme, and of the levels of engagement of key stakeholders. Thus the structure of the individual initiatives and their implementation follows a common development and management approach, so that those involved in the delivery of a number of initiatives have a common framework within which to operate rather than different ones.

6.9   Making strategic change effective

Establishing a comprehensive change architecture is the first step when faced with ambitious change, and the next priority should be getting the immediate implementation decisions right. These will vary across organisations and change situations, but certainly the resonance of change proposals, change accelerator decisions and some aspects of leadership (for example, the early briefing, training and engagement of 'early adopters') are all capable of immediate decision, and often also of local-level decision and action. Making sure that these 'change levers' are understood and used effectively can create a positive impact on some of the longer-term leadership and culture issues. Does such an approach guarantee success? No, of course not, but it does seek to equip those involved with a framework within which decisions can be made, which will help to increase the likelihood of success.

Clarity is key, if as a leader I am told that to lead change successfully I must change my leadership style, that feedback may be valid and can help. However, there is much that can and should be done immediately that will help and thereby encourage me to feel positive about leadership style change. All too often, leaders attend a succession of leadership programmes without moving their leadership forward because it is being viewed in isolation, and not being integrated with the real organisational world. In this book we seek to provide tools to help people use leadership as a real opportunity to develop their own performance, as well as that of their teams and organisations through day-to-day activity and managing change.

In practice, therefore, resonant and convergent design for change are all-important. In reality, organisations seek to achieve change within the culture that prevails and with the leadership team in place, noting that best practice involves using the changes to both shift the culture and to invest in leadership development, and noting that in some cases whole leadership teams are replaced, certainly at senior level and particularly in turnaround situations. Nevertheless, the real point is that resonance and convergence are characteristics of change plans that can quickly be given effect. Without efforts focused on achieving behavioural change within a leadership team or to the corporate culture independently even if we take the right change choices (resonant and convergent designs) and implementation decisions (the accelerator principle) the results are likely to be less effective and certainly longer-term in delivery.

In summary, therefore, to craft a successful/sustainable change design (both in terms of the changes to be implemented and the implementation plan and its management) the following principles need to be followed to give the highest likelihood of success:

(i)   *Balanced* in terms of the components of change architecture being in place and the necessary skills, resources and capabilities being available and/or accessible to the organisation.

(ii)   *Economy of effort/energy* to ensure the maximum overall impact. This requires that the approach to change is balanced, convergent and integrated, both across change initiatives currently under way but also with existing organisational arrangements including the management of 'business as usual'.

(iii) *Integration*, of change activities and initiatives, including the accelerator principles.

(iv)   *Benefits realisation*, a key aspect of change management practice, including effective change leadership and change culture.

(v)   *Solutions approach* focused on the definition, agreement to, measurement and adherence to a simple and enduring set of objectives and outcomes.

(vi)   Finally, a *convergent* approach to the design and operation of change-related activities to maintain consistent focus on those objectives and outcomes.

Clearly, all of these principles taken together subsume the ideas about stages of change, involvement and communication. Resonant solutions are often highly unlikely to emerge without the appropriate involvement of those involved in the change, those individuals being likely to indicate the key areas of resonance. The principles identified here also go to a higher, organisation-wide level of analysis looking at how to manage strategic change most effectively as a bundle of change initiatives being introduced in an organisation where many other changes are going forward concurrently. Logically, what is needed is a framework of principles and ideas to help us handle the trade-offs that follow.

This is the reality for most organisations of any size and scale, and/or for organisations operating within networks of clients, alliance partners and so on. Overall, without convergence there can only be continued under-performance because there can be no sustained effort in agreed directions – going back to the point about alignment of effort being critical to high performance. The more ambitious the changes being introduced, the more important are these principles.

The approach presented in this chapter represents a clear departure from existing practitioner-focused models of change management. It starts from the position that current preoccupations with ideas relating to participation, communication, involvement, leadership and culture are a necessary but not sufficient basis for planning and managing corporate-wide change. The 'people-centred' approach to change management is an attractive one in many ways, but it is limited from a strategic viewpoint. A senior executive wishing to achieve substantial change within an organisation must plan a 'bundle' or portfolio of changes that deal with the personnel, process, structure, governance and the other factors indicated. Change cannot be delivered by acting on a single factor on its own; a holistic approach is the only route to success. Why? Because organisations are holistic entities made up of different interacting components, and change initiatives must reflect this. The problem is that because one individual leader can rarely change all the factors influencing the success of a change initiative, it is essentially a group activity.

Changes required might include new technology, new routes to market, new structures, the appointment of people to new roles, new business models and many, many more. These will be introduced in an organisation within which many other change initiatives are currently under way. The questions are many:

- How many changes can be implemented?
- How should they be timed?
- What resources will be needed?
- Are those resources available? If not, can they be obtained?
- Are the various changes consistent?
- Can we manage the changes to maximise the possibility of linkages between them?
- How many people are involved?
- How, whom, when, and why?
- Is the intended change likely to be irreversible?

None of these questions can begin to be resolved when our focus is on each individual changes, one at a time; considering each as standing alone just will not work. Yet none of the existing theory on how to manage change takes multiple changes as a starting point, apart from, of course, the work on programme management that shows how to manage portfolios of projects.

Building, then, on programme management thinking, what is needed is a 'change map'. This would show all the intended changes over a given period to be integrated into a holistic change project plan. Drawing up a 'change map' allows those leading changes to see more readily their own contribution to longer-term strategic objectives of the organisation. Doing so would be a source of discipline likely to help senior management to ensure that key change initiatives do in fact converge, and that no critical areas are missed.

For senior management, working on this together would also increase the chances of achieving long-term objectives, confirm accountability and make co-ordination and prioritisation easier. The change maps need to be kept simple, and organisations that create them, though they do not necessarily use the terminology adopted here, limit them to portraying only the major strategic changes. Thus you may have six long-term objectives, six key themes within which change initiatives are organised; for example, business models, new routes to market, talent management including development and reward, leadership development initiatives, and world class organisation built around Six Sigma and enterprise resource planning (ERP). Within those six themes, a number of key initiatives are identified. The purpose of the map is to guide rather than to constrain action, so flexibility is key.

These themes are then communicated, sending critical messages across the organisation about what is important, and thus aligning effort, as mentioned earlier. This communication signals to everyone that these are the priorities, demonstrates how

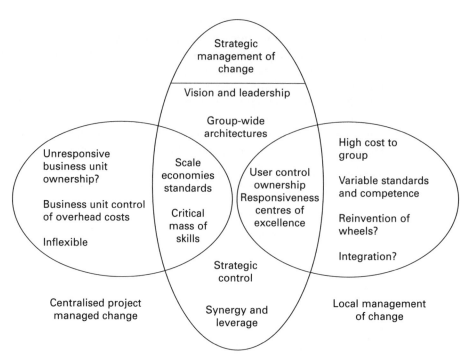

Fig 6.1 Balancing centrally driven versus locally determined changes

they are linked, sets out the benefits, and shows the intended 'fit' between these initiatives and the longer-term strategic objectives. Of course, communication is ongoing and there should be regular communication to keep both leaders and staff up to date. Further, other changes and 'business as usual' activities can continue, particularly those undertaken at the local level to respond to local, market or other circumstances. The communication must also be two-way, to enable the collection of feedback data on the progress of changes in different areas and discuss any problems, so that strategic plans can be updated accordingly.

The likely differences between strategically managed change and local managed change are set out in Figure 6.1.

6.10 Leadership as 'contested terrain'

If leadership is about achieving change to the organisation, this role is both problematic and 'contested'. Inevitably, people's views and interests change over time. In addition, the details of any particular set of changes evolve as leaders proceed through an implementation process that can take months or even years. The circumstances also change. Change leadership is partly a matter of dealing with constantly shifting 'targets'. Change is necessarily associated with conflict. The decisions of leaders often have , or are perceived to have, important consequences for the personnel involved and that often causes disagreement. Thus it is that our conception of leaders as 'change leaders' must take into account the contested nature of leadership as practised.

Naturally enough, the social, political, technological and cultural changes associated with the technological revolutions the world has experienced since the start of the nineteenth century, alongside globalisation, and other particular pressures of the twentieth and twenty-first centuries have created conditions in which traditional bases of authority have been undermined. It ought to cause little surprise to any of us that in our current media era, reputation and image play a part in how we judge leaders and the quality of leadership. Not least, we are influenced by many years of investigative journalism that has been examining leaders and their performance critically – and political, cultural, business and public sector leaders above all. But not just examining the results their organisations achieve during their incumbency; they are also looking for evidence of personal consistency. The politician who campaigns for a measure in the field of policy but who then behaves inconsistently is criticised on that basis. So, for example, a politician who implements laws to limit the operation of tax management practices designed to help companies or individuals minimise the tax they pay who can be shown to have paid tax lawyers to minimise his own tax liability will be criticised for doing so. The thrust of the critique may vary from country to country, and culture to culture, but criticism is now expected by leaders, whether it is considering Jack Welch since retiring from GE, or Henry Ford III or Sir Richard Branson, or any of a number of famous corporate leaders.

Such thinking does impact on the way that we judge corporate leaders, so much of our judgement about them is related to 'performance' and 'authenticity'. Do they create a 'performance' as leaders that resonates with key stakeholders? While this may be partly about leaders' traits, it will partly be about their ability to project their ideas, personality and energy, and partly about the decisions and choices they make. The humblest, most introspective leader who makes the right decisions may still have impact. Nevertheless, this combination of performance and decision-making creates a sense of confidence, energy and success, which is often associated with our perceptions of what leaders should be like and therefore can become the core of the judgements made about them.

Leaders seek to connect people, thus engendering collaboration as they embark on changes, and the perceived 'authenticity' relates to the level of 'fit' between the performance of the leader as an individual 'change leader', the example thus created, the level of engagement thereby developed, and the energy and commitment that is then devoted to achieving the changes. In that sense it really is a 'performance' worthy of those in the acting profession.

Let us take an example from 2008. The opening of Terminal 5 at London's Heathrow Airport was widely seen as a disaster. There were long queues at check-in, cancelled flights and lost luggage. Staff were unable to find the car park and arrived late for their shifts. There was wide media coverage, with well-known celebrities' names attracting yet more attention. Who was to blame for this fiasco – British Airways (BA) or the airport operator, British Airports Authority (BAA)? Allocating responsibility for these problems would certainly be complex, but some weeks later, the CEO of British Airways, William Walsh, announcing a set of good financial results, also announced that he was refusing to take a bonus (reputed to be worth £750,000) because of these difficulties. Walsh appeared to recognise that there would be a clear lack of credibility attached to his reputation and the image of BA should the bonus be announced in these circumstances.

So it is when 'authenticity' comes into view. Whether we refer to 'authenticity of behaviour' (Goffee and Jones, 2005), ideas of consistency, coherence and 'fit', or the notion of ' resonance' as articulated by Goleman *et al.* (2002), we often judge leaders in relation to the credibility of the decisions and actions they promulgate. This was covered in our review of this model of leadership in Chapter 2. Thus Goleman *et al.* (2002) note:

> One sign of resonant leadership is a group of followers who vibrate with the leaders' upbeat and enthusiastic energy. A primal leadership dictum is that resonance amplifies and prolongs the emotional impact of leadership ... The glue that holds people together in a team, and that commits people to an organisation, is the emotions they feel.

The only caveat that may be justified here is the notion that people may partly be engaged and committed by the power of ideas rather than by emotional ties alone. And high levels of commitment from staff demonstrate that. So through the choices leaders make, the priorities they decide upon, the scope they provide for people, the presentation of opportunities and benefits, and the power of their presentation, then the higher purpose is thus created. Thus resonance stems from more than the 'emotional intelligence' of the leader, which is in effect the Goleman *et al.* argument, even though it will be part of what leads to this commitment.

However, the ideas of Gary Klein (1998) – and see Campbell *et al.* (2009) – conceive leaders making decisions in novel situations based on two cognitive processes, namely 'pattern recognition' and 'emotional tagging'. Faced with a new situation, we make assumptions based on prior experience and judgements, and our views are significantly impacted by emotional information stored in our memories related to the patterns we recognise. Thus if people have experienced a positive emotion in the past in relation to a pattern that they now recognise, or believe they recognise, in a novel situation, then this combination is likely to affect their decision positively.

Therefore, with this argument, resonance may require 'emotional intelligence' but it may also need more than that to create the commitment we seek. All of these ideas must encompass the way leaders behave and what they do, in terms of decision, choice and action. It follows that, to understand leadership in terms of these ideas of followership, authenticity and resonance we also need to understand the knowledge, assumptions and intelligence that form the basis of leader decisions. If followers respond to their leader's 'upbeat and enthusiastic energy' this seems likely to be related to ideas about what to do, and not just to the energy itself.

A final point on followership ideas is worth making. It is possible to argue that senior leaders must be concerned about followership, but not to the extent of only pushing ahead with decisions that no stakeholder group will criticise or resist. Arguably, leaders need to work on identifying other leaders at all levels to support their decisions and subsequently implement them. In effect, this relates to the notion of leaders sponsoring people in change, as shown to be powerfully important during implementation by Kelman (2005) (see Chapter 1, above). Here we see the power of 'distributed leadership', the need to identify, develop and support leadership at all levels of an organisation, particularly where transformation is needed. Senior leaders cannot do it all. As Kelman says, 'most respected co-workers' can be impacted more substantially in achieving change than can middle managers. One task of the leader in a period of change is to encourage people to engage with change, so that he or she thus creates an organisation that is 'ready' for change.

Leadership can also have a 'political' role in terms of an organisation as a political system, comprising groups of people with different interests, sometimes labelled as 'interest groups'. The task of the leader is to bring forward the means either of satisfying or marginalising 'interest groups' in respect of the changes the leader seeks. First, the leader seeks to understand each group's likely response to the proposals. Second, the groups' relative power and influence over the suggested changes are considered. Depending on this analysis, strategies would be sought, based on what appears to be an appropriate mix of involvement, education, consultation, communication, incentives, negotiation or even coercion. Such an approach needs to be taken seriously. Carnall (2007) summarises the politics of change as relying on the deployment of action based on political resources (authority, resources, information flows, the agenda), processes (negotiation, mobilising support and bias, ceremony and ritual, and the exploitation of professional 'mystery'), and various forms of action and decision (budgets, careers, succession plans, and performance review). However, there is too great an assumption here of certainty and stability regarding what will change, and of the impact of change and in respect of interest groups, both in relation to membership and the definition of shared interests. Such an analysis may make sense in a highly unionised situation, of course, but in any event the model of change leadership reviewed at the end of this chapter subsumes the political approach within a rather richer view of how leaders preside over change situations.

6.11   Leadership and the analysis of 'change readiness'

Decisions relating to 'change readiness' are an important aspect of change leadership. Getting an organisation ready to implement the changes required to give effect to a new strategy proposed by senior leaders is clearly 'change leadership'. But this means more than building receptivity on the part of staff to any particular set of changes; it also means the willingness to persist with them consistently over an extended period. This is a key component of successful leadership. Also, the leaders have to create the organisational 'space' and 'sponsorship' for people's efforts to help make change work. This consistency represents a real contribution to 'followers'.

Conversely, leaders who are forever articulating new ideas and fresh initiatives, can create a seemingly endless stream of change initiatives that tend to leave people confused as to priorities and unable to see any change through to a successful outcome. The modern concern over 'delivery' often turns on how leaders respond to pressures on themselves by creating yet more internal initiatives, which in turn often actually limit the organisation's capability to deliver the change that really matters.

Creating a small number of initiatives that can clearly be seen as being linked to the achievement of critical deliverables, delivery of long-term strategy, and preparing the organisation for the future is key. Some senior executives describe this as being about creating a clear 'line of sight' between change initiatives and the future 'operating model', and argue for simplicity and for robust strategies to get the organisation to the 'target operating model'. The Toyota case study that follows illustrates these ideas.

Case study   Toyota

The change theme of this chapter can be illustrated by examining the basis on which Toyota was a leading innovator in the automobile industry. The success of Toyota's business was obvious enough. For example, in 2008 it was one of the world's ten most profitable companies, with profits running at double those of its nearest competitor. At the time of writing the market presents profound challenges to the automobile sector. Toyota has been reporting losses but it is clear that all major car manufacturers have been affected by the downturn, and many around the world are seeking state support. Despite the emerging recessionary picture, however, May (2007) has analysed the principles Toyota employs, and then examines the practices which, he argues, explain the success of Toyota to date.

But the core idea is to root all decisions in the design of cars and production systems in the search for elegance. Elegant solutions are the basis of convincing market positioning, requiring the minimum amount of effort, and number of steps or messages to achieve the greatest degree of clarity. As Sherlock Holmes was made to say, 'When all the more complex solutions have been discarded, the simplest must be true.' Elegant solutions are often based on simple, single ideas.

The Toyota Lexus brand is a good example. Toyota worked at making continuous improvements over forty-five years before launching the luxury model; two years later it had displaced Mercedes-Benz and BMW in the North American market. Toyota pursues perfection by defining the ideal end state and working backwards, always asking 'What is blocking perfection?' The Lexus was instigated as a secret project, codenamed F1, in the 1980s, with the objective of beating BMW and Mercedes-Benz. Over six years, 1,400 designers and 3,700 engineers developed 900 engine prototypes and 450 test models. The LS400 was launched in 1989. As rated by a lead industry journal it was five decibels quieter, 120 lbs lighter, 17 miles per hour faster, had better petrol utilisation and was significantly less expensive than the other two makes.

The project was begun through the ambition of the company's chairman, Eiji Toyoda, to build the best car in the world, competing with Rolls-Royce, Mercedes-Benz, BMW, Cadillac and Jaguar. The company possessed the relevant experience. It just needed a plan, which was as follows:

(a)   Bring together a first rate team of engineers and designers.

(b)   Set the target – to test-drive the competition and then focus on the true 'best in class' models (the Mercedes S Class and BMW 7 series).

(c)   Understand the customer – the team researched the customer from a Southern Californian base, test-driving cars and using inputs from anthropologists, psychologists and focus groups. The research showed that image, quality, resale value, performance and safety, in that order, were the basis of the buying decisions.

(d)   Back in Japan, begin work on competitor models and the design. The team leader set challenging goals which the designers and engineers involved thought to be impossible. Not least, while particular goals (for example, top speed) looked to be attainable, the combinations (for example, top speed and fuel efficiency) seemed impossible.

(e)   Engage people in working groups cutting across departments and divisions, with team leaders being held accountable.

(f)   Launch with a compelling name, logo and description. In this case 'The Relentless Pursuit of Perfection'.

To take one example of the problems facing Toyota, let us consider the question of complexity. It comprises three features: inconsistency, overload and waste. Inconsistency is the enemy of reliability and predictability, and derives from irregularity, interruption and imbalance of supply. Overload limits performance, functionality and effectiveness, and derives from stress and strain and under-capacity. Waste involves the use of resources without achieving value, and derives from too much capacity, overdesign, defects, redundant processes, bureaucracy, handover delays between sub-systems or stages on the process, poor communication, and lack of horizontal process. Thus complexity is the antithesis of elegance. Much of what causes complexity is the output of real decisions, albeit these are often the legacy of earlier decisions.

How, then, can we deploy these principles of elegance and consistency, and related practices? Toyota sought to do so by drawing on the creative power of its people. One million ideas each year have been claimed to emerge from Toyota's employees, with leaders accepting these ideas through team members at all levels. The solution will be accepted if it meets the following criteria:

(a)   The team focuses on a current issue or objective.

(b)   The idea must be from within the team's own area of responsibility.

(c)   The team delivers a no- or low-cost solution which can be piloted in thirty days.

(d)   The team uses a systematic problem-solving methodology.

(e)   Value must be achieved.

(f)   First experiment, then capture learning to create a compelling case for change.

There are compelling contradictions inherent in this approach. The company seeks simplicity but creates complex networks. It is organised as a well-defined hierarchy but encourages employees to question and challenge. It pursues operational efficiency relentlessly but often appears to use time inefficiently. Toyota moves slowly but can make step changes such as the launch of the Prius in Japan, in 1997, incorporating a hybrid engine. Takeuchi *et al.* (2008) argue that these contradictions are created by three 'forces of expansion' leading to change and improvement (namely, the setting of impossible goals, the focus on local customisation, and an approach based on experimentation). To stabilise the company, three 'forces of integration' are embraced (namely, values, a commitment to long-term employment and the development of its employees and open communication).

However, there were problems under the surface, though not with the Lexus. A number of design faults became apparent in 2009/10 related to the Camry and the Corolla. As a result, Toyota had to recall around 7 million cars globally for repairs or updates. These faults were alleged to have resulted in more than thirty deaths caused by sticking accelerator pedals. By 2011, this problem had seriously damaged the brand name that Toyota had in relation to quality and safety, and calls into question the degree to which the initiative undertaken above was fully effective.

Economic impact

The recall came at a difficult time for Toyota, as it was struggling to emerge from the recession and had already suffered from a resultant decrease in sales and the low exchange rate from Japanese yen to US dollars. On the day that the recall was announced in the USA, it was announced that 750 jobs were to be cut at Toyota's British plant at Burnaston, near Derby. It was estimated that each Toyota dealership in the USA could lose between US$1.75 million and US$2 million a month in revenue, making a total loss of US$2.47 billion across the country from the entire incident. Additionally, Toyota Motors as a whole announced that it could face losses totalling as much as US$2 billion from lost output and sales worldwide. Between 25 January and 29 January 2010, Toyota shares fell in value by 15%.

According to analysts, Toyota owners (including owners of cars not recalled) could also be affected economically by the recall, as the damage to Toyota's reputation could have a negative effect on the resale value of used cars.

Manufacturing changes

In addition to its recall efforts, a new global quality committee to co-ordinate defect analysis and future recall announcements was declared by Toyota in early 2010, along with a Swift Market Analysis Response Team ('SMART') in the USA to conduct on-site vehicle inspections, expanded event data recorders and readers, third-party quality consultation, and increased driver safety education initiatives. Industry analysts noted that the recall response was a challenge for the The Toyota Way manufacturing philosophy, because the recalled parts were not caused by factory errors or quality control problems, but rather because of design issues leading to consumer complaints. As a result, a better communication of consumer issues with management was needed, and the global quality committee aimed to be more responsive to consumer concerns.

Competitor reactions

One day after Toyota's announced sale suspension General Motors (GM) began offering a US$1,000 cash rebate targeted at Toyota owners. By 1 February 2010 Ford, Chrysler and Hyundai were offering similar incentives.

Case study questions

1 Does this represent an alternative way to practise leadership? If so, how?
2 How important is it that leaders seek clarity and simplicity in all they do?
3 Describe the Toyota way. Why was it successful?
4 How do you think Toyota can have let such serious mechanical faults slip through their 'Relentless Pursuit of Perfection' system?

Sources: Spear, 2004; Takeuchi *et al.*, 2008.

Case study commentary

Clearly, there is a recognition of a continuing dynamic at work. There is no final solution in complex and challenging environments. Everything is temporary, and subject to challenge and change. The task of the leader is to create the context within which challenge is legitimate and can be harnessed while at the same time creating the organisational stability needed to leverage advantage from the results. Efficiency alone is a necessary but not a sufficient condition of success. Once a design is complete, the company needs to employ it to high levels of efficiency. But not to the extent that the drive for efficiency pushes out innovation and improvement, however, as may have been illustrated by the recall problems in 2009/10.

The pivotal role of various senior leaders is also relevant here. Crucially, the organisation sought to create a process of distributed leadership, both to source ideas to achieve the ambitious targets it set, and to energise teams to work on and solve problems. Analytically, however, the behavioural concepts alone cannot explain the full success that occurred, nor even the ideas of authenticity and resonance in relation to leader behaviour. These must be part of a model of leadership that blends these elements with technical, business and organisational concepts to decisions about priority, ambition and targets to find the causes. In other words, once again getting the people and the process to align. To achieve this we must blend ideas about value, advantage and success into an emerging leadership theory. The challenge is to develop a framework of change leadership where there is a focus on both the thinking driving the change proposals as well as how leaders create appropriate change processes.

In essence, a key task of the leader from a strategic perspective is to set out forward strategy that makes sense to people given the resources available to the organisation. Words such as alignment, elegance, simplicity, resonance, value and authenticity each reflect part of this challenge. Strategy means change, and change requires that we move from one set of ideas and concepts about what our organisation can achieve to another. In effect, we need to adopt a new concept of what is achievable. Thus leaders must change minds – their own and others. Central to this will be the analysis of the level of ambition to pursue in the new strategy. On the one hand, leaders must judge ambition in terms of what the market requires of them; and this may include new or substantially changed markets. But they also need to show that the proposed ambition is feasible to those whom they expect to implement it. This may be challenging but it needs to make sense if the vital engagement of key people is to be achieved.

Markides (2000) provides an interesting perspective on ambition by arguing that success derives from the exploitation of a unique strategic position. No position can remain unique or unassailable by competitors for ever, but nevertheless the ambition to achieve a unique position is a key driver of success. Position is defined as the clarity through which customers are served with a range of products or services through particular delivery systems. These comprise market channels and product/service offerings combined with support, financial, maintenance and disposal services. This then combines to create the 'operating model', which becomes the means by which an organisation deploys its business model in one or more markets. Typically, organisations become successful not by playing dominant organisations already operating in the market at their own game, but rather they 'change the rules of the game'. Thus Canon in photocopiers, EasyJet in air travel, Dell in computers, Amazon in books, CNN and Sky TV in broadcasting, First Direct in banking, Komatsu in earth-moving equipment and Starbucks in coffee have achieved prominence in their businesses through being distinctive. This was a key driver of the 2002 UBS strategy of 'Aligning the Integrated Firm' – in other words, seeking a unique position in the banking market by delivering a seamless service to clients from all parts of the bank across the world. This strategy was said by analysts in 2005 to have contributed up to 10–15 per cent of the market capitalisation at that time.

Daring to be different involves risk, by questioning the status quo by which everyone else operates, by posing and answering new questions to identify and enter new market segments or radically improve the current offering via restructuring and re-engineering. For Markides (2000) this requires the adoption of a new mental model for the organisation and its leaders. It requires that organisations break the current mental model, removing barriers to innovation and developing new positions through learning and adaptation.

Under Jack Welch (see Tichy and Sherman, 1995; and Welch and Welch, 2009), GE developed new ways of thinking about their business model. A domestic appliances manufacturer that can cut the cycle time between receipt of order and delivery by 75 per cent has clearly changed significantly. Hampden-Turner (1996) examines this problem through an analysis of value creation as involving configurations of value. Products possess two forms of value. One is the immediate market value as measured or indicated by price. The second Hampden-Turner calls integral value, the value of the product in relation to other products now or in the future. This encourages leaders to view the issue at the systems level. Faced with problems, we often seek to deal with the symptoms rather than the underlying cause. Thus an organisation faced with high procurement costs incentivises purchasing staff to cut expenditure. This leads to pressures on suppliers, which in turn leads to quality and delivery problems. This may in fact have the unwanted effect of increasing the total cost. Further, an increasingly complex cost control system or procurement system designed to reduce costs can, in the end, effectively increase costs by reducing the speed of decision-making, adaptability, alignment and responsiveness to customer needs.

6.12   A model of change leadership

Higgs and Rowland (2001) developed a model of leadership combining skills/competencies and the idea of 'Being yourself'. Taking each in turn:

(a)   Skills and competence – here Higgs and Rowland list vision, engagement, enabling others, inquiry and development.

(b)   Being yourself – here they refer to authenticity (of behaviour), integrity, will, self-belief and self-awareness.

However, Higgs and Rowland (2001) had reported on the development of a change leadership capability framework, seeing this as a 'quest for change competence'. Here, the model was limited to competence clusters, as follows:

Change initiation	Change learning
Change impact	Change execution
Change facilitation	Change presence
Change leadership	Change technology

And looking at the above, the inherent difficulties with models of this type start to emerge. First, all the competencies are described as fundamental to 'change leadership', yet one of the eight is labelled 'change leadership'. More important, the competency indicators relevant to change presence includes authenticity and resilience, but in addition the word integrity is used. Thus it is difficult to see how Higgs and Rowland (2005) can really claim that skills/competence is being assessed independently of 'Being yourself' when both are viewed through a behavioural lens.

However, it is clear that the overwhelming majority of the listed change competence clusters relate to knowledge and choices. These relate to the case for change; scoping of the breadth, depth and sustainability and likely gains from change; insight in relation to change dynamics; personal advocacy; change planning; goals, resources and metrics; knowledge generation; and the skilful application of change theories, tools and processes. So it is clear that what leaders know and how they choose to deploy that knowledge is an important aspect of change leadership.

The implication of this conclusion may also be that the role of change leaders in identifying and then sponsoring people within teams to drive change might be at least as valuable as any other ways they choose to implement change. This is, however, one that is rarely used in day-to-day practice by organisations. Relying on the line management structure, seeking to cascade change through the existing culture appears likely to 'blunt' the impact of change as it passes down through the organisation. This often produces the situation where senior leaders and their direct reports are engaged with the change, know what to do and why it is being done; however, further down the organisation there is less clarity, less engagement and therefore less is likely to happen as a result of this blunting effect. The use of champions at all levels in the organisation, and employing effective communication systems can counteract this effect.

Rowland and Higgs (2008) argued that what leaders do is central to understanding change leadership. They identified eight practices: four necessary and four distinguishing in their formulation. By nominating four as distinguishing practices they argued that their data suggested that these four practices were what set those leaders apart who could create sustainable change. The practices were as listed below.

6.12.1 The necessary practices

(a) Insight and comprehension – creating clarity about why change is needed and the gains change will achieve.

(b) Building an 'organisational blueprint' – creating the relevant organisational architecture for governance, structure and control, alongside work building informal networks supportive of change.

(c) Building capability – developing skills for change, creating connections across the organisation to support change, creating coherence in terms of goals, outcomes and metrics.

(d) Maximising performance potential – growing the organisation's talent, learning how to trust people, building an understanding of the business model.

6.12.2 The distinguishing practices

(e) Attractor – creating and articulating, even embodying in behaviour, a widely held and shared sense of vision, purpose and identity for the organisation.

(f) Edge and tension – testing and challenging assumptions and practices.

(g) Container – channels the ideas emerging from edge and tension into positive action, managing the anxiety and turbulence created by changing and building organisational 'cover' for change.

(h) Transforming space – promotes learning and productive reasoning, again to deploy the concept of Argyris rather than their own, as a basis for growth and improvement, thereby withstands pressure to maintain the status quo, not wasting time and resources on change.

Rowland and Higgs (2008) went on to note that these eight practices, but particularly the four distinguishing practices, appear to be based on some fundamental beliefs held by change leaders. These were: that you can trust people to do the 'right' thing; that the leader is the responsible agent but must lead via a process to which others are contributing. So, from this perspective, the answers to any problems are to be found inside the organisation, and that risk-taking is acceptable, given the belief that the answers to problems will emerge naturally.

However, they are also clear that the issue is one of balance. Thus the distinguishing practices can either be underdone or overdone. This is one part of their formulation that is difficult to accept, even though the basic idea is plausible. What do they mean by 'overdone' or 'underdone'? How are these situations measured, and what is the interrelationship between each necessary practice, or in relation to the other three distinguishing practices? In their book, Rowland and Higgs presented it practice by practice. To take one example, on the 'attractor' practice, being overdone, they note that people may feel that the direction is dubious; the unknown may feel risky for many people rather than exciting; over-zealous behaviour can be seen as arrogance; and stories and missions lack substance and a connection to the reality of the situation.

To obtain real and significant answers we need to know how high-performing change leaders do better than low-performing ones. This is explicit in Rowland and Higgs' methodology. So, to achieve this as well as what particular leaders say about themselves or what they say about the way that people respond to them as leaders, we need independent assessments of their ambition and performance. Only then can we assess the real achievements of change leaders and make judgements about the balances they have sought and if these were effective. Thus we certainly accept the Rowland and Higgs (2008) concept of balance.

To measure success is potentially possible by assessing the value added through the success of the judgement and the balancing of differing stakeholder ambitions in achieving the collaboration needed to deliver advantage. So, to be successful in change leadership certainly requires the use of the distinguishing practices discussed above. But the case studies in this chapter show that more than this is involved to ensure success. In reality, change leadership requires the engagement of people to create new value through the ideas and opportunities created by developing networks, and leveraging new situations or opportunities, or both. These need to be agreed and appropriate resources identified and applied to exploit them. The approach is likely to indicate the ambition of those involved in the change. The National Trust case study below illustrates this.

Case study   **The National Trust**

The UK's National Trust was established in 1895 as an organisation with the legal powers necessary to hold property for permanent preservation.

Despite its success in substantially growing its membership since the late 1970s, making it a large membership organisation, it found itself, if anything, less influential nationally than it had been from its establishment. A series of attempted changes since the late 1990s created little impact, but encouraged a clear sense of discontinuity arising from the feeling that, despite its recent success in increasing membership, the Trust was if anything less able to deliver its 'mission and purpose'.

A series of major changes were undertaken between the year 2000 and 2008, deriving initially from an organisation review established in late 2000. There was also a number of ideas focused on the future which ran through the thinking of senior level executives at around the time the organisation review was put in place. It was felt that the Trust was not 'punching its weight' at the national level. The organisation is a major landowner but felt it lacked influence on the national stage on issues of relevance to its purposes. In a world char-acterised increasingly by collaborative working and connectedness with other stakeholders, the ability to reach out, to set agendas and to create influential contacts with central govern-ment and other national bodies appeared increasingly to be a necessary but not always achieved part of the National Trust's approach to achieving those purposes.

This led to ideas about how the Trust ought to operate. On the one hand, it needed to be organised around single-point contact with government and other agencies. It also needed to be well connected, influential and capable of representing relevant interests locally, regionally and nationally. But to make that possible it needed to be viewed as being respon-sive to local needs and concerns. This implied a decentralised asset management model with a 'light touch' management approach. Throughout the various discussions associated with the organisation review, the idea of the dilemmas this posed and the balances required often emerged. Sometimes described as the 'tight/loose' or 'centralisation/decentralisation' dilemma, it is not an uncommon question, which organisations often struggle with in prac-tice. This is also a classic challenge of the global corporation – the global versus the local dilemma. How to balance central direction with local responsiveness was bound to be an issue facing the management board as it grappled with the challenge of achieving national-level prominence.

The director of personnel, acting as review leader, established a review board consisting of seven members drawn from the management board, and a project group which was to organ-ise all the work involved in the review including appointing and then supervising the work of a leading consulting firm which carried out much of the work. There was extensive consul-tation with staff – not least following an invitation to submit written evidence/ideas/views, over 2,000 submissions were received in the form of notes, letters, emails and longer reports. In addition, the consultants reviewed a wide range of internal documents and visited various National Trust offices and properties, interviewing staff in each case, with over 100 staff in total being interviewed. The review board met regularly to establish an appropriate level of project governance and to produce an agreed strategic view of the future organisation. The project group and the review board exchanged data regularly.

Following completion of the review, various working groups were established, each led by a senior executive and focused on a particular issue arising out of the implementation of the recommendations. In parallel with this activity, the Human Resources team was engaged in an extensive process of recruitment, job matching, grading and relocation of employees. This was necessary to move existing employees into the new structure and was paralleled by the process of moving people from current locations into new ones, some of which were on short-term lease while a new headquarters building was being constructed at Swindon; this opened in 2005.

In all of this, the work of one particular working group was particularly important. This group, led by the newly in-post director general, was looking at the new behaviours thought to be needed in order to create a new culture for the organisation. Subsequently, many of those involved agreed that progress had been made. Performance and accountability had improved, and real momentum for change could be identified.

In the light of the financial pressures arising from an epidemic of foot and mouth disease among cattle and from rising pension costs during 2003/04, the Trust concluded that it needed to focus on two financial targets for 2006/07, namely to achieve a 'net gain' of at least 20 per cent on surplus – that is, the excess of ordinary income over ordinary expenditure, and to achieve a General Fund operating contribution of at least £20 million. To quote from the National Trust 2006 Annual Report: 'Excluding one-off Organisational Review costs, the Trust achieved a Net Gain of 18.7% in 2004/05'.

It is impossible to disentangle the various causes of this improvement in terms of making an assessment of the financial and operating impact of the review; but by 2008 many senior executives of the Trust concluded that the review was a clear signal that change was not merely to be debated but would now be followed through. Overall, the broad purpose of the review was to create an organisation that was 'fit for purpose', simpler and more effective, particularly with regard to decision-making. Judged as one of a series of organisational changes, it seems possible to conclude that the review did make a positive contribution to that forward movement of the organisation.

Sources: Research interviews conducted Autumn 2007 to June 2008; National Trust documents; National Trust annual reports, 2006, 2007.

Case study questions

1 Identify the change strategies adopted by the review board. What steps were taken to engage employees and volunteers working at Trust properties or in other parts of the organisation?

2 To what extent was the coherence of the organisation review changes a matter of changing external circumstances?

3 Assess the role of the newly appointed director general in taking forward these changes.

Case study commentary

It is clear that substantial efforts were devoted to creating clarity about why change was needed, and on rethinking structures, staffing, competence requirements and appropriate ways of working, support services and decision-making. Staff at all levels were provided with various means of engaging in the process, including access to the review board via the director of personnel, interviews, letters and email comments, ideas and contributions, and various regional conferences. Attention was also paid to developing informal networks and identifying proposed outcomes, goals and metrics.

The proposed changes to the Trust's national structures were reviewed thoroughly to ensure that managers at Trust properties around the UK could readily access appropriate professional support – in conservation or land management services, for example – and could obtain quicker decisions. Moreover, effort was directed to reworking job descriptions, appraisal and performance management parameters and processes, and designing appropriate training. All of this was undertaken with 'New Ways of Working' as the end vision. In this way, 'necessary practices' were delivered.

But what of the 'distinguishing practices'? The new director general personally took over 'New Ways of Working' to engage directly and take responsibility for helping to define the new culture of the Trust. One report on earlier and stalled changes bemoaned the existence of a 'culture of optionality' existing in the National Trust. There were many professional staff and volunteers who were seen as being able to ignore or opt out of changes while suffering no consequences of any kind. Here, the director general was signalling her own determination to see these changes through and the expectation that senior leaders would do the same.

Experience with some of the new structures quickly showed that in some key respects they had led to various problems emerging. These were carefully reviewed with thorough consultation and a detailed technical evaluation; for example, of conservation services performance, with professional experts as well as property staff views being taken into account. Further updating changes were subsequently made. The director general was willing to challenge assumptions and practices arising out of the review recommendations. She also channelled ideas into positive action in relation to finance. The review recommendations were widely advertised as being intended to have a neutral financial impact. In reality few believed this claim, as the changing financial circumstances led the top team to put in place actions designed to deliver surpluses. There is a general acceptance that the serious way in which the review was implemented, including the relocation of the head office, prepared the ground for these later changes. This relocation had been recommended and put off previously. Now that it was implemented and staff found themselves working in what was claimed to be an 'iconic' new building, combined with the determination with which these matters were managed, built resonance for these changes. There was seen to be a real coherence between the original review changes and later changes in response to the new financial circumstances.

It could be said that the 'distinguishing practices' can therefore also be observed. The willingness to re-think the original review recommendations indicated a willingness to take changes seriously, focusing on delivering the Trust's goals and on taking responsibility for governance, management and resources and their effective use in pursuit of National Trust objectives. This made sense to people and created coherence and 'line of sight' across the Trust organisation and between its day-to-day management and its long-term goals. The role of the most senior leader, the director general, in taking personal responsibility for achieving culture change appears to be most important here, stressing the value and criticality of visible senior management leadership during times of significant change.

6.13   Summary

Change leadership is a key part of the role of leaders. Organisations quite naturally change all the time, and at times they need enforced change; only with effective leadership can this be achieved. Leading change successfully requires that leaders and employees are able to make sense of radical and ambitious programmes of change. Clearly, 'mental models' and new rules of the game are important here, If radical change requires balance, integration and simultaneous actions, then the role of change leaders must be to ensure that these features are achieved in practice. There is no reason to assume that these features will emerge naturally across the various activities in which people are engaged in an organisation undertaking radical change. They have to be planned and driven. This is not an argument for grand strategy or a centralised, top-down approach, as these would not be conducive to learning and experimentation. Integration is a component of successful breakthrough or radical change, and this leads on to the idea that success may require the capability to adopt incremental change in each element of the organisation. Success goes to those who can create advantage by improving their performance significantly, and disrupting opponents by doing so. Integration becomes the ability to put these simultaneous changes together.

In effect, change leadership is ultimately a matter of judgement and balance. Further, these judgements will probably affect the organisation over a period of years. They include the ability to decide on the changes to be attempted, leveraging existing resources and new platforms, of technology or business models, or both, and a high degree of connectivity between strategic thinking driving a change programme forward and the change architecture deployed to achieve it (Carnall, 2007). It is these decisions and choices that lie at the core of change leadership and its effectiveness.

Looking at case studies adds significantly to any behaviourally focused ideas of change leadership. While 'space' is vital, and the role of the leader in creating space for people most important, any reading of either the Toyota case study or the summary of GE under Jack Welch indicates that a set of decision principles, robustly and convincingly applied is just as important in change leadership as behavioural change. The simplicity and symmetry of the driving ideas in both of these cases appear to be part of their attraction. The idea of 'primal' leadership as introduced by Goleman and his colleagues (2001) may be conceived by them in emotional terms but in our view it needs to be related to a cognitive framework that judges the power of the ideas that leaders use to take the organisation forward. These are defined by the simplicity and economy of ideas involved and the degree of fit between ideas and proposed actions, along with the conviction with which these ideas are put into place.

So we view change as a learning process and a key challenge of change leadership in relation to the need to unblock barriers to learning. This is clear from the National Trust case study. During periods of change, ideas must be developed to allow new value possibilities be identified and shown to create options for various stakeholders to pursue their own ambitions as part of a collaborative effort. Here the change leader is seeking to develop, or at least work within, a framework of market incentives and social capital. Both are needed if significant change is to be created, because that needs patience as new ideas rarely work well initially. Those involved often need to work hard to find the right formula, often in a situation where the benefits of that effort will not be delivered for some time. This is the fundamental purpose of 'transformational space' (that is, the freedom – often only temporary – to try out new ideas free from the immediate constraints of performance management, which might otherwise dissuade people from trying new ideas in case they fail. Transformational space implies an acceptance that transitional costs are likely to be associated with any change implementation). The objective is to create sufficient organisational 'cover' and support to allow time for the process of learning to proceed, even if often by trial and error. Ultimately, this is the real test to change leaders: their ability to create such space, deal with risk and demonstrate their conviction about the change. Any attempt to understand change leadership needs to incorporate the assessment of actions of this kind.

We see this particularly in the National Trust case. Here, the initially presented view regarding the financial aspects of the change recommendations was unconvincing to many. But circumstances changed, and in addition some change recommendations had 'unintended consequences'. The newly appointed director general led the 'New Way of Working' initiative and demonstrated the integrity and openness of the top team by admitting that all was not proceeding to plan. The change plans were then modified in the light both of the new circumstances and the unintended consequences. Here, the 'distinguishing practices' of the change leadership model can be seen in operation, and these further changes helped people make sense of the organisation review changes.

The concept that enables us to connect these ideas is called 'productive reasoning'. In Argyris's view, this focuses on performance and problems, not on people. Thus productive reasoning is the means of engendering learning and change. The role of change leadership in this context is to remove the blocks to learning and to encourage 'active learning'. The Toyota case shows that this does not necessarily apply to senior leaders alone. The practice of 'distributed leadership' is important. The role of change leaders is to energise and drive learning so that change can take place. Productive reasoning then becomes the basis for learning and change, and enabling this learning is a key contribution of leaders. Based on the deployment of powerful and convincing ideas related to value and ambition, however, the creation of 'transformational space alone will not deliver change. Creating it is important but it will not in itself deliver change; it must be accompanied by a compelling vision, justification and a plan about what to do next. The National Trust case illustrates this combination in that the changed financial circumstances created the context within which financial gains had to be achieved. The determination with which the organisation review changes were implemented and followed through made clear that 'optionality' was no longer an alternative. Everyone, especially the leaders, was expected to adhere to collective responsibility and make the changes happen even if initially they were personally sceptical. The move into the new headquarters building was seen as symbolic of a new beginning, and the emerging financial strategy was evidently easier to argue for and implement as a result of the political and practical messages that were sent.

So, from all the research and debate, is there a simple 'road map' for successful change that organisations can implement in the real business world? There are suggestions. We know that, in an increasingly challenging world, organisations must undertake change in new ways. No longer can change initiatives take years to implement, meander through confusion and lack of focus, and never quite deliver the predicted benefits. Change initiatives are effectively a risk to an organisation, but a risk that must be taken to adapt to changing environments and deliver the best service to customers. The longer change initiatives run, potentially the less effective the implementation and the greater the risk both in terms of wasted resources and diversion of effort from key deliverables. To be successful, change, now more than ever before, must be rapid, engaging, focused and deliver measurable benefit.

This has significant implications for future change initiatives that proposed by organisations, and the role of leaders – in particular the CEO and top team. The launch of change activity must be high impact and high engagement – and it must be right first time. From the experience of one of the authors of leading change in two major global organisations, there are some basic principles to help make change successful in the new world.

There is often a split between those who think that the process side of change is most important and those who think the people side is. In reality, you need both, so the argument is irrelevant. It indicates four key factors in successful change: review frequency, project team capability, management and staff commitment, and the additional effort required. The data show that frequent reviews and measurement of progress is vital: every six to eight weeks for a simple change and every two weeks for a more complex change. The change management team must be the best people for the task, there must be real commitment from those impacted by the change to make it happen, and people must have the time and support to deliver successful change as well as do their 'day' job. These factors were developed into a questionnaire that was able predict the likelihood of success for the initiative. This, used at review points, gives a good measure of progress and potential risk. Interestingly, to look at change from the opposite direction – that is, what makes it go wrong – there is an curious mirror image. Robert H. Miles (2010) looked at why change slows and potentially fails. He identified a number of factors, which we paraphrase for clarity: *over-cautious leaders and avoidance of reality* – there is no full acceptance of the need for change among leaders; *lack of management commitment and co-operation* – not all the leaders are on board, and those that aren't are not confronted; *too many initiatives* going on, thus confusing the situation; *disengaged staff* not wanting to let change happen; *a loss of inertia* – post-launch blues, and possible over-confidence; *carrying out the change or doing day-to-day business, but not both* – both need to be done, however.

From the experience of one of the authors, applying these principles in one major global change initiative having not used them in a previous one demonstrated how much difference they made – the latter initiative won several awards and became a Harvard Business School case study as a result. This suggests that a number of assumptions we have made in the past are perhaps not as valid as we had thought. Thus, significantly, to gain high employee commitment, management has to obtain emotional as well rational buy-in. Neither is sufficient in itself for success, however, as emotional buy-in alone will not deliver high commitment unless supported by rational buy-in. In reality, senior leaders, and even many experienced change managers, do not allocate any significant element of their time to the emotional aspect, which must have some influence on why many change initiative do not fulfil their potential, that if 43 per cent of the leverage capability present to make change work is not used, then it is less likely to succeed.

Taking this all together, it gives us some powerful guidelines for successful change in the new and challenging world of the twenty-first century. So, in the new world we need to follow some simple guidelines on effective change:

1   *High profile launch and keep the momentum up* – launch with a bang and have everyone engaged and ready to change within three to four months.
2   *Confront reality* – management and staff must accept the need for change.
3   *Change for all* – everyone must commit to change; both rational and emotional buy-in must be present.

4 *Best leaders to lead change* – those delivering and leading change must be the best people for the task, not merely the people who have time on their hands.

5 *Keep it simple and focused* – have one or two clear initiatives that be simply communicated and everyone can focus on.

6 *Frequent progress reviews* – check you are making real progress and identifying risk every few weeks.

7 *Combine change with business as usual* – enable staff to do their 'day' job and make change happen at the same time.

Thus the role of the CEO and line leadership is key in any strategic change and it should not be passed over to HR to drive. If they do this it will be quickly be viewed as just another HR initiative and lose credibility. CEOs and line managers must make the case for change, build engagement with it, use the best people make it happen, and then drive it personally with their line managers, supported by HR. Within a few weeks a CEO can ensure that change is a success, or doom it to failure, by their actions. CEOs should never forget that bad change is actually worse than no change for their organisations.

Ineffective, confusing and distracting change initiatives are viewed by many leaders and employees as a depressing reality of organisational life that saps their enthusiasm and commitment. Change should be a challenging and inspiring journey to a new and better world that is undertaken willingly. Change initiatives should build inspiration, not desperation.

Questions

1 Why is change critical to organisational success? Have you personally experienced both successful and unsuccessful change? What made the difference between success and failure?

2 Who is key to successful change? Senior leaders? Line managers? HR? Who should be doing what to make change effective?

3 What makes you as an individual prepared to put effort in and change? What part of your decision is emotional and what rational?

4 What makes a good compelling vision for change in your view? Should it be operational, strategic or both?

7 The ethics of leadership

In an increasingly complex business environment, organisations and societies interact in a variety of ways. The decisions made by those in organisations have an impact on the wider community, be it regarding product safety, environmental pollution, consumer protection, employment policies, executive remuneration or other areas – matters we are concerned with as aspects of the relations of organisations with society in general. Irrespective of whether the organisation is public or private sector, the interaction between the organisation and the wider community on a variety of levels is important for both.

Clearly, the public sector organisation, such as a police service or a health authority, must interact with the community, but private sector organisations have to do the same through customers, employees, supervisory or regulatory bodies and the wider public as potential customers in the market. Certainly, the very existence of public service organisations implies a requirement to deliver some services that it is likely a private sector organisation would not wish to do, or should not be allowed to do for good governance reasons, and thus only a public body can provide.

For example, the setting up of regulatory bodies to oversee capital markets generally is undertaken by public organisations, not private ones. The same applies to the armed forces, police and diplomacy personnel. In each of these areas it is largely accepted that market-based solutions to the provision of services would be inadequate or bring associated risks that would be considered unacceptable. The 2011 downgrade of the USA's credit rating by the Standard & Poor's (S&P) rating agency refocused the debate around this and S&P's previous role prior to the financial crisis in rating debt products. Should a private sector (and thus profit-driven) organisation have responsibility for either the rating of debt products that underpin financial markets or to gauge the creditworthiness of nations, which has an impact on the lives of millions of their citizens?

Thus there is debate about where the demarcation line ought to be set. In some countries, some prisons are privately provided, using state funds. Similarly, private-sector-provided health care is common but by no means universal or without controversy. Moreover, often even some aspects of the armed forces' provision is partly provided privately, such as, for example, some logistics and training.

Few today hold the view that the only purpose of private business enterprise is to generate profits, though this remains the primary objective of the business. It seems sensible to avoid over-simplification. It is hard to accept the view that a business exists solely for the benefit of the shareholders. Suppliers, employees, customers, the local community, and potentially the government representing the wider community, all have an interest. Similarly, some might suggest that it is increasingly difficult to assert that the sole justification of a public sector organisation is in public service.

7.1   What is social responsibility?

There are many opinions on the issue of organisations and their social responsibility, and this chapter will review the key arguments and opinions in this debate. Social responsibility is the concern of organisations regarding the welfare of society at large through its obligations beyond those directly connected to the organisation as shareholders, employees and customers. Direct responsibility exists for those groups, and is often governed by minimum standards or governance regulations; for example, employment rights, or health and safety. But some regulation will enforce wider social responsibility – for example, via pollution and regulation to control uncompetitive or restrictive market activity. Thus an organisation not only has direct obligations to shareholders, employees and consumers, but also a wider social responsibility to the community.

The organisational leaders of today, especially as their roles become more strategic, have to consider their actions in relation not only to their direct responsibilities but also to the wider social ones. The importance of the social responsibility element is increasing as more effective communication and deeper scrutiny of organisations' action globally is now both possible and actually happening. Actions undertaken in one part of the world with suppliers become known by consumers of the end product across the globe, and they make decisions based on the application of their communities' standards to the behaviour of the organisation in the other location. The rise of Fair Trade goods is a clear result of this, as are the frequent scandals of major sports or footwear brands, or their suppliers, being caught using under-age employees, or treating their workforce badly. Virtually every major brand that sources from developing economies has been found wanting at some time when viewed by the standards of responsibility of its consumers.

Thus the organisational leader needs to think beyond the organisation's value and standards, or those of where the work is being done, and build other societal values into his or her actions. It would also seem that the standards of the final destination community are the key ones, where they are the highest in terms of expectation, not the ones on the value chain. But is this an unnecessary burden on the organisation? Will the pursuit of business self-interest naturally lead to benefiting the community as a whole?

Some suggest that organisations exist through right of privilege given to it by the community: to own property, to employee citizens and to make money for shareholders. These are regulated though corporate laws determined by society itself, so logically society can change its expectations of what is acceptable and endanger the existence of business. This is the exercise of control directly by the community, but there is a wider and community driven pressure. For example, if the consumer thinks the organisation has behaved badly for some reason and chooses to withdraw support by not buying its products this will affect profitability. So communities exercise both direct control, via regulation, and indirect control, via commercial pressure. This impinges on organisations, and thus also on their leaders. Leaders need to be aware of this and respond to it to maintain the viability of the organisation.

This is particularly the case where the behaviour of the organisation falls short of the expectations of the community within which it is based, or where its consumers are living, even if that behaviour occurs elsewhere. Fair Trade and the sports goods industry have already been mentioned, but there are many other examples, such as poor environmental controls by oil companies in developing nations, the dumping of toxic chemicals, and the poor treatment of staff. This is likely to lead to activity by pressure groups, who work to control and monitor the behaviour of organisations. These groups will have an impact on the organisation's public image and cause a rapid loss of public support. It is clear that if organisations do not meet a particular set of community standards of behaviour then the community will withdraw its support and have a serious effect on profitability.

However, the control society imposes on organisations must be weighed against the need for an environment where business can flourish. Too much control could damage business and industry, and thus have a negative effect on a community – for example, through unemployment. This is the argument that has often been used by organisations for over 150 years to object to any form of government intervention. But when the government, driven by popular opinion, feels that steps must be taken then this is where social responsibility is enforced and business has to find ways round it. For example, the protection of employees against death or injury at work, the limits on the lowest age that people can start work, and the ability to join a union were all objected to by business initially, on the grounds of lost profitability but forced on them by governments, and driven by social pressure. In all cases the businesses still managed to operate. Therefore a balance must be sought between society recognising the reasonable needs of business but business also recognising that profitability is no justification for behaviour that a society views as unacceptable.

Furthermore, social responsibility creates an improved environment. Examination of the work of the leading early industrial pioneers of social responsibility such as Robert Owen, Joseph Rowntree in the UK, and, since 1980, Amgen in the USA show that where business did mitigate the apparently pure profit motive by taking action on social responsibility – for example, by creating better employee conditions or a broader contribution to society at large, then this might lead to longer-term business benefits. So while such actions had a cost they were more than compensated for by rises in sales, production and/or quality. Further, as the quality of life improves, wages are high, more free time is available, then purchasing power is increased. As incomes grow, so does the increasing demand for goods and services. This is not just a phenomenon from the nineteenth century; the growth of the middle class in India and other emerging economies, with increasing disposable income, shows that where organisations balance profit and social responsibility correctly the society is able to grow and improve the quality of life, which in turn drives further economic demand and development.

7.2   Using social responsibility to improve brand

As well as being challenged seriously by consumers if it falls below expected standards, if an organisation is seen to adopt a proactive attitude towards the community in which it exists and exceed industry standards, often its brand image will be improved. As a result, many organisations invest significant sums in projects they hope will gain positive approval from both consumers and the community – for example, by improving the environment and increasing educational opportunities through sponsorship schemes.

But for some organisations it is not that simple. For a range of organisations, their core business is considered by some in the community to be essentially anti-social – for example, tobacco companies, arms producers, and parts of the mining or oil industries. The anti-smoking campaign has raised public awareness of the health risks involved in smoking, which has led to restricted publicity: a ban on television advertising and restricted press advertising, health warnings on tobacco and cigarette packets, and there is continued debate about cigarettes being linked to sports activities via sponsorship, which subtly offers widespread exposure through TV coverage. Here, by the global nature of the sponsorship and therefore the differing restrictions by country on tobacco advertising, the organisations have been able to 'sidestep' some bans and place their advertisements on television in countries where formal advertising is banned.

The interesting point here is the way in which different communities view the activities of business, which means that what is acceptable and what is not varies from place to place. Strategic leaders in organisations need to recognise this, and act accordingly, remembering that the 'key' community is the one where the consumer makes his or her decision to buy, or not.

So it is possible to see the relationship between what the public will accept, how it can control business, and how far the community can go before driving the business away and thus destroying the financial return to the community that the business creates. This is the catalyst for organisational relocation driven by being able to obtain lower costs, lower taxes or lower regulation by moving elsewhere. This is happening all the time as a result of long-term economic trends; for example, the movement of textile manufacturing from Europe to Asia over the twentieth century in search of lower wage and material costs. But this can also be driven by shorter-term public pressure. This was seen in the public pressure in the UK to increase taxes on banks after the 2006–10 financial crisis, where banks that had been 'bailed out' by the taxpayer continued to pay large bonuses to some staff while other members of the community suffered income reductions or redundancy as a result of the banks' actions in creating the crisis. When the UK government made clear its intention to raise taxes on banks, a number of them threatened to leave London and move to to places with lower tax levels. With the potential loss of significant tax revenue, the government carefully negotiated a tax level that was not as high as many in the community would have liked but which did increase tax income from banks without driving them away. This demonstrates the balance required between community and business needs.

From the organisations' point of view, the arguments against social responsibility generally centre around profit maximisation: 'Profitability must be the criterion of all responsible business decisions'. This comment is from Peter Drucker (1999) and was earlier put more strongly by Milton Friedman (1972), who argued that social responsibility is not the province of organisations. Friedman believed that the responsibility of a private-sector corporation was to its shareholders and that it was management's job to make as much money as possible for them. He contended that social responsibility would reduce the return to stockholders. Money spent on social considerations would erode profits, which in turn would raise prices, lower wages and have a negative impact on society. Others have argued that organisational leaders are not trained to assess social needs, so this falls outside their responsibility or capability. However, as has been seen above, shareholders do expect organisational leaders to manage issues around social responsibility, bearing in mind the long-term sustainability of the organisation's profits.

7.3   Ethical issues

The need to delivery social responsibility for an organisation translates into ethical decision-making for the organisation's leaders. They must decide on the benefits of social responsibility, set against any potential costs to the organisation. Ethics relate to the set of standards by which actions are judged to be right or wrong. For example, if an organisation does not respond to public pressure to limit its pollution of the environment, then this has been judged on ethical principles by the public for causing pollution and will be further judged on the degree to which the company responds to those concerns. There are therefore two stages to the ethical judgement made by the public: the first is whether the organisation conforms to the public's expected standards behaviour; and second, if it does not do so, how quickly does it change its position and its attitude, having been found to have breached those standards. If the organisation is sensitive to public demands and responds accordingly, then that is seen to mitigate the impact of the initial breach. If the organisation procrastinates and objects, then the public's attitude may rapidly become highly negative.

Where organisations do not act ethically they run the risk of damaging consumer goodwill and incurring the disapproval of their peers. Gitman and McDaniel (1983) suggest that business ethics come from five sources: *religion*, which stresses the dignity of humanity under God; *philosophical systems*, which claim that reason produces ethical norms; *cultural experience*, which provides values that society expects to be upheld; *legal systems*, which should prevent violation of socially accepted ethical standards; and *professional codes*, which are derived from corporate codes. Codes of ethics are important to the organisational leader as he or she takes responsibility for the organisation. As such, an individual leader may find that his or her personal ethics conflict with those of the organisations. The issue becomes a case of how the individual can balance his or her views and beliefs while maintaining the interests of the organisation. This can be compounded by senior management's sensitivity and overprotectiveness about the organisation, and resulting restrictions on the degree to which employees can speak freely. Over-regulation will produce suppression and is likely also to result in a reduction in open communication internally, as well as reducing employee morale and subsequently performance. Organisational leaders must balance the needs of the organisation against the basic freedoms of the individual to hold their own ethical positions and express that of others appropriately.

7.4   Personal business ethics

If an organisation has to make a number of its workforce redundant, who makes the decision on who will go, and how is that decision made? The decision will hinge on both the ethical principles of the organisation and on the values and beliefs of the individuals making the decision. Gitman and McDaniel (1983) constructed a set of principles that might be taken into account when making such decisions: fair treatment of others (justice); the individual's right to be accurately informed of the situation (truth);

standing up for what one believes in, even if this has unfavourable consequences (courage); independent thinking and expression (freedom); impartial justice when making decisions about others (fairness); and including others, such as trade unions and employees, in the power process (sharing). Most organisational leaders today believe that social responsibility is an ethical issue, where they bear responsibility for both the individual and the organisation through social obligations at work as well as to the organisations role in society at large.

7.5 The leader's ethical dilemma

The role of the individual leader is key in the ethical decision-making process, either as an individual or as part of a management team who jointly decide on the organisation's policy. We need to examine the ethics of leaders' decisions and behaviour, and how to help potential leaders develop the ability to make such judgements effectively. This is not a simple balance between the leaders' own ethical positions; rather, it is a complex balance of a number of factors, such as:

1 The individuals' own ethical principles.
2 The views of other colleagues if there is to be a joint decision.
3 The business interests of the organisation.
4 The views of community as a whole in which the organisation operates.
5 The views of the key stakeholders – shareholders, employees, consumers.
6 The presence of regulation or governmental policies.
7 Anticipated changes in any of the above in the future while the action being considered is likely to be undertaken.

There is often an assumption that leaders have to decide between right and wrong – both in the moral context and in that of general organisational decision-making. That is not always the case, however, as leaders often have to judge not between right and wrong but rather between two rights. In many ways this is the most challenging of leadership dilemmas, because the understanding of how leaders come to choose between two or more options, each of which are likely to create positive outcomes, is the basis for consistency of vision, strategy and leadership purpose throughout the organisation.

Clark and Clegg (1998) argue that the paradigm underpinning management knowledge is changing. This is fundamental to any treatment of leadership, both from the viewpoint of leadership development but also in the context of judging the ethics of leadership. Basing their analysis on various sources (notably Naisbitt, 1982, 1997; Tapscott and Caston, 1993; Hamel and Prahalad (1994); Cannon, 1996; de Geus, 1997), they join Collins and Porras (1996) in noting 'the tyranny of the OR'. In essence, they call for an acceptance of paradox, the reality that decisions are rarely 'black and white' in the real world, and that there is more 'grey' than black or white in the majority of leaders' decisions.

The concept of 'the tyranny of the OR' requires people to accept the idea of fixed choices – either change OR stability, low cost OR high quality, shareholder return OR social responsibility. One can be idealistic and driven by values, or pragmatic and driven by economic motives, but not both. They argue that an 'intelligent' organisation embraces the paradox that OR is not the best answer: that the route to sustainability lies in the acceptance of AND instead. Following de Geus (1997), they argue that the paradigm shift now under way is from a world of organisation dominated by 'capital' to one dominated by 'knowledge'. This accepts that social responsibility and ethics can operate with profit and be balanced successfully, and that 'knowledge' is now the source of profit as much as 'capital' via the exploitation of human ingenuity, innovation and knowledge. Here, people are seen as sources of creativity and as the knowledge base of the organisation. Hence the phrase 'human capital'.

7.6 Ethical standards

Ethical standards are relative and may vary from place to place and over time. There may never be an absolute 'right or wrong', and there may be no clear and accepted standard over ethical questions at any given point in time (Badavacco and Ellsworth, 1989). This is demonstrated clearly by the different levels of employee protection – for example, health and safety, as operated by different countries and regions across the world. Each country thinks its solution is appropriate for its community.

Ethical standards are impacted by various factors. For example, personality – that is, the authoritarian personality (see Adorno *et al.*, 1950) – demonstrates a set of principles regarding behaviour that they view as acceptable. In addition, further development of ethical standards emerges out of various processes of socialisation – at school, in the early years of work, through professional groupings and so on. Family and social groups are also important factors in determining patterns of behaviour.

The evaluation of behaviour as being good or bad implies the existence of norms or values generally accepted in a given context which creates a frame of reference. Typically, four approaches exist, as follows:

- *Naturalism* – takes as central the issue of self-interest, accepts ethics as being context specific and therefore 'local' in the sense that in varying localities differing circumstances create different responses. Thus what might be acceptable in a desert may not be acceptable in an urban environment, for example.

- *Rationalism* – argues the existence of universal principles and ideas to underpin ethical ideas. Based on the notion that, through the application of reason and logic, it is possible to identify ethical standards.

- *Utilitarianism* – here it is thought that the right outcome promotes the common good. This requires agreement on what this means, but this principle has been used since the eighteenth century, when it was put forward by Jeremy Bentham, the British philosopher. Raphael (1994) restates these principles, including ideas such as promoting the happiness of oneself *and* others, of doing no harm to others, of telling the truth, of treating people fairly, of sustaining promises and undertakings, and of acknowledging the worth of others.

- *Formalism* – based on the idea that often a means–ends perspective can be applied to human situations. This can underpin the justification for the regulation of corporate behaviour via governance processes, regulations, rules and operating procedures.

What outcomes are these different approaches likely to lead to in response to a real situation? This can best be illustrated through an example. The work of Hosmer (1987) sets out the following within which to judge the ethical quality of a decision:

(i)   Various features of the *decision context*, including the organisation's culture, the economic context, the broader social and legal context, and beliefs and values.

(ii) Ethical standards, whether stated or tacit.

The components of the decision situation itself, and then the decision outcome, are also a factor. The decision situation will almost certainly comprise a dilemma for a decision-maker. Following Sucher (2007), we see that there are four types of dilemma worth noting:

(i)   *The challenge of right versus wrong.* Thus a situation in which accepted codes or norms have been breached, and the question is what to do about the situation. Right and wrong decisions nearly always end up as shades of grey – a case of bribery, for example, but then questions may arise about the strength of the evidence; for example, the fact that at the time of the action the option taken might have been argued to have been acceptable, but only through hindsight is now not the case. As an example, referring back to the Shackleton case in Chapter 1, he mistakenly relied on ponies rather than on dogs, despite advice. A modern example is the payments made to senior figures in Middle Eastern governments by some defence contractors to ensure they won contracts. This was seen as acceptable business practice in the region at the time, but in the context of Western practice was questionable, and by the time it was made public in 2009–10 was viewed quite clearly in both UK and the USA as bribery.

(ii) *The challenge of right versus right* Often more than one available option will meet the criteria that those involved use to judge a decision outcome. Much more difficult are decisions where there is right on both sides. For example, in the case of diversity, if political parties set quotas for particular groups – women or ethnic minorities, say – they are typically seen as undermining the principle of meritocracy. There is right on both sides – developing meritocracy or developing diversity. In organisations, leaders often face 'right versus right' challenges, such as balancing the needs of employees and those of shareholders, or short-term profit for which the leader will be incentivised versus long-term viability, for which they will not, for example.

(iii) *A moral dilemma.* Where there is an irreconcilable 'right versus right' issue this creates a *moral dilemma*, where either one right must be subsumed to another or both cannot be maximised and a balance must be struck.

(iv) *New or changing principles.* As time passes, new moral principles are developed, or existing ones extended, and this has an impact on what is acceptable. Thus what was right in the past may now be viewed as wrong – for example, the view taken of smoking at work and how increasingly this has been controlled since the 1990s as a result of changing perceptions of what is acceptable.

In the run-up to contentious events – for example, the war in Iraq from 2003, there is always a debate about 'right versus right' problems, and similar issues occur in organisations. In a televised debate between two British politicians regarding invading Iraq, they were asked why they voted as they did on the decision to commit UK forces in a coalition with US forces. One had voted for and one against the decision. The factors they cited revolved around:

(i) Integrity, principle and self-respect in relation to sending troops to war.

(ii) Logical consistency, in relation to differing policy positions at different points in time.

(iii) Public acceptability of the course of action.

(iv) Perception of the national interest.

(v) Doing the best for their own political party and government (in the case of one respondent) – from both an organisational and personal perspective.

(vi) The concept of a 'just' war, and what the criteria for that were.

(vii) The level of risk they perceived in the balance between success and failure.

This set of principles seems to be reflected in the corporate world as well as the political, through some key judgements. Decision-makers ask 'Is this proposed action—':

- In my best interests?
- In the best interests of the organisation?
- In the best interests of the wider community?
- Likely to succeed or fail?
- Conform to the wider community's generally accepted principles of behaviour?
- Conform to my personal principles?
- Be visible to others in the organisation or community?

The corporate leader is likely to use the same set of questions as is any other individual who is making a decision. The variation occurs more in the weighting given to each factor than to individuals using a different set of factors. Thus if it is an individual decision that has little impact or bearing on the organisation or community and is not visible, then personal interests will be highly weighted, but the greater the visibility and impact on others, the greater the extent they must be borne in mind. At the most basic level we all want to get our own way and maximise our own benefit, and the degree to which we have to mitigate this is driven by the significance of the other factors we have to consider.

7.7 Moral codes

Badaracco (2006) links 'right versus right' choices with the whole question of moral codes, and the initially appealing idea that leaders need a 'clear moral compass' to guide them in the choices they must make. He notes:

> A moral compass is useful for straightforward questions of right and wrong. In most organisations, however, the hardest choices rise to the top, because the questions that can be resolved with simple rules are delegated to others. And many of the hardest questions, in organisations and in life, are conflicts amongst several competing responsibilities. But when right conflicts with right, the needle

in the proverbial moral compass switches back and forth and offers little guidance to leaders.

Yet we are inevitably attracted to the idea that leaders should have clear ideas to enable them to deal with crises, pressure and uncertainty. It is often thought that leaders whose decisions are driven by deeply held values and beliefs are more likely to withstand the pressures presented by the environment, stay the course and achieve success in the long run. The only issue here is that there is a fine line between a leader who is determined and one who is arrogant and refuses to listen to the views of others. Determination to deliver the outcome of a bad idea is not what is wanted in leaders. Thus the importance of the initial decision is critical.

Just as life's challenges are many and varied, so different leaders have different moral codes, and these are likely to be dynamic and complex. This creates an obvious difficulty. One leader's consideration of complex options may look like a lack of clarity of purpose to another. Moreover, in discussing 'dreams', Badaracco describes healthy dreams as those which set ambitions that are achievable within the available resources. How can leaders judge what should be done with available resources, what is achievable with those resources and, if required, how can more resources be obtained and at what cost both financially and organisationally?

For example, an organisation might seek to dominate its market sector using a strategy combining organic growth with mergers and acquisitions. As it grows it may become an important player in its sector but while this good for the organisation, it leads to other problems, such as an increase in financial and other organisational costs, and creates a more complex organisation that is more difficult to lead. Thus growth, while good, has costs, including ethical ones, that have to be considered.

People follow leaders not just because of their moral codes, and in many cases the complexity of both individuals and organisations, especially those with significant cultural diversity, mean that many differing codes may exist, and that different ones may be used at different times. As mentioned earlier, corporate conduct acceptable in Asia, say, may not be seen as acceptable in Europe or the USA. Historians and biographers of figures such as Hitler and Stalin note that ordinary people tended not to blame these leaders personally for things that went wrong but saw them as being misled by advisers offering poor or self-interested advice. So leaders are inevitably judged not only by their moral codes but also by the quality of decisions in terms of the business and social value. Thus a moral leader who makes bad decisions could be seen as being worse for an organisation than a leader with few values who gets things right. For some people, morality is of no use when the situation is so dire that personal survival is at stake and the ends justify the means.

Badaracco (2006) goes halfway with this argument. In his view, given a complex set of moral codes and issues of right versus right, the 'best' leaders are those who ask themselves tough questions. He lists five questions for leaders, or aspirant leaders, to test the quality of their moral codes:

1 **How deep are the emotional roots of my moral code?**
   Here he examines the extent to which moral codes are rooted in family experiences and that of the immediate social group or community. He notes that some successful leaders come from family backgrounds characterised by parents who 'fail', but there are also leaders who embody the worst traits of an otherwise 'good' society

and do not have a sound moral code. It is his view that deeply rooted personal emotional codes are very inaccessible. Badaracco is referring to a community-based set of ideas which deem a set of behaviours and choices to be based firmly on a 'good' moral code and indicative of 'character' that derives from an individual taking up various moral codes during their development from childhood.

2 **What do my failures tell me?**
The key point here relates to the question of excess presenting risk. Just as Miller (1990) identifies in his book, *The Icarus Paradox*, a leader's strengths, if taken too far, may reveal vulnerability. There are two key issues here: first, the ability to tell when a strength is becoming a weakness – for example, determination becomes arrogance, attention to detail becomes perfectionism and so on – is important. This is the basis for the Hogan Derailer model, where this trend is examined in corporate leaders via a test. Second, is the ability to admit to and learn from failure. Some leaders have the ability to deny that even the most obvious failures *were* failures, and even if they do admit this, many don't learn the lessons and therefore repeat them. This ability is a key indicator of leadership potential and is one of the predictors of capability at a higher level, but it is surprising that the number of leaders who have reach higher levels too obviously were not measured against this criteria.

3 **How have I handled ethical surprises?**
Badaracco urges us to look for patterns here. Possession of a sound, if complex, set of moral codes is likely to result in patterned rather than highly variable responses to moral or ethical challenges. Thus leaders can be judged in terms of clarity, motivation and dominance around their moral code. The latter is the most important. Does the moral code ultimately determine decisions and actions, or do personal and organisational imperatives take priority? But this still does not resolve the 'right versus right' problem.

4 **Do I have the courage to reconsider?**
This perhaps a key leadership test, as at any point leaders may take the wrong course, and when they realise that this is the case, what should they do? Press on to maintain their image, which will lead inevitably to failure, or admit the error and move on to success? These dilemmas are complex. The real question is 'Are leaders open to learning and willing to reconsider?' Following Badaracco (2006) 'these individuals (leaders with character) have strong moral codes – strong enough to be open and curious, to ask themselves challenging questions, and to recognise the moral and practical complexity of their level'.

5 **Can I crystallise my convictions?**
Even if the leader possesses a moral code but is unable to either make sense of that or to convince others of its validity so that they can act on that insight, it is likely to lead to failure. Finally, the key test of both character and the leader's moral code is the ability to communicate in ways that resonate with the values and beliefs of those around him or her, a return to the idea of resonance. Thus leadership is a relational matter, and as morals are complex not simple, just as life's dilemmas are complex, simple codes are unlikely to be effective. More often than not the issue is deciding 'right versus right', not 'right versus wrong'. Leaders may hold deeply rooted convictions, but so will those around them and they need to be sensitive to the moral codes, views and concerns of those in the organisation and the wider community, both emotionally and intellectually.

Steare (2008) defines 'ethicability' as a behaviour-based definition where the focus is on acting ethically. His states that this requires individuals to consider the environment within which they operate, including other people. They need to seek to achieve objectives, but at the same time bearing in mind the impact of the options available and the other problems or dilemmas they might cause.

So the decision on what is right, and thus on the course of action, is decided not only by reference to any rules that may apply but also the possibility of harm to others and whether those involved would judge it to be right, fair and reasonable. So the focus is on the consideration of others involved, which leads inherently on to the leader taking a relational perspective.

7.8 The 'relational' perspective

Building on the work of Jaques (1963) and Stewart (1982), we can view this issue from the business decision perspective. Stewart noted that 'managerial manoeuvring room' may be defined in terms of three elements: demands, constraints and choices. The leader's freedom to choose and act is shaped by the interaction of the demands and choices applied to or available in the organisation in that situation and at that time.

Demands are definitions of what leaders are expected to do, and relate to the tasks built into the role and the accountability applied to them. Demands therefore derive from the environment and key stakeholders, the governance and regulatory arrangements within which the organisation operates, colleagues' expectations, and their own aspirational ambitions, goals and values.

Demands can be goal- or relationship orientated. Leaders are normally expected to build relevant cultures, foster positive attitudes and be catalysts for change, and the leadership role includes adjusting the organisation's response to the demands placed on it if the leaders or others feel the organisation is 'not fit for purpose'.

Conversely, constraints provide the boundaries within which leaders operate. They are determined by the organisation's structure, culture, operating models and access to resources. Such constraints are dynamic and change over time. Constraints create routines, including cultural routines that represent acceptable ways of operating or acting. They provide stability and order, and therefore predictability, becoming part of the 'psychological contract' with employees. Changing these alters this contract and therefore has to be 'sold' to the employees in a way that demonstrates the leader's moral code and requires relational skills.

Choice refers to the decisions managers make, choosing from the options they conceive as available to them, Organisational slack, a free resource, has long been seen as linked to the ability to innovate (March, 1994). Choice therefore represents the opportunity for leaders to create desirable consequences through the decisions they make. Thus the actions of managers can be judged either in terms of consequences (goal-orientated) or in terms of appropriateness in relation to rules and norms, identity and the organisation viewed as a community.

Limiting that judgement to the delivery of objectives, that is, consequences, creates the risk that there will be less co-operation and more opportunism. The organisation is likely to be less able to adapt to changing circumstances. Complex and challenging environments require adaptability driven by individual and team learning. This is conditional on trust, openness and co-operation (see Chapter 1; and Gratton, 2007), which require that the options leaders decide upon must have the capability of aligning to the individuals' and organisation's rules, norms and moral codes. If they are not aligned, this essential co-operation will be missing. This is a key element in the building of employee engagement to improve organisational performance – that leaders are sensitive to employees' views and align with them where possible.

This co-operation is vital to success, in particular where the relationships between actions and consequences are unclear, or where preferences are themselves changing. Adaptive approaches become even more important in such situations. In the real world this happens all the time and is quoted in the organisational change literature as 'experience based design' (see Carnall, 2007). Because of the significant time pressures under which senior managers operate, there is a tendency for action orientation – one has to do something as soon as possible – though it might be rather optimistic to equate this with being an experiential or learning-oriented approach – it is more likely to be a 'knee jerk' reaction in some cases. This is well summarised by the number of senior leaders who have had to be taught that 'doing nothing' is a valid option in any situation and not an abrogation of the leadership role. 'Wait and see' is often better than 'act in haste'.

Nevertheless, practitioners argue that the test of appropriateness is a better basis for judging managers and leaders in relation to the circumstances and the leaders' identity. The critical question is: 'Would a leader like me have acted as I did in these circumstances?'

This is derived from the key test of behaviour within the Anglo-Saxon practice of law; that is, would a 'reasonable' person, in a given set of circumstances, have acted in a particular way? But this requires leaders to have full knowledge – self-knowledge, a full understanding of the situation, and an understanding of others and their situations. But there are inherent risks here – frequently lack of full knowledge, and leaders being too keen to exert their influence to deliver objectives. Argyris (1982, 1985, 1990, 2004), in a series of contributions has demonstrated the difficulties a leader can encounter where he or she seeks to reinforce his/her own identity, say, as a decisive manager. See Chapter 6, above.

In summary, judgements about the choices leaders make must be measured against consequences and appropriateness, and the more reflective leaders are at both the individual and on a group level, the better these judgements are likely to be. Consequences – the outcomes – relate to the efficiency of means–ends sequences. Evaluation here is likely to be based on rules, order, predictability and stability. Evaluation criteria are more likely to emphasise change and adaptability, but this is not necessarily true, and in many cases it is the outcome that is viewed as the most important element. Over-emphasis on achieving change can also be counterproductive – too much change can cause significant damage to organisations. This is particularly the case where the change is not really needed, as in the case of a new CEO making changes for changes' sake, where it is not well planned or where the previous change is not yet fully embedded. This too-rapid change is a problem where change planning fails to reflect adequately a realistic timetable (Carnall, 2007). This may cause confusion, cynicism, 'change fatigue' and poorly implemented change strategies.

Badaracco (2007) offers a way through this dilemma by observing that leadership is constitutive commitment; leadership is more than just what leaders do, more than satisfying stakeholders and the pursuit of revenues, it is a set of experiences that help leaders to define themselves. People who have become successful leaders rarely do so easily, without periods of failure, self-doubt and personal challenge. Leaders find challenge valuable because they learn more about themselves than they do in periods of stability, calm and success. Even failure has some benefit in learning. It is often said that a leader who has never experienced failure is potentially a bad leader: 'It is not what happens to you in life which defines who you are, it is what you do with what happens to you in life' is a common cry. Badaracco (2007) concludes:

> These critical incidents tend to occur after the first years of a career. Their bosses think they have talent and experience. They have a job they care about, and it fits their dreams and hopes. They have faced demanding situations and believe they have a sound moral code. But then they face a critical test of character and competence that reveals whether they can take responsibility, for themselves and for others!

From an entirely different perspective, Dweck (2008) casts light on these ethical issues from the perspective of what constitutes success when working in various 'callings' in life (for example, parenting, business, sport, school and relationships). Her work is based on focusing on what people believe about themselves. She began her work on 'mindsets' by looking at how people cope with failure, which she examined by observing how students dealt with 'hard problems'.

Basing her premise on the observations that people have the capacity for lifelong learning, she notes that the major factor in whether people achieve expertise is not related to a prior and fixed level of ability but rather 'purposeful engagement', through two mindsets:

- The Growth mindset, based on the belief that one's core capabilities can be enhanced and grow through learning and experience. People characterised by this mindset are likely to be constantly stretching themselves, accepting challenges, taking responsibility.

- The Fixed mindset, based on the belief that one is unable to change, and therefore there is no need to try to adapt to changing situations or to change oneself in any way.

Her conclusion is that people with a growth mindset are more likely to possess self-awareness and self-knowledge. In her research, Dweck demonstrated that people find it hard to assess their own abilities accurately, but that 'it was those with a fixed mindset who accounted for almost all the inaccuracy'. Howard Gardner (2004) concludes that exceptional people appear to possess the talent of identifying their own strengths and weaknesses. Further, those with a growth mindset are much more likely to believe they can learn new things, change substantially and, indeed, even change core elements of the person they are, and how they relate to others.

It is worth noting that few leaders would say that they have a fixed mindset, but they might well demonstrate such behaviour to some degree. Lack of self-awareness of one's impact on others naturally breeds a fixed mindset, as the individual cannot assess the impact that he or she is having. The key issue is one of trying to get leaders to be able to move along the spectrum from a fixed mindset towards a growth mindset if they do not do so naturally. This can be driven, as will be seen later, by a

Talent issues

	Fixed mindset	Growth mindset
Appropriateness **Stakeholder pressure**	Likely to be unable to take responsibility for stakeholder demands (Large, complex bureaucracy)	Likely to respond to stakeholder demands, resolving dilemmas creatively (Satisfy complex and changing needs customer)
Consequences (outcomes)	Likely to leverage change, new markets quickly and effectively Satisfying immediate needs but find complexity hard to handle (for example, retail supermarkets)	Likely to frustrate and lose adaptive creative people (for example, research organisations)

Fig 7.1   An overview of growth and fixed mindsets

number of interventions such as coaching, mentoring, 360° feedback, but becomes more difficult to achieve as people become older and more set in their ways.

Dweck (2008) goes on to develop this thinking in the context of business and leadership. She suggests that Ken Lay of Enron was an example of a fixed mindset leader, while Jack Welch of GE, Anne Mulcahy of Xerox and Lou Gerstner of IBM were growth mindset leaders. In her discussion, Dweck relies extensively on the Level 5 leadership notion as deployed by Collins (2001) in his 'Good to Great' model. Briefly, Collins' work suggested that successful leaders are less likely to be egoistical, charismatic, 'larger than life' figures, at least in today's complex business world. Rather, they are likely to be people possessing the growth mindset, as Dweck characterises the Collins notion, committed to learning and improvement. She also refers to the idea of a fixed mindset or growth mindset workplace, raising questions about culture and values at the organisational level – again reflecting the challenge of moving organisations, as well as people along the spectrum from a fixed to a growth mindset.

Combining a number of the ideas we have considered, we have created an overview, as shown in Figure 7.1.

As suggested earlier, the ultimate test of leaders is whether they are effective in the core task they face. For a corporate leader perhaps so long as they preside over a period of profitability and share price growth, they are considered to have been successful. For the CEO of a publicly funded hospital, say, so long as activity rates have increased, more people are being treated, patient outcomes have improved, and financial stability maintained, then the same applies. Thus the outcomes are achieved and no further questions need to be asked. Essentially, we accept that the ends justify the means.

But is it that easy? For example, take the case of the hospital. If those outcomes were achieved by the hospital only treating certain types of cases; that is, simple cases where good outcomes are easily achieved, then how great an achievement is that really, and is there not some moral question about only taking on easy cases if that leads to problems for those sent elsewhere with more severe problems, such as someone needing help having to wait – or be transported many miles to a different hospital? Leading teaching hospitals carry out medical research in many fields, and in order to do so they take on the most challenging cases. Inherently these have a higher chance of failure, but do we want research to be hindered, and would we suggest that a hospital should turn away difficult cases merely in order to get good results?

In a simple situation, excellent performance easily leads to excellent outcomes and that is a sufficient basis for judging a situation. But in more complex 'right versus right' situations, complications abound. The greater the simplification of complexity conducted in the leader's analysis of the problem, the greater the risk that the solution will either not work or have a negative impact somewhere. Thus good leaders must have the capability to embrace, manage and deliver through complexity.

Cuilla (2007) argues that 'Ethical leadership entails the ability of leaders to sustain fundamental notions of morality such as care and respect for persons, justice and honesty, in changing organisational, social, and global contexts.' She also makes a crucial point that leaders do not have to be power-hungry psychopaths to act other than ethically. Leaders are ordinary people in business, government, not-for-profit organisations and elsewhere, and they will make mistakes – they are not born a perfect leader and need help to learn and develop into one. This simple fact is often forgotten by organisations – young, growing leaders don't know what they don't know – be that related to process, people or ethics. They need guidance, and organisations fail to do this at their peril. The impact will be felt for years to come and at significant risk to the bottom line and the organisation's future.

7.9 Adaptive leadership

It is worth noting Heifetz's (1994) work on 'adaptive leadership', because in this context it provides a basis for looking at 'ethical leadership' in that it examines the way that leaders help 'followers' to deal with challenging or conflicting situations. The adaptive leadership perspective involves balancing competing values – values of employees, the organisation and the wider community. Leadership comprises the use of authority by creating 'space' or a 'holding environment' for people to enable them to adapt.

Adaptive leadership requires leaders to be willing to take responsibility for arguing that people in challenging or conflicting situations need to accept less than they aspire to in order that a compromise can be achieved and progress be made. Where polarised attitudes have developed this is often very difficult, as positions taken by the parties tend after a time to be linked directly with the values of those involved. So while initially the issue may have been a technical one, it then becomes one that challenges the individuals' views of what they now believe to be right, and backing down in any way challenges their principles and ethics – the ethics that say 'I believe I am right so why should I compromise?' These are perceived as ethics, but in reality they aren't, and ethics is a cover for refusing to admit that one might not have all the right on one's side – again, back to the 'right versus right' problem.

To solve this problem, adaptive leaders create a 'holding environment' within which they create trust and empathise with the need for all involved to accept 'loss' or compromise if a solution is to emerge; that to do so does not challenge individuals' ethics; and that such behaviour actually conforms to the organisation's ethics. The leader's responsibility is to help the followers in coping with these challenges driven by change and personal growth that they feel threaten their ethics or values.

For Northouse (2004), there are five principles of ethical leadership:

(i)   **Leaders respect others** – in essence, treating others as human beings of value and worth in themselves.

(ii) **Serve others** – while this is often discuss as a 'follower-centred' approach, for example following Senge (1990) in his formulation that one key task of the leader is to be the 'steward' of a vision that is not merely self-centred. Service to others is the key here, albeit the literature tending not to make a sharp distinction between employees and clients, or for that matter other stakeholders. Interestingly, the motto of the British Army Officer training college, the Royal Military Academy Sandhurst is 'Serve to Lead', and the importance of this is strongly emphasised in officer training.

(iii) **Ethical leaders are just** – Northouse begins by equating justice and fairness and then goes on to argue that a leader's top priority is to treat all subordinates in an equal manner. However, he notes that where individuals are treated differently, the grounds for that difference needs to be clear, reasonable, fair and based on sound moral values.

(iv) **Ethical leaders are honest** – he quotes Dalla Costa (1995), who argues that honesty means 'do not promise what you can't deliver, do not misrepresent, do not hide behind spin-doctored evasions, do not suppress obligations, do not evade accountability, do not accept that the 'survival of the fittest' pressures of business release us from the responsibility to respect another's dignity and humanity'. However, that does not mean that the leader must tell everyone everything. The leader has a duty to the organisation that he or she must exercise, and this may require that they know things that their subordinates do not, and which cannot be disclosed to them until authorised. That is no contradiction to the ethical leader, nor does it make them less ethical. Provided they act as ethically as possible within the bounds set by the organisation, and if they feel those bounds are unacceptable, to make this clear to their superiors, they still maintain their ethical leadership position.

(v)   **Ethical leaders build community** – if leadership comprises the processes of influencing others to achieve a common goal, then it is necessary for leaders to develop the engagement of employees to do this. To be effective, this needs to apply to all team members, not just a few of them, and thus the creation of a community is essential for organisational effectiveness. Burns (1978) placed this point at the heart of the transformational leadership model.

Northouse (2004) rightly notes that much of the work on which he had relied to argue these five principles is anecdotal, and based on opinion not evidence. But like many such observations, if it reflects the reality of what we see around us day-to-day, and if it provides resonance, then it has value even if it is not evidence-based.

Northouse bases his analysis on Rawls' 'Theory of Justice' (1999) and reviews Heifetz (1994) on ethics, and he also includes in his book a chapter entitled 'Leader-Member Exchange Theory'. In the latter, he notes that most leadership theories are focused from the leader's own perspective or the 'follower' perspective or the context.

Exchange theory takes a relational approach. It focuses on the interactions between leaders and followers.

In discussing exchange theory, Northouse makes extensive use of Graen (1995), in particular a 'Leadership-making model', which views the leader–follower relationship as going through three phases: 'stranger'; 'acquaintance'; and 'partner'. In the latter phase, the roles of leader and follower are negotiated, influence is reciprocal between both, exchanges are of a high quality, and interests are group-focused more than individual.

This links to the work of Heifetz, where 'adaptive leadership' involves the leader being willing to take responsibility, for creating the 'space' within which people can come to terms with tough decisions. In both the Graen 'partner' phase and the Heifetz adaptive leadership process, the leader brings a positive contribution to the relationship by buying time for negotiation and an exchange of views with followers. If roles are negotiated and influence is reciprocal that is very different from simply being follower-centred. In adaptive leadership, the leader creates 'space', by using his or her own authority and credibility to 'buy time'. When tough choices must be faced there will always be pressure for rapid choices and immediate action. Those to whom the leader reports will probably apply pressure on the leader to make a decision and take action as soon as possible. Creating 'space' for followers to come to terms with the choices they are facing, where consequences are difficult, probably because valued outcomes have to be given up, involves 'managing' or 'coping' with that pressure. In simple terms, 'bad' news needs to be digested, the situation 'reframed' and a new plan developed before successful action can follow.

Viewing leadership as a relational process between leader, followers and others, one is forced to face reality, which many leadership models tend to minimise. Where tough choices are to be made, it is unrealistic to believe that the leader's contribution is only a vision that empowers others. The leader will seek to present a viable vision of the future but he or she has to do much more – because otherwise the relationship is not reciprocal, just one-way street. It is the reciprocal element that is critical in the relationship.

7.10   Responsible and ethical leadership on an industry-wide perspective

The crisis in the financial sector in the late 2000s should never have happened. Following Enron, WorldCom, Tyco and others, the implementation of Sarbanes–Oxley and similar regulations combined with tighter internal systems were supposed to prevent any repetition.

But this defies the evidence of history. Gresham's Law, named after Sir Thomas Gresham, the sixteenth-century British financier, postulates that 'Bad money drives out good'. It suggests that there is an inherent pressure within any trading environment for people to do things they shouldn't, either through greed, peer pressure or to meet the expectations of those more important than themselves. As was proposed earlier in this chapter, the view of some is that as long as the outcomes are delivered, no one cares how it has been achieved: the traditional 'the ends justify the means' view of life.

In modern, complex and globally distributed organisations, effective risk management is of increasing importance, but in difficult times there is pressure on client-facing staff to 'get business in' at any cost to help the organisation survive, or to beat competitors. This leads to a temptation by leaders to cut corners, not to ask too many questions, and to assume an introspective view of the world where ethical behaviour is seen as an obstruction to the achievement of objectives.

This approach was taken up by some involved in creating the financial crisis of 2006–10. The results of which led to profound consequences for the sector around the world. The level of connectivity created by globalisation triggered the crisis, when confidence was initially lost and the whole system locked up, minimising liquidity, which led to failures occurring. The 'subprime' mortgage market problems, the complexities created by the creation of 'collateralised debt obligations' and a lack of confidence on the part of banks to lend to other banks led to a crisis of confidence in financial institutions generally. No single explanation of how this came about has emerged, more that it was a number of interconnected factors that all came together at one time to create a 'perfect storm'. But the causes need to be identified and agreed to establish conditions from which confidence can be rebuilt, and rebuilt it must be for the world's markets to recover.

The cause most commonly cited in the media is what is termed 'irresponsible lending' by a banking industry driven by the pursuit of profit. But the claim that this caused the whole thing is far from the reality or the situation, but a useful escape route for politicians and regulators who also had some responsibility. They claimed that it was also caused by the 'bonus culture'. But some observers would suggest that while there was some bonus-driven behaviour, the key to the creation of the potential for disaster lay in policy decisions by governments, central banks and regulators, which created relatively inexpensive and too easily accessible credit. This built a house of cards that was always fated to end in a 'bust'. The only question was, when.

Certainly, reviews of what went wrong have identified the granting of credit to those who could not afford it, in particular in the US mortgage market, as a key factor in the creation of the crisis. Evidence from legal action initiated in mid-2011 by the US Federal Housing Agency against 17 international banks shows that those banks repeatedly breached their own rules to ensure that mortgages were granted to people who could not really afford them. It shows that surveyors were pressured to over-value properties. Thus the mindset in these organisations was one of maximising the bottom line at all costs, even if this meant breaking one's own rules, breaking the law and breaking the basic principles of ethical leadership.

The assumption was that, as property values rose inexorably – as they had been doing for a number of years – then, where no equity existed for the lender initially, this would grow over a few years, thus creating a safe investment. Therefore, granting a 100 per cent mortgage to someone with a low income was seen as being acceptable as it made money for everyone. Further, in the US, many mortgage sales staff were remunerated only on commission, thus if they did not sell they starved. Here the balance between the profit motive, effective risk management, ethical behaviour and social responsibility was not just unbalanced but had ceased to exist. Some mortgage brokers just saw selling these mortgages as the only way to survive on commission. For them, survival could logically be expected to beat ethics in the real world, but for their organisations and leaders there was no excuse.

There were other systems failures, such as the inadequate pricing of risk when these investments were sold on. The risks taken were not properly priced by rating agencies, which led to products that were assumed to be low risk actually being high risk. Further, there are suggestions that, rather than corporate leaders not understanding risks in the process they *did* understand them but attempted to disguise them when selling-on mortgage-based products to others. In addition, there is evidence that senior leaders failed to ask basic questions about how so much money was being generated so fast. Another factor was that many leaders didn't understand how the system worked but they did not want to look stupid by asking questions of more junior staff: a triumph of the protection of self-image over corporate good governance.

There are examples of organisations that lost potential business as their tighter, and thus more effective, compliance requirements took longer to process new business compared to their less risk-averse competitors. Those organisations, rather than standing firm, loosened controls to make sure they didn't lose out to their competitors, thus feeding the cycle. This led to situations where legal, but unethical, behaviour or lax risk management slowly became the norm in those parts of the major international banks whose trading led to the crisis.

Another weakness of the regulation of the financial sector was that it was regulated by legal entity – that is, by what the organisation was defined as, not by what it actually did – so even where an activity created a risk, if it was not within a legal framework requiring regulation it was not regulated. This is where many of the problems occurred – in unregulated business. In unregulated areas, then, the moral compass is the only possible way to set out a code of ethics and reduce potential risk, as regulation does not apply.

Even where risk was identified, and senior leaders were warned, often the 'whistleblowers' were told to keep quiet or leave. No one who questioned the viability of the unrivalled profits pouring in was tolerated. Even though the Codes of Corporate Governance around the world generally recommend that boards of listed companies should have some form of supervisory committee, this failed to restrict excessive risk-taking and short-term orientation of leaders at all levels where these securities were being traded.

Admittedly, in the parts of the banks where securities weren't being traded – for example, private banking and retail banking – the behaviour of leaders and staff remained both responsible and ethical. This is interesting, because it shows that both ethical and 'unethical' leadership can exist in the same organisation. This links to the degree to which leaders who see others failing to meet the standards of behaviour required are empowered to challenge them. Having strong organisational values is of little use if nothing happens when someone flouts them. In financial services, few saw the problems building, and even fewer challenged what was going on.

Overall, it was this culture in those parts of the banks trading badly, not incompetent pricing, understanding of risk or the bonus culture that was the key problem. This was driven by a lack of a strong, ethics-based leadership, driven from the top, which created a strong moral compass where staff would not have accepted subprime mortgages, repackaged them and sold them on to unsuspecting buyers for maximum profit. Thus short-term revenue and market share growth would not have been encouraged rather than long-term value to the business.

As a result of this unethical behaviour, many say that the reputation of the banking sector is now in tatters. Can this reputation be rebuilt? Yes, if the financial services sector firmly returns to values based on ethical principles shared with the rest of society. Banks need to balance ethical principles with encouraging entrepreneurial endeavour as a key engine of change within the world economy.

7.11   Rebuilding industries post-crisis

How can this be delivered? One approach is to construct more effective corporate governance – effectively enforced ethical behaviour. Yes, this can be done but there is a risk. While many countries have adopted corporate governance frameworks over recent years it is also true that many exhibit a 'tick box' mentality, where compliance is with the letter rather than the spirit or the intentions behind the framework. This applies to all organisations, not just to banks.

In all organisations, the objective of regulation is to apply good governance principles from outside. However, this is based on assumptions that regulators or non-executive directors, acting on behalf of shareholders, are able to monitor and control the organisations' actions. After the financial crisis, cries of 'it must never happen again' prompted increased regulation, but this maybe counterproductive in the future. Greater transparency and more robust risk management practices are both part of this, as is the role and position of internal and external audit and board committees. The core problem is that these don't necessarily prevent things from going wrong in the first place, they just stop them getting out of hand once they have started.

Too often there is an assumption that optimum risk minimisation is delivered by regulation and tight compliance systems – effectively enforced ethics. Tight control systems may reduce risk but they can restrict the organisations' ability to adapt to change, and to respond quickly to customer needs. Further, they can slow or prevent the development of innovative products or processes that reduce operational costs or increase profit. The equation is assumed to be that risk may be kept low, but one has to sacrifice flexibility and responsiveness. This is a classic 'right versus right' problem – less risk but a slower response time.

Here the core concept of ethical leadership and the moral compass are vital. They stop employees and leaders doing things wrongly in the first place, they ensure that everyone knows what is right and what is wrong, and that the organisations' definitions of this match those of the community and stakeholders they serve. But to make the banks move to this model, and to do so for real rather than as a 'tick box' exercise, requires a deep period of self-analysis and then change from the banks, with a wider dialogue about the banks' role in society.

A spirit of inquiry and learning must be created about ways to deliver more effectively the sustained growth of value, re-establish trust and create a culture where ethical behaviour is as important as profit. This must come from the top, with new reward strategies to reinforce it, re-thought training and development, and new criteria for promotion and dismissal. No single blueprint yet exists. What is needed is careful and thoughtful dialogue, and evidence to support an emergent strategy for the future. This dialogue expends the concept of 'space' introduced earlier, from being an internal tool to a much larger and wide-ranging process that reconsiders the core principles on which the organisation operates in relation to its stakeholders and society. It is not just about an internal resolution between leaders and followers.

7.12   At the organisational level

Building an ethical leadership code is vital and poor ethics do have consequences in the real world. Often not driven by the high-by level moral questions about right and wrong in society but more simple practical issues such as 'Should I cut corners in the process to save time or money?'; 'Would it really matter if the maintenance didn't get done this month and waited until next?' 'Would it really be a bad thing to underplay the risk to the client if it would get me the business?' and so on There are many examples of both recent and past corporate disasters that can be attributed to the failure of organisational control systems where at the most basic level someone decided to do something they shouldn't, or didn't do something they should have done.

Even in areas where you would not expect such failures – for example, the military services – as the size of the perceived benefit increases by acting wrongly, the chances of failure of the organisation's values also increases. The decision to break personal and organisational values is effectively a cost–benefit one based on the factors set out earlier in the chapter.

In any event, even with tight systems, in the drive to earn money, or not to disclose mistakes, it is not difficult for a reasonably clever individual to subvert control systems should that be in his or her interest. Individuals such as Nick Leeson (Barings, $1.3bn) and Jérôme Kerviel (Société Générale, $7.0bn) proved that. But perhaps if there had been a stronger moral compass, these individuals might have not done what they did.

Embedding the ethics and values of the organisation in the entire employee population via the moral compass not only has the effect of reducing risk but also adds value by supporting other key principles of good operation, such as encouraging staff to:

■ Deliver excellent customer service.

■ Find ways to save money.

■ Work out better ways of doing things.

■ Sell your organisation's qualities to customers, potential staff and the wider public by the demonstration of ethical behaviour.

From the perspective of the CEO, chief legal officer (CLO) or chief risk officer (CRO), the benefits of a strong moral compass are to make their jobs easier. Law and morality are not always the same thing. Reputational risk can be created by perfectly legal activity that fails to comply with current social norms. CLOs cannot properly advise CEOs if they are leading an amoral organisation. Laws are passed and the CLO can only tell the organisation what they mean, when they have been breached, and what will happen as a result. So the legal function can help the organisation to keep out of trouble by ensuring it obeys regulations and does not break the law, but it cannot ensure that it stays out of trouble by doing the right thing and being ethical.

The real risk of a lack of moral compass, and thus ethical leadership, is in those areas where risk, or potential risk, exist, but where regulation and control systems are not present. This is of particular importance for reputational risk, where despite an activity being legal if it is perceived by employees, stakeholders, customers or the wider community as unacceptable, it is indeed risk. As has already been said, it was in this type of area that the banking crisis began; the development of leading edge financial products in a little regulated environment where the generation of profit was the be all and end all irrespective of the ethics of what was being done, or indeed, the business logic based on the claimed lack of sustainability of the model.

Investor attitudes may also add pressure on organisations to compromise the moral compass, in particular those institutional investors who want to maintain year-on-year increases and in return create an expectation that organisations feel obliged to meet. Some non-financial sector senior leaders may assume smugly that they are safe from such risks, but they are not. Things go wrong, and badly wrong, elsewhere as well, so the moral compass founded on ethical leadership is valuable everywhere. Ask Exxon about Valdez; BP about Texas City and Gulf of Mexico; and Union Carbide about Bhopal.

Variation in regulatory environments globally adds to the risk, 'the butterfly and hurricane effect' – the flap of the butterfly wing represented by an improper conversation with a customer in Africa, if not dealt with then and there, after a time becomes a hurricane elsewhere, through class actions, large fines, reputational damage and the termination of careers from the USA through the EU to Asia Pacific. Such is the increased risk of globalisation. Again, back to Bhopal and Valdez. But this could potentially be prevented by ethical leadership and the moral compass; where wrong is wrong no matter where you are.

Statistically, more goes wrong lower down the organisation than at the top, but the perceived impact is often less. In reality, one cannot stop things going wrong. As a group CRO of a global bank said to me in 2006, 'We know statistically in this organisation of 80,000 someone, somewhere must be doing something wrong every hour of the working day. The systems should catch it before it gets critical, but with strong ethics and values it doesn't even start. And that would make me sleep much easier at night.' Sadly, he didn't know that the ethics and values of others elsewhere in the organisation were not as strong as his, or the financial crisis would not have hit the bank.

But the ultimate and most devastating indictments of the failure of moral compass and ethical leadership are the examples of senior management ignoring, sidelining or even dismissing those who warned them about building risk because it did not fit with the delivery of their current business strategy. Examples of this are now creeping out into cold light of day in the financial sector globally, and they also exist elsewhere.

But its not just about big mistakes, as these problems often start on a very small scale. Small acts of unethical behaviour and examples of unethical leadership can be chipping away unnoticed for years, slowly damaging an organisation. If unchecked, these can fertilise the creation of a culture where mega disasters can germinate. Most of the major disasters we recalled earlier grew from small beginnings and were left to grow more and more potentially damaging. Even if they don't grow bigger, the impact of many smaller issues that, for example, give a negative view of an organisation to 15 per cent of its customers may not have an immediate effect but over time the damage will have a bottom line impact.

So who helps to create this moral compass and ethical leadership? It is a critical strategic leadership issue that defines the way the organisation and everyone in it behaves. Making it happen is a partnership between the CEO, CLO/CRO and the HR department. HR has an important role to play in making the moral compass work. In recruitment, HR makes sure the right people come into the organisation, it makes sure they are inducted to be aware of correct behaviour, it should ensure promotion and remuneration to reward that behaviour. The only problem is that if every day the individual's line manager is sending signals that contradict this, all the work that HR does will be diminished and the compass fail. So the line manager influences the individual's behaviour, but who influences line manager's? Simple – his or her boss and the CEO, so they are also key to an effective moral compass. A demonstration of ethical leadership from the top is key to success. the CEO as the driver and example, CLO/CRO as the monitor, HR as the facilitator, and every line manager in the organisation as the implementers and examples of good behaviour.

The moral compass needs to be aligned with the organisation's business strategy and the values by which the strategy is delivered. This is the combination of the delivery of objectives and the ethical elements set out earlier that meet and deliver those objectives ethically. The values must be developed by staff as well as senior management, and be simple and understandable so that staff will take ownership and use them operationally day to day – like most people, employees don't like being told what their ethics are. Further, people tend to attach greater importance to emotional connections of what is right or wrong than to operational risk systems; the former belongs to them as individuals, and the latter to the organisation. That perceptual difference is critical in determining behaviour.

The compass has to be embedded the organisation's ethics by using all touch points between organisation and individuals – for example, communication events, appraisal, development activity, discussion with line managers and those chosen to be examples of success. The steps that organisations should use to create or confirm its moral compass are relatively simple:

- Create new values or reaffirm old ones if they are valid. Do this by working bottom-up to create values and behaviours to which everyone can commit.
- The values are the overarching principles – the behaviours that everyone does day-to-day to make them a reality – that good ethics is good business.
- Integrate this into all touch points with staff.
- Make sure all line managers buy into it, demonstrate it and expect it of their subordinates.
- Appraise and reward people positively if they do it.
- Champion people that do it well as examples to others.
- Measure it via organisational processes and systems.
- Include customers and clients in discussions about how it can be improved.

The problem with reality is that the environment is dynamic and ethics change over time, so the moral compass and ethical leadership must reflect this. New or unregulated activities will emerge, society's views of ethics change, and a moral compass is likely to have the flexibility to respond to this much more than fixed regulation that takes years to implement.

In the final analysis, having a strong moral compass underpinned by ethical leadership in an organisation not only minimises risk but also improves performance via better employee engagement from better leadership. It increases trust and respect, and the external brand image of the organisation benefits in the market as customers see it at work. Further, in practical terms, the moral compass is an extremely cost effective way of minimising risk compared to more formalised systems.

7.13   Creating space for dialogue

Progress on organisational challenges requires a 'space' within which key players and stakeholders can participate in a dialogue that tries to make sense of the newly emerging environment, or out of a crisis, so it is possible to move forward. This needs to build a powerful shared interest among all, to work together in order to establish a new basis for taking forward organisations built on fundamental values, including the idea of 'responsible and ethical leadership'.

In the case of complex environments, where a whole industry, such as banking, has challenges, there is a requirement for a wider definition of 'space' to include dialogue from academics from a range of disciplines and institutions, and industry key players along with politicians, senior policy-makers, regulators and so on. This 'space' provides a stimulus to research and reflection that would offer the opportunity to review the emerging situation in an evidence-based way. This would also tend to focus on long-term issues, whereas internal 'space' and dialogue often focus more on the operational and local issues. Implicit in this where problems of an ethical nature have been raised, such as in financial services, includes the rebuilding of trust and ethical leadership via a moral compass.

Such dialogue has occurred in relation to financial services via G20 heads of government in 2009–11; via the central bankers and Basel III over the same period; and locally in the UK via the Independent Banking Commission, which recommended the 'ring fencing' of banks in September 2011. All of this demonstrates the creation of 'space' to enable free and open discussion and the development of future strategy between all significant stakeholders. Within this, the academic content has been strong, and in particular from finance–focused institutions such as Cass Business School.

Similar discussions have taken place on a less public level in the oil industry, related to the Gulf of Mexico incidents in 2010 and the associated issues of conduct, safety and ethical leadership they raised. This was especially important in relation to the subsequent proposed expansion of oil exploration into highly environmentally sensitive areas such as the Arctic and Alaska.

We see similar 'space' and dialogue occurring in relation to the hardwood timber industry, mining and air accidents. Where an industry either faces unexpected disasters or challenges, or is seen to be falling short of its responsibilities to a community or its declared standards of behaviour, such dialogue is needed. Thus 'space' is critical for organisations to realign their strategies, operational delivery and leadership behaviour around the basic principles of ethical leadership that most in society expect.

7.14   Summary

It is clear that the practice of leadership is complex, that leaders face complex problems, and that ethical behaviour is one key to long-term success. To be successful, the leader not only needs skill and knowledge, intuition and experience, plus a little luck, but all of this needs to be underpinned by a set of ethical principles that reflect those of the community within which they function.

In this chapter we have examined the question of leadership against the issue of the wider responsibilities of organisations. Corporate leaders find themselves urged and potentially required, by social policy and legislation, to take into account wider interests. While there are various theories to explain these pressures and to examine how organisations can respond, senior corporate leaders are now, more than ever, subject to external scrutiny on these issues by stakeholders, including investors and even the community. Unacceptable behaviour to drive the bottom line is now often seen to cost more in reputational or legal risk than the potential profit it might deliver. The risk of problems in this area increases where leaders maintain an inward-looking and short-term perspective, which slowly diverts their view of what is ethical and responsible from that of the wider community. This has been seen in many cases of corporate disaster or misbehaviour, from Exxon Valdez to Exxon itself, from Bophal to the 2008 financial crisis, and from the Gulf of Mexico to Chernobyl. In all of these situations someone did something they shouldn't and the organisation failed to prevent it turning into a major issue. Had ethical leadership and moral compass been present these events probably would not have happened.

Thus the decisions and choices leaders make need to take into account issues, factors and principles well away from the immediate operational drivers or current environment. Their actions may be judged by others far away or at a different time, who will measure them against basic principles of ethical behaviour and social responsibility and not just on how much benefit the organisation might have gained. Having a strong moral compass is not only good for the organisation but it is actually good for business too. The leader who ignores the importance of ethics and having a moral compass does so at their peril.

Questions

1 Does leadership have an ethical element? If so, what is the leader required to do to make it effective?

2 Does the principle 'my word is my bond' have any relevance for leadership in the twenty-first century?

3 Can an organisation have ethical standards, or only individuals? What creates an organisation's standards and values?

4 Do you observe the same values at work as you do with friends and family? If there is a difference, why is this?

5 Do organisations have a moral responsibility to those to whom they might not have a legal responsibility?

6 How do the ethics and brand of an organisation interact?

8 Politics, power and perception

8.1 Introduction

Throughout much of the twentieth century, research into organisations looked at how to increase performance, productivity and profitability most effectively. A number of ways were investigated, from work or organisational design, effectively the analysis of *process*, and motivation and analysis of the *people* involved. In most cases this research focused internally. The impact of the conflicts of the early twentieth century, in particular the Second World War, led to rapid increases in research to find ways to deal with problems presented by such conflicts. These included creating systems to select candidates for officer training from a large potential population in the rapidly expanding armed services. Other examples were maximising productivity in factory systems being rapidly expanded to manufacture military output on a vast scale. After these events that required total focus from all involved, subsequently, when economies returned to more normal production, the satisfaction of employees and customers came to be seen as central to improved performance. Further the development of the 'public service' in many countries after the Second World War led to the study of this new type of non-commercial organisation.

After the end of the Second World War in 1945 many observers argued that the Cold War, conflicts around the world and the growing pressures of global competition alongside the demands of what US president Dwight Eisenhower famously called the 'military-industrial complex' added substantial and continued impetus to the research effort. This led to the impressive growth of business schools in the USA and elsewhere. Professional schools such as law schools, medical schools and similar had been established in the late nineteenth or early twentieth centuries, but the emergence of business schools after 1945 was a feature of the educational 'landscape' during the latter part of the twentieth century.

The twentieth century has been labelled by some as 'the American century' as the USA's capitalist organisations became dominant in sectors such as automobile and aircraft manufacture. Moreover, US culture came to be almost the defining culture for big cities around the world, albeit in a slightly adapted form. American business, diplomacy and military power eventually reached a leading position across the world, balanced only by the Communist bloc led by the USSR. For a period of nearly 50 years the balance of political and military power was held in place politically by the two superpowers, the USA and the USSR, but the clear economic power was held by the USA. The rise of the European Economic Community (later Union), from the late 1950s began to counter this to some degree, together with the growth of Japan. On the political and military side, the collapse of the USSR in the late 1980s allowed the USA take on the role as the only political and military superpower. However, the USA is challenged increasingly on the economic front from the EU, and more particularly from the new 'tiger' economies of China and India.

Yet within USA there has been significant forced change in the position of business relative to the rest of the world. It is clear that while US business continues to deliver economic success there are nevertheless many US organisations struggling to survive and prosper in mature sectors such as automobile manufacture or heavy industry. Further, the cost advantages provided by low wages in Asia have had a significant impact on industries such as clothing manufacture. The impact of this has been to initiate a number of world trade problems resulting from the US and others 'defending' their industries from perceived unfair competition. Further, where such competition has had an impact this has led many thoughtful business leaders to raise new questions about the operation of both organisations and global markets.

As long ago as the mid-1980s, Turner (1986) traced an interest in corporate culture related to both the decline in standards of manufacturing quality and design in the USA, and the challenge to the economic supremacy of the USA, from Japan in particular. He argued that the culture concept offers a new way of understanding organisations. The use of corporate culture appears to offer analytical possibilities for explaining the success of Japanese companies at least in the 1960s and 1970s. Of course, there were other feasible explanations, not least the rebuilding of Japan and Germany post-Second World War to equip their industry with more modern equipment, systems, labour laws and trade unions. However, these were deemed to be insufficient in themselves to explain the observable differences in performance and success between the two.

Literally hundreds of research studies seeking to explain organisational performance by looking at structure, innovation, technology, size, adaptation and so on tended to reveal statistically significant correlations (between the US and Japan or in general). For a clear summary of this literature see Child (1984). However, it was also true that the factors studied provided an explanation of only part of the variance in the dependent variable, commonly a 'bundle' of performance measures. Researchers concluded that some other factor, not being measured, was producing the additional variation. It was not long before it was concluded that the missing variable was culture.

Further, it is difficult to conclude that the leadership qualities of business leaders are sufficient to explain corporate success, but how else could the growth and decline of organisations under the control of the same leader by explained. Moreover, the Icarus phenomenon (Miller, 1990) suggests that within the success of an enterprise lie the seeds of its eventual decline and demise. This links well to the suggestions that organisations need different types of leaders as they move through their organisational cycles.

To those reviewing the differences between US and Japanese organisations and their success it seemed clear that leadership, alongside other unknown factors, must be brought into play if more accurate explanations were to be developed. Herbert Simon (1957) had noted this point in his book *Administrative Behaviour*, based on his experiences during his involvement in managing the US armament programme in the period 1941–5, that leaders often find themselves 'satisficing' because optimal decisions turn out to be illusions in the midst of the interplays between rapid growth of output, lack of information, lack of resources and so on. His assertion reflects what we have learnt from experience and what observers have long recognised: that leaders work within a real world where the 'best of all possible worlds' rarely applies and decisions are made based on often inadequate or inaccurate information. Thus pragmatism and 'taking an educated guess' become the way that leaders make day-to-day decisions, driven by a combination of the objectives they have and the circumstances in which they find themselves.

Of course, such a view possessed powerful 'face validity', looking at what was happening. Just as the 'frontier spirit', thought to engender values of self-reliance, independence and enterprise, had been instrumental in the growth of American business, so observers now sought similar explanations for the success of Japanese enterprise in 'consensus management', Japanese style. In addition the adoption by Japanese corporations of American ideas such as total quality management (TQM), combined eventually with the 'Toyota Manufacturing System' incorporating ideas that came to be known as 'lean thinking', 'kanban' and so on, added further factors for differences in performance.

While the explanation ultimately relates to changes in the way that work is organised, the argument for why Japanese enterprises achieved advantage by making these changes first was seen to include culture as one important source of explanation. While some will argue that the devastation of the Second World War meant that international investment in both Germany and Japan led these two economies to having capital equipment for production that was on average newer and therefore more productive than that of their competitors, and this was the key to their success. New ideas were perhaps also more easily introduced in these economies; for example, quality circles in Japan which may, in turn, have led to the development of more powerful ideas such as *kaizen* and just-in-time (JIT) strategies (see Chapter 5, above).

Thus, from the historical comparisons between US and Japanese organisations we can show that culture does have an impact on performance at the strategic level, and we can see the same at the micro level. Evidence of various studies can be found in different parts of this book that, when taken down to the level of the individual, if a positive culture exists in the team as a result of the actions of the leader then, irrespective of organisational culture or activity, these teams perform better than where such a culture does not exist. Thus to some degree organisational culture is an aggregation of the cultures of all the teams within the organisation, some good and some bad – and thus performance levels will reflect this. The role of senior leaders is therefore to set out the best possible culture as an example for all, in the likelihood that if it is taken up by all the teams in the organisation and supported by organisational systems, good performance should naturally follow.

Just a simple example should suffice: Corporate Leadership Council's (2004d): 'Engaging the workforce' survey (50,000 employees surveyed at over 50 organisations). The top 50 drivers to increase discretionary effort included the following – and each has the capability to increase commitment by at least 20 per cent to 30 per cent. The line manager:

- Demonstrates commitment to diversity – driver rated 4th in importance in obtaining increased effort.
- Demonstrates honesty and integrity – driver rated 5th.
- Respects employees as individuals – driver rated 18th.
- Cares about employees – driver rated 20th.

- Defends direct reports – driver rated 24th.
- Makes sacrifices for direct reports – driver rated 27th.
- Inspires others – driver rated 31st.
- Places employees interests first – driver rated 35th.
- Trusts employees to do their job – driver rated 44th.

It should also be noted that from within the top 50 drivers of higher discretionary effort, only two drivers do not relate to the actions of the line manager within the team as leader. So culture is as much about what is happening at the micro level as much as at the macro level.

8.2 Organisation culture

Organisation culture is commonly defined as the attitudes, values, beliefs, norms and customs that distinguish an organisation from others. Organisation culture is intangible and difficult to measure. In fact, there are many ways of defining this term. Elliot Jaques (1952) referred to 'customary and traditional ways of thinking and doing things', noting that new employees must learn to adopt them sufficiently to gain acceptance in the organisation. Schwartz and Davis (1981) note that culture is both about beliefs and expectations, while Lorsch (1986) refers to the beliefs of 'top managers'. Conversely, Kotter and Hesketh (1992) note the importance of community and its preservation within any definition of culture, effectively arguing that the urge to create identity and ensure survival are what gives the culture impact. It is also worth reminding ourselves again here that teams and departments also have subcultures, and these, albeit on a smaller scale, conform to the same principles as the overarching organisational culture. Further, these team cultures, when aggregated, naturally create the overall organisational culture. To understand culture we have to think micro as well as macro.

Johnson (1988) set out a 'cultural web', noting a number of components that help in the definition of organisation culture:

(i)   *The organisation paradigm*. What an organisation does; its mission; its values; how it defines itself.

(ii)   *Control systems*. Processes in place to monitor performance and/or behaviour. Role cultures have many formal controls, rules and procedures, for example.

(iii) *Organisational structures*. Reporting lines, hierarchies, work flows.

(iv)   *Power structures*. Who makes the decisions, how widely spread is power, and on what is power and influence based?

(v)   *Symbols*. Logos and designs, office allocation, car parking and other tangible and intangible means of differentiating people.

(vi)   *Rituals and routines*. Meetings, reports, budget and performance review processes.

(vii) *Stories and myths*. Convey messages about what is important and valued in an organisation.

While not denying that organisations are cultural entities, it ought to be noted that the underlying consequences of having a strong culture could be to stifle any variation from the existing culture or progression to a new culture when circumstances require it. In any event, organisations are certainly only rarely capable of being understood as a single, homogeneous culture and this is often at a surface level. There are several examples of organisations perceived to have strong cultures: for example, GE, Goldman Sachs, Hewlett Packard and many Japanese organisations. If we take Goldman Sachs as an example, there is without doubt a very strong overarching 'Goldman's' culture, but underneath there exist sub-cultures where the overarching culture is applied in different ways. You would not expect those in the IT, legal or HR functions to have all the same cultural behaviours as those doing mergers and acquisitions work, or trading. In general, these cultural variations relate to functional activity differences and the behaviour adopted within those areas based on the same cultural principles.

This brings with it the prospect of cultural differentiation and adaptation via what would in effect be a process of evolution. Evolutionary explanations of change attract some interest (see below). However the idea that a leadership team can change the culture of an organisation is very contentious, but certainly impacts upon it. Parker (2000) observes that many of the ideas behind organisation culture theories are not new, depending as they do on the well-known tensions between cultural and structural, or informal and formal, explanations of behaviour in organisations.

Going back to some of the earliest studies of culture, we note that one of the explanations for the famous Hawthorne research (undertaken between 1927 and 1935) lies in a cultural explanation different from those suggested by Roethlisberger and Dickson (1939). The Hawthorne experiments began as a consequence of an earlier study carried out in the same factory looking at the impact of lighting on the productivity of workers engaged in tasks demanding physical skills. Gains were observed as lighting levels were increased. Then lighting levels were reduced. Even so, further gains were recorded, and these only slowed when lighting levels were reduced to the level of moonlight! Social factors were believed to be the explanation.

Subsequently, the famous 'relay assembly test room study' was set up to investigate these factors in greater depth. The initial experiments had changed the incentives for production, from individual based to team based, so the more the team as a whole produced, the more everyone got paid. Other changes were also tried, such as providing food during breaks, shortening the day by 30 minutes, moving workstations, and keeping the work areas clean and unobstructed. Again, all had some effect. The results of this were reported in great detail (Roethlisberger and Dickson, 1939). Taken together the results of this and later studies at Hawthorne were taken as a demonstration that social factors explain performance more fully than various economic explanations including the operation of incentive schemes. These social factors are 'in-group' factors such as 'group pressure', whether that is in a positive and mutually supportive way, or through peer pressure to perform. Thus the social explanation did not relate to factors we might associate with a higher-level factor external to the team in the form of corporate culture as such.

There have long been various contending explanation for these results (see Sofer, 1973 for an excellent summary) offers an explanation of interest to those interested in cultural factors. We should also not forget that these experiments were carried out within the social and economic environment of 1930s USA. The relay assembly test room operators were female workers in the Hawthorne factory, a Western Electric factory in outer Chicago. The majority were recent immigrants whose English language skills were relatively poor and they were often the main income earners in their families. Economic pressure and the experience of being a relatively recently arrived immigrant and therefore not fully socially adjusted may well offer an explanation as to why group pressure was so important. The group incentive scheme was clearly an important part of the reasons for the group pressure, so it is difficult to conclude that no economic explanation applies. Certainly, output increased in the relay assembly test room. However, the Roethlisberger and Dickson book, while it was published in 1939 shows the data only to 1929. Whitehead (1936) published the relay assembly test room data to 1934. From the beginning of the Great Depression of 1929 output fell away, thus reinforcing the likelihood that while social factors were important there is the possibility that these factors mediate the operation of a group incentive scheme, and that from 1929 onwards the key motivation was that of limiting output. Note, however, that other, operational factors may explain falling output from 1929 onwards. We cannot tell from the available data but what we can conclude is that a combination of social, cultural and economic explanations is needed.

So there is an intersection of various economic, social and contextual variables as well as social group factors related to the 'informal' organisation idea. Of course, we have long known that the 'real world behaviour' in an organisation operates differently from the formally prescribed rules, procedures and so on. In order to 'get things done' people develop 'shortcuts'. From there it is not difficult to see how corporate cultures may emerge. A combination of the operation of formal systems and processes and informal organisation could reasonably be expected to result in the development of tacit understandings about what is and is not 'acceptable behaviour' in any given organisational situation. The important point to note here is the intersection of factors at different levels: individual, organisational and contextual. If this is how culture arises we should also note the Deal and Kennedy (1982) observation about 'strong' and 'weak' cultures.

A strong culture exists where employees respond to changing situations consistently with their alignment to the values of the organisation or objectives; the Goldman Sachs situation quoted earlier is an example of this. There is a high degree of predictability in this regard. Conversely, a weak culture exists where there is little alignment with organisational values or objectives. Here control must be exercised through extensive procedures, rules and formal systems. Where the culture is strong we have the possibility, identified by Janis (1972) as 'groupthink'. This happens when people do not challenge current thinking, but also where the group will take riskier decisions than would any individual member acting alone. There is a strong belief in the organisation's values and a tendency to create negative stereotypes of competitors, the latter leading to a belief in the inherent advantages of the organisation on the part of its members. In turn, this leads to riskier decision-making. It is worth noting that, generally, strong cultures tend to out-perform weaker cultures (Kotter and Hesketh, 1992). But also that this strength and resulting 'groupthink' can lead to inward-looking and arrogant attitudes that sow the seeds of the organisation's own destruction.

This leads on to some interesting questions: Are strong cultures most likely to emerge in a period of growth? Is that when organisations with strong cultures perform best? Could not the Hawthorne research be an example of a strong culture in operation but one in which the contextual factors were both conducive to the development of a strong culture and likely to support effective performance because of the alignment between employee objectives and needs, and corporate goals?

8.3 Models of organisation culture

Looking in more detail at the models of organisational culture may help us find answers, or at least indicators of the answers, to the above questions. Various influential models of culture are as follows:

(i) Hofstede (1968), identified five characteristics of culture in his study of national cultural influences:

- *Power distance*. The extent to which, in a given national context, people expect there to be differences in the level of power across groups and between individuals. A high power distance score represents an expectation that some people can wield substantial power. A low score is an expectation of equal influence over decisions.
- *Uncertainty avoidance*. In essence, a national attitude to risk taking and coping with uncertainty.
- *Individualism versus collectivism*. People are either concerned primarily for themselves, or act as a member of a group, subordinating individual to group goals.
- *Masculinity versus femininity*. The contrast between male values of competitiveness, aggression and ambition and feminine values emphasising the value of others and of developmental rather than simply economic goals.
- *Long-term versus short-term orientation*.

Using attitude data from a major multinational organisation, Hofstede was able to show national differences for these factors.

(ii) Deal and Kennedy (1982) defined organisational culture in a more pragmatic way, as 'the way things get done around here'. On the face of it, this is based on organisational reality. However, the fact that different organisations do things differently is hardly being definitive about an organisation's culture. The organisations concerned may deploy different technology and therefore do things differently. So, what do they do differently? Surely similar comparators where culture is the main difference is more helpful? Does that mean they had different cultures at the outset? More helpfully, they go on to define measures of corporate culture depending on two factors:

- *Feedback*. The speed of feedback and the scope of it have an impact on behaviour in an organisation.
- *Risk*. The level of uncertainty applying to an organisation.

Using these factors, Deal and Kennedy proposed four types of culture:

- 'Tough-guy' or 'macho'. A culture in which rewards are high and feedback immediate. Fast-moving financial and investment companies might be typical of this culture, but Deal and Kennedy noted that this can also emerge in front line areas of hospitals, sports organisations and police forces.
- 'Work hard/play hard'. A culture emerging where risks are high, but more typically in large organisations compared with the previous culture type.
- 'Bet your company'. A culture in which big decisions are taken but it may be years before the results are known. Typical of this type are power utilities, oil exploration, aviation and mining.

■ Process culture is one in which people are given little or no feedback. Often this is because services delivered to clients are complex, with many departments and individuals involved. Examples might be social services organisations, the public sector such as local government, or parts of the administrative elements of health provision.

The strength of this model is that it deals with corporate culture in a relatively pragmatic way, which can be identified easily in the real world. One issue is, however, that when culture types are defined, then the types should be independent of each other, but within organisations they tend to combine to some degree. For example, in a hospital you could expect to see possibly as many as three of these cultures being demonstrated by significant groups – for example, clinicians, management, administrative and support functions. In some of these groups there would even be a mix of these cultures within the group. Thus, in practice, it is very difficult to define particular organisations by using these culture types.

(iii) Handy (1984) built on the work of Roger Harrison in developing a model of organisational culture in which he describes four culture types:

■ *Power culture*. A culture in which power influence and decision-taking is concentrated among a few key people and positions. The organisation is controlled from the top through networks and teams, rather like a web. Decision and action are quick and decisive, and there are few formal systems, procedures and rules.

■ *Role culture*. Here, people as role incumbents or role holders have clearly defined authority within previously defined parameters. Power derives from position and/or expertise so long as the expertise is recognised and legitimated organisationally.

■ *Person culture*. This culture comprises an organisational setting designed around individual performance – for example, a ballet or opera company, investment bank, law firms or consulting firms. Handy suggests person cultures exist where each individual ranks his/her own performance as being superior to the organisation.

■ *Task culture*. This exists where teams are created to work on and resolve particular problems. Power derives from expertise so long as that expertise is needed. Organisations with matrix structures and multiple reporting lines will often be characterised by this culture. This is typical of complex major organisations such as GE, Shell, BP, British Telecom or major global financial organisations such as Citigroup.

Here the culture types are defined independently of each other and linked to a questionnaire developed by Handy. However, as was suggested with previous models, in practice multiple cultures exist inside organisations even if there is a 'general' overall cultural theme. If most complex global organisations are examined, be they energy suppliers, financial services, logistics, aviation or others, they have all of the cultures suggested in different parts of their organisations. This may just be differences that have occurred by chance, or that have been initiated deliberately to align to customers segments, regional cultures or business models.

For example, a well-known global technology services group is organised into sector groups to win and manage business; capability groups to facilitate solutions development; and central functions including information services, finance and human resources to provide shared services. Further, a business transformation group exists to provide thought leadership, and client service teams come together as teams to serve clients. Are many organisations in reality too complex for these models to be the basis of useful solutions?

Perhaps what we are saying is that, in reality, any organisation needs multiple cultures within it to be effective in different areas, based on what that area has to deliver and to whom, but that it also needs a general 'overarching' culture that sets out core principles by which the sub-cultures deliver what is required.

(iv)   The work of Ed Schein (1996) defines organisational culture as 'the residue of success'. Of all organisational attributes, this is the hardest to measure and therefore the most difficult to change. Once changed, however, Schein argues that the impact of that change will be long-lasting, outliving products and services, leaders and founders, buildings and other physical attributes.

Schein describes culture at three cognitive levels. The first and simplest are those aspects of the organisation that can be observed directly and experienced by anyone. The second level deals with those aspects of culture professed by participants only. Here we talk about mission statements and the like, but also about employee and client surveys. At the third level we deal with tacit assumptions, 'unspoken rules' and the like. Much of this latter element is rarely discussed openly in the organisation. Schein even suggests that much of this exists without the conscious knowledge of those involved. This seems likely only in the sense that we are talking about unspoken rules so deeply embedded that we no longer think about them. However, work on the impact of the subconscious in conscious decision-making would suggest that perhaps we seriously underestimate the power of things we do not consciously think about.

Here, Schein is proposing an analysis also developed earlier by Argyris and Schön (1978) in their discussion of 'espoused' theory and 'theory in use'. The latter distinction comes from observing differences between what senior executives and others say is important and what their behaviour actually signals to be important; that is, 'what I say' versus 'what I do'. Often this behaviour in organisations is paradoxical, and in some cases causes significant confusion and cynicism if a conflict exists between the two.

In such situations, newcomers to an organisation may take a long time to settle into the culture as they receive conflicting messages. However, this is also a serious issue in respect of the perception of all employees. Where leaders are seen to demand one type of behaviour but contradict this by their own actions it creates not only confusion but also a significant loss of credibility and perceived integrity for those leaders. More important, it explains one factor that impacts on why culture change is so difficult in practice. Some writers working within the critical theory perspective are also deeply sceptical about whether culture change can be achieved. However, despite this, it is clear that organisations certainly report successful culture change initiatives, which have been documented in detail.

(v)   For Trompenaars and Hampden-Turner (2007), each organisation has its own unique culture, probably created unconsciously, based on the actions and behaviours of senior executives, founders and other core people, those who built it originally and any who subsequently changed it. Culture is an acquired body of knowledge about how to behave, shared mind-sets and cognitive frameworks. Their model uses the sources of national cultural differences in corporate culture on a number of dimensions, as follows:

- *Universalism versus pluralism* (do we focus on rules and procedures or rely on our relationships when we seek to get things done?).
- *Individualism versus communitarianism* (do we think organisations should focus attention on individuals or on groups?).
- *Specific versus diffuse* (are relationships superficial and transactional or deep and go beyond the workplace?).
- *Inner directed versus outer directed* (is action focused inside the organisation or externally?).
- *Achieved status versus ascribed status* (value is seen in who people are or in the positions they hold).
- *Sequential time versus synchronic time* (attention to people and problems in sequence or jointly).

The connection between this study and Hofstede (1968) is evident enough, but it seems clear that Trompenaars' work has application to corporate culture generally. Thus, for example, where formal status is important in defining people's worth in an organisation, there have to be real questions about how easy it would be to introduce change, as change would be likely to undermine those definitions of worth. From experience, this is a real issue in the delivery of significant structural change in organisations. People become mentally tied to things such as their grade or rank, and view it as something personal rather than something that is merely an organisational label. While Trompenaars' concern was with the sources of national cultural difference, it seems clear that the model also reveals much about corporate culture.

It is clear that attitudes to risk, the feedback people receive and the timescales associated with feedback are important factors in understanding the emerging complexity to which Schein (1996) points. The mechanism through which cultures are formed is important, because while the factors identified by Schein are clearly important, they seem unlikely to explain the emergence of long-lasting cultures. For example, we know that attitude to risk is unlikely to remain stable over time between generations of employees.

One interesting element in the consideration of culture is the attitude to risk-taking. The response to failure is a key factor in how culture impacts on organisational performance. Where there is a 'fear of failure' culture, the impacts on the organisation are not just on present performance but also on future performance. A short-term approach combined with a narrow functional or departmental orientation, together with centralisation and autocratic management styles, are factors that tend to create a powerful limit to risk taking.

Further, managers moving rapidly through careers, having a succession of roles, and often not having to discuss their approach to leadership errors, do not develop the interpersonal skills they need. They find facing up to performance issues difficult. Therefore, when forced to do so by those same short-term pressures, they often do it inadequately by not tolerating mistakes. This further reduces risk-taking by employees fearful of the consequences of any mistakes.

Over time this can create an organisation where no one is prepared to take risks at all, with the consequent cessation of innovation, change and operating outside the rules to maximise customer service if required. The process has thus become more important than the output.

Where any problematic culture like this has emerged, changing it needs significant and powerful initiatives to make the organisation move forward. It seems clear that, to change a culture, not only must one work on structure and processes but also on the mindsets that exist within the organisation. The solution seems to be by getting people to recognise 'where they and the organisation are', 'where they want to be' and 'how to get there'. That must be done by encouraging people to focus on shared problems, developing new solutions and supporting their successful implementation. Demonstrating that taking measured risks is acceptable and essential is vital.

Where positive elements of the current culture are mainly behavioural or restricted to certain parts of the organisation, we can help the creation of new mindsets across the whole population by identifying and quantifying 'tacit' knowledge that already exists in the organisation, converting it to new, explicit knowledge and encouraging its spread and use in problem solving. Thus new possibilities are created – engendering mindset change not by destroying the current mindset but rather by adding new ideas based on building on the best of the past by focusing on solutions and not on failures. Thus the new world is created as a vision of a better place based on an accurate assessment of the current position together with a 'road map' of how to get there together.

(vi) Goffee and Jones (1996) offer another approach to the analysis of culture. For them, culture is about the presence, or absence, of community. Building on the ideas of social theorists such as Émile Durkheim, they argue that *sociability* (the extent to which people like each other, and mix with each other in and out of work) and *solidarity* (the extent to which there are shared goals) are important components of corporate culture. These two dimensions lead to the identification of four cultures. We have modified the Jones and Goffee model here. In this adaption, where sociability is high but solidarity low we have a team culture. Going back to our idea of differential cultures between teams and the organisation, the solidarity within the team might be high while solidarity for the organisation as a whole is could be low. This is a typical scenario, where a good line manager is able to inspire the team even if the rest of the organisation does not have such a high standard of team cohesiveness. This happens naturally in many organisations, depending on the capability of line managers. Across the organisation, in areas where sociability and solidarity are high, one can see a network culture emerging, characterised by easy and effective vertical and horizontal communication. This is the secret of an effective matrix structure. This indicates that, for maximum effectiveness, culture and structure must be mutually supportive.

More important for these authors, the issue is about identifying whether an organisation has a culture that is positive to change – in other words, adaptive. A positively orientated culture is more likely to be an adaptive one. Here, they rely partly on Kotter and Hesketh (1992), who identify values and behaviour common in adaptive versus non-adaptive cultures:

■ *Adaptive cultures* are customer focused, value people, value change and improvement, focus on the needs of stakeholders, innovation and an open-minded approach.

■ *Non-adaptive cultures*, value structure, orderly decisions and clear process, risk aversion is high, and the silo mentality prevails because of the emphasis on process and structure.

Here, the idea of culture change through incremental steps rather than a single jump starts to develop. Mindsets and structures cannot be changed overnight, and from analysis of successful change programmes we know that successful change can take years to complete. The time taken from the acceptance of a need to change to the change becoming an accepted part of everyday practice and embedded in the culture could be between three and six years, even if it is successful, and often these initiatives are not a success, for reasons explained elsewhere.

Case study   **Sony Europe**

Like many complex global corporations since the late 1990s, Sony has experienced a range of issues within its core businesses, partly relating to a weakening Japanese economy, and partly competition. This led to a series of restructuring exercises, as many as five in nine years, and other problems regarding the launch of new products. There were strategies to simplify and create focus through its business on to its core activities and customers. To this end it has 'downsized', 'outsourced' and 'off-shored' its many activities. It has focused on the 're-' words; that is, re-emerged, realigned, restructured and reorganised. While the group continues to seek improved operational performance, it seeks in particular to encourage entrepreneurial behaviour and innovation, and to speed up its processes. Here we see the concept of the overarching culture that is often the 'heart' of the organisation, frequently linked to the organisation's historical roots or purposes. All of this is based around the desire to inject new energy into Sony's 'product engine'. With an ambitious aim 'to become the leading digital entertainment brand of the 21st century', a debate began on issues relating to leadership and culture.

The appointment of Howard Stringer as CEO was presented to the organisation in this way: he and his team were to 'wake the company up'. Once celebrated for innovation, Sony was by 2000 viewed as a laggard in an increasingly digital world. The brand was still strong, but financial results less so. The business remained heavily silo based, and Stringer was quoted as saying 'We've got to find ways to drill holes in the crust.' The focus is on breaking down the silos, listening to customers and focusing on success in the market. Again, he is quoted as follows: 'Sony United is like an airplane. The cabin class is united. The business class is getting united. It's the first class I have the problem with.' In this he refers to a significant number of long-serving senior employees devoted to developing good products but less focused on customers. The culture values product launch, starting up new ventures rather than having the disciplined leadership needed to focus on customers.

So, on the one hand, the culture is defined by its early successes in bringing forward new, world-beating products, and while not short of ideas it is no longer able effectively to respond to customers' tastes and requirements. The drive to change must re-energise the organisation, develop leaders more able to understand customers, and be more effective in strategy execution and delivery. This is a good example of a product-driven culture that was effective via the provision of world-beating new products but lost sight of what customers wanted as the market changed and competition increased. Thus the culture must change and adapt, not only to internal issues but above all to external pressures brought about by change in the market that the organisation seeks to serve.

Sources: D. Braun *et al.* (2005); 'Recharging Sony', *Fortune*, 12 June, 2006.

All too often, when we consider culture we look at companies that need to break away from the 'dead hand of bureaucracy'. With Sony, no doubt some of this applied, but the main driver was to develop leadership capability to convert a ready source of ideas into competitive advantage and business success.

Case study questions

1 Why is it difficult to balance innovation and efficiency?
2 How important is the role of the new CEO for culture change?
3 What aspects of the culture of Sony should be maintained?
4 Should the CEO change the culture, or should others decide what the new culture needs to be? What is the balance between the input from those at the bottom of the organisa-tion getting customer feedback and those at the top creating the strategy?

Of the culture models we have reviewed here, probably Trompenaars' is the closest to providing a sound analysis of this case. Do we focus on our internal capabilities or our relationships when we seek to get things done? Is it right to value people solely in terms of the status they have achieved or on what they can now achieve? Does Sony need to be more externally directed in its efforts?

But each of the models points to the differences between adaptive and non-adaptive cultures, which is often the key determinant of the organisation's ability to change to meet new challenges (see Section 7.9 'Adaptive leadership' in Chapter 7).

8.4   Leadership, power and corporate politics

The impact of politics within organisations is much quoted in day-to-day conversa-tion – the view that some decisions are taken for political rather than performance reasons; the advancement of individual agendas rather than those of the organisation. All of us have seen examples of this during our careers, where decisions that defy logic – that is, contrary to the optimum outcome for the organisation – appear to have been taken. Here it is possible to divide these into two main categories: one where the defying of logic has been unknowing (for example, by accident, incomplete data or subconscious emotional bias) and those where there was a decision to know-ingly take other than the logical course – political action.

Leaders and others employ a variety of resources as they engage in the politics or organisation (see Table 8.1). They may have positional formal authority (or may be perceived as having such), direct control over resources or other capability to in some way influence the actions of others. The use of resources as a weapon to negate efforts

Table 8.1	The components of organisational politics		
	Resources	Process	Form
	Formal authority	Negotiation	Politics of
	Control of resources	Influencing	Budgets
	Control of information	Mobilising support	Careers
	Control of agenda	Mobilising bias	Succession
	Control of access symbols	Use of emotion	Information
		Ceremony and ritual	Organisational structures
		Professional 'mystery'	Appraisal

by other leaders is widely seen. For example, if an initiative driven by one leader requires a certain type of resources if the leader who has control of those resources can withhold them, perhaps by claiming that other priorities must prevail, then that initiative will be delayed or fail.

Control of information, agenda and access are all important political resources, and the phrase 'information is power' is common. This relates to the power to control not only what the organisation does now but also the development of policies for the future. This point was made well by Henry Kissinger when he described the new role that President Nixon and he had agreed for the National Security Council at the beginning of Nixon's first term:

> A President should not leave the presentation of his options to one of the Cabinet departments, or agencies. Since the views of the departments are often in conflict, to place one in charge of presenting the options will be perceived by the others as giving it an unfair advantage. Moreover, the strong inclination of all departments is to narrow the scope for Presidential decision, not to expand it. They are organised to develop a preferred policy, not a range of choices. If forced to present options, the typical department will present two absurd alternatives as straw men bracketing its preferred option – which usually appears in the middle position. A totally ignorant decision-maker could easily satisfy his departments by blindly choosing Option 2 of any three choices which they submit to him. Every department, finally, dreads being overruled by the President, all have, therefore, a high incentive to obscure their differences. (Kissinger, 1979)

The task of the leader in any organisation is multifaceted, and the ability to lead is linked to the ability to exercise power. Thus there is a relationship between leadership, the constructive management of conflict, corporate politics and power. The following concepts from French and Raven (1959) seek to identify the following five social bases of power:

(i)   *Legitimate power*: deriving from the manager's position and therefore formal authority.

(ii) *Expert power*: deriving from the knowledge and experience of the individual (thus a doctor can influence a patient's behaviour because the doctor exerts expert power when giving advice).

(iii) *Referent power*: deriving from the ways in which people identify with others (this often involves a charismatic individual).

(iv) *Reward power*: deriving from the individual's control over rewards such as pay, promotion and task assignments.

(v) *Coercive power*: deriving from the capacity to sanction individual behaviour – but often of use over short periods only.

Thus power is not simply a matter of position, that is, it is more than legitimate power. Leaders appear to vary in their motives and thus exercise power in the different ways outlined above. Power is inherent in any bargaining, negotiation and political process, and the effective use of power is central to effective management and leadership. Kotter (1978) suggests that individuals who make effective use of power are likely to possess the following characteristics:

- Be sensitive to what others consider to be legitimate behaviour, acquiring and using power.
- Have good intuitive understanding of the various types of power and the methods of influence.
- Tend to develop all the types of power to some degree, and use all methods of influence.
- Establish career goals and seek out managerial positions that allow them to develop and use power successfully.
- Use all resources, formal authority and power to develop greater power.
- Engage in power-orientated behaviour in ways that are tempered by maturity and self-control.
- Recognise and accept as a legitimate fact that, in using these methods, they clearly influence other people's behaviour and lives.

8.5 Power and conflict

The exercise of power by leaders is often directly linked to either the avoidance of conflict or the mitigation of conflict when it arises. Conflict is essentially driven by differences – differences in perspective, judgement, opinion that lead to a difference in relation to action – thus conflict is often initiated by the decision-making processes. So within the organisational context it is the conflict over action that can be the most disruptive. Conflict essentially blocks action until it is in some way resolved. Some very short-term conflict may be good as it results in the discussion of a range of opinions or possibilities during the development of those options. This often leads to more effective decision-making by a group than by a single individual. But it can, if entrenched, delay action and lead to ineffective outcomes. Conflict arises around decision-making, so an analysis of decision-making may offer some insight.

Decision-making is often neither a rational nor an orderly process – particularly so in periods of change, characterised as they are by uncertainty and the involvement of emotions. We now know a considerable amount about the process of decision-making – enough to know that a wide range of individual, group and organisational factors can affect the activity (see Janis and Mann, 1976; Hickson *et al.*, 1986). Selective perception, uncertainty, organisational politics and time pressures are only some of these factors. In addition, individual perception, emotional attachments and personal interests also impact on decisions.

Moreover, decisions are not discrete events – they are fluid. A group of people 'decide', but during implementation the decision is often effectively modified, scaled down or delayed to meet the circumstances prevailing at the time. A symptom of this is the frequent 'backtracking' displayed by senior executives on decisions made with colleagues in a meeting which either they didn't fully support despite their agreement, or they have underestimated the resistance they will face. Decisions have both intentional and unintentional consequences. A decision is often part of a wider 'stream of decisions', connected either directly or indirectly, because they are part of the same programme or project, or because implementation influences other things. The McKinsey 7S model illustrates this well.

In any event, leaders can improve their decision-making capability by *choosing the problems to work on*, the battles to fight, when to act and when to wait. They can develop a broad and detailed *knowledge of the organisation, its clients or customers and its people.* They can try to *develop their own self-awareness and influencing skills.* As leaders rarely start from an ideal position of having all the time, resources or information they want to be effective, they must *focus on the manageable, practical and time relevant, and prioritise.* Thus it is crucial to focus on manageable decisions that can be executed in reasonable times and to a reasonable quality. Perfectionism is in effect a delaying tactic, as the perfect outcome or time for action never comes – there is always some reason to delay or seek more data before making the decision. Organisational structures mean leaders cannot be everywhere or do everything – they must rely on others to implement their decisions; that is the whole point of building organisations – specialisation of effort to produce the product that no single individual can produce alone. So this means that leaders must create opportunities to help people develop, improve performance and focus effort on what delivers the best return for that effort.

At more senior levels, where leaders can exert strategic influence they can build an environment where it is more likely that the right decisions will be taken. These relate to:

1 *Set and sustain values.* This creates the framework within which all decisions in the organisation should be taken.

2 *Support problem solving and risk.* If genuine mistakes are punished in any way this creates a fear of failure that will lead to no risks being taken for fear of punishment. This effectively means little or no action will occur, inflexibility will build, management by process will take over, there will be a lack of innovation, change or development; in other words, stagnation. Further, as it will be seen that risk increases with responsibility, no one will be keen to take on more senior roles, with a consequent lack of capable leaders for the future.

3 *Design systems to support action.* The most important thing is to get on and do things; to get action. Action drives new ideas, learning and development. Pilot schemes are always a useful tool to test the approach. Plans, targets and milestones should be clearly defined and consistent with a well-understood longer-term strategy. This should run from both the strategic to the operational level.

Corporate Leadership Council (2004d) data show that if an individual has a line of sight from his or her objectives to those of the organisation, this can increase executive effort by up to 28%

8.6   Blocks to decision-making

Decision-making is a critical leadership capability, not only to deliver objectives but in particular to enable change. And change requires creative solutions to what are generally new problems. There is never any shortage of ideas about how to deal with problems and making decisions. However, finding new and creative solutions through creative decision-making is more difficult. Ideas from Adams (1987) consider some of the blocks to creative problem solving. Understanding the blocks is useful in helping to counter them, to allow creative decision-making that will enable change.

8.6.1   Perceptual blocks

(i)   *Stereotyping*. We make assumptions about things based on what we expect or want to see. Over recent years there has been an increasing awareness of stereotyping, and this cannot apply only to people but also to situations. We sometimes assume that situations are similar when in fact they are not, leading to the wrong outcome from decision-making.

(ii)   *Difficulty in defining the real problem*. A team of consultant designers was briefed to design an apple-picking machine. A number of solutions was put forward, but none seemed feasible – in general, all the machines were too big and unwieldy. It was a month before a team member said: 'Our problem is that we are focusing on the wrong problem – we should look at the design of the tree.' Eventually, a new strain of apple trees only a few feet high was created. The problem of designing the machine then disappeared. The height and spread of apple trees had finally been seen as the problem, not the design of an apple-picking machine as such.

(iii)   *Tendency to look at the problem area too closely*. All too often we define problems very narrowly, which leaves people looking at, in effect, only part of the circumstances that led to the situation. Again here, the issue becomes one of not dealing with the whole problem, just part of it.

(iv)   *Inability to see problems from other perspectives*. There is evidence of 'trained incapacity', or seeing problems through the lens of professional training. This seems to apply across a range of professionals, such as doctors, lawyers, accountants and engineers. Obviously, seeing problems from different viewpoints is likely to result in more possible solutions and a greater opportunity for consensus – this is why mentoring is such an effective developmental activity: it provides a new perspective for individuals to contemplate what they might previously not have considered.

(v)   *Saturation and irrelevance*. Data may come in large quantities, or in large quantities only occasionally, or arrive accompanied by irrelevant and distracting data. It can be difficult to distinguish the relevant information from all the available data.

(vii) *Failure to use all sensory inputs.* We need all the data we can get, but do we really use everything that is available to us? Thus, when trying to decide on a new organisational structure for a new venture, we should try to find other organisations facing similar problems. How have they solved them? What evidence can be found from external sources with easy access – for example, the internet?

8.6.2 Emotional blocks

(i) *Fear of taking a risk.* In some organisations, because of the organisational culture there is a considerable fear of making a mistake, potentially as a result of the sanctions taken against those who have made even small, genuine mistakes. The result is that people either try not to make a decision, or go for the safest outcome if they have to.

(ii) *Incapacity to tolerate ambiguity.* The solution of a complex problem is a messy process. The data will be misleading, incomplete, full of opinions, values and so on. While creating solutions, plans and so on requires that we eventually establish order, attempting to do so too early may mean that we overlook promising ideas. This is the 'jumping to early conclusions' problem.

(iii) *A preference for judging rather than generating ideas.* Judging ideas too soon can lead to early rejection. The onus of proof is all too easily placed on the person who suggested the idea. Yet if the idea is novel it may be ill thought out at such an early state, and may not present a good 'fit' with the hazy and incomplete data at that time. Thus rejection is easy. We should recognise that finding reasons to say 'no' is easier than finding reasons to say 'yes' – particularly if we are poor risk takers who are intolerant of ambiguity!

(iv) *Inability to incubate.* An unwillingness to 'sleep on the problem', often because there seems to be pressure for solutions: 'We must have a new pricing policy because the sales department is pressing for one.' In planning the process of managing change, we should allow enough time for ideas to incubate.

8.6.3 Cultural blocks

(i) *Taboos.* Issues that cannot be discussed and therefore cannot be faced are taboo. For example, at some engineering companies it is impossible openly to challenge the continued relevance of existing expertise.

(ii) *Focus rather than fantasy.* Adams (1987) makes the point forcefully that psychologists have concluded that children are more creative than adults. This might be explained by adults being more aware of practical constraints; however, as Adams says, 'another explanation, which I believe, is that our culture trains mental playfulness, fantasy and reflectiveness out of people by placing more stress on the value of channelled mental activities'. Certainly there is now evidence that creativity is, for some people, trained out by formalised education.

(iii) *Problem solving is a serious business.* Linked to item (ii) is the notion that humour has no place in problem solving. And yet humour is often based on the process of associating apparently unrelated ideas. Creativity is similar, in that it often involves the association of unrelated ideas or structures. Adams argues, therefore, that humour is an essential ingredient for effective problem solving.

(iv)   *Reason and intuition.* It is apparently often believed that reason, logic and numbers are good, and that feelings, intuition and pleasure are bad. Adams suggests that this is based on our West European Puritan heritage and our technology-based culture. This raises the question of how this point applies in cultures without a Puritan heritage. This has been complicated by the tendency to assign these characteristics to gender, namely, that men are logical, physical, tough and pragmatic, while women are sensitive, emotional and intuitive. Creativity demands a balance of these characteristics.

(v)   *Tradition and change.* Traditions are hard to overcome, particularly when people do not reflect on their traditions and their present problems/dilemmas at the same time. We need tradition –much of our personal commitment and motivation is based on our traditions. We need to respect tradition but we also need to recognise the need for change. Adams distinguishes primary and secondary creativity: primary creativity generates the structures and concepts that allow the solution of a family of problems; while secondary creativity deploys these structures and concepts to develop and improve a particular solution. He argues that primary creativity demands more intuition, humour, feeling and emotion, while secondary creativity seems more likely to be associated with logic and reason – as the structures already established are deployed systematically to solve specific problems within a new and well understood field. Secondary creativity involves applying rules, but primary creativity requires that existing rules be ignored, to enable new rules to be generated.

8.6.4   Environmental blocks

(i)   *Lack of support.* We have already seen that a non-supportive environment is not conducive to innovation, nor to creative problem solving. Change is often seen as threatening, and new ideas are easily destroyed, by ignoring them, by laughing at them, or by over-analysing them too early.

(ii)   *Not accepting and incorporating criticism.* Those with good ideas can create blocks, too, by not being willing to accept criticism. The ability to accept criticism builds an atmosphere of trust and support, and leads to improvements in the final outcome.

(iii)   *Bosses who know the answer.* Many managers are successful because they have ideas and can push them through. But only if such a manager will listen to subordinates will he or she be able to maximise his/her creativity. Group creativity is nearly always better than individual creativity, so long as the individuals involved have sufficient knowledge of the issue being discussed.

8.6.5   Cognitive blocks

(i)   *Using incorrect language.* Whether mathematical or professional (for example, accounting, marketing, HR and so on) or visual. Using inappropriate language can hinder creativity in problem solving – and this includes using technical language or jargon that other groups of people won't understand.

(ii) *Inflexible use of strategies.* There are many strategies available; they are often used unconsciously, but not necessarily to best effect in problem solving, perhaps because of the various blocks we have already discussed.

(iii) *Lack of the correct information.* This is clearly a limiting factor. But again balance is needed. Information makes you an expert, which can mean that you think within the lines of that expertise, possibly closing you off from creative solutions. Further, the issue of waiting for all the information to be available before making a decision – procrastination – is another problem.

8.7   Working through the blocks

Adams (1987) describes this as 'block busting'. Various techniques are available. Here we need to do no more than list one or two very briefly. More details can be found by referring to Adams' own account. Identifying the blocks in the first place makes dealing with them subsequently much easier! A questioning attitude is therefore very effective. Further, various thinking aids can also be applied, including attribute listing, 'checklists' and list making. Being able to 'suspend judgement' as an individual or in a group can also enhance creativity. Another useful technique is 'synectics' (Gordon, 1961). The following actions seem to encourage creativity in problem solving:

- Stay loose or fluid in your thinking until rigour is vital.
- Protect new ideas from criticism.
- Acknowledge good ideas, listen, show approval.
- Eliminate status or rank.
- Be optimistic.
- Support confusion and uncertainty.
- Value learning from mistakes.
- Focus on the good aspects of an idea.
- Share the risks.
- Suspend disbelief.
- Build on ideas.
- Do not evaluate too early.

The following actions seem to discourage creativity:

- Interrupt, criticise.
- Be competitive.
- Mock people.
- Be dominant.
- Disagree, argue, challenge.
- Be pessimistic.
- Point out flaws.
- Inattention, do not listen, use silence against people.

- React negatively.
- Insist on 'the facts'.
- Give no feedback, act in a noncommittal fashion.
- Pull rank.
- Become angry.
- Be distant.

Still more limits or 'blocks' can be listed. At the individual level people may engage in 'satisficing' or 'incrementalism': accepting satisfactory solutions and/or making only incremental or limited changes to previous policies. At the group level, we have 'groupthink' and 'risky shift'. 'Groupthink' is characterised by complacency and a lack of critical evaluation of ideas (Janis, 1972). 'Risky shift' is a condition observed in experimental groups, where groups seem likely to take more risky decisions than the individuals involved might have wished, because of a diffusion of responsibility, perhaps, but still without critical examination.

At the organisational level, various typical responses can be identified. Some we have already seen. People seem to 'distance' themselves from problems. Where organisations are highly centralised, responsible managers may be 'out of touch'. An 'illusion of reliability' can prevail in existing techniques or among people, the assumption being that 'we are the best so we must be right' The Greeks had a word for this – *hubris* – meaning overbearing arrogance. Highly specialised organisations can lead to parochialism, the tendency to conceal dissent or disagreement, and to problems of communication (Wilensky, 1967). Solutions to all these limits to thinking involve opening up the problem-solving process, being willing to change and allowing the 'block busters' to operate. The ideas are clearly there, among the people in the organisation – the challenge is to encourage them, to help them find expression, then to evaluate realistically, to apply, learn from experience and then to change.

In essence, the various counterproductive norms focus decision-makers' attention on the simple issues, often the things that can be measured quantitatively, rather than the crucial issues – frequently the blockages to change and improvement. This reinforces a risk-averse culture leading to people 'covering up' mistakes, for example. In what some would call the 'virtuous circle' of change successful experience of change reduces anxiety, lessens resistance, encourages measured risk taking and leads to more change. This is positive, but the challenge is how to avoid the counterproductive and encourage the productive behaviours.

Janis (1989, pp. 235–64) presents a range of ways in which these counterproductive dynamics can be avoided. His advice includes ways of maintaining scepticism about the 'obvious' solution as well as of limiting criticism of 'wild' suggestions. In particular, he argues for a willingness to make 'temporary' arrangements with other groups in order to buy time. Admittedly, his focus, and therefore his examples, deal with national-level policy development, but there are equivalents in the organisational area – for example, in the context of mergers and acquisitions, where joint ventures are involved, and in difficult technological change situations. Basically, the approach Janis favours is to take any and all measures likely to lead to a more systematic approach to planning, decision-making and implementation. Some of his recommendations relate to leadership style and some to the structure of decision-making, but all are designed to create or facilitate this more systematic approach.

8.8   Organisations, decision-making and rationality

We often assume that what happens in organisations is logical and rational. Leaders weigh the options and come up with the best solution for the organisation – or that is the assumption. The problem is that we all know that this is not always a true reflection of reality, where both decisions and behaviour sometimes seem to fail to conform to any rational rules. Is what happens within our organisations always rational, and do we believe that effective organisations are 'rational' organisations? Are organisations designed and managed on rational lines? Can the thorough application of a systematic approach to change planning and implementation lead to a 'rational', perhaps 'optimal', result rather than the ad hoc actions driven by events that we often see? It all depends on our definition of rationality.

As an example, the idea of 'clinical' rationality is often seen as dominant within health care systems. Here the decisions of doctors govern the pattern of care provided to patients and the use of resources which take a consistent approach to treatment that is driven by experience and established process. This does not mean that all doctors have the same views, beliefs or attitudes, or that they would argue for the same vision of health care. People are not automata, without autonomy or freedom of action.

So at the outset we must make clear that our definition of rationality owes nothing to the concept of scientific method, where a process is either rational and conforms to pattern, or irrational and does not. From the organisational rationality perspective there is no simple division between rationality and irrationality, the former based on 'science' – that is, established process and logic – and the latter on emotion, feelings and personal perspective. In the dynamic of a changing environment – for example, a budget cut or the advent of a new technology – people will reflect on the consequences of the change, developing new responses and decisions based on reason. People develop a framework of reason based on knowledge and experience. Herein lies both its success and weakness, however – that the framework of each individual is different and perception of even the same past events may also be different. These then emerge through the processes of thought, emotion, action and decision-making into the 'real world' of the organisation. This suggests that there are various 'sources of rationality', which lead to men and women to construct different perceptions, different arguments about, and drawing different conclusions in respect of, the changes that affect them.

Any definition of rationality must allow for the differences in perception, uncertainties, vested interests and a multitude of other factors that influence us in the world in which we live. Weick (1979, p. 98) summarises the position succinctly: 'Rationality is best understood in the eye of the beholder. It is his aims and how consciously he sets out to accomplish them that constitute the clearest, most easily specified component of rationality.' Weick supports our view, and that we all see, day-to-day, that people in large organisations are unlikely to employ the same rationality; rather 'organisations will have several different and contradictory rationalities'. Herein lies the reason why many of us find that discussion about the problems an organisation faces can reveal many different perspectives and even seem to be, at least initially, confused and confusing. Thus often, before decision-making can even start, a common framework and language for looking at the problem needs to be established.

The literature abounds with theories of decision making ('garbage-can model': March and Olsen (1976); 'satisficing': Simon (1957); and 'incrementalism': Lindblom (1959)), which reflect this general problem faced by organisations at different times and in different ways. Bryman (1983) suggests that there has been a 'retreat from rationality' as a consequence of attacks on the rational systems model of organisation. The first, exemplified by Weber's writing on bureaucracy and by the classical school (see March and Simon, 1993), takes the view of organisations as goal-seeking, functional systems operating in a closed system. In recent years, the second – the development of the 'contingency' approach – viewed organisations as having the same basic objectives and systems of operation, but taking an open system approach. This open system view (Scott, 1981) has been subjected to critical scrutiny from at least four directions: the 'garbage-can' model, institutional, political and Marxist approaches. Bryman (1983) concluded that scholars in the fields of management theory and economics are now uneasy about their 'rationalist infrastructures'. Such approaches assume rationality, placing particular emphasis on notions such as utility and profit maximisation, taken from economics. But more recently many others, such as many leaders operating in organisations day-to-day have started to ask themselves 'How rational are our organisations in reality, given what happens in them and some of the decisions taken?'

Bryman (1983) noted that this is an extreme form of rationality, and then went on to discuss 'soft' rationality, incorporating ideas such as Simon's (1957) notion of 'satisficing' and Watkin's (1970) discussion of 'imperfect rationality'. He concluded his discussion by noting the methodological and conceptual weaknesses of the alternative views of rationality presented, and of alternative models such as the political or Marxist approach. For example, when Bryman discussed one empirical study by Bowers (1970) of the capital investment process, which found the economists' version of rationality to be of little empirical use, he concluded that *purposiveness* had greater usefulness. Here lie reasons for hope, he seemed to suggest.

Landes (1967, p. 204) provides us with a clear definition, based on the idea of purposiveness:

> Rationality may be defined as the adaption of means to ends. It is the antithesis of superstition and magic. For this history, the relevant ends are the production and acquisition of material wealth. It goes without saying that these are not man's highest ends; and that rationality is not confined to the economic sphere.

So rationality is a way of doing things: the application of the principles of rationalism to action, rationalism being defined as the doctrine that the universe of perception and experience can be understood in terms of thought or reason, as against emotion, intuition or extrasensory modes of apprehension.

Within organisations, leaders are likely to adopt the 'means to an end' definition of rationality; however, we depart from Landes' equation of rationality and the doctrine of rationalism. We need to recognise the limitations of this in respect of real behaviour in real organisations. We cannot pretend that men and women do not use intuition as well as empiricism. Some may use one or the other to a lesser or greater extent, but to assume that people operate purely on the empirical does not bear examination. Weick's (1969) position on this point is probably more realistic and therefore of value in dealing with organisations and leaders in decision-making.

Returning to organisational politics, the notion that political models of organisation represent an attack on rational models of the organisation needs to be considered. To recap our position here, we are saying that the ways in which leaders make decisions in organisations is critical; we are asking about the degree to which those decisions are taken on the basis of commonly held rational analysis; individual rational analysis that may be different between individuals but still essentially rational; or some element of irrational analysis based on political or emotional drivers; or a combination of all of the above. In understanding the balance between these and how culture impacts on the ultimate mix, we hope to understand how decisions are made, and how change is achieved, so that we can fine-tune the way things are done to improve future outcomes.

Close examination of alternative modes of decision-making proposed by Pfeffer (1981) makes this point clear. He compares rational, bureaucratic decision process/organised anarchy and political power models. For *rational* decision-making the ideology is seen as being 'efficiency and effectiveness'; while for *political power*, the ideology is 'struggle, conflict, winners and losers'. Decisions from the former flow from 'value maximising choice', and from the latter from the result of 'bargaining and interplay among interests', but this is hardly a satisfactory distinction. The question is: what is it that the 'interests' bargain over?

Definitions of appropriate action, policies, means/ends sequences and strategies will form the basis of any answer to this question. By working on the principle that the political power model demands the analysis of various interests, we immediately adopt a rational model – by virtue of the analysis of the interests themselves. Thus this model differs from the rational model only in that the proponents of the rational model are seen to model choice in essentially unproblematical terms. But Bryman (1983) makes it entirely clear that only proponents of the 'hard' version of rationality could be accused of that. Thus the apparent difference collapses in all but the most extreme of juxtapositions. We conclude that the extreme or 'hard' definition has never had much application for those concerned with the management of organisations. But it is worth noting the growing number of studies examining the work of F. W. Taylor, which cast doubt on whether Taylor, for one, ever believed in such a straightforward view – see Rose (1975) and Merkle (1980).

However, by distinguishing 'hard' and 'soft' rationalities, Bryman seems tacitly to admit that the latter is not properly 'rational'. Here he appears to be following Landes, equating rationality with rationalism. To do so is to adopt too limited a view of rationality. The concept of multiple rationalities does not imply a 'softer or weaker' view. Poorly understood it might be, but we believe it is possible to establish, empirically, rationalities in use.

People in organisations attempt to make sense of the confusion they see around them as they experience it, and to do this they employ a particular rationality, so to understand their perspective we must understand the rationality behind it. In other words, the very simple concept of 'understanding where the other person is coming from'. This concept is very simple in principle but very difficult to get right in practice. On the surface, at the individual level, by asking the individual to explain his or her views and by asking open questions we can dig down and discover some of the answers – indeed, this is the basis of the mentoring process. However, this may not reveal some of the other factors that influence the person's view and of which they may be unaware – emotional bias and subconscious programming. However, at least it is a start. But as an overall principle, if we are to understand the variations in perspective, often of the same events or problems, we need to find, through open discussion, the underlying rationalities. Once these are out in the open they can be integrated into a common framework for moving forward to an agreed decision.

Rationalities are not fixed in time. They change as a dynamic response to environmental, group or individual changes. Such changes would represent a watershed in the 'life' of the organisation, team or individual. These moments happen for all these groups, in particular during periods of substantial upheaval – this has been seen in the response of both individual leaders and organisations as a result of the world financial crisis in 2006–10. Some organisations failed, some changed dramatically to enter the 'new world' that had been created, some previously successful leaders were unable to adjust and thus failed, while others not seen as the best before the crisis were seen to flourish after it ended. Leadership behaviour and organisational behaviour changed as the rationalities altered, driven by the new environment.

With so many possibilities and a dynamic situation, how do we understand and take action for the benefit of both leaders and organisations going forward? We need to identify the frames of reference that explain the choices and decisions of people within a given organisation and time frame. This is, in principle, not a difficult activity; for example, the study of past events, whether historical or business case studies, is only effective when one understand the perspectives and thus rationalities and subsequent decisions of those involved – whether that is Lord Nelson at the battle of Trafalgar or the merger of Glaxo and SmithKline in 2000, say. An individual's or organisation's particular 'rationality' comprises the 'rules of action' that are deemed suitable for given circumstances. Thus to find the answer we need to observe the choices that people make, and the reasons they give for making those choices over long periods of time, examining many of the decisions in order to establish a pattern that indicates the 'rules of action' and 'frames of reference' in use. Using a similar example, the previous approaches to different battles used by Lord Nelson show a set of common 'rules of action' developing based on his rationalities. Similar patterns can sometimes be seen in organisational behaviour over a period of time.

Important consequences flow from the existence of alternative sources of rationality within groups of people and organisations, such that there is then no common framework to identify vision or objectives and take decisions as circumstances change. So for each individual or group, the apparently rational strategy for 'getting things done', for deciding on action, for enabling employees to perform at their best, or other things, has counter-rational consequences associated with it when viewed from the perspective of others.

It must be stressed that by counter-rational we do not mean irrational or emotional. What may be seen as rational by one person maybe viewed as counter-rational by another, but they would not accuse the other person of being emotional or irrational, just that they are looking from a different perspective. So counter-rational behaviour may be highly rational from the viewpoint of the individuals concerned, given their situation, the power and resources, objectives and politics, and so on. By counter-rational we simply mean based on different sources of rationality.

Argyris (1982) provides us with a good example of this situation. A group of senior university administrators attending an executive course were examining a case study on a particular college that included a set of recommendations for the future of that college, produced by a working group of senior academics and administrators from within the organisation. The college working group had been asked for 'concrete recommendations' for action.

The executive course members were asked to evaluate the recommendations made by the college's working group. When doing so they criticised the recommendations, expressing the view that they were vague and cliché-ridden, the typical output of a committee that had not been well briefed. It is interesting that such an evaluation of working groups, working parties or committees is not uncommon. Argyris suggests that this is based on several assumptions about organisation and management, linked to rationalities:

(i)   The first assumption is that by giving people specific goals it will lead them to make decisions and undertake actions that are more relevant and specific to the prevailing situation – in this case, to make review recommendations.

(ii) The second assumption is that goals will motivate people or, if not, will at least make it easier to confront them on their performance.

(iii) It is assumed that effective control of performance requires the objective monitoring of performance.

Underlying these organisational and leadership assumptions as set out by Argyris is the fear that people will not do what the organisation or the leader wants them to, or not to the standard they require, without rules, regulations, systematic procedures, objective performance monitoring and control as the basis for order. In other words, unless a compliance control and measurement system is in place, people will not do what they are asked.

However, this implies a belief that rules, systems, monitoring and control are not themselves obstacles to progress that make it harder to 'get things done' and are thus actually self-defeating. But we know this to be false, as from experience we often see systems that are counterproductive to the outcome they seek. We think of bureaucracy, 'red tape', over-complexity, measuring things for the sake of it and other well-known organisational issues associated with self-defeating control systems. So the 'imposition' of systems to drive rationality to enhance output can in reality degrade it.

For example, appraisal systems in organisations often fall into this category. The aim of the system is to measure effectively the performance of employees in order to assess pay, promotion, development needs and other things the organisation needs to know. The systems are designed mainly by experts in HR who are familiar with the technical principles, and in designing the system they seek to obtain the most accurate possible answer. To do this they try to measure a large number of variables relating to the performance of individuals. This is then turned into a form for line managers to complete when they appraise staff. The only problem is that the line managers are not technical experts in this field, so often they do not understand the principles behind it or the reasons for some of the questions. The managers often vary their interpretation of the measurement criteria, and the number of questions the experts want answered is so great, perhaps up to 40 questions per person, so the line manager rushes to complete the appraisal. The result in many organisations is that appraisals are either not completed at all, are partially completed, or completed using rushed and inaccurate data. Thus an attempt to create a process that seeks to deliver the most accurate answer fails by virtue of its complexity to achieve that end, and the real quality of the outcome is poor. Evidence suggests that using less accurate but simpler systems actually provides better results because the system is being used in practice by more people, with better completion levels and greater accuracy, thus the less accurate system is actually more effective.

Here we refer to what R. K. Merton (1940) called the 'dysfunctional' consequences of bureaucracy, and what March and Simon (1958) referred to as the 'unintended consequences'. For Merton, a bureaucratic structure exerts constant demands on officials to be methodical and disciplined. To operate successfully there must be reliability, conformity and discipline. However, adherence to the rules, originally conceived as a means, becomes transformed into an end:

> Discipline, readily interpreted as conformance with regulations, whatever the situation, is seen not as a measure designed for specific purposes but becomes an immediate value in the life-organisation of the bureaucrat. This emphasis, resulting from the displacement of the original goals, develops into rigidities and an inability to adjust readily. Formalism, even ritualism, ensues with an unchallenged insistence upon punctilious adherence to formalised procedures. (Merton, 1940, p. 16)

Thus over-conformity to the rules in practice actually obstructs the purposes of the organisation. This is known to us, familiarly, as 'red tape'.

If we look again at the example given above of the executive courses reviewing the recommendations of the college administrators and faculty, how did Argyris explain the apparent paradox? The original diagnosis by the executive course was that the working-party recommendations were vague and unusable, and that more specific goals and directions combined with methods of monitoring and controlling performance would overcome this difficulty. However, should, in reality, such a strategy be implemented, the members of the working party might feel mistrusted and constrained, and the very creation of more specific goals would in itself be counter-productive as effectively it determines the outcome before the debate has taken place.

In any event, Argyris (1985) pointed out that faculty members and administrators within a college are likely to have different objectives and rationalities, and will potentially not work together effectively on critical issues. Thus for a successful outcome there is a need for integration between the two groups, the members of which are trained in different ways, work to different rules, with different methods and styles, and are likely to emphasis different views of the college. There are likely to be advantages in keeping goals vague. Specific goals could be interpreted as being limiting, not allowing creativity and perhaps resulting in emotional reactions that inhibit performance. Thus actions that appear to be rational, such as setting specific goals, may lead people to produce counter-rational consequences. This confirms a process similar to our appraisal example – the creation of self-defeating systems – maybe summarised by the well-known saying, 'the road to hell is paved with good intentions'.

Argyris suggests that these counter-rational consequences can emerge in three ways:

(i)   First, if individuals do not feel any personal responsibility for causing the problem they may not see it as their responsibility to solve it. So they may distance themselves from the difficulty.

(ii) Second, in situations where there are very difficult issues to discuss: for example, people may be worried about the future, motivation may be falling, people feel mistrusted, and people to find these issues difficult to talk about openly even if they know they exist. According to Argyris, this can get to the level that 'counter-rational' behaviour is so difficult to discuss that all agree that the issue is 'taboo'; the classic 'elephant in the room' scenario.

(iii) Third, people may prefer counterproductive advice: that is, advice that reinforces the counter-rational behaviour. For example, in the example we examined above, the executive course members suggested that the college president should play a game of deception to save face for himself and the faculty, and to keep his options open. They proposed that he accept the report, and thank the working party, but at the same time arrange for a new committee, or implement specific actions. Such behaviour would, of course, reinforce the difficulty of discussing any problem, and the distance the working-party members create for themselves from the issues being discussed. This is clearly an action aimed at avoiding making explicit the issues and/or the working party's difficulties in producing a good outcome. Thus everyone comes out of it looking as if they have done as much as they could, even though no effective solution has been delivered. This is a classic demonstration of what happens in organisations sometimes.

Forrester (1969) discussed this problem when he referred to the 'counterintuitive' behaviour of complex systems linked to people; for example, urban systems or large corporations. He stated that people in general have been 'conditioned almost exclusively by experience with first-order, negative-feedback loops which are goal-seeking and contain a single important variable'. In other words, primarily we seek to obtain a specific result from what we do, and draw the conclusion that if we cannot do so then the cause of that problem must be closely related in space and time to what we wanted to do. He argued that complex systems appear to be the same; that is, they appear to present cause and effect close in time and space. However, causes of a problem may not be as simple as we think; they maybe more complex, and/or may actually lie in some remote part of the system of which we are unaware, or perhaps be caused by something in the distant past, and not close to the event we witnessed. What appears to be cause and effect may actually be 'coincidental' symptoms.

This is a frequent problem in organisations, where symptoms are confused with cause, and a number of problems-solving tools seek to address this, the most basic being the use of the 'so what?' question to dig down or back from result and symptom to cause. We can easily find examples in most organisations – here is one in an organisation where such junior staff were complaining that they were not receiving the development from their managers that they expected. A survey in the organisation by the leadership institute, Roffey Park (Roffey Park, 2008), found that about 75 per cent of respondents thought this to be the case, and the conclusion was that the line managers did a bad job at that time in developing people's skills. But more than 80 per cent of line managers said that they were developing people. The conclusion to be drawn from this is that there are different rationalities involved here, and there must be a difference between what the line managers were delivering as development and what those receiving it thought they should be getting.

When line managers were questioned, they said that they were sending people regularly on development programmes. However, the junior staff said they didn't want that – they wanted to be developed by their manager on the job. But no one had told the line managers that this was what they wanted – and the junior staff either assumed that the managers knew it, and the juniors didn't want to complain that they weren't getting what they needed. Also no one had told the line managers that development on the job was specifically part of their work. Further, few had had their own skills developed to enable them to do this. This situation had been going on for years, and it was assumed by senior management that development was happening, as no one had complained until the survey discovered that it wasn't. No junior staff had complained as they didn't know what they should have been getting, and they didn't want to complain even if they suspected it, and line managers didn't know they were supposed to be giving it, and didn't actually know what 'it' was. Senior management assumed silence was good rather than bad. So the problem, even when identified initially, was thought to be caused by bad line managers at that time when in fact it was a long-term legacy issue related to clarity on line manager responsibility and training, together with the briefing of junior staff.

Action to dispel symptoms in a complex system will often leave the underlying causes untouched, as is seen in the initial assumptions made above. Forrester (1969) claims that intuitive solutions to the problems of complex systems will be wrong most of the time. He also suggests that change programmes will often have an effect that is less than originally anticipated because they tend to displace existing internal processes.

Pressman and Wildavsky (1973) describe a programme aimed at developing employment opportunities for ethnic minority groups in Oakland, California. The federal government committed US$28 million to the project during a four-year period, with little result as far as the aims of the project were concerned. Their evidence suggested that the majority of the benefits derived from the programme went to people other than members of the ethnic minority groups. We do not need to interpret this as failure, but rather as an example of counterintuitive behaviour.

People in organisations, whether representing themselves or their groups, tend to advocate views and positions with a degree of certainty that discourages further enquiry. Moreover, they tend to act in ways that inhibit the expression of negative feelings. There is often a lack of clarity between 'constructive feedback' and 'criticism for its own sake'. In many environments there is a desire not to upset others, even if only for the reason that you don't want the same to be done to you in the future if you make comments about others' work, views or rationalities.

Sometimes we offer presentations in such a way as to emphasise that there is nothing new or radical in a set of proposals. People appear to design their behaviour to appear rational, and the more skilled even manage to make the emotionally and irrationally driven seem eminently rational! The power of the human mind is amazing in creating perverse logic to justify actions. Thus individuals focus on what they argue to be necessary and attainable goals, realistic means and clear objectives. All this is to suppress issues that might upset other people. Moreover, people tend to control meetings to maximise winning, minimise losing (at least in the short term), minimise the expression of negative feelings, and keep others rational. Following Argyris (1982), we summarise these ideas in Table 8.2.

Table 8.2	Ineffectiveness/effectiveness patterns

	Behaviour	Response	Outcome
Drivers of ineffectiveness	Not defining goals	Confusion and unfocused outcomes	Limited testing
	Maximising 'winning' and minimising losing	People become defensive, inconsistent, feel vulnerable, act in manipulative ways, mistrustful, lack risk taking or take very high risks, withhold information, adopt power-centred behaviour	Issues not discussable
	Minimising the expression of feelings		'Distance' themselves from issues
	Appearing always to be 'rational'		
Drivers of effectiveness	Depend on people	Builds confidence, 'self-esteem'	Effective testing
	Allow tasks to be jointly controlled	Creates learning and trust – team spirit	Informed choice
	Make the protection of feelings a joint responsibility	Leads to less defensive relationship and group dynamics	Internal commitment
	Discuss issues, performance and problems, not people	Open confrontation of issues, open discussion of positions and rationalities	Creation of consensus framework to move forward

Source: Argyris (1982).

All this can have important consequences. People attempt to 'distance' themselves from critical issues and events or norms as 'undiscussable' and to offer advice which, while ostensibly aimed at increasing rationality, actually inhibits it. All this blocks the production of valid information for diagnosis and decision-making. Yet these behaviours are most prevalent just when valid information and discussion are needed – when people are dealing with difficult and threatening problems. In other words, as the pressures of change increase the likelihood of defensive behaviour increases, which in turn reduce the ability to manage the change. This is why successful change is so difficult – you need people to behave in a way that is opposite to the one they naturally feel they want to do – to open up and share rather than to close down and keep quiet.

Argyris (1985) suggests that we are dealing with a powerful set of individual, group, organisational and cultural forces that are mutually reinforcing. As these forces are multiple and driven by a range of different factors, they naturally create contradictions. Yet these contradictions can be identified, resolved and action taken to deliver success. But this will be based on routine performance, on stability, which can mean that people do not feel it necessary to pay attention to the deeper issues until the impact of these contradictions becomes so powerful that the stability itself is under threat. Now the organisation is seen to be in a crisis. Drastic action is possible; 'turnaround' becomes the objective. These factors will all influence the process diagnosing the need for change. In essence, therefore, we need to deal with the 'blockages' before we can identify, let alone make progress towards, the organisational changes that are needed.

Sadly, as Argyris makes clear, people can become highly skilled at maintaining these patterns of ineffectiveness because it seems, from their perspective, to protect them when in fact it is making their situation worse. Argyris calls this 'skilled incompetence' (see Argyris, 1990). He demonstrates the relevance of this to major programmes of change by reference to a study of six large US corporations which had invested heavily in change programmes which had not worked, in which the authors found the following evidence:

- Inflexible rules and procedures.
- Managers not understanding customer needs.
- Managers not committed to, or skilled in handling, change.
- Inter-group problems.
- Poor communication.
- Lack of strategic thinking.
- Top managers evidently believing that declining revenue was only temporary.
- Low levels of trust. (Beer *et al.*, 1988)

Here we have the classic 'blockages' to change restated. Argyris goes on to argue that characteristic solutions to these problems seem purposely to avoid the problem, by self-defeating tinkering with symptoms rather than addressing the real issues. A structural solution will not deal with the real issues, nor will a solution that emphasises a clearer definition of roles and 'better' communication, because neither deals with the causes. His main idea to deal with such problems is to get those involved to 'map' how decisions are actually made as a means of recognising their own 'skilled incompetence' – that is, spotting the errors in the process that led to the problem. He refers to work by Putnam and Thomas (1988) on a performance-related pay system which was ineffective because too many people received high ratings. A common problem in organisations today – caused by line managers not wanting to have difficult and honest conversations with individuals about their performance and rather taking the easy option by making the below average into the average, the average into good, and the good into very good. At the core of which is likely to be differences, perceptions and rationalities that they wish to avoid discussing.

The problem is that if this happens over a period of years all the ratings 'creep' – for example, one international bank had, in one area, 70 per cent of people classified as good or very good over two years but had falling profits for the same period. In response, the CEO dictated that there had to be a specific justification to the next level of management for individuals to be graded higher than 'competent' into 'good' or 'very good'. Thus, for the line manager, the difficult conversation with the individual, if not held, would be replaced by a difficult conversation with their own boss. Not surprisingly, most opted for the conversation with the individual.

There is a further element that needs to be considered between the rational and emotional sides of how people respond. There is a clear emotional component to responses to change, decision-making and personal performance. In its research, the Corporate Leadership Council found that an employee's decision to give a higher commitment was 57 per cent rational and 43 per cent emotional (CLC,

2004c). In terms of the elements that drive this, the results showed the maximum potential impact on commitment of excellence in each area. Of the rational element, a good team could raise commitment by 26 per cent, a good manager by 36 per cent, and a good organisation by 22 per cent. Of the emotional element, a good job could raise commitment by 34 per cent, a good team by 47 per cent, a good manager by 73 per cent, and a good organisation 37 per cent. However, the results showed that the rational element is the foundation as this can increase emotional commitment by up to 57 per cent, effort by up to 26 per cent, and retention by 36 per cent. A negative rational element will override positive emotional one. Similar figures apply to retention.

Above all, this shows that there is an emotional element to the ways that people behave, and that leaders must take this into account to be effective. This also stressed the importance of the individual's immediate leader, as, of the total factors, nearly 80 per cent was influenced directly by actions taken by the line manager.

8.9   Summary

In this chapter we have examined ideas relating to corporate culture, politics, power and perception. This is underpinned by some of the organisational dynamics based on the complexity of behaviour, and in particular, rational behaviour. We have shown how these ideas help us to understand some of the challenges faced by leaders as a result of the context in which they work (for example, the corporate culture) and/or, at least in part, those as a result of their own behaviour and that of others, relating to rationalities, emotional responses and the difficulties in analysing problems in the real dynamic world of organisations. This shows how complex many organisational decisions are, and how imperfect can be the processes we often use to get our answers.

So the focus of this chapter on culture, politics and power has dealt with what many conceive to be the 'dark side' of organisations, a part that cannot easily be analysed, identified or 'pinned down'. Thus, while traditional logic-based analysis gives us some part of the decision picture it is only part of that picture, and the fuzzier elements, made up of perception, power and politics, cannot be ignored even if they are difficult to deal with. Actually, much of what happens in organisations is examined more effectively within a framework devoting more attention to these areas. Further, as power and politics are more appropriate to understanding how choices are made and framed, and link to legitimacy overall, culture models seem to provide a more useful form of framework to get to grips with what happens day-to-day in organisations. This therefore emphasises the need for approaches to leadership that focus on the way management is practised in the organisation. Moreover, the need to position such efforts within the real organisational context is obvious enough. These also need to take into account that despite the fact we do not like the idea, emotions do play a part and these must be dealt with and leveraged, just as with the rational elements. Only by working in this way, grounded in reality, can we hope to make progress.

Questions

1   What does 'organisational culture' mean to you, and how does it impact on your actions and behaviour in the real world?

2   Do organisations have one culture, or many?

3   What is the impact of politics in organisations? Is it always negative?

4   Do perceptions matter more than reality?

5   How often have you seen observation leading to incorrect inference and perception? Why does this happen?

6   Do you think decision-making by leaders could be better, given inherent bias? How could that be achieved?

7   What is the key driver of leaders' decision-making and organisational culture: the common good or individual self-interest?

9 Knowledge as a leadership resource

9.1 Leading change by leveraging knowledge

The global organisational environment is changing faster than ever. We are living in an era when organisations constantly need to reshape their ideas merely to survive. But to achieve sustained success it is not sufficient merely to manage existing operations in a better way: organisations need to do things radically differently to secure an advantage over their competitors in a world where replication of product and process it relatively simple. Thus, in the future, organisations need to focus more on re-engineering markets rather than on re-engineering processes, and not on restructuring the organisation but on transforming it. Increasingly, this is undertaken co-operatively, working with partners and customers to develop new forms of market intelligence. This requires co-ordinated leadership and that in itself provides a competitive advantage, because while process and product are becoming easier to replicate, it is difficult to replicate leadership capability, as to do this successfully takes years, not months. Thus good leadership at both the individual and organisational level not only facilitates change, and building competitive advantage is itself a competitive advantage.

If you recognise one or more of the following pressures increasingly impacting on organisations, then the need for frequent, if not radical, transformation is clear:

- The transition from growth to maturity in developed economies, leading to overcapacity, more competition and fewer, larger players.
- The need to compete against global leaders, even in once secure local markets.
- The challenge of managing a shift from a wide competence/local market focus to a narrow competence/international market focus.
- The entry of small, aggressive competitors into niche segments, using these as a springboard to challenge the market leaders.
- The shift from integration (ownership or control of all elements of the value chain) to specialisation (leveraging capability in one key element of the value chain).
- The shift in power or added value from one player to another in the value chain (from manufacturers to distributors or suppliers, or vice versa).

These are critical issues for competitive organisations. Organisational transformation is a philosophy that challenges established practices and boundaries in a fundamental way. It involves challenging 'the rules of the game'.

9.2   Changing the rules of the game

'We've restructured, we've de-layered, we've got close to our customers, we've achieved zero-fault manufacturing and service capability. Now what do we do for an encore?' Questions like this indicate that 'business as usual plus' is no longer an adequate means of achieving sustained competitive success. In future, this success will go increasingly to organisations that are able to achieve radical change, either internally or externally, or, more probably, both. *This is the central idea of the organisational transformation philosophy.* This approach to competitive strategy is based on five key propositions:

(i)   Discontinuity in the market is more likely to result from *radical* rather than *incremental* change, and this is likely to be driven as much by companies themselves as by social and economic factors.

(ii)   Coping with strategic change needs to move from an emphasis on forecasting to creating an organisation that can respond quickly to change.

(iii) Approaches to gaining and sustaining competitive advantage need to shift from *erecting barriers* (vertical integration, proprietary technology, piling up fixed costs to create scale and so on) to *overcoming or ignoring them* (through outsourcing, building strategic alliances, and the aggressive elimination of fixed costs).

(iv)   The basis of strategic thinking therefore needs to shift from an 'as is now' perspective of market attractiveness and competitive capability to a *'changing the rules of the game'* view, thus destabilising entrenched players.

(v)   The role of leadership in this context is to affirm that *'it's achievable'* (provide a vision), rather than *'it's impossible'* (the controller/pessimist).

By changing the rules of the game, a organisation may be able to wrong-foot competitors to such an extent that they may never recover; this can be achieved by driving radical change either internally or externally. Thus the competitive breakthroughs of the future are likely to go to organisations that can transform either their market or the organisation itself, or both. As has already been suggested, this involves radical rather than incremental change, or both together, and needs vision and leadership to bring it about. But before organisational transformation can realistically be contemplated, a sound strategic plan must be developed on which subsequent actions can be built.

Understanding leadership requires that we understand how some organisations and leaders are able to organise activities to gather, analyse and make sense of market intelligence in ways that enable decisions ultimately leading to competitive advantage. In some circumstances, advantage relates to the possession, or at least control of, physical resources, routes to market, mailing lists and other valuable data or delivery channels; in many ways, it relates to gaining a better understanding of market need and how best to satisfy it profitably.

For some twenty years or more, ideas such as organisational learning, the learning organisation and knowledge management have attracted substantial attention. Long linked to the obvious impact of scientific knowledge, clearly 'knowledge', in one sense, are those 'outputs' derived from the application of rigorous scientific methods, tested and validated within a community of scholars and presented in books, reports and research papers. But increasingly, within a broader framework we use explicit and tacit knowledge, where the latter relates to the knowledge an 'experienced practitioner' may develop over a number of years. Note, however, that various approaches for the definition of 'knowledge' bring other distinctions into play, such as:

■ Explicit versus tacit.

■ Individual versus collective.

■ Event versus procedural.

■ 'Embedded' knowledge.

■ 'Encoded' knowledge.

Organisational elements relevant to understanding how knowledge management might work include corporate culture, leadership, information technology, human resources, control and organisation design and role descriptions/definitions. Mertins *et al.* (2003) define knowledge management as follows:

> Knowledge management includes all methods, instruments and tools that contribute to the promotion of an integrated core knowledge process – with the following four core activities as a minimum: to generate knowledge, to store knowledge, to distribute knowledge and to apply knowledge – in all areas and levels of the organisation in order to enhance organisational performance by focusing on the value creating process.

Scholl and Heisig (2003) reported the results of a Delphi study on the future of knowledge management. The study involved 45 'experts' in the first round, with 25 involved in the second round. Looking at the most challenging, theoretical or research issues for knowledge management, the study identified the integration of knowledge management in organisational processes as key, not least because some other organisational challenges identified clearly relate to this issue. Thus the connection between learning and organisational success, knowledge sharing, including identifying who has the knowledge and motivating these individuals to share, the knowledge management framework, and organisational learning and its contribution to success all appear to be different aspects of this same issue.

Clearly, there are also other issues, including those related to technology and the creation of a knowledge management infrastructure. Again, integration appears to be a key issue, as discussed under leadership development in Chapter 3. The emphasis is clear – even with good leadership or knowledge inside organisations, if that is held only by individuals and not integrated to add value to the organisation, then the full value of potential benefits will never be achieved. There is a clear tendency in this data to argue priority for human rather than technical factors in knowledge management. IT-related issues, while being important, are not seen as the most important source of constraint on the development of the necessary infrastructure for knowledge management. In other words, going down to the most practical level, if people do not want to share knowledge, even if there is a world class knowledge management system, they won't. If they do want to contribute, even if there is no system set up they will find a way to share and transfer knowledge.

That being accepted, the survey also looked at the most challenging practical problems associated with knowledge management. Here, three main categories predominate. The first could be labelled '*cultural*', because it relates to the barriers created by conventional thinking, the need to create a 'new mindset' for management, and related issues of raising awareness and motivating knowledge management.

The second could be labelled as *organisational* because it comprises issues such as the ability to assess and validate knowledge, the capacity to identify who possesses relevant knowledge, and convincing and motivating individuals to share that knowledge with others. It also incorporates the need to allocate sufficient time for knowledge management for individuals, and the creation of organisational processes to capture knowledge efficiently.

The third relates to *technical* matters. Here we look at the instruments and practices involved, standards for knowledge management, knowledge-management-orientated databases and other IT systems, including the use of an intranet, internal systems and groupware. In addition, this includes the development and use of tools, such as artificial intelligence tools, 'second life' and knowledge trading, knowledge-creation tools, portals, and even emails as a means to facilitate knowledge collection or transfer.

But where does leadership link into knowledge management? Knowledge management is a key element of leadership, as leadership requires knowledge to make decisions, and without it leadership would be ineffective in that even good leaders would, because of the lack of sufficient information, potentially make the wrong decisions. To enable good knowledge management, a series of theoretical and practical problems must be considered and addressed.

Knowledge management is inherently nothing new to society or organisations. The application of 'knowledge' within formal and informal processes established to share knowledge for mutual benefit has long been a feature of organised activities. The medieval apprenticeship system involved knowledge transfer, and the Livery Company system in the City of London is an example of this. Books on accounting were printed in Italy in the fourteenth century, and the development of the War College model in Europe and the USA placed evolving technology and the development of knowledge at the centre of military power. Haxel (2003) noted: 'In Henkel's [a manufacturer of chemical products] research departments, "knowledge management" has a tradition going back more than 150 years. Sharing knowledge also means publishing and protecting knowledge. Henkel applied for its first patent in 1896.'

Nevertheless, the quickening pace of new technology, new and emerging markets, corporate restructuring and regrouping has provided new emphasis on attempting to create new strategies by seeking to enhance the ability to leverage knowledge. Nonaka *et al.* (2008) sought to understand knowledge creation and knowledge management in general terms. For these authors, the key aspect for understanding knowledge management is 'the dynamic capability to continuously create new knowledge out of existing … capabilities rather than from a pre-existing stock of knowledge'.

They note that, traditionally, knowledge is 'justified' true belief, with the emphasis on the word 'justified', implying that knowledge is socially generated, or 'relational'. They suggest that there are two types of knowledge: *tacit* and *explicit*. Explicit knowledge relies on rules, formulas, routines and procedures, drawings, specifications, manuals and databases. Tacit knowledge is rooted in the process of putting rules, procedures, routines and manuals into practice. Tacit knowledge is personal experience, in human cognition and in values, beliefs, ideas and emotions.

Nonaka *et al.* propose a three-element model for knowledge creation by organisations. Each element plays its part, and none is given priority in the model. The elements are:

(i)   The conversion of tacit to explicit knowledge.

(ii) The shared context of knowledge creation – specifically the platform, tools and approaches in use, but also the broader world of knowledge.

(iii) Knowledge assets.

Most interesting is their idea that 'knowledge assets' moderate how (ii) performs as a platform for (iii). On the face of it, this presents a problem. How can knowledge assets moderate anything? Moderation implies judgement and therefore human agency. To know whether the 'platform' is performing appropriately is to imply standards of performance that must, to some extent at least, imply external standards and benchmarks.

What do knowledge assets comprise in their model? They are as follows:

(i)   Experienced knowledge assets – essentially tacit and shared through common experience – skills and know-how, product knowledge, business relationships.

(ii) Conceptual knowledge assets – explicit knowledge 'contained' in images and languages – design, brand equity, product concepts.

(iii) Routine knowledge assets – tacit knowledge routinised and embedded in the organisation – the organisational culture (defined often as 'the way we do things around here'), routines, operational knowledge (for example, that the service interval for a particular motor car should be a specific mileage).

(iv) Systemic knowledge assets – databases, patents, licences, specifications, manuals.

It is not obvious how these assets can act to moderate anything. However, people clearly are involved and so it would be based on their judgement of whether any moderation could have occurred. Nonaka and Takeuchi (1995) are explicit in saying that knowledge is often created with outside constituents. Customers and suppliers are obviously very important here, but they also refer to social, cultural and historical elements. For them, the knowledge context is complex and everchanging. The 'platform' may set a boundary for interactions among individuals, within the organisation or between the organisation and individuals, including customers and suppliers. Yet they argue that the boundary is open.

Here, Nonaka and Takeuchi began to get to the key of knowledge creation when they linked the idea of open boundaries with the four modes of knowledge conversion they identified:

(i)   Socialisation.

(ii) Externalisation.

(iii) Combination.

(iv) Internalisation.

Each of these was discussed in terms of the knowledge the company holds and they noted that:

Taking a snapshot of the knowledge assets that the organisation owns at one point in time is never enough to evaluate and manage knowledge assets properly. Indeed it is likely to be impossible to know all the knowledge assets available in the firm at any point in time. The process is far too dynamic for that to be possible.

While the knowledge creation process cannot be managed, senior and middle managers can play appropriate roles in an attempt to optimise the process. These authors argued that senior leaders need to provide a 'knowledge vision', and view this as defining 'what kind of knowledge the firm should create, in what domain'. They noted that the knowledge vision must transcend the boundaries of existing products, divisions, organisations and markets. But in their discussion of knowledge creation and knowledge vision, their arguments and examples are all internal to the firm. But in reality firms need to bring in new knowledge from outside, as it is the ability to deliver what the external customer wants in the context of the external environment that is key to organisational success. Thus good external knowledge is critical.

No doubt Nonaka *et al.* would accept this need, and this is suggested in their point about openness. But is that sufficient? For Snowden and Boone (2007), the answer is no. In their view, you need also to consider the decision context in which knowledge is to be applied. They identified five such contexts, as follows:

(i)   Simple context – here, stability and clear cause and effect is the norm, and reaching a good answer requires nothing more than the application of agreed 'rules'.

(ii)   Complicated contexts – these contain multiple 'right' answers. Clear cause and effect sequences apply, but not everyone sees them.

(iii)   Complex context – here it is hard to identify the right answer.

(iv)   Chaotic context – cause and effect is shifting continuously as the dynamics impacting these relationships are changing.

(v)   Disorder – in which it is difficult to discern which of the above applies.

Case study   **Knowledge management at NASA**

The National Aeronautical and Space Administration (NASA) was established to run the US space effort. They realised at the outset that knowledge and project management were essential disciplines if complex, highly technical space missions were to be successful. The early years at NASA are characterised by the evolution of solutions to new problems. Lessons learned from the earliest missions, such as the Apollo missions, led the US space programme to be seen as an innovator in this area, even allowing for disasters such as that of the Challenger accident.

Identifying, selecting and then successfully developing project managers was a challenge recognised early in NASA's history. However, just as important has been the transfer of 'lessons learned' through successive projects. As each project manager found him/herself facing a new mission, it was clear that effective project leadership involved leveraging the expenses of the team. However, various mission failures, beginning in 1988 and then the Challenger tragedy, provided new emphasis on the application of a knowledge management approach to project management.

The Challenger tragedy led NASA to make an enormous effort to learn lessons. Numerous 'tiger teams', commissions and boards were convened to resolve specific problems. Emerging from this effort was the concept of the Program and Project Management Improvement (PPMI) programme – the forerunner of NASA APPL (Academy of Program and Project Leadership). PPMI set out to enhance project management. It was readily recognised that sharing knowledge across projects was very important, as essentially lives potentially depended on it.

While PPMI was to provide project managers with sound skills, this would be followed up and developed by a series of assignments to ever more challenging assignments. PPMI was conceived as promoting the development of people through parallel efforts – formal training, on-the-job development, capturing and disseminating past experiences, studies of current requirements and skills, and the documentation and dissemination of current and new programme and project management methods. Given the large, long-duration, high-profile and expensive nature of programmes and projects at NASA, this fitted well into the NASA context. The Apollo, Shuttle and Viking missions and the Hubble Space Telescopes offered challenging programmes within which development opportunities, that were progressively more challenging, would readily be provided.

By the early 1990s, new budget pressures began to be experienced, not least because the US federal government was beginning to implement reform programmes aimed at enhancing the efficiency and effectiveness of government organisations. A program excellence team (PET) was established in NASA to streamline policy and processes. When it began its work, the average time between authorisation of missions and actual launch was eight years, and typically, programme cost and time overruns were around 60 per cent. Various factors contributed to these problems, including inadequate statements of requirements, a reliance on unproven technology, funding issues, complex organisation structures and interface issues, requirements 'creep', and an approach to purchasing not focused on cost.

There had been 30 studies initiated by NASA to assess their problems. These causal factors had been identified many times but yet had been repeated. A series of organisational arrangements were instituted to enhance the role of knowledge management to ensure that existing knowledge was leveraged throughout the organisation. Previously, the training and development culture emphasised curriculum but lacked an emphasis on metrics focused on performance and outcomes. Going forward, knowledge management was imbued with concepts and tools relating to competence, capability, knowledge sharing and performance standards, alongside innovative delivery and learning solutions.

Continued development along these lines initiated the establishment of a training 'academy' and partnerships with the Project Management Institution and universities such as the Massachusetts Institute of Technology (MIT). In 2003, the Columbia tragedy provided a new impetus and included changes emerging from the Accident Investigation Board which led to the establishment of an Integrated Learning and Development Board. Central to these changes were factors such as a shift from training evaluations to mission evaluation, from event-driven to outcome-driven focus, from 'one best way' to competition, from developing individuals to developing teams.

Knowledge sharing is a vital process, enabling the accumulated reservoir of critical knowledge to be harnessed. It was important to ensure that NASA shared lessons learned, transferred best practices, captured data and developed leadership skills and capabilities. To these ends, the Agency recognised the 'experienced practitioner' as the basis of knowledge creation and sharing, and that mission success was achieved by leveraging knowledge in project teams. Forums for leadership development and networking were also essential, but key was for the Agency to explicitly value, recognise and reward knowledge sharing. Much of this effort works through processes designed to build dialogue, using activities such as Master's Forums, Transfer Wisdom Workshops and the ASK magazine (which compiles best practice from practitioners), alongside the Leaders as Teachers and Mentors initiative.

Sources: NASA Academy of Program/Project & Engineering Leadership website: http://appel.nasa.gov; NASA 2007 Annual Performance Report.

Knowledge management therefore comprises the leveraging of wisdom, experience and explicit, formalised knowledge to enhance responsiveness to environments, stakeholders and innovation. At one level it relates to the ability to engage current, unrealised knowledge, or to develop knowledge potential by sharing already realised knowledge in new combinations to allow the organisation to respond to new challenges. Ultimately, knowledge management is the formalisation, capture and leveraging of knowledge to produce a higher-value asset (Stewart and Stewart, 2001).

Knowledge 'storage' is critical. Where does knowledge reside? In the brains of individuals, on paper, in databases, in other electronic formats and documents. There is a multiplicity of knowledge repositories and one challenge is to develop and use technology to put them all together. Leadership can play a key role in securing the leveraging of knowledge, and this requires the creation of a culture that emphasises collaboration and trust so that sharing can take place.

The role of leaders in knowledge management is partly about establishing a 'knowledge vision' as suggested earlier, but also in recognising and responding to the organisational constraints that apply:

(i)   *Culture* – the culture of the organisation is a powerful force, and research has shown that the more successful companies have been those that have regarded knowledge management (KM) as a cultural issue, one of people and processes rather than one of technology. Culture is often defined as 'the way we do things round here', and changing the culture to one where people openly share knowledge may be the biggest challenge modern organisations face.

(ii)   *'Knowledge is power'* – there may be a feeling within the organisation that to give up knowledge means giving up a valuable lever, so there is a reluctance to share information and knowledge.

(iii) *Reward systems* – do the reward systems reward individual achievement and contribution? What kind of performance is rewarded? Does this mitigate against collaboration and sharing? How are people recognised for sharing knowledge? Should reward systems be changed to reflect team contributions?

(iv)   *Misunderstanding* – KM may mistakenly be assumed to be another technology project that doesn't involve anyone else but the information technology (IT) department. There may also be confusion with other initiatives, such as business process reengineering (BPR), total quality management (TQM), document management and records management. It is important to ensure that everyone understands the concept, and this may require a significant investment in training, coaching and educational programmes.

(v)   *Technology* – though we are in the 'information age', be aware that even today there are people who are uncomfortable with technology and reluctant to embrace the benefits it can bring to their day-to-day operations. However, many organisations use technology (intranets or groupware) to mobilise knowledge, to speed the flow of information and to help manage knowledge better. However, it is an enabler and not a driver. Some early KM initiatives focused too heavily on the technology without paying enough attention to the people and cultural issues, and consequently failed to realise the benefits expected.

(vi)   *Information overload* – we live in a world where we constantly receive and have access to more and more information, sometimes collecting information for information's sake. A focused information management strategy will ensure that data that have been identified as being of use should be accessible at the right time, in the right place, in the right format and to the right people.

(vii) *Time* – downsizing and de-layering sees fewer people doing more work – are employees given the time to participate in sharing activities? Does the infrastructure support and facilitate knowledge sharing? Is searching and exploring the internet regarded as 'real work', or is it seen as something that should be done in your own and not the organisation's time?

(viii) *Awareness of value* – most fundamentally, people often do not see the knowledge they hold as being relevant to the problems the organisation faces.

The importance of learning has long been recognised. De Geus (1997) outlines two ways of describing a firm. One is as a money-making machine, seeking revenues and profits. The second is as an institution focused on realising its full, long-term potential. In the latter, a key emphasis is on learning, and on learning as being a relational process requiring trust and collaboration. From the case studies of BP, UBS and others – for example, GE – clearly think of the two views as being compatible – the issue is partly about time horizons but also partly about the use that leaders make of people. Are they merely a resource to be used, and replaced? Or are all the people in an organisation part of the same community, with the possibility of a shared goal focused on long-term potential and benefit for all?

9.3   Strategic leadership as a learning process

To be credible to those engaged in day-to-day leadership activity in organisations, a model of strategic leadership needs to deal with these change issues in a practical way. While it may be necessary to re-engineer processes to reduce costs and improve service, that is insufficient to gain competitive advantage because competitors can do the same by copying what has been changed. To be successful, the organisation must create new strategies aimed at transforming their area of operation – whether this is food, medicine, education, entertainment, transport or whatever. In the modern world, renewal demands that we do more than identify how to do more, better and using fewer resources.

Kay (1993) attempts to identify the origins of corporate success from distinctive structures of relationships between the organisation and employees, customers and suppliers. Continuity and stability in these relationships, engendering trust, allow for a flexible and co-operative response to change. At the core of Kay's analysis lies the concept of added value. This, he argues, derives from the architecture of the firm, derived from the structure of relationships referred to above, and the application of distinctive capabilities in particular markets. Continuity and stability provide for the development of organisational knowledge (of its identity, vision, distinctive capabilities and invisible assets – Itami, 1987), the free exchange of information, and a readiness to respond quickly and flexibly to changes in the world.

The distinctive capabilities that provide the basis of competitive advantage are architecture, innovation, reputation and strategic assets. Architecture is both internal (the corporate structure and management processes) and external (networks of relationships with suppliers and other organisations – joint ventures, strategic alliances and so on). Strategic assets are the inherent advantages a corporation may possess (for example, licences, access to scarce factors), which cannot easily be copied.

But many people forget that good leadership capability itself is also a strategic asset that is difficult to replicate over a short timescale, as is the full engagement of employees behind the organisation's delivery. The creation of high-quality leaders aligned to even a current organisational strategy who then engage everyone in the organisation to maximise performance could easily take two to three years to accomplish this. During this period the organisation will be performing better than competitors. If, on top of this, an innovative strategy is added, the benefits will be greater still, even though the change to the new strategy will involve more time. So the ability to lead and implement strategic change in an organisation is an asset in itself that can be developed.

Leading strategic changes successfully requires us to take an organisation-wide approach. Change creates stress and strain (through overwork, the challenge of leading change in an uncertain world, the pressure of dealing with other, often anxious, people, the inherent uncertainties all are subject to in some degree and so on), both for those who support change and for those who are either indifferent, opposed or fearful of change.

Organisational learning is a vital component of effective change. Following the work of Quinn (see, in particular, Quinn, 1992) organisational restructuring and strategic change should be based on effective diagnosis and bench-marking, information and incentive systems. A key point, however, in achieving strategic change amid organisational circumstances that exist in many organisations that are increasingly unlike traditional hierarchical structures, is that 'managed incrementalism' is a strategy for change implementation designed explicitly to manage risk. However, this does not need to imply that change is slow, random or gradual. Frequent increments, taken together, can produce significant change over time.

Concepts such as transformational leadership, entrepreneurship and the learning organisation each embrace these ideas. Major changes are typically implemented as major programmes organised around simple themes (for example, 'right first time' for total quality programmes, or 'next steps programme' for major programmes of culture change). A good example is that of 'time-based competition'. The key principle is that the management of time – whether in production, in new product development, or in sales and distribution – represents a powerful source of competitive advantage. This idea spawned another – that of 'business process reengineering (BPR)'. At the core of both is a strategy for change employing analytical techniques to dissect what the organisation does, seeking continuous improvements to work and information flows, and to the use of time. The emphasis is on the organisation doing the work itself, using its own people, and empowering people at all levels to achieve change. Benchmarking is a key analytical technique used in such programmes, as are techniques such as 'pilots' and 'breakthrough teams'. According to Stalk and Hout (1990), breakthrough teams should be given radical goals such as reducing the time by half to carry out a process, so that that assumptions will be challenged. Bottlenecks, breakdowns, failures and unmet customer needs all become opportunities to learn. All of this implies radically new ways of thinking about the organisation that can make significant process improvements.

Learning implies the willingness to experiment. In reality, substantial or ambitious changes cannot readily be 'packaged' as final, fully worked-out plans that are not subject to amendment or change. A natural process of trial and error will inevitably be involved as the process moves to implementation. Going back to the military saying that no plan survives first contact with the enemy, this will lead to adjustments, some chosen, but others driven by circumstances and with no element of choice. This is learning. Even where employees are fully convinced of the new strategy there needs to be room for adjustment over many issues as the overview approach of the strategy comes into contact with the detail of operational reality. This requires a willingness to suspend judgement, which in turn involves a willingness to trust senior leaders. Social capital is a concept focused on understanding the basis for cultures characterised by high levels of trust, and has relevance here.

9.4　The concept of 'social capital'

One formulation of how to achieve economic success amid these pressures relates to the concept of 'trust', or social capital. Some of the most influential recent work in this area is that of Fukuyama (1995). For him, one solution to the problem of scale lies in the emergence of networks, such as businesses held together by family ties, cross-ownership, long experience of joint working and so on. In particular, he points to the advantages of establishing long-term relationships between members of a network. All of this is now known as supply chain management. Fukuyama argues that networks based on reciprocal obligation enable scale to be achieved without the problems of size and alienation referred to above. These networks appear to have emerged in societies with cultures that encourage high levels of trust (for example, Japan, South Korea, Germany, northern Italy). In 'low-trust' societies, stable networks can be created via cross-ownership but they will certainly be more difficult to sustain. Social capital may be thought of as the degree or extent of organisational cohesion created out of reciprocal obligation.

Increasingly, major corporates are beginning to work on the briefing of 'social capital' via value-added strategies. Here, the organisation is defined as a horizontal value stream supported by other activities (for example, marketing development, senior management, finance). Each part of the organisation has performance parameters defined in terms of value to its customers. Organisations use competence models and assessment, 360° feedback techniques and the balanced scorecard as a means of putting this into effect. The objective is to identify what each activity contributes by way of value to its customers, measure that and feed that information openly to the people involved in the activity, their customers and senior management. Part of the role of management is to help each activity to drive its performance forward in terms of these parameters.

A longer-term task of senior management is to identify and access the capabilities needed for the future. There are few organisations that have actually deployed a coherent system of the type outlined here, but there are many examples in telecommunications, financial services, health care, manufacturing, and the utilities of organisations working on such approaches. Traditionally, we think of and operate organisations as structures of hierarchical authority whether what we are describing is based on functional or divisional structures. Rarely were organisations as simple as that. The formal structures and organisational charts do not describe behaviour within organisations, which is why sociologists created the distinction between 'formal' and 'informal' organisations, where the latter term describes how people work with, through and around the formal organisation in pursuit of various objectives, their own as well as the organisation's.

Increasingly, leaders recognise the problems of aligning the formal and informal referred to above, and, in particular, when related to change. This has led many try to complement the traditional 'top-down' models of change with 'bottom-up' models as a means of making implementation more effective. But both are essentially 'vertical' models – that is, the focus is on how the organisation arranges its internal affairs, how authority is used, and how information is transmitted. If the objective is to drive change that is designed to ensure increased value added for customers and clients, then the traditional organisational pyramid structure needs to be rethought, because value added flows horizontally.

This led many thinkers on change to ask how we could have previously thought through the leadership of change without thinking horizontally if the aim was to maximise value added. Many concluded that we are in the midst of a paradigm or mind-set change in relation to how to organise economic activity. New forms of organisation are increasingly being discussed or developed. Networks, virtual organisations and homeworking are all variants that organisations are testing to see whether they improve performance. There are two points to note:

(i)   Increasingly, there are two approaches to change in use: a planned approach and a market-based one. In the planned approach, the direction, objectives, stages, milestones, change methods and so on are decided, but in the market-based approach it is sought to motivate people in pursuit of a particular direction, desired objectives, preferred patterns of behaviour and so on, but there is less concern with milestones and so on. This is a topic to which we shall return, but the basic argument is that too much attention being paid to targets and milestones creates expectations that can lead to fewer results than might be achievable if the overarching effort to achieve the targets actually distracts from the effort to add value in practice. Effectively, the target is more important than the outcome. In the market-based approach, market mechanisms are used to motivate changes in behaviour. So long as adequate resources, information and support are provided, this often leads to dramatic changes.

(ii) It appears that innovations, such as the virtual organisation, networks, alliances or homeworking, create the potential for isolation (an increased reliance on networks and alliances increases the tendency for people to be working remotely from others, with an associated tendency to isolation). Thus cohesion becomes a crucial issue. New forms and sources of group cohesion are needed if the traditional sources of department and structure are no longer present.

More generally, economists now argue that social capital is essential to success. Social capital can be seen as the extent of social cohesion and is firmly linked to a sense of social solidarity, shared values and common commitment. If these are high, then we have a high level of social capital. In an increasingly fragmented organisational world, social capital becomes a crucial determinant of success and advantage. In other words, social capital is what makes people work together for a common cause, and without it they are just a group of individuals and an organisation effectively does not exist.

This is why social capital is vital. It is interesting to note that these characteristics are also generally valuable in other circumstances: mergers demand them, and lean production requires them. In reality, the changed focus of action moves from vertical concerns over control and co-ordination to a horizontal concern for value added. This creates the circumstances in which trust is essential to success. Fukuyama (1995) puts it this way:

> It is possible to argue that in the future the optimal form of industrial organisation will be neither small companies nor large ones but network structures that share the advantages of scale economies while avoiding the overhead and (other) costs of large, centralised organisations. If this will in fact be the case, then societies with a high degree of social trust will have a natural advantage. Networks can save on transaction costs substantially if their members follow an informal set of rules that require little or no overhead to negotiate, adjudicate, and enforce. The moment that trust breaks down among members of a business network, relations have to be spelled out in detail.

In fact, managing networks, professional practices, alliances and joint ventures, virtual organisations and lean production all share these characteristics. This is a reflection of our own experience – we all know this to be true – in situations where we have worked with people on a basis of mutual trust that have been successful, we know that all aspects of the process to get things done works better and faster than where such trust does not exist. This is one reason why the military build an ethos of total trust between leaders within that environment – so they don't have to waste time checking that the other person knows what to do, knows what the overall objectives are, and will deliver their part of the process on time. And if things go wrong they know that their colleagues will get the problem resolved and not start blaming others.

In the non-military world, Castells (1996) comes to a similar conclusion. For him, 'the main shift can be characterised by the shift from vertical bureaucracies to the horizontal corporation'. This shift is characterised by seven main trends, as follows:

(i)   Organisation around process, not task.

(ii)   A flat hierarchy.

(iii) Team management.

(iv)   Performance management based on customer satisfaction.

(v)   Rewards based on team performance.

(vi)   Maximisation of contacts with suppliers and customers.

(vii) Information, training and retraining of employees at all levels.

These ideas derive from a recognition of the limits both of the original functional/ hierarchical model and attempts to modify this model via the Toyota lean production model or later equivalents such as Business Process Reengineering – effectively, in Castells' view, making the wrong way of doing this more efficient. It is still not the best way to achieve value added, but it is less bad than it was before.

In fact, regardless of the use of hierarchical, matrix or network organisation models, the concept of value added provides the psychological and organisational 'glue' from which to create cohesion. We shall develop this view in a later chapter, but here two sets of principles may operate. Organisationally, the work of each of us is helped through understanding and seeking to maximise the value of the work of others whose input is needed for our work – that is, we need to make sure that those whose work we need to be successful are doing the best job they can. This idea of supply chain management is based on a process view of organisation. Ultimately, cohesion arises out of a shared sense of purpose. This is achieved from the perception that each contributes to the achievement of those purposes, that is, that we all will deliver both the ends and the means.

We seek effective performance from collaboration. This allows for speedier flows of information, which in turn bring benefits by, for example, providing for low levels of inventory because replacement of stock can be handled quickly. Collaboration also has another benefit in that it tends to drive proactive rather than reactive co-operation. This is key – if I have an idea that I think will benefit you I will proactively seek you out and tell you. In the normal organisational world the tendency is that I will wait for you to ask me if I have any ideas that could help you. Thus, and this is the key to success, the whole organisation is more responsive to customer needs. The case study of Zara below illustrates the benefits that can be achieved by such an approach.

Case study	**Zara**

Zara, the fast-growing Spanish fashion clothing retailer, owned by Inditex Group, is based in Corunna, Spain. It merchandises 10,000 new items each year, replenishing 650 or more shops in 50 countries twice a week. It manufactures 40 per cent of its own fabrics and 50 per cent of its own clothing. It designs new collections in 4–5 weeks and can manufacture in one week.

At Zara, inventory amounts to 10 per cent of annual sales and is less than those of Gap, Benetton, Matalan or H&M. It can design, produce and deliver a new garment in 15 days. This 'fast fashion' business model is based on constant exchange of information across the Zara supply chain. This includes customers, store managers, marketing staff, designers, production staff, buyers, sub-contractors, warehouse managers and distributors.

Zara has a single, centralised design and production centre in Corunna. It runs three systems in parallel, for women's, men's and children's clothing. By doing so it trades off the possibility of capacity under-use against the benefits of speed and small batch sizes. It does not see running out of stock as being a problem. By focusing on short lead times and small batch sizes it reduces both inventory and working capital. Running three systems in parallel (which include dedicated design, sales, procurement and production planning staff), it incurs higher operational costs but the supply chain is more responsive. Zara's 200 designers work in the midst of the production process, thus allowing for easy consultation and decision-making. Cross-functional teams can consider prototype designs, choose a design and agree resources for production and distribution within a few hours.

A flat, team-based, proximity-based organisational arrangement emphasises speed, responsiveness, rapid change, low inventory and low risk. Unsold items account for 10 per cent of inventory compared to an industry norm of 17–20 per cent. Zara customers visit stores frequently, creating high traffic volumes and meaning that Zara does not need to advertise.

The senior executives who designed the business model understood the nature of the relationships between capacity utilisation, demand variability, and speed. In particular, they appear to work on the basis that where demand variability is high (as in fashion) declines in the speed of response to demand changes are directly linked to any attempt to enhance capacity utilisation at the centre. Their conclusion appears to be that, on balance, it is better to lose some capacity utilisation in pursuit of sales.

More recently, Inditex has announced that its results show continued, if reduced, levels of growth. The demand for affordable, designer-inspired clothing is holding up well in the current recession, Zara is not experiencing the sharp revenue and profits decline so characteristic of the sector. However, the planned rate of expansion is being reduced by 15 per cent.

Sources: Ferdows *et al.* (2004); Tiplady (2006); Mulligan (2009).

Case study questions

1 The Zara business model emphasises responsiveness through information sharing. How is this encouraged?

2 Senior leaders have created a very successful business model by 'breaking the mould'. They have done some things differently from their competitors. How important might this be for employees' commitment to the organisation?

3 Is this an example of 'problem'- or 'mission'-oriented leadership in practice?

Case study commentary

In one sense, Zara illustrates a different version of a systems approach to devising a business model. Rather like Toyota, this company understands what it needs leaders to specify, and what is best left to others. Each employee is treated as an 'expert' in the contribution they make, and each is expected to provide an input where they have the capability to do so. The firm concentrates on creating the conditions under which that can happen. Here, leadership focuses on ensuring that experts can contribute. It emphasises a business model creating value across the supply chain. It is not difficult to conclude that a shared sense of purpose does arise out of these organisational arrangements. If this shared sense of purpose does arise, creating organisational cohesion, then success flows partly from the deployment of a business model based on employee engagement – the result of cohesion, and a 'holy grail' that many organisations seek.

Crucially, though, the idea of organisational cohesion here is more than an emotional notion. Rather, we argue that it comprises an important cognitive element and this partly relates to the decisions and actions of leaders and the sense they create among their people, but also to the degree of conviction they demonstrate. Where ambitious changes are brought forward it is important that followers find themselves convinced that the changes make sense.

This links back to the Corporate Leadership Council data quoted previously, showing that while there is an emotional element to employees deciding to give high commitment that will only work if it is underpinned by a rational argument. The data show that a leader's rational explanation alone is not sufficient to maximise employee commitment, recalling the 57 per cent rational and 43 per cent emotional structure of the decision. The emotional element must be present. But it also showed that unless the rational is present the emotional on its own will not obtain effective commitment.

Much of the success of the Walt Disney Company relies on the way it manages its assets, both tangible and intangible: the film library and the brand name, including the Disney Channel. Using its in-house film-making capabilities, it produces major box office hits such as *Beauty and the Beast* and *Aladdin*, which it then exploits vigorously both as films and often via merchandising – for example, via computer games and toys. At least in part this success arises out of strategies designed to exploit existing resource bases.

This is particularly relevant to this chapter, for two reasons. The focus on exploiting resources drives forward the importance of value added as a strategic management concept – and the linked concept of synergy. Second, much of the success in change management situations comes from leverage and connectivity. Where changes aim to leverage existing resources and capabilities, and where there is a higher degree of connectivity between existing resources and processes – and these are put in place to manage change – there is a higher likelihood of success in strategic change.

Success may actually flow best from a combination of ambition and conservatism. This is the contradiction of the type we saw when discussing the Toyota case study in Chapter 6. Ambitious strategic objectives are more likely to convince stakeholders, and employees in particular, when combined with implementation strategies that leverage existing as well as new capabilities. This leverage refers to the exploitation of combinations of assets, resources and capabilities, both existing and newly acquired or developed. From the change perspective, if everything needed is totally new, then perhaps the best answer is to set up a new organisation rather than to try to change an established 'legacy' organisation, as the change management required will be significantly less and thus the chances of success higher. This is evidenced by examples of major global organisations setting up new subsidiaries to deal with new technology, products or markets beyond their original structures.

So it is important to understand how leaders can judge whether ambitious strategic plans are capable of being implemented within an existing organisation, or whether the changes are so fundamental that a new organisation will be necessary. Previous work on leadership largely ignored the question of how to judge whether a given level of ambition can be achieved within existing structures or cultures, and it is important when examining how best to effect change through leadership.

This is partly a matter of risk and how ready the organisation is as a platform for change. This is best decided in a structured way via the 'readiness for change' checklist, and via the idea of an implementation success index comprising four components:

(i)   Is there a critical mass of support from key stakeholders?

(ii)   Is there a sufficient problem orientation within the change process?

(iii) Is there sufficiently robust programme management?

(iv)   Is there sufficient focus on clear goals?

Our capability to develop and deliver ambitious change programmes is about the ability of the change architecture we put in place to deliver the infrastructure and culture needed quickly enough. Is the reason radical change programmes often fail related to resistance to the change or to inadequate change architectures or a combination of the two? The change plans may not be delivering the needed infrastructure quickly enough to meet the rate of change required, which may be largely externally imposed by forces such as competitive pressure, or government action in the public sector.

Kanter (1983) provides some clues in discussing 'inspiring visions'. In her opinion, 'inspiring visions' include a dream of what our world will look like when we achieve our goal, but she also believes that success will follow only where the change leaders' passion matches their aspiration, as judged by how strongly they feel about the aspiration, how convinced they are of its accomplishment, how excited they are, what sacrifices they are prepared to make and so on. But that merely applies to the individual leader, and change needs the many not only the few to make it happen. Also, is the direction of change correct or optimal? So another dimension is, can the leader and change advocate enlist backers and supporters, ultimately providing a reality as well, by gaining support from key stakeholders? This links back to the discussion of 'social movements' in Chapter 1, as the social movements approach depends on leadership but also on the ability of leaders to exploit distributed models and ideas. A good example here is Barack Obama's exploitation of web-based methods in the 2008 presidential campaign.

But essentially stakeholder acceptance is an indicator of acceptability as much as of ambition, so for the sake of clarity about what leaders in change must do can we estimate more accurately the level of ambition in any set of strategic change ideas and the likelihood of success?

McGrath and MacMillan (2000) set out profiles for technical uncertainty, 'competitive insulation', that is defending the competitive advantage expected in a new venture, and the assumption-to-knowledge ratio; in other words, the proportion of the knowledge needed for a new venture based on assumption rather than hard evidence: how much is fact and how much guesswork? Clearly, therefore, it is right to include the level of ambition involved in any set of changes, effectively the degree to which changes are radical as opposed to incremental, in any readiness for a change index. The question is, are there other issues or areas that need to be included?

Jack Welch, formerly head of General Electric (GE) is one business leader frequently identified with ambitious, transformational strategy. Tichy and Sherman (1995) refer to his determination to stretch the business in terms of the level of ambition to be pursued. Viewing any organisation as a 'business engine', of which high levels of performance can be demanded, Welch adopted what by now has become known as 'the market leadership rule'. As noted in an earlier chapter, heads of business units in GE were told that they would need to gain first or second position in their sector, in terms of market position, or the business would be divested. Behind the market leadership rule there lay objectives such as that of achieving well above average returns on investment, and gaining distinctive competitive advantage by leveraging strengths relentlessly. This is often seen as a 'succeed or die' strategy that some say drives performance through a element of fear and may cause higher levels of risk-taking as a result.

These ideas have now moved on substantially, as can be seen in Prokesch (2009). Now GE provides a four-day programme, entitled 'Leadership, Innovation and Change' (LIC) to whole management teams in the various businesses. This seeks to accelerate the pace of change by focusing on the team's business with the whole management team. It can create a common language of change and a shared views of barriers to change and how to tackle them. Moreover, the whole team can address issues of priority and create an initial action plan to which all are committed. This series of programmes ran over the period 2006–08 and a total of 2,500 people in 260 management teams participated. GE describes this effort as a journey, and as 'unfinished business'. Interviewed as part of the Prokesch paper, the CEO, Jeffrey R. Immelt commented as follows 'I always say, "Drive change and develop other leaders." LIG gave me a way to do both at the same time.'

But it could be argued that radical change can be achieved by a more effective understanding of economic activities as whole systems. Organisations operating in a supply chain are within a complex web of activities, and often consequences within such webs are counter-intuitive. Take the following example, as described by the CEO of a global logistics business. His company operated at a port, at which they landed goods from a ship from the USA daily. The cost of doing so each day was £1 million. He noted that the 'dwell time' – the time the landed goods remained in port – was five days. By focusing on reducing this dwell time he was able to reduce the frequency of shipping to once every two days, thus making substantial savings. When he first proposed the idea there was major opposition, on the grounds that this reduced customer service, as it was suggested that less frequent deliveries would delay response to customers. But in fact by reducing 'dwell time' he enhanced customer service directly and was able to invest some of the savings in customer service enhancement! The resistance was a reaction to him challenging a long-standing and accepted mode of operation that everyone else had assumed was unquestionable.

This is connected with the ability to recognise and harness discontinuities, both externally and internally. Gilbert and Strebel (1989) refer to the idea of 'outpacing', which they define as 'The explicit capability of a company to gain product leadership and cost leadership simultaneously.' In effect, they argue that those seeking radical change cannot afford to adopt traditional, single-pace strategies. Success in radical changes comes to those who can integrate approaches that have traditionally been seen as incompatible. This is likely to result in a change that outpaces competitors – changing 'the rules of the game' in the industry or sector. Their observation of 100 companies identified common capabilities for successful organisations:

- The ability to innovate.
- The ability to configure and deliver a competitive offering.
- The ability to do so at a competitive price.
- The ability to perform these moves simultaneously.

Gilbert and Strebel illustrate this with the case of Nintendo. Through their ability to develop and deliver hand-held electronic games, Nintendo became the largest toy manufacturer globally in 1988, not having been in the top 10 in 1983. Gilbert and Strebel explain this in terms of the ability to develop hand-held games – attractive to young people thanks to high-quality images – to drive down costs via supply arrangements, and at the same time to price competitively. Similar conclusions might also be offered to explain the success of the clothing company, Benetton, and the chain of Scandinavian furniture stores, IKEA.

The key point here is that, to be successful, radical change demands balance, integration and simultaneous actions. Ansoff and McDonnell (1990) contrast American and Japanese models of decision-making, noting that Japanese managers operate parallel activities – that is, they begin to launch implementation activities before decisions are finalised. At the time that Ansoff and McDonnell's book was published, American managers would not do so, thus putting more pressure on the decision process, which often led to less commitment to the decision and less effective implementation. This resonates with the conclusions of Clark (1995). For him, organisations where knowledge is a premium, which operate in uncertain and complex environments, cannot be managed by planning and 'command and control'. Rather like Rubinstein and Furstenberg (1999), Clark sees too much planning as a real weakness. For him the answer is 'simultaneous, cheap explorations of multiple options' and not trying too hard – evolving options from the ground up rather than imposing them via a grand strategy. For Rubinstein and Furstenberg, more effort devoted to problem-finding leads to less effort in problem-solving later, and more early changes mean fewer changes later on in a development cycle. Again, these ideas appear to overlap, one with another. But perhaps the key difference to note is the Gilbert and Strebel focus on simultaneous change in the various competence areas relevant to a business. This links to the experience all have had in change initiatives – that hours of meetings to finalise every last detail often creates an implementation plan so detailed that it falls apart at once when put to the test of the real world, and is inflexible, or it takes so long to agree the final version that the world the changes and it is out of date even to the degree that the sponsors have given up and left the organisation!

But can organisations take this approach too far by moving too fast, and too radically? Are there circumstances in which they need to spend more time in planning, designing and analysing before they act? Handfield (1995) raises this question in what he refers to as 'the dark side of concurrent engineering'. So the bigger question really is whether some organisation changes actually require incremental rather than breakthrough change. For Handfield, the key issue relates to the technology. If it is a new technology, he argues that an incremental approach is the best. Indeed, he also suggests that his evidence points to breakthrough methodologies being attempted more often where the product development involves an incremental change with an existing technology; that is, where the technology is well defined. This is not very different from ideas D'Aveni (1994) offers for the hyper-competitive firm, which requires multiple moves to escalate the cost/challenge to imitators. But he argues that in a more volatile environment it is crucial to seize the competitive high ground in a series of small steps – small steps, multiple moves, simultaneous change, integration. The concepts of both clearly overlap.

So the question about the interaction of ambition and change becomes quite complex. But the measurement of both is always relative – we compare ourselves to our competitors, they are the benchmark. We also compare the extent to which intended changes are based on the following:

(i)   Leverage of existing resources and other platforms.

(ii)   A high degree of connectivity between the strategic thinking driving a change programme and the change architecture deployed to achieve it (where connectivity is defined as the extent to which concepts and practices, thinking and application are linked explicitly and interconnected).

(iii) Scalability.

(iv)   Integration of simultaneously conceived and delivered changes.

The important point relates to the need to develop a new understanding of what the organisation might achieve through the implementation of new strategy via more disciplined thinking about value and a recognition that the organisation and its leaders must articulate a new 'value proposition' that is convincing to those involved. To achieve this, leaders must think this through, respecting a need for simplicity, resonance and alignment in order to create a compelling vision. But thinking ability alone is not sufficient. Leaders also need the skills to engage people practically in changing the way they work, so change leadership skills are critical.

9.5   The learning organisation

Ideas and concepts such as 'organisational learning' and 'the learning organisation' are used widely in connection with knowledge management. Senior managers often express a wish to create 'learning organisations', though few know what these are, or what they entail. It is another useful corporate 'sound bite'. At various points throughout this book we argue that effective change must involve learning, and readers, from their own experience, would probably agree. But what does this mean in relation to organisations? How important is it? It is clear that managers may learn as part of the process of change, either about themselves or about the organisation, its environment and other factors relevant to delivering objectives. But can an organisation 'learn'?

The reason for interest in this question is the observation that organisational techniques appear suddenly, rather like fashion. The current management 'fad' is often quoted and the phrase 'learning organisation' is thrown around with enthusiasm. Moreover, the use of various management techniques ebbs and flows over time. Often it is possible to see today's latest technique as comprising old ideas recycled, repackaged and projected as novel to gain attention, or so it seems. In reality, it appears that organisations adopt fashionable techniques but are then unable to incorporate them as a sustained way of improving performance, and this failure to implement techniques effectively and derive benefit from them leads to change fatigue and cynicism on the part of staff. As a result, they then tend not to implement subsequent initiatives launched as they suspect it is better to see if they work elsewhere first. This reinforces the chances of failure until it builds into a vicious circle of change designed to improve performance but in the end actually reducing performance.

So organisational learning clearly is of interest in change and performance improvement. If only individual learning takes place, however, when people leave an organisation the learning they have achieved goes with them. This happens a great deal in practice, and little or nothing is done to ensure that, before departure, the intellectual capital the organisation has invested in the individual is recovered and retained. On the other hand, some learning is often reflected in changing procedures, patterns of behaviour, evolving culture, and 'stories' within the organisation. It is fair to say that these do change and that therefore learning is 'captured' in some way so, in that sense, organisations do learn.

The central point is whether we can observe systematic changes in behaviour and culture over time. If we can, there is clearly a basis for arguing that while the process of learning may be individual, the consequences may be more wide-ranging within the organisation. Thus, if the individual learning processes lead to enduring changes in behaviour and culture in teams and throughout an organisation, then the learning is 'captured' at the broader level. So we can refer to 'organisation' as opposed to individual learning, and organisations which seek to encourage the 'capture' of learning could be said to be 'learning organisations'. However, there is no accepted model of organisational learning and, moreover, not everyone agrees about whether an organisation can learn. There are two arguments to consider here:

(i)   This debate may be largely irrelevant to those concerned with developing organisational practice in the real world.

(ii)   Many ideas about 'organisational learning' are incomplete.

In any event, Weick (1995) noted: 'Scholars of organisations have developed theories that not only don't work for them but won't work for others.'

The focus of this part of the chapter is on how an organisation can be designed, systems created, and a climate developed to encourage learning, and thus effectiveness.

9.6   Changing perceptions of organisations

We have already seen in Chapter 2 that our perception on how organisations are described, designed and experienced is changing. This is a result of technological, market and competitive changes and socioeconomic challenges. Part of the change in perception is associated with the impact of rapid, often discontinuous, change, and attempts by those involved to find ways of dealing with this increased pace and complexity. In addition, issues such as managing diversity, cross-cultural influences, gender, environment and corporate social responsibility are creating new challenges to rethink the concept of 'the organisation'. Finally, the challenge of the long-term switch from a 'career for life' model for most employees to a more individually centred concept of a portfolio career adds a new impetus to learning as a key skill: 'learning how to learn'.

New ways of describing organisations are now beginning to replace more orthodox approaches. Peter Senge (1990) maintains that it is now necessary to think more carefully about what is meant by 'learning' and 'organisation'. His work challenges practising managers to recognise that 'mind-set' is a crucial aspect of learning:

> The most accurate word in Western culture to describe what happens in a learning organisation is one that hasn't had much currency for the past several hundred years. The word is 'metanoia' and it means a shift of mind. To grasp the meaning … is to grasp the deeper meaning of learning.

The NASA case study (see earlier in this chapter) and the underpinning activities in the UBS case (see Chapter 4) show that, over the long term, organisations can use information 'learned' to make changes along the developmental path set out in Kolb's 'learning cycle' (Kolb, 1984).

Van der Erve (1994) argues that evolution is the engine of corporate success. He argues that evolution requires that we understand the changes impacting upon us *and* know how to deal with them. Evolution involves a succession of differentiated 'life forms'. Clearly, organisational change involves a differentiation of products, target markets, internal capabilities, employee attitudes, customer groups, internal talent, and area that benefits from differentiation. A chairman of Nestlé once offered the following prescription for successful change and growth: 'Be first, be daring, and be different.' But it is unlikely that this can be achieved by chance. Corporate success demands a high order of cognitive capability or, to follow Argyris and Schön (1974), the capacity for 'double-loop learning, the capacity to break the mould, to challenge the established norms, policies, objectives, resource configurations and corporate architecture'.

All of this argues for the notion of paradigm shift as an important element in seizing advantage. Capra (1986) defines a social paradigm as 'a constellation of concepts, values, perceptions and practices shared by a community which forms a particular vision of reality that is the basis of the way the community organises itself'. He goes on to argue that the social paradigm which drives 'the modern world' is evolving from a mechanistic and essentially fragmented view into a new paradigm through shifts on various dimensions, as follows:

- From a focus on the part to the whole.
- From a concern with structure to process.
- From revolutionary to evolutionary change.
- From objective science to an understanding of how we learn.
- From hierarchy to network as the metaphor for knowledge.
- From truth to approximate descriptions.
- From domination and control of nature to co-operative approaches.

This list is a simplification of the original Capra text to summarise these ideas. Currently, many we could consider to be in the midst of a shift in the mindset or paradigm relate to economic activity that now emphasises networks as learning and collaborative resources, emphasising optimal solutions and, above all, process and learning through evolution. All of this depends less on a need for certainty to precede action and more on the use of action as a means of achieving certainty. Van der Erve (1994) describes this paradigm shift in this way:

- From quantification and certainty to differentiation and uncertainty.
- From parts to the whole.
- From organisation to enable tasks to 'self-organisation' to enable creation.
- From single-loop to double-loop learning.

This shift in the paradigm has led to changes in the language of business, which, in turn, has provided the possibility of new solutions. Where previously people talked of organisation, tasks, systems, products, technology and customers, they increasingly talk about competencies, capabilities, added value, performance management, process design and information flow. This has happened as a consequence of increased competitiveness in the world since 1970, where increasingly, when faced with tough competition, the successful organisation is the one that changes the rules of the game. Hamel and Prahalad (1994) conclude: 'Market research and segmentation analyses are unlikely to reveal such opportunities. Deep insight into the needs, lifestyles and aspirations of today's and tomorrow's customers will.'

Linking this to major change, this paradigm shift has moved our thinking about how to achieve change. Where once the concern was with 'top-down' or 'bottom-up' change, with most of our discussion being about why change programmes fail, and how to use involvement programmes as a means of buy-in and success, some organisations now seek the following, as set out in the bulleted list below. These are often delivered or discovered via cascade communication programmes, change workshops, performance management programmes, and the use of market mechanisms:

■ Providing people with a new frame of reference about the company, its performance, its markets and so on.

■ Uncovering hidden or 'tacit' knowledge (see below).

■ Learning by scoping perceptions.

■ Circumventing destructive politics.

■ Seeking rapid change via differentiation.

Achieving a shift in mindset, then, is first and foremost a cognitive task undertaken within a social context. While communication, involvement and empowerment will form a part of the process, *unless* people in the organisation are prepared to engage with the cognitive challenge they are unlikely to succeed. In turn, this implies that certain skills need to be deployed and developed, and particular organisation characteristics to be in place to ensure success.

Another interesting theme emerging in strategic change literature is the focus on 'conversations'. The argument related to 'conversations' runs as follows: change is introduced, managed and experienced by people within the organisation, which is given its most obvious expression by conversation between people. Central to the research are conversations undertaken as part of a change effort, whether organised formally or not – the discussions around the coffee machine as well as the formal workshops. Researchers seek to understand how these 'conversations' lead to the development of a commitment to change being made. For example, Beckhard and Pritchard (1992) described a 'vision-driven change effort' at Statoil in Norway. A key stage of the process developed as follows:

> The top managers have set up a series of meetings to develop and review jointly the corporate values and principles for managing and acting. The meetings include the top management team and other senior managers as participants. The top leaders believe that, as with the vision, it is crucial for these values and principles to be 'owned' by the entire senior management. They hope the outcome of these meetings will be the commitment by the organisation's leaders to use these principles and values as the guide to their behaviour.

Clearly, then, conversation serves various purposes.

Ellinor and Gerrard (1998) show how the use of dialogue can help people to talk through issues in ways conducive to achieving change. They define two forms of dialogue:

(i)　Convergent conversation, which narrows discussion down toward a single perspective, opinion or answer.

(ii)　Divergent conversation, which expands discussion by allowing for a multiplicity of perspectives.

The key to this is to engage in each at the appropriate time: (ii) early on in discussions about change; and (i) when deciding on agreed actions. Emery and Purser (1996), Bunker and Alban (1996) and Jacobs (1994) look at how best to gain a critical mass of people involved in change discussion in order to evolve a sense of inclusion and subsequent commitment. Following Jacobs in particular it is clear that the period of divergent dialogue about change needs to be significant before attempts are made to close down and move to a more convergent dialogue, even though many people engaged may seek closure more quickly. It is possible to identify four types of conversation from a functional perspective:

(i)　Conversations for 'making sense' of the issues that change needs to address.

(ii)　Conversations for making choices.

(iii)　Conversations for reaching commitments about change.

(iv)　Conversations over revisions to change plans.

These Ellinor and Gerrard (1998) describe as a learning cycle. They go on to observe that the 'sense-making' conversations have the deepest impact on the content of any emerging set of change proposals. They note the importance of divergent and convergent conversation, but also note that we may observe conversations that are about either innovation or replication. That is, that at some stage the changes under discussion are genuinely innovative. Sooner or later the changes become replication, as the organisation seeks to rule out change. Where the talk is innovative, divergent conversations are needed because this facilitates the widest search for ideas, but also finally more convergent talk, as this allows for a focus on the innovation to be put in place. Conversely, where replication is involved, convergent conversation can create a sense of community and commitment. Clearly, managing discussions, whether informal or structured as part of change events, workshops, conferences and so on requires attention being paid to these categories and ideas.

All of these ideas are seen in some way in the development of successful change in high performing organisations: the divergent discussions being developed slowly into a convergent discussion where an agreed course of action is decided. The making sense of the need to change, the choices around how to do it, obtaining the commitment of the staff, and the constant revision as set out above, are all elements of successful change.

9.7　Disciplines for the learning organisation

Senge (1990) indicates how such an approach can be generated and identifies what he calls *five disciplines* as the key characteristics that everyone must develop if they wish to create a learning culture that produces an organisation capable of facing the challenge of making sense of emerging complexity.

The five skills or characteristics are:

(i) *Systems thinking*: everyone must learn how to view things as a whole, and that one set of events impacts on others.

(ii) *Personal mastery*: for Senge, this is 'the discipline of continually clarifying and deepening ... personal vision, of focusing ... energies, of developing patience, and of seeing reality objectively. As such, it is an essential cornerstone of the learning organisation – the learning organisation's spiritual foundation.'

(iii) *Mental models*: these are about 'learning to unearth ... internal pictures of the world, to bring them to the surface, and hold them rigorously to scrutiny'.

(iv) *Build a shared vision*: this is about everyone holding a shared vision for the future. Leadership is the key to creating and communicating the vision. However, Senge sees leadership being about creating structures and activities that relate to a person's total life activity. The leader creates a vision but is prepared to have it reshaped by others.

(v) *Team learning*: teams, not single individuals, are the key to the successful organisations of the future, and individuals have to learn how to learn in the context of the team.

The key observation here is that, when an organisation faces increased complexity in its environment, caused perhaps by competitive and technological change, there is a need to rethink. This implies the principle of the 'mindset' shift as being key, as discussed through this chapter, and the learning that facilitates this.

Hurst (1995) argues that, faced with complexity, a performance organisation needs to become a learning organisation if change is to be achieved. To this end an emphasis on recognition, networks and teams replaces tightly defined tasks, control systems and rigid structures. One of the necessary conditions, Hurst argues, is a crisis – that is, a clear failure of the status quo that cannot be rationalised away, hidden or denied. He argues that all organisations go through an ecocycle comprising eight stages:

(i) Strategic management.
(ii) Consolidation.
(iii) Crisis.
(iv) Confusion.
(v) Charismatic leadership.
(vi) Creative network.
(vii) Choice.
(viii) Innovation.

It is true that some organisations will fail in some way, thus prompting a crisis of some sort, but what Hurst's model implies is that this drives a renewal process through which an organisation recreates itself – more specifically in which people rethink what they are seeking to achieve, with whom and how, and thereby recreate the organisation. Whatever else this may be, it is certainly a learning process of some kind. Again, back to NASA, the reflection and reappraisal of what the organisation does, how and why after a crisis.

How does this ecocycle model relate to the 'coping cycle' model discussed in Carnall (2007), in which individuals deal with significant shocks, bad news or negative events. In effect, the coping cycle model deals with the process associated with a single change, whereas the ecocycle model presents similar ideas (that is, initial shock, denial and confusion, followed by adaptation and change) in a circular fashion in order to add the dimension of renewal.

Over the medium term, change can be part of an overall renewal process. For this to happen, organisational processes may need to be rethought, but at the heart of this learning process are the people within the organisation who are either stimulated, helped or hindered by the circumstances facing them. One challenge is 'fit' between individuals and the organisation if we wish to engender learning and renewal – for example, are the people who performed well in the 'old world' going to do so in the 'new' one?

One of the frequently mentioned but little analysed issues in strategic change is that of 'timing'. It is often claimed that timing is vital for successful change, and this can be seen in the UBS case study (see Chapter 4). The timing of certain events drove the need for change. In many cases, the timing of change is determined primarily by events, the change being the organisation's leaders' response to those events. Hurst's (1995) views of the organisational ecocycle provides one way of viewing the question of timing. Hurst's own summary of his model's key features are listed below:

(i)   Change is continuous.

(ii)   The pace of change varies, sometimes smooth and linear, sometimes rapid and non-linear.

(iii)   Renewal requires destruction. In a resource-limited world the only way to create new structures, opportunities, possibilities is to dismantle structures which are currently claiming the resources.

(iv)   Emerging structures and processes are a product of a multiplicity of factors including constraints imposed by the environment.

(v)   However, the organisation's people are self-conscious 'actors' capable of rational action.

While the reader may refer to Hurst (1995) for a full treatment, suffice to say that the essence of the ecocycle model is to argue that organisations go through crisis and renewal involving three phases:

(i)   Emergent action.

(ii)   Rational action.

(iii)   Constrained action.

The model starts with the initiating factor being the recognition of a market opportunity that turns out to be repeatable. Hurst gives the example of Nike, a company initially established in high-performance track and field shoes, which was able to expand quickly as it moved from basketball to tennis, American football, soccer and many more activities. Also an early mover in the use of endorsements by top athletes, the company exploited a huge, untapped market. By contrast, the 1980s saw increased specialisation between sports, new materials and designs combined with flexible manufacturing. Nike was then assailed by competitors such as Reebok in the aerobics market.

In effect, therefore, Hurst argues that behaviour, action, is *rational* at the outset, as a company seeks to enter a given market, *constrained* as it proceeds through the product life cycle (not least by competition) and then *emergent* as the need for renewal emerges, often because a crisis has occurred or has to be precipitated before significant change can be achieved.

The similarity between the Hurst and the van der Erve views is obvious enough. Both are evolutionary models that, in effect, argue that 'nothing fails like success' – that is, given a successful formula which then begins to underperform, it is very difficult to get an organisation to do more than seek incremental improvements that fail. Clear differentiation is what is needed. For Hurst, the cycle is a learning cycle. What he does not analyse is how the learning is captured such that the organisation could be said to have learned, but what he does do clearly is to show business development and corporate change as a social process within which learning must be embedded.

9.8   Convergence and the learning organisation

Pulling these ideas together, a number of points emerge, the most important being that if an organisation is to achieve long-term benefit from the learning achieved through change, then appropriate processes are needed. So an organisation needs *convergent systems* designed to capture and create knowledge – this could be done by using the IT infrastructure's capacity to capture knowledge, using the management structure and systems design to focus on the encouragement of learning, using the corporate development processes to achieve learning, and applying it in new circumstances. All of this needs to be 'energised' by appropriate leadership, vision, rewards and 'mental maps'. This was the underpinning approach used by UBS (see Chapter 4) to transfer knowledge about the organisation and the services it provided to senior leaders, who were previously only aware of the services they provided, and to energise them to apply that knowledge to deliver to customers in a new, aligned way not done previously, and improve business performance.

So, to achieve this, organisations need a process that facilitates 'productive reasoning' is effectively hard cognitive work that identifies and challenges assumptions, collects and analyses data, then challenges the status quo, opening up tacit knowledge and converting it to explicit knowledge, bringing in new knowledge and thinking through the unintended consequences of systems, decisions, the status quo, new ideas and all within the context of the community that is the organisation. New techniques in the field of cognitive modelling can help in training these cognitive capabilities, but at its root the issue is about overcoming the organisational defences against 'productive reasoning' which tend to have the effect of blocking change.

Following Nonaka and Takeuchi (1995) organisational learning can be seen as those processes we use to capture and convert tacit knowledge into new explicit knowledge and/or to obtain new explicit knowledge. Tacit knowledge is important because when organisations are faced with problems and challenges, solutions, certainly good ones, rarely emerge overnight. Normally people within the organisation have begun to recognise the problems and started to conceive solutions but usually these are incomplete solutions and not fully thought through. They represent tacit knowledge. So the organisation need a process to 'collect' that emerging knowledge. The solutions needed to achieve that may need new knowledge as well, for example, a new technology.

The key is to seek new, explicit knowledge. Doing so, i.e. capturing and converting tacit and explicit knowledge to integrate it into our business system (into our strategy, structure procedures, product portfolios, etc), helps the process of shifting mind-sets by adding new possibilities. Here mind-set change is unlikely to result from directly challenging people's current ideas. Rather it follows by adding new ideas, and therefore creates new possibilities that allow a change of mindset. In other words the 'old world' has its own rules and perspectives which limit change and unless these are added to by new ideas the mindset change required to conceive the 'new world' is unlikely to happen.

This view has something in common with Orgland's (1997) concept of 'vision influencing'. He records a lack of clarity of the role middle and junior managers played in a major process redesign change undertaken by a consumer goods manufacturer. He notes that when asked to contribute to a process redesign project driven by consultants, 760 employees submitted nearly 1000 ideas. Whilst we cannot judge the extent to which the 'bottom-up' dimension was substantial, it may well be that, by adding new ideas and concepts, the process redesign methodology opened up new possibilities for these managers, thus helping with mind-set change and initiating new ideas.

Therefore, the ability to capture and work with knowledge is a pivotal capability creating:

1 A knowledge base – *capture* and *convert* tacit knowledge to explicit knowledge and create *accessibility* to this knowledge.
2 A knowledge base often *organised* to achieve:
   (a) open *access* to all
   (b) effective *sharing* of information – conferences, meetings, etc.
   (c) focus upon *technology*
   (d) *integration* across corporation
   (e) systematic capture, analysis and retrieval of *customer* information.

This is a reality in some organisations. For example, Kao Japlin's leading household and chemical products business handles 250 customer calls a day and now has 350,000 customer questions / complaints stored in the system, which can be analysed and recalled using 8000 keywords by customer name, product, division, date, geographical area.

9.9   Summary

In a rapidly changing organisational world achieving transformational change is a key challenge for leaders. Meeting this challenge depends upon the ability to capture and leverage knowledge. In turn this assumes an organisation has put in place the capacity to learn. Stakeholders view an organisation from varying perspectives and perceive the changes and challenges likely to impact them in different ways. The organisation which can makes sense of the 'landscape' within which it is working and see how that 'landscape' is changing so that it can change itself appropriately can 'rewrite the rules of the competitive game'.

In this chapter we look at issues of leadership, knowledge and learning, linking them in the sense of viewing strategic leadership as essentially a learning process. We explore this through the NASA case study and by looking at the concept of 'social capital'. We then go on to link these ideas to the emergence of networks which in turn we consider by looking at the Zara case study.

We then argue the case for looking at organisation change from a perspective taking account of creative conversation and dialogue as a means of generating learning in the complex circumstances in which we now work. This implies a need to make sense of complexity and to create convergence in learning such that we can develop 'productive reasoning'. In essence then leadership involves hard cognitive work. Whilst at its most basic leadership is a relational activity it is also a hard intellectual task as well.

Questions

1   How much of an organisation's 'knowledge' is really under the control of the organisation?

2   How can organisations better leverage the knowledge of people?

3   In your experience, how could organisations better share knowledge between people?

4   How much impact does shared knowledge really have – is this about being sociable or does it have specific benefits? If so, what might the latter be?

5   Should knowledge be moved across an organisation horizontally as well as vertically?

6   Can an organisation 'learn'? How can this be led, and by whom?

7   How does knowledge enable collaboration?

Systems for organisational leadership development

10.1   Why take a systems approach?

The purpose of this chapter is to consider how to integrate leadership development into the overall strategy for developing the organisation. It is ironic that all too often leadership development investment appears largely to be divorced from efforts to develop the organisation. Developing people as leaders of potential for subsequent promotion has the obvious advantage that in this way one provides for succession, but using leadership development as a key lever for strategic change can achieve much more. Why invest in leadership development unless doing so changes the way leadership is practised? If the latter is achieved this will help to transform the organisation and engage the best and brightest of a 'talent pool' in the future of the organisation. Integration then becomes an important feature of effective programmes.

The key objective for any organisation in undertaking leadership development is to improve its performance. This is often manifested in a strategy that relies on the hope that the development of individual leaders will, by some means, and if applied to enough people, deliver this. However, this strategy is unlikely to be effective and lacks the ability to focus resources on the development of the people and teams that will deliver the highest return and what is critical to the organisation's success. It is therefore inaccurate, ineffective and more costly than having a strategy aimed at developing leadership specifically for organisational benefit. This failing has been picked up by a number of other writers; see, for example Ulrich and Brockbank (2007).

To be effective, leadership development must apply not only to the individual as a single leader but also to the whole leadership group of an organisation. It is only by knowing which individuals to develop, and in what way, and then viewing and leveraging the skills of leaders as a group rather than just as individuals will the organisation be able to maximise its performance. The delivery of organisational objectives is essentially a team process, not an individual one. No individual can deliver all the organisational objectives. As organisations must be made up of more than one individual, then delivering the optimum outcome must inherently be a team process.

This is often forgotten in the context of leadership development, where the needs of individuals often have precedence over those of the organisation. It is only where the needs of the organisation are pre-eminent over those of the individual that the organisation will meet its full potential. That is not to say that individual leaders are exploited, as this would reduce their performance, but when development is being provided, the primary objective must be to benefit the organisation, and through that the individual, not the other way round.

Leadership development from the organisation's perspective should be to create not only good individual leaders but also an aligned leadership team that can then focus the effort of all staff on to key deliverables. The performance elements of this were covered in Chapter 4. Here we shall cover the system prerequisites that need to be in place to make this possible, and in this chapter we set out a road map to deliver them.

Essentially, it is about two key elements:

(i) *Making sure that you have the right person in the right place at the right time*, so you have the leader who is the best for that role. Further, this is not just in one role but in every important role across the organisation. If that is not happening, then it is impossible to build on the foundation of good leaders in key places to encourage high performance from everyone through their leadership. Obviously, having the wrong person in the wrong place at the wrong time in an organisation seems laughable; however, a short reflection on our own experiences tell us how often organisations somehow manage to achieve this rather than the optimum outcome! The costs and risks for organisations of getting this wrong is significant, especially at the senior level.

(ii) *Making sure that individual leaders act as part of an integrated leadership team*. The development of leadership as a group relates to the ability of the organisation to withstand the challenges to which it is subjected inevitably by changing environments. To continue to function and flourish, the organisation must have leaders who are bound together by common process and belief. The military spend a lot of time and effort in developing this to ensure the integrity and efficiency of their teams in even the toughest of circumstances.

This binding of the leadership team together is vital to make the organisation effective and sustainable. If, when the pressure builds up on leaders from both inside and outside, they cannot continue to function effectively and deliver their own objectives or support their colleagues in the delivery of theirs, the organisation will fail. An organisation is an integrated delivery chain, and should any one link be allowed to fail then the whole machine fails. Thus one of the key objectives of leadership development for the organisation is to create effective, well integrated and mutually supportive leadership groups at all levels of the organisation that are able to deliver objectives no matter what the challenges.

This problem is reflected in the individualistic view of leadership in organisations as shown in Figure 10.1, where individual leaders operate their own functions with minimal integration. They don't see their role to operate as a fully integrated team just to deliver their own objectives. This leads to less effective operation and higher error risks especially at points where the functions interact.

However, integrated teamwork, where the alignment of effort by the leadership group on key deliverables is consistent across functions, is likely to minimise risk and maximise delivery (see Figure 10.2).

The need to see leadership as an integrated and integrating process is thus vital to success. Particularly where the objective encompasses 'changing the way leadership is practised in the organisation' and through the right analysis incorporates interventions for doing so, of which leadership development is a part. Organisations, both public and private, face an ongoing need to provide 'streams'

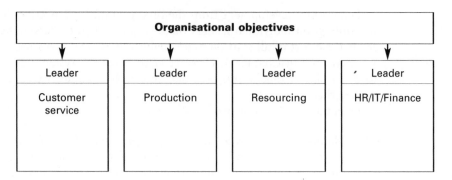

Fig 10.1 Individualistic view of leadership in organisations

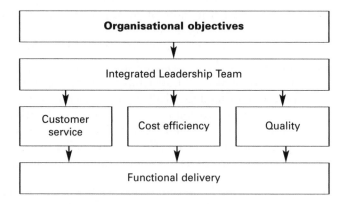

Fig 10.2 Alignment of effort by the leadership group

of people taking on leadership roles as well as technical experts at all levels of the organisation. Thus the objective is threefold. First, to recruit, identify, develop and motivate talented people to provide leadership in key roles in the organisation; second, to ensure a base level of leadership capability elsewhere; and third, to ensure that throughout the organisation all leaders share a common framework of values, ideas and concepts, including a shared understanding of business models (doctrine) and objectives.

The recognition of the importance of this is now becoming clear to CEOs as well as to human resource departments. In the modern economy it is a commonplace to argue that knowledge is a key competitive advantage, so the 'war for talent' continues to concern organisations, both public and private. Irrespective of economic cycles there is always competition for the best talent in labour markets or industries. The assumption made that, in tough times, the 'war for talent' declines because of the availability of people from a pool of unemployed is patently false. The best talent is never unemployed, and in tough times the best talent is a means of ensuring that your organisation survives.

A survey reported in 2005 by McKinsey noted respondents identifying these capabilities as 'most important to your business's growth over the next ten years':

- Ability to innovate: 43%
- Ability to allocate the best talent: 25%
- Ability to manage a global corporation: 17%
  (sample size 9,347)

For example, a research report published by Deloitte in 2009, entitled 'Managing Talent in a Turbulent Economy: Playing both Offense and Defence', surveyed managers. The percentages listed below indicated they would increase expenditure on the areas indicated despite there being a need to cut costs in their organisations because of the economic downturn:

- High potential employee development: 37%
- Leadership and management development: 36%
- Sales/customer service: 29%
- Security and risk: 26%
- Induction/transition support: 24%
- Try to bring in more talent to their organisation: 40%
- Worried about the loss of talent: 43%

Thus having the best talent and developing it is seen as an important objective. It must also be made clear that here the term 'talent' does not only mean leaders, but anyone whose skills and ability can add significant value to the organisation, thus functional and technical experts as well as leaders and potential leaders are included.

10.2   The leadership delivery system: basic principles

To make sure that the right people are in the right place at the right time there needs to be a system to make this happen. Having such a system will then also ensure that development is aligned to general, long-term organisational strategy and shorter-term key deliverables. This system is essentially a machine that matches supply and demand for leaders, and to a wider degree, though not covered in this book, the workforce planning required to match the overall human capital supply to organisational demand. In simple terms, then, it's about working out what you have versus what you will need and trying to fill the gap. The critical deliverables and the tools to deliver them are:

1 Identification of current leadership supply through:
   (a) performance measurement systems – appraisal, performance management; and
   (b) potential measurement systems.

2   Identification of current demand through:

   (a)   initial identification of 'key' roles that present potential organisational risk; and

   (b)   other roles.

3   Identification of future demand based on business strategy through human capital planning.

4   Matching of current supply to current demand – to reveal any current risks.

5   Matching of current supply to future demand – to reveal leadership development demand.

6   Mitigation of any current risk.

7   Leadership development for future need:

   (a)   generic for responsibility level – development of skills appropriate for all at a certain level

   (b)   specific for role – development of skills appropriate for the role.

This assumes that there is base level leadership competence within the organisation; that is, all leaders at all levels have the basic leadership capability of getting a good performance from employees. The system detailed above is there to assess that capability, match it to demand and move it to the optimum location, having fine-tuned it to match the specific needs of the relevant role. If this base capability is not in place, then additional leadership development must be delivered to address the shortfall, effectively to mitigate the current risk.

The structure set out above can be applied to the identification and development of leaders at any level of an organisation, not just at the top. While most organisations tend to concentrate on the top people, world class organisations apply this at all levels. This is because, if it is applied at all levels of the organisation, there is a system where, from bottom to top, individuals would be developed, their ability to take on more responsibility assessed, and if appropriate they would be promoted, thus moving them up the organisation step by step, or moved laterally to develop their experience. This ensures, where it is practical, having the right person in the right place at the right time at all levels, with the performance improvements that would naturally accrue. This is the underlying principle of the talent or leadership pipeline concept set out by Charan *et al.* (2001).

The system proposed is made up of transition points at which individuals need to think about changing the way he or she leads to meet the requirements of the new role, as follows:

- Managing self to managing others
- Managing others to managing managers
- Managing managers to managing a professional function
- Managing a professional function to managing a profit centre
- Managing a profit centre to managing a business

The model sets out what the leadership requirements are at each level, and at each level leaders need to adapt their style, time allocation and skills. This provides a good indication of the development required to enable leaders to take on their new roles and the criteria they should be measured against in order to see if they have the capability of fulfilling the role.

In more detail we have:

- **Managing Self to Managing Others**
  When individual contributors, in particular, specialists (for example, IT experts, scientists), move up to take a line manager's role in the organisation, the key challenge will be shifting from the paradigm of 'doing' to 'getting things done'. Key deliverables required for this transition are: planning work, filling jobs, assigning work, motivating, coaching, and measuring the work of others. Key skills and knowledge required for the new level are: delegation, basic management concepts, time management, project task management, supervisory skills, and coaching skills.

- **Managing Others to Managing Managers**
  The key challenge at point includes cutting down on individual tasks to identify high return on investment (ROI) managerial work that only you can do. Key deliverables required for this role are: selecting people to transit through the first level by assigning managerial and leadership work to them, measuring their progress as managers, and coaching them. New skills required are likely to be: appraisal skills, coaching and mentoring, an understanding of strategic issues, handling conflicts, and team building.

- **Managing Managers to Functional Manager**
  At this level, senior managers get ready to manage their function at the corporate or business level. They need have cross-functional understanding and be effective at inter-team working, presenting a good business case for the resources they require. They have to create a functional strategy that supports the overall corporate strategy and ensure that their function delivers on business needs. They need to possess the skill to communicate with colleagues outside their functional specialism; team-building, cross-functional teamwork, negotiation and influencing skills as an ambassador for the function; functional strategic planning and implementation skills; participating in business meetings; presentation skills; performance management; basic financial management; and project management.

- **Functional Manager to Business Leader**
  Here the functional expert takes on his or her first general management role. Key challenges would be making a shift from looking at the future based on cross-functional activity being brought together to create a delivery or value chain to ensure profit is created. The leader here needs more strategic and cross-functional, integration and team management skills. His/her direct reports need to be built into an integrated team, but for the first time they will not all be from the same function but have widely differing agendas. New skills likely to be needed are: strategic planning skills, cross-functional team management, networking skills, facilitation skills, management of meetings, communication and presentation skills, results focus, performance management, financial planning and evaluation, profitability management, understanding of all functional management areas in the strategic perspective, and ability to integrate and lead complex projects.

- **Business Manager to Group Leader**

  The expertise in managing one business does not guarantee success in managing a group of businesses/business units. Here the issue is not to integrate functions but to let business managers get on with their own tasks. Group leaders need to manage a portfolio of businesses, understanding the business cycles they are in, and providing longer-term support for growth and development. The new skills needed are likely to be good strategic financial management, risk management, human capital management, business strategy, marketing, integration, portfolio management of the businesses, decision-making skills, influencing skills, and value-based leadership.

- **Group Manager to Enterprise Manager**

  The enterprise manager is the top of the pipeline here the focus is on values rather than skills, shifting from strategic to visionary thinking and operations to a global overview. The key skills required here are long-term/visionary thinking, trade-offs between vision and operating objectives, external stakeholder management, and setting the internal cultural agenda. New skills required not previously in place would be insight, to build an organisation through vision, exposure to global trends and directions, prioritising in complex and fast-moving environments, mentoring, effective delegation, and value-based leadership skills.

Thus the pipeline concept as discussed above has several benefits:

(i)   It sets out the key deliverables at each level of leadership – clarity of role and responsibilities.

(ii)   Allows identification of individuals who can meet those criteria – succession planning.

(iii) Enables effective development of leaders to meet those criteria – development alignment to business needs.

(iv)   Provides role clarity and clear career paths for the individuals – more effective working and more motivated staff.

(v)   Provides a 'reality check' to those who wish to advance faster than their capabilities – effective expectation management, especially for high potentials.

(vi)   All the above will generally reduce the time taken to move individuals up the pipeline as a result of the more effective delivery of identification and development to specific levels of leadership roles.

(vii) Generally ensure that your leaders are developed as well as possible before they take on the role, thus they will not need remedial development once in post to maintain their competency, as in many organisations.

This can be summarised in Figure 10.3, which sets out what must happen at each level of staff throughout the organisation.

There are, however, issues around the operation of organisations where there are a significant number of specialists, and where those specialists may at some times in their careers be in leadership roles and at other times in specialist roles. This requires an adaptation of the model to permit two different career paths, one specialist and one leadership, where cross-over is possible when appropriate. This is illustrated in Figure 10.4.

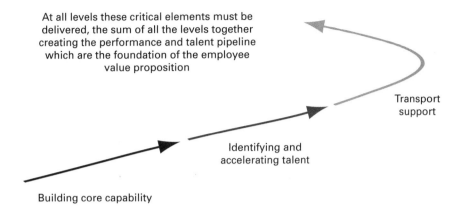

At all levels these critical elements must be
delivered, the sum of all the levels together
creating the performance and talent pipeline
which are the foundation of the employee
value proposition

Transport
support

Identifying and
accelerating talent

Building core capability

Fig 10.3 What must happen at each level of staff in the organisation

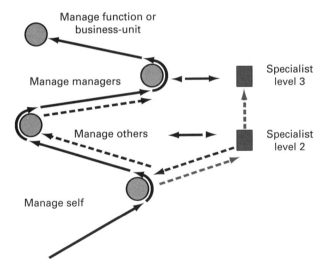

Manage function or
business-unit

Manage managers

Specialist
level 3

Manage others

Specialist
level 2

Manage self

Fig 10.4 Organisational career paths

At the 'managing self' point, the individual would be expected to make a choice
on the level of specialisation, and take the specialist path if they wished. But after
some development of knowledge they would be able to return to a leadership
pathway.

10.3 Roles and responsibilities

Having identified the components of the pipeline process at each level this allows us
to allocate responsibility for their delivery. This lies within the aegis of HR, senior
management and line managers. In chronological order:

- HR to create the tools required to make the system work.
- Line managers to collect the data required by assessing performance and potential effectively.
- Senior managers to assess key roles, leadership role requirements and future needs based on strategy.
- HR to reconcile the match between supply and demand, and identify gaps at each level.
- HR to assess current leadership capability against base level competence and identify risks.
- HR to propose strategy to fill identified gaps and leadership capability shortfalls.
- Senior managers and line managers to implement strategy.
- HR to provide support and facilitation.

The purpose here is to identify the relevant HR issues and responsibilities of management, showing how they are relevant to leader development. In this chapter we do not propose to present a full treatment of any of the areas considered. The issue of space alone makes that impossible. In any event, there are excellent texts available. Rather, our purpose is to set out, first, the links between areas of HR activity and leader development, and subsequently that for management. The key areas of HR practice are as shown in the list below.

(i)   Build a system to measure both performance and potential – to enable identification of talent – supply side.

(ii)   To assess future need for individual posts and generally – demand side.

(iii) To match talent available with talent needed for key posts and generally – identify gaps, possible succession plans and plan development to make up shortfalls.

(iv)   To assess current leadership capability and assess risk – to identify any remedial action required.

(v)   To provide support and facilitation – for example, development programmes, team development interventions.

The key areas for management practice are:

(i)   Effective measurement of performance and potential.

(ii)   Assessment of future leadership needs (senior management).

(iii) Implementation of development strategy – including development on the job or via other business-linked activity.

No doubt some readers will at this point be asking why the implementation of the leadership development strategy is the responsibility of management and not HR. The reason is simple. It is known that the best development often takes place on the job, where it is automatically job relevant, or aligned directly to business need– for example, via a special project. Both also deliver immediate benefit to the organisation rather than having a time lag and transferability challenges that some off-the-job development might have. Such development is delivered by the line manager or other managers, and not the HR function. With development off the job there needs to be careful planning to ensure that the content is relevant to the role and aligned to business need, so that the time taken off the job to deliver the development is counterbalanced by the subsequent additional performance on the job.

10.4   Step 1: Identification of current leadership supply – measurement systems for performance and potential

The effective measure of performance is important for the organisation to find the 'right' people. Assessment is thus a part of this process. Clearly, the key points to make relate to the role of assessment in the leader development 'journey' for each individual. Appraisal, different sources of feedback and assessment centres are often used as part of talent management and development planning. Is it possible to create valid assessments of past performance? And how can we assess potential? This is viewed as 'contested terrain', in particular on the issue of potential. However, it is becoming clear that even potential can be assessed much more accurately by tools now available than by the traditional 'back of an envelope' list used by and provided by senior managers based on whom they favour at the time.

The difference between potential and performance, and the impact on organisations is important. Performance relates to what has been achieved in the past, and potential is effectively what could be achieved in the future. This distinction is important, as the delivery of past performance in one role is not necessarily a predictor of future potential in another. Indeed, data from the Corporate Leadership Council in 2003 would suggest that up to 71per cent of those who are high performers do not have high potential and thus are likely to fail to meet the requirements of leadership at the next level (Corporate Leadership Council, 2005). Interestingly, there are 7 per cent of high-potential staff who are not high performers, so high performance is not always a prerequisite for someone to have high potential as a leader at the next level.

An effective leadership development system assumes that the assessment of actual and potential performance is feasible and is being applied systematically to all employees. What we know in practice is that performance management systems are often well established, but not always fully effective as a means of assessing current performance, let alone potential. Further, the subsequent process by which development is aligned to either future individual need, or certainly future organisational need, is even less sure. It is the quality of the assessment that is critical and while the design of the instrument is in the hands of HR its effective use is the responsibility of line managers.

Berger and Berger (2010) report studies of 350 organisations involved in 'some type of successful talent management', reporting that they typically employ five-point scales based on competence models to measure performance and/or potential. Berger and Berger conclude that most organisations prefer simple models, which are 'apparently successful', the implication being that there is a lack of rigour. However, this does not say there is no value here. There is a clear balance to be struck between the theoretical means to measure to highest accuracy and the reality of an organisation trying to meet its day-to-day objectives. In reality, any attempt to implement a complex 'HR best practice' performance and potential system that has the potential to produce, if properly used, a totally accurate measurement and result, is doomed to failure. This is because the data input for such systems inevitably come from line managers making judgements about their subordinates. Thus, to be accurate, the line manager must be willing and able to make an effective judgement within a time frame that he or she considers to be acceptable within the context of his/her other work.

The reality is that an assessment process that is totally accurate but takes the line manager two hours to complete per person reporting to them is not going to be workable. They will either not undertake the task or do so but to get it completed quickly will put in invalid or ill-considered data. Thus failing to match the tool to the day-to-day organisational reality will make a highly accurate tool produce inaccurate results because of poor-quality completion or low completion rates. In any event, the results will be questionable.

The solution is to produce a tool that measures as effectively as possible within the time constraints of the average line manager, so that as high a percentage as possible will complete the task accurately. Thus, while the accuracy of the simpler tool is lower than that of the more complex one, the quality of completion and the completion rates mean that the overall data quality is better.

The more the measurement/assessment of performance and potential is practised, and shared, the more likely it is that the capacity to develop it further will emerge. Therefore, over time the measurement system can be refined and added to so as to improve accuracy. This represents a constant rebalancing of the ability of the line manager to have the time and capability to measure performance and potential effectively, set against the ideal means to do so that provides a fully accurate answer, the latter being seen as the 'perfect world' solution that may never be reached, but may be aspired to. This is because the diminishing marginal returns of further accuracy improvement compared to the time and resources required to obtain them means that organisations are unlikely to pass the point where the effort of getting additional accuracy outweighs the risks of not getting it.

So clearly, the need to attract, recruit, develop, retain and motivate the best people is important, and HR directors become very concerned with evidence of failure in this regard. This is especially so as there is increasing interest among CEOs in the provision of good leadership and effective talent management as a means of delivering better organisational performance.

10.4.1   Performance

Thus two measurement systems are required: one for performance and one for potential. The measure of performance should focus on the delivery of objectives. This is likely to be in terms of whether they were met or exceeded, and the manner in which they were delivered; that is, in compliance with the organisation's values. This may be measured against a number of scales, or just simply 'met', 'not met' or 'exceeded'.

Berger and Berger (2010) argue that only a minority of employees are superior, or have delivered high levels of performance. Berger and Berger refer to them as 'superkeepers', and view them as role models for success that the employing organisation cannot afford to lose or fail to leverage their ability and potential. They suggest that only 3 per cent to 5 per cent of employees are 'superkeepers'. There are also employees who regularly deliver above-average performance expectations; these they label as 'keepers'. These typically represent 20 per cent to 25 per cent of the workforce. This is reflected in a number of studies linked to employee engagement which suggest that suggest that high employee engagement leads to higher levels of discretionary effort being expended by staff. In most organisations, this group tends to be about 20 per cent to 25 per cent. However, there is an interesting relationship between leadership, employee engagement and the development of both performance and potential.

10.4.2   Potential

The effective measurement of potential is more difficult, but effective assessment focuses on the presence of behaviour that is predictive of the successful assumption of further responsibilities. In general terms, the presence of the following has been found to predict an ability to take on additional responsibilities, namely, being good at:

- Engaging others – getting things done effectively through other people.
- Learning ability – learning from experience to improve performance of self and others. Manage change – being effective in any situation, whether slow- or fast-moving.
- Strategic understanding – understanding, using and improving the whole organisation.

These can, again, be measured either by simple questions asked of line managers and others about the presence of these behaviours, or by more complex systems such as assessment centres. In general terms, the greater the number of objective data sources obtained, the more accurate the likely outcome.

10.4.3   Other factors – ambition and mobility

In addition to performance and potential being present to move up the organisation, the individual must have the ambition or desire to progress and develop, using the opportunities the organisation offers. This is another key point, where the individual's optimum wishes need to be balanced against the needs of the organisation. Further, this must be combined with being prepared to be mobile should that be necessary. This is also a time-related factor, in that at certain times in their careers individuals may or may not wish to take up the opportunity of promotion, development or career moves for personal reasons, such as family commitments. However, not wishing to move into a new role or location at a certain time does not mean that the individual will not wish to do so in the future.

10.4.4   Groups likely to be identified

The identification system is likely to identify a number of different groups – high performers; high potential; both high performance and high potential; normal performers; and below normal performers. The organisation then has to resolve the issue of what happens next for each group in terms of ongoing development. In the simplest terms, the decision concerns whether the individual should stay in the same role or progress, as set out in the leadership pipeline. However, there are a number of variations that give other options, which can develop leaders other than by promotion up the pipeline: more responsibility in same role; a lateral move into a more challenging role; or a move to a new area to broaden experience. High performers often stay in their original roles, as unless they have been assessed as also having potential, it is a risk to give them greater responsibility.

For simplicity, many organisations use a matrix or grid system to identify which category individuals are in for planning purposes. These grids commonly use performance rating levels as one axis and assessment of leadership potential on the second axis. These, then, are visual representations of leadership potential, normally in the form of a 3x3 grid, but they can be made more complex, as a 4x4 grid or larger. The benefit of increasing the complexity of the grid is of dubious value other than for the amusement of HR professionals, as the positioning of individuals on the grid sometimes gives the impression of greater accuracy than the quality of the data can support.

10.5 Step 2: Identification of current and future leadership demand

For most organisations there are two important areas of demand for leadership: the overall demand, and the demand for key roles. So there needs to be an assessment of the overall numbers of leaders that will be required for the next three or so years, and within this identification. of where there must be specific coverage as a result of the levels of risk for the organisation if these key roles are not covered.

10.5.1 General

The general leadership demand is based on normal manpower or human capital planning. This takes into account the current organisational structure with leaders at each level and then compares this with the predicted structure in two to three years time, based on the business strategy. It identifies general number of leaders required and their functional types at each level.

10.5.2 Key role identification

On the demand side, Berger and Berger note that typically only 8 per cent to 12 per cent of organisational positions can be defined as 'key' because they cannot be left vacant for any significant period without damage to the organisation, and thus these need to have qualified emergency back-up and longer-term candidates available through succession planning.

Key roles are likely to vary over time with changes in environment and organisational strategy. A role that was key at one time – for example, heading a business unit in an emerging market – may, once the market is stable, not be such a critical role. Thus key roles should be reviewed on an annual basis by organisations to see if they are still vital. This is essential, as there maybe new roles that have appeared, or existing roles that may have changed which now meet the requirement of being 'key'.

10.6 Step 3: Matching of current supply to current demand, and matching of current supply to future demand

The gap between current leadership and future needs is, then, the basis for building a leadership delivery system. There maybe areas of the organisation that will be expanding during this period, and some that maybe contracting. The plan should

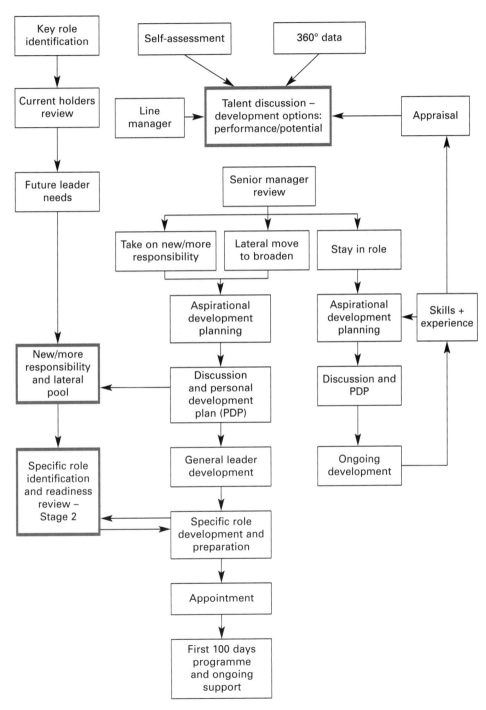

Fig 10.5   The demand and supply of talent

include this. It would also be expected to cover all leadership positions in general numbers terms and the key positions in more detail, with possibly identified successors – for safety, normally more than one individual per role.

10.6.1   Succession planning or specific role planning

Succession planning/specific role planning is a key element matching supply to demand, and thus in talent management and leadership planning. This is where organisations of any significant size need to provide for successors to people in key posts. This obviously applies to the most senior posts in the organisation as being 'key' but the principle also applies at all levels and positions. While 'key' roles must be covered, general organisational effectiveness suggests that there should be successors potentially available for any role where a vacancy might cause damage of any type. In addition, as well as emergency back-up there should also be longer-term planned successors, as often the short-term coverage available is not always the ideal solution. Here, as elsewhere, the effort put into mitigating the risk must be a reflection of that potential risk.

Succession management systems are used to describe the likely pattern over time of 'openings' – that is, existing posts to be filled as a result of retirement, resignation or promotion of the incumbent – and new posts. This pattern is 'matched' by the development plans of all talented people, undergoing a range of postings and development tasks and so on intended to equip them for one or more of these openings. There are also the unexpected vacancies that naturally occur by chance because of people making decisions relating to issues about which the organisation has no knowledge or cannot influence – for example, family or health issues.

Succession planning is a complex process that is subject to the ever-changing circumstances in organisations, changes in strategies, unexpected departures or illness, restructuring, changes in performance or the mobility of successors. Generally, for key roles organisations will conduct annual reviews to ensure that any changes have been reflected in their succession plan, so that full coverage is maintained and risks minimised.

10.7   Step 4: Development planning

From the organisation's perspective, leadership development planning is not just about developing individual leaders for their roles, but also about developing them to be part of the overall leadership group that act as a team to maximise the performance of the organisation.

Having further segmented the population into different performance and potential groups, it takes little thought to conclude that investment in rewards, training, coaching will necessarily achieve higher returns if the focus is towards superkeepers, keepers and key positions. Talent management activities are normally based on a recognition of the need to focus effort along these lines to maximise return on investment (ROI). Development of leadership would normally follow the pattern of initial generic development to meet the requirements of the role level, as in the pipeline concept, and then development that is specific for the role. The latter would probably be developed probably on an individual basis via coaching, mentoring or other development on the job, the former potentially in groups with colleagues via development programmes initially followed by 'on the job' training via their line manager.

However, leader development is not always about development for the next role. In many cases in the first instance it focuses on equipping leaders to perform more effectively in *existing* roles, in which they may be recent appointees, where the role might have changed, or where basic capability is not apparent.

More broadly, however, and where succession management is practised, roles are viewed as a succession of challenges and experiences developing people for future positions. In this sense, therefore, succession practices become an important part of the rationale for leadership development. It represents part of the leader development process in that the series of appointments 'building up' a career pathway are intended to be developmental in any event.

10.8 Step 5: Development delivery – organisational effectiveness as well as individual effectiveness

In much of this book, and indeed in many other books, the development of leadership capability focuses on the development of individual leaders. As this chapter deals with the creation of a system to supply leaders for the benefit of the organisation, there is also a need to focus on the development of leaders as a group in addition to their identification and positioning as a group. This was alluded to in Chapter 3, which dealt with the development of leadership from the individual perspective. The development of group leadership capability has an obvious limitation on the way it can be done as it must be a group exercise. Thus no matter how good the individual leadership development, unless it enables the capability of the individuals to work with their peers as a team it will have little effect on improving the performance of the whole organisation. It may have a positive effect on the performance of the individual leaders but it will not spread wider, and the presence of a number of well-run teams that don't interact well, while being better than badly-run teams, will not produce the benefits of teams led by leaders who integrate their performance across teams to produce more efficient outcomes.

Thus to develop organisational leadership capability only group-based activities will be effective – for example, within development programmes, or team-specific activities. However, the assumption that on-the-job development is not effective for group development is incorrect. Teams can be developed on the job as well as individuals. Most team-based development is done in two types of environment:

(i)   Development of individuals brought together as a team for a development programme as a team within the time period of the programme.

(ii) Development of an existing team that will continue to deliver for the organisation as a team in the future.

10.8.1   Individuals working as a team during a programme

This is the most often used development tool as it is generally nearly impossible, and potentially a risk, to take a whole leadership team away at the same time. Here, groups of similar-level leaders, but often with different experience or expertise, meet and have to work as a team during the period of the development programme. This is likely to be over a period of at least one day or more, to ensure that effective discussion and relationship development takes place. The objectives in such cases are primarily:

(i)   To build an understanding of the wider organisation – structure, strategy, customers, challenges.

(ii)   To discover common ground – experiences, clients, business ideas, challenges.

(iii)   To build networks – to enable the group to interact for both personal and organisational benefit after the event.

(iv)   To identify and or address issues affecting the performance of the organisation or its constituent parts – what are the challenges they face, how can they help each other, sharing of best practice and ideas and so on.

(v)   To challenge current thinking – to challenge the current status quo in thought, structure, strategy or other areas, thus encouraging innovative approaches to be implemented by the participants.

10.8.2   A team being developed for the future

Here the group is a pre-existing or future team that is being brought together to develop its effectiveness. This is could be achieved either through short, on-site sessions with external input – for example, one two- to three-hour session, or a longer off-site intervention. Obviously, having an entire leadership team away at the same time is difficult, but in reality this can also have a positive effect on the development of their deputies or successors, who are then training on the job while the leaders are away. Likely objectives are:

1   To identify issues restricting team performance, how to improve it or identify team development needs.

2   To identify how to improve organisational performance through the team.

3   To address specific challenges or issues the organisation or team currently faces.

4   To build an emotional link between team members, team spirit, to create stronger team bonds and focus on delivery.

An example of the individuals working as a leadership community and gaining individual development is set out in the example from AstraZeneca in the section below regarding leadership in action.

Further developing leaders and changing the ways that leadership is practised is a key theme of this book. Any discussion of leadership development, in theory or in practice, needs to encompass both ideas. But understanding context is also important. When discussing leadership development innovations in the corporate context there is much to learn from the application of interactive methods, simulations and exercises including 'gaming', based on established data around either 'doctrine' (see Chapter 11) or 'business models'/operating models. This can be of particular value for teams where these present 'real' scenarios and enable executives to practise planning, decision-making and 'command' skills and capabilities as a team. In an arena where 'tough' decisions are needed, on which decisions affecting more than one organisational unit, strategic business unit, decision and so on are involved, these become important capabilities.

10.8.3   Enabling the pipeline to be effective

The pipeline concept, as set out previously, is a simple representation of what is required to ensure effective leadership at all levels of the organisation. However, the practical implementation of this is much more complex. Analysis of the components set out in Figure 10.6 suggests that provided these things are in place, the pipeline will work effectively. These core components linked directly to the leadership pipeline are predictable, but they form part of a more complex jigsaw, the greater part of which being in place, the greater the chances of success.

However, the other components that also need to be in place to maximise the effectiveness of the pipeline, or indeed even to ensure its successful operation, are set out in the full jigsaw (see Figure 10.7). Organisations that have the most successful leadership development systems ensure that the additional components detailed in the figure are aligned to the leadership development objectives, or those leadership objectives aligned to them as appropriate. If this is the case leadership development becomes part of the organisation's systems and culture and is not perceived as a disconnected HR-led initiative, which seems to happen in many organisations.

The construction of a framework that aligns many of the components above is an indicator of a successful leadership development strategy aligned to organisational need. The leadership in action examples of both UBS and AstraZeneca demonstrate the implementation of that principle, where significant effort was put into creating an environment where the pipeline would work, and not just implementing the pipeline processes and hoping they would work.

10.8.4   Categorisation of leadership development system capabilities

Within this context it is possible to measure organisations' progress in implementing organisational leadership development systems. For simplicity, from experience of the realities in many organisations, four categories should suffice:

(i)   *Starting the journey* – putting in place the initial core components; for example, succession planning and perhaps development programmes. Often initiated as a risk management response; for example, to having a key role left open

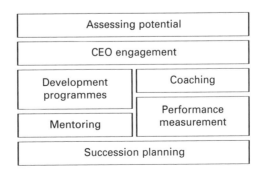

Fig 10.6   The leadership jigsaw: the obvious components

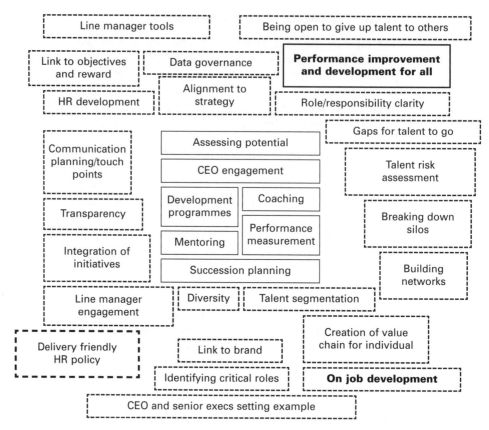

Fig 10.7   The leadership jigsaw

unexpectedly. These would be to identify key roles and ensure that successors are present to fill them. HR is having to drive the leadership development process.

(ii)   *Finding their feet* – discovering that talent needs to be identified and a system created to deliver not just immediate successors but also successors further down the line. A plan to implement the leadership pipeline is normally adopted at this stage. Development programmes are now in place to develop successors' capabilities, and possibly a potential leader identification process. Leadership development is probably still seen as the responsibility of HR.

(iii)   *Strategic veneer* – there is a leadership development system in place, but often primarily for top management and those with high potential above middle management only. The pipeline does not extend to the bottom of the organisation. While most of the key leadership development is in place for the elite few, the majority of the organisation's staff do not gain any significant benefit nor improve their performance as a result. A realisation that leadership development cannot be just be undertaken by HR off the job, and some level of CEO leadership and line manager involvement is planned on the job, and development will be starting to happen.

(iv) *World class* – the leadership pipeline runs and works well from top to bottom, as set out in the previous sections. Line managers are fully engaged at all levels and everyone, not only those with high potential, is being developed and performing to the full. All the components in the leadership jigsaw are in place, aligned and integrated with the leadership development system and vice versa. Here the organisation realises its potential, as do the leaders and employees.

Case study   **Leadership in action: leadership development after M&A – the formation of AstraZeneca**

This leadership in action study reflects some of the processes by which leadership development can support organisational performance improvement and cultural change after mergers and acquisitions (M&A). The same general approach is also reflected in the case study on UBS at the end of Chapter 4 where similar objectives were met. The commonality of the two suggests there are consistent objectives that can be met by developing leaders in groups as well as individuals.

Two companies, Astra and Zeneca, merged in 1999 to form AstraZeneca, to become one of the world's largest pharmaceutical companies. Both companies were largely pharmaceutical businesses and roughly the same size (around 20,000-plus employees in each), and both had a long history of organic growth. Note, however, that Zeneca had been created out of the break-up of Imperial Chemical Industries (ICI) in the early 1990s.

In 1998, Astra, a Swedish based organisation, was ranked eleventh worldwide in its sector, with strong portfolios in cardiovascular and respiratory products. Zeneca, based in the UK, was ranked nineteenth worldwide, with a portfolio including cardiovascular, anaesthetic and anti-cancer therapies. Both had delivered growth, shareholder value and innovation in the past.

The main business objectives post-merger were identified as those of achieving merger integration while sustaining business focus, delivering synergies, retaining key talent and creating a new culture while continuing to grow value. The newly created AstraZeneca senior team decided that leadership development might play a vital role in cultural integration. This led to the definition of the GOAL programme (Growing Our AstraZeneca Leadership), which had three objectives:

(i)   To support the development of a cohesive culture.

(ii) To develop leadership capability both in cadres of managers and individually.

(iii) To enhance the ability to work cross-border.

Seven leadership capabilities were identified as part of the process, but the top team recognised that, for objective (iii) to be handled, people, through GOAL, needed to work on issues such as how to build trust quickly, how to work with differences, how to operate remote teams, and how to move flexibly between groups.

Driven and sponsored by the top team, an 'action learning' methodology supported by 'learning coaches' was adopted. Programme design included three-day and two-day workshops with a Business Challenge Group (BCG), using an action learning approach. People from Astra and Zeneca were mixed in cohorts, thus encouraging an AstraZeneca 'mindset', building networks and encouraging shared ownership for changes emerging from the BCG work and for the emerging new common culture. By the end of 2002, some 900 managers had attended the programme, which was perceived to have helped managers to work on the dilemmas of leadership and change in the emerging business.

The GOAL programme was followed by a Developing Leaders programme, designed for the 'talent pool' and intended to accelerate these individuals' development, equipping them to move into more senior roles. The objectives were:

(i)   To deepen understanding of the health care industry, trends and implications for AstraZeneca and its leaders.

(ii)   To deepen understanding of the business model, strategy and key objectives.

(iii)   To enhance the ability to lead change and to work effectively with a range of colleagues from different disciplines and cultures.

(iv)   To increase the capacity for learning.

(v)   To enable young leaders to reflect on their own leadership styles, career aims and development needs.

Between 100 to 150 people went through the programme each year in the immediate post-merger period. While open programmes were considered, the demands of this period were such that an internal programme was established. This facilitated shared work on leadership and change by developing leaders across the business, as well as engaging senior executives with that work. The active engagement of senior leaders was pivotal to the success of the programme, a feature similar to the UBS experience, where again senior management involvement was crucial for success.

Other activities included an additional senior induction programme for new leaders in AstraZeneca working in global roles. Designed to take them quickly through their 'change curve', it also enabled the top team, who were involved in the programme, to hear about the company from a fresh perspective. Again, the 'leaders developing leaders' principle in action. As has already been noted, the content of this process was very similar to the approach taken by UBS to align the legacy cultures post-M&A, when also improving performance and building a single brand.

10.9   Aligning development with organisational direction – the 'outside-in approach'

The importance of alignment to organisational need of any leader development programme was set out earlier in the chapter, both in terms of the development of individual capability to carry out the role but also the ability to be part of a leadership group. In 'Building a Leadership Brand', Ulrich and Brockbank (2007) set out the concept that, to be effective, leaders need to reflect the brand attributes of the organisation, thus suggesting that leader selection and development should also be linked to brand. Certainly, this links back to the principle that the external brand values of an organisation should also be reflected internally to ensure that there is no mismatch between customer and employee brands. Such a mismatch can lead to disenchantment among employees, where their treatment does not reflect the brand promise. So this is essentially reflecting inside what is outside, and thus linking the two.

Ulrich and Brockbank also comment in similar ways about the core issues identified in this book, the low level of effectiveness of leadership development in most organisations: 'Leadership practices are piecemeal and seldom integrated with the firm's brand, let alone the daily operation of the organisation.' We would argue that until these practices are integrated with the daily operation of the organisation, they cannot be linked to the brand, as they are essentially disconnected from what the organisation is trying to achieve. This is confirmed by the fact that it is mainly organisations that have been reasonably successful in both brand building and leadership development that have been able to move on to the leadership brand approach.

So leadership brand building occurs in a number of leading organisations that have achieved reasonable success, and this is then built on by using brand-related input – for example, from customers or investors – to align the leadership, and thus the organisation, more closely to what the customer wants. This step is difficult for many organisations, even those already doing well. Asking investors and customers to come in and give open feedback on the quality of the service they are given is a step that challenges senior leaders to give up control of the agenda and be open to some difficult truths. For example, in UBS in 2004 there was significant debate about the pros and cons of allowing customers into development programmes to express their views to developing leaders. However, it was decided that the possible shock of what might be said would be outweighed by the long-term benefits of being able to (a) improve customer service quickly; (b) identify issues that only customers had seen: (c) build deeper relationships; and (d) identify new products and services.

Prior to taking these kinds of steps, some foundations must be in place. These are described as the 'Leadership Code' by Ulrich and Brockbank, and consists of the following requirements of leaders:

- They must fully understand the strategy and position of the firm for success with customers.
- They must be able to execute – to create systems that work, deliver results and manage change.
- They must be able to motivate, engage and communicate with staff.
- They must be able to develop talent and groom employees for future leadership.
- They must be able to learn, demonstrate integrity, have emotional intelligence, make bold decisions and engender trust.

Then, when these are in place, Ulrich and Brockbank suggest that the development of leaders should focus specifically on the brand, via:

(i)   Identifying the prerequisites of leadership:
  (a)   the fundamentals – quality product or service
  (b)   the brand differentiators – what makes our product or service special to our customers.
(ii)   Connecting leaders' abilities to the reputation the brand tries to establish.
(iii)   Assessing leaders against the leadership brand.
(iv)   Let customers and investors develop leaders.
(v)   Track long-term success.

They cite evidence from a number of major organisations which shows that those with a strong leadership brand within their industry consistently had higher price/

earnings (P/E) ratios than the industry average. Examples of these are: GE, Johnson & Johnson, PepsiCo, Boeing, Disney, Procter & Gamble and Toyota.

Obviously, this is difficult for organisations where there is a poor or unclear brand, so it could be argued that the organisation has to have progressed well to have such a clear and strong brand before it can develop its leaders further. If the company has achieved this success, then that itself must be in some part a result of effective leadership.

Ulrich and Brockbank (2007) argue that alignment with brand is a better option than alignment with CEO behaviour, which appears in many organisations. Here, leaders sometimes model themselves on the behaviour of the CEO in a desire to mimic that behaviour to obtain advancement. They suggest that sometimes the CEO does not always model the brand well, and often leaves within a shorter time frame than would allow for any brand changes to occur. Thus getting leaders to reflect the brand attributes rather than the CEO alone is likely to be better in the long term. But this is a reflection of the common failing of some at senior management level, which is the 'Don't do as I do, do as I say' phenomenon, which dooms many transformation initiatives to failure from the start.

10.10   Organisational leadership development in the global context

There are enough problems for organisations based in one location to develop best in class leadership, but as geographic and business diversity increases this becomes even more difficult. Consider a company, operating internationally, which seeks to be global but to deliver locally. Corporations in this category include Wal-Mart Stores, Goldman Sachs, Citigroup, IBM, Pfizer, General Electric (GE), Chevron, Petronas, Sony, Johnson & Johnson, HSBC, Microsoft and many others. Why do they require a global structure in any case? Why not operate as a group of locally based organisations within a holding group structure? There may be a number of factors for this, but one certainly will be the principle of economies of scale, scope, with the possibility of sharing scarce resources and learning, including the ability to transfer knowledge and competence.

This benefit does have commercial value. In many cases, creating such a global framework with local delivery has not only been seen in the M&A environment but a number of diversified groups have also adopted this approach in an attempt to further increase return on investments. One example is the Generali Group of over 100 local organisations with at the outset only profit and loss (P&L) accountability to the Group. They were brought together as a co-ordinated group, starting with their first strategic plan in 2003 that sought to better leverage the group as a whole.

The McKinsey report (McKinsey Quarterly, 2005) mentioned earlier in the chapter identified the capabilities needed to be an effective competitor, including the ability to gain and deploy local knowledge, the capability of global integration and co-ordination of operations, and the transfer of learning and knowledge. Turning to the pressures forcing corporations to develop local leader respondents indicated that the key drivers here are:

Operational effectiveness	52%
Languages and cultural issues	50%
Corporate values	46%
Legislation or government influence	41%
Cost reduction	32%

Thus there are a number of drivers here pushing towards localisation, which may then require further efforts towards integration of operations within a global framework. Here, many other factors apply, not least the ability to pool purchasing power, the need to integrate IT systems, the pressure to deploy supply chain management on a global scale, shared services and competencies, harmonising HR recruitment and development processes, and the impulse to develop and sustain corporate culture. But often forgotten here is the creation of leaders – for success in the 'global/local' structure, leaders must have the capability to deliver a high quality, locally tailored service while operating within the framework of a global business. This takes a special capability, both in terms of managing process and people, that needs development.

To take one example provided by the McKinsey report mentioned above, HSBC seeks to develop its leaders globally. With great care it identifies, develops and oversees the career development of a selected group of 'high-performing' people. HSBC conducts regular international training programmes to develop executives capable of operating anywhere in the world. It offers leadership opportunities across 81 countries. This process is reflected in a number of global organisations; see examples of AstraZeneca and UBS already discussed.

Against this backdrop it is evident that leader development serves various purposes. It is partly about identifying and then nurturing and developing a talent pool. But, just as important, it is about developing localisation but not at the cost of lower integration with the global framework. Given that localisation is important, the potential for differences to emerge needs to be countered by efforts to integrate. Developing high-performing people with international experience is part of that process. Providing international programmes such that members of the 'talent pool' – that is, future leaders – work within shared development programmes, developing common experiences and languages (of management, banking and so on), all help to create understanding and integration, and to sustain an overarching corporate culture.

10.11 Working collaboratively in the organisation: the 'domains' of leadership

To maximise the benefit of leadership development for the whole organisation, both locally and globally, we must go beyond situations such as those set out in section 7.9 'Adaptive leadership', in Chapter 7. New thinking with regard to leadership development suggests that further progress can occur collaboratively. James *et al.* (2007) examine how to facilitate collaborative learning for school leaders. This has implications for the development of leadership groups in other fields and organisations.

James and colleagues define 'distributed leadership' not as a set of personal attributes or styles, but rather as a set of practices or ways of being leaders. It is therefore a new way of practising leadership, based on the idea that leadership is practised at all levels of an organisation. This is commonplace among leadership thinkers and seems hardly worth claiming as 'central to most post-traditional leadership models' (James *et al.*, 2007). However, these authors are pointing to something that is emerging in organisational practice: a focus on collaborative working. They argue that collaborative work at least implies changing from peer competition to peer collaboration, which must be learned but is easily overstated. The ability to handle the dilemma of competition and co-operation is not very new or unusual in organisations, mainly because, in most cases, performance appraisal is individual, even in situations where team objectives exist rather than individual ones.

All groups create settings within which individuals seek to resolve this dilemma. Sports teams are a classic example. This is not to agree that resolution is easy, but rather to note that it is not a new observation. Moreover, the resolution of this dilemma is fundamental to most leadership development effort. James *et al.* (2007) point to the work under way in BP in the 1990s onwards, and described in the case study included in Chapter 1, and indeed by the other case study organisations covered in the book. James and colleagues point to distributed or shared leadership as an important component of transformational leadership and to Kets de Vries' (1999) point that however much leaders encourage the participation of others, there is sometimes a need for clear direction and priorities delivered in an authoritative way, much of this confirms what Vroom and Yetton (1973) put forward in their 'decision tree'.

In this context, the challenge of top leadership becomes more complex, and here they refer back to the adaptive leadership model to argue that the role of leaders is to manage differences, conflicts of interest and tensions inherent in organisational life. Finally, they note the importance of leaders creating a 'holding environment' or 'breathing space' within which people can experiment, learn by trial and error, resolve tensions and so on.

They illustrate this thinking by looking at school leadership through a UK schools-based collaborative learning project. At its core this requires schools in a locality to work collaboratively and with other organisations. They note the tensions inherent in this work. School leaders often play a potentially controversial role locally. Should a school's output be deemed to be failing, in terms of pupils' results on tests, then their position is one of failure in a very public position. In addition, schools compete for resources at the local level, with high performing schools obtaining more resources.

Nevertheless, the National College of School Leadership has established a Networked Learning Communities (NCC) programme through which learning networks have been established, comprising groups of schools engaged in knowledge sharing and innovation. A pilot project comprised a group of school leaders, each facilitating a collaborative leadership learning group. The learning model recognised three fields of knowledge:

(i)   The knowledge of the participants.

(ii)   External, public and validated knowledge available from research or best practice experience.

(iii) Knowledge constructed from the collaborative working.

James *et al.* (2007) present no data on outcomes, but they do comment on what they claimed was learned from the experience. This was mainly related to the start-up and facilitation of these learning groups, and about group dynamic issues. Important as both these sets of factors may be, the study set out to demonstrate the role and importance of collaborative leadership as part of organisational work, in this case in the UK school system, and it casts little light on that issue.

It is worth looking at the contextual conditions most likely to be appropriate to collaborative leadership. Snowden and Boone (2007) link the complexity of the circumstances they face to leader decision-making. Complexity is implicit in the James *et al.*'s observation that collaborative leadership is particularly relevant for transformational work. Snowden and Boone divide the situation in which leaders make decisions into five contexts: simple; complicated; complex; chaotic; and disordered. The first four require leaders to diagnose the situation facing them and to act in ways that appear to respond logically to the context.

Simple contexts are the domain of 'best practice', while complicated contexts are the domain of 'experts', because 'best practice' solutions may be insufficient. The need to consider a range of options becomes important. For complex contexts, emergence becomes important. No fail-safe options are likely to be available in these situations and most probably teams of people must improvise in real time. Here creativity, brain-storming, dissent and diversity are of paramount utility. Chaos demands a rapid response. In this context the leader must act to establish order, to resolve the immediate problems to stop the losses and so on, again the need for the stabilisation of the situation and 'breathing space' before the development of action plans.

In some organisational settings this would be deemed the province of 'command', more of which we shall encounter later in this discussion. In a chaotic situation, the first response is decisive action because the losses (of revenues, margins, property, life or reputation) must first be stopped. This is reflected within the development of military leadership. Only when the risk has been reduced to acceptable levels does it become appropriate to attempt to make sense of the situation and decide how to respond over the longer term. Snowden and Boone (2007) conclude that business schools equip leaders to operate in ordered domains, which are either simple or complicated, but within which known decision-rules will operate. In unordered contexts, either complex or chaotic, however, leaders need more than just intuition and intellect. For these commentators, leaders need a deep understanding of context, a willingness to share power and the ability to recognise when to do so, and the ability to embrace complexity and paradox combined with a flexible leadership style. They note also that leaders need tools and approaches to guide them. This takes us back to adaptive leadership, and this point is reinforced by reference to the case example they use.

In January 1993 seven people were murdered in a suburb of Chicago. The Deputy Chief of Police found himself dealing with several situations at once. The grieving families and a fearful community both placed demands on his time. Additionally, he had to run a busy police department as well as take questions from the media, which had swamped the town. He sought to stem any critical panic via the media, keeping the community informed while he sought to use experts to help solve the crime. At the same time he created forums for business owners, high school students, teachers and parents to hear the facts, and to raise and share concerns. He sought to allow solutions to emerge from the community rather than to impose them. All of this is compatible with the adaptive leadership model considered earlier.

Why does complexity create such a challenging environment for leaders? While the answers to this question may appear to be obvious, it is important to understand them because doing so allows us to consider how leaders might seek to deal with situations of this type. Roberto (2013) identifies why firms ignore the early, and therefore often initially weak, indicators of threat to markets or reputation. Initially, these amount to ambiguous threats to their situation, and leaders often fail to recognise these early signs, for various reasons:

1 *Cognition*. Following Roberta Wohlstetter's well-known analysis of the failure at Pearl Harbor, they note that existing cognitive anchors are part of the problem. Wohlstetter (1962) refers to this as our 'stubborn attachment to existing beliefs', and we suppress the data that are inconsistent with those beliefs. Thus we notice and give prominence to data that confirm our existing views, while dismissing any data that contradict them. Thus it is that, before an important deal, those involved will judge the financial data with an optimistic mindset.

2 *Group dynamics*. Long known to have real relevance here, certainly since the publication of Irving Janis's (1972) *Victims of Groupthink*, the 'groupthink' atmosphere within which participants feel insecure, perhaps through working on critical projects without a sufficiently clear charter, budget, reporting structure and so on, may lead to a climate within which members do not feel comfortable raising questions or dissenting views. This is a key element within the development of leaders as a leadership group or team. Self-delusional groupthink is a significant issue within leadership teams. It is essential that some system is in place to deliver a 'reality check'.

3 *Organisational culture*. As organisations mature, the emerging culture may operate in ways that limit the response to threats. In scientific organisations, in which decisions are data-driven, it may be difficult to focus attention on the early signs of impending difficulty if no data are yet present. If in addition an organisation has experienced a long period of continuous success, this will reinforce this tendency – 'we got it right in the past so we must be right now'!

In summary, then, we cannot content ourselves with the traditional distinction between management (doing things right) and leadership (doing the right things) as a means of establishing a basis for understanding leadership. We need first to consider management, leadership and command, and then consider the context within which each will predominate, recognising that in any given setting all three play a part.

Following Snowden and Boone (2007), we identify various domains. These are 'best practice', 'expertise', 'experience and judgement' and 'crisis management and improvisation'. Each of them predominates in the leaders' most likely/effective response to the context with which they are linked. As the contexts are increasingly characterised by less order (that is, the behaviour of stakeholders and of 'systems', so they become increasingly less predictable as one moves from simple to chaotic contexts) the domains shift. At each stage the prior domain is subsumed.

Take the chaotic domain as an example. The key priority in a chaotic situation is to deal with the immediate threat: of death, damage to property, civil disorder, economic collapse, loss-making and service disruption. Thus when the queues of passengers checking in at Heathrow Airport reached numbers which could not safely be accommodated in the departure hall as a consequence of the security measures adopted immediately after the attempted bombing of an airport terminal in Scotland, temporary accommodation was improvised. Only subsequently would leaders seek ways of working together (that is, security services, the airport operator and the airlines) to find ways of coming to terms with the new threat situation. In that setting, therefore, the context moved from chaotic to complex to complicated as leaders found ways of dealing with the realities they faced. It is within the context of military leadership that chaotic conditions are more likely because of the pressures of warfare. Therefore significant effort is made to develop the capability to deal with such situations, unlike in the leadership development for the non-military.

A further vital point here relates to the question of 'path-dependence'. Decisions are 'path-dependent' to the extent that future decisions are affected by the outcomes of prior decisions. Clearly, in simple settings, where 'best practice' and 'alignment' are deemed to be important, decisions are highly 'path-dependent'. In a complex setting, decisions are significantly less 'path-dependent' because innovative solutions and approaches may be needed. In the chaotic context, 'path-dependence' is higher, simply because the response is likely to be based on command and rely on improvisation needed quickly and therefore using immediately available recourses, even if in novel combinations! This has further implications. Improvisation demands a deep understanding of existing practices. Improvisations are often, and readily, misunderstood. The soundest basis for using improvisation in the stresses of a chaotic situation is where the teams involved share a deep understanding of the procedures and practices, forming the basis of those improvisations as well as the purposes the improvisations are seeking to secure. This is illustrated by the case study below of Apollo 13, and confirms the value of organisational and team or group leadership development in addition to individual leadership development.

Case study   **Apollo 13**

Few of us are unaware of the Apollo 13 space mission, not least because of the video version of this near disaster averted by the courage and capability of those involved. Importantly, however, while disaster was averted on the basis of a series of improvisations or 'work-arounds' as engineers and others sought procedures to take into account what had gone wrong, it was clear that all this effort built on depth of knowledge, well-established procedures and long training, both on simulations and as lived experience.

The first moon landing mission (Apollo 11) was prepared for in great detail. Procedures were available two months prior to launch, followed by a series of simulations from which weekly updates of the rules and procedures were agreed in the period running up to the launch. Simulations were in two phases: nominal and contingency. The nominal training occurs early in the simulation period. It is used to establish crew–controller interactions and timing, establish the 'go/no-go' decision points and exercise procedures for the mission. The contingency training tests the crew–controller decision process in a mission environment. Complex problems are presented on the basis of training scripts, carefully prepared to test strategy, knowledge co-ordination and teamwork.

This is a challenging training mission because ultimately people are being trained to deal with something that up to that point has never happened. Working the simulator for 12 hours a day, the training team worked 14 hours a day, with the extra time being devoted to reviewing strategy, knowledge, co-ordination and so on, identifying gaps and developing new simulations to train these gaps. Mission readiness is evidently a complex condition, combining in particular the confidence of the flight team in their ability to handle the countdown, given a deep understanding of everything that is known and now set out in the procedures.

At 55 hours and 53 minutes into the Apollo 13 mission, astronaut John 'Jack' Swigert was ordered to undertake a cyro stir of the service module tanks (a cyro stir is a process involving stirring the gas stored in cryogenic tanks to maintain the gas in what is called 'supercritical density'). This led to a spark in tank 2, which in turn created an explosion as a consequence of a combination of a design fault in the heater circuit. Immediately, multiple indications of problems developed, both in the spacecraft and at mission control, and events occurred in rapid succession. Not least of the issues was to determine whether the problem (whatever it was) was real or an instrumentation malfunction. Some people in mission control 'worked the problems' while others maintained their own particular systems, providing brief but precise reports. Then the mission controller, Kranz, stated that the problem became clear. James 'Jim' Lovell (another of the astronauts) reported 'We are venting something out into the – into space – it looks like a gas!' An explosion had destroyed vital systems. This created a 'no-go' situation for the moon. Now survival was the only aim, depending entirely on mission control and its abilities.

From here, Kranz and his team were working on how to preserve sufficient power to get the astronauts back to earth. Faced with a proposal to jettison the lunar module, Kranz rejected that idea because he wanted to keep all options open. He needed to create time to work out procedures for the return. Fundamental to a successful recovery was trust between the crew and mission control. But Kranz and his team had to put together procedures in a few hours that would normally take weeks of work. Involving his own team, others in mission control, and engineers in the manufacturers' factories alongside the simulation staff and crew members rehearsing the procedures, the vital decisions involved rejecting two options which appeared to offer a faster return because they were deemed too 'time-critical' and left no downstream options. Some of the decisions Kranz described as intuitive, in particular the decision not to use the main engine.

Most important, Kranz was aware of the need to build confidence within his team. Signs of lack of confidence and disagreement among them would create a situation in which senior management must intervene. They briefed the crew continually on manoeuvre procedures, mission rules, consumables and the return strategy just in case communication was lost. Kranz reported having continually stressed to the controllers and the crew that the burn was not critical. There was confidence in the proposed procedure because it was a variant of a lunar module engine rocket burn that had been undertaken during the Apollo 9 mission.

As a result of quick thinking and co-ordinated effort, the astronauts were safely returned to earth.

Source: Kranz, 2000.

Clearly, many of the decisions here were 'path-dependent'. Just as clearly, Kranz and others were very aware of the need to make decisions to secure the immediate survival of the crew, and then to make decisions which combined improvisations to secure a re-entry/return strategy while keeping options open. The well-established, rehearsed and tested mission control and crew capabilities, and confidence in procedures and rules were vital to success here. New procedures were to be improvised. All knew that none would be fully acceptable without testing in the simulators, and with the staff and crew involved having a deep understanding of the procedures and processes involved. An open process was deployed because it was essential to instil confidence in all those involved. In this situation, we see an example of the process within which learning is essential, but which is firmly based on well-tested procedures. Leadership development in a military context represents another example of this approach.

10.12   The impact on organisational leadership of HR practice

As noted earlier in this chapter, the measurement of performance and potential, the matching of demand and supply for leaders, and the delivery of development is the foundation of any effective leadership development strategy in an organisation. This has to be supplied by a combination of activity from HR, line managers, senior managers, and the individuals themselves.

This is designed to deliver the organisation's talent and leadership strategy, which is a key part of the HR and the wider organisational strategy. The importance of clear alignment and line of sight between the leadership strategy and overall corporate planning cannot be over-emphasised. This linkage ensures and forms a key part of the HR strategy that supports the overall corporate policy.

It is clear that the HR function has a critical role to play in the development of leaders and leadership in organisations, and that this is executed with a combination of policy and practice. Within the practice there are both transactional and transformational elements. In this context, these can be viewed as:

■ Transactional – the delivery of basic HR services at the operational level; for example, remuneration, recruitment and policies, primarily to keep the organisation running day-to-day.

■ Transformational – the delivery of strategic advice and services to improve business performance in the future from an integrated organisational perspective.

There is much discussion about the evidence that HR practice, especially in the field of leadership development and other transformational activity, makes a difference to organisations and their performance. Work by Ulrich and Brockbank demonstrates a link between HR delivery and organisational impact. Their Human Resource Competency Study from the University of Michigan in 2003 studied the business impact that differing HR competencies delivered, and how effective they were. While not a book on HR capability, the data reveal some interesting perspectives linked to leadership development. The study found that normal day-to-day HR service delivery had an 11 per cent impact on business performance, while the delivery of strategic HR, which has talent and leadership development as a key component, contributed 43 per cent. Thus it is clear that effective strategic HR linked to developing the performance of people through good leadership can have a significant positive effective on an organisation.

However, Wall and Wood (2005), who concluded that various studies of the impact of HR management practices on organisational performance suffer from various methodological limitations for us to consider the relationships proposed as being demonstrated beyond doubt. More seriously, Godard (2004) noted the rather simplified nature of the high-performance HR systems position. However, it must be noted that Godard's position is itself over-simplified. He compared 'high-performance systems', ideas and practices with, what he proposed, was formerly 'good management practice'. The question is whether there was, and is, much in common between what was 'good management practice' and what is now 'high-performance systems thinking'. Arguably, the latter is, at least in part, a process of making 'good management practice' more explicit, not least by consultants converting it into more defined systems. Thus his comparison is of limited value. More seriously, however, the work of Hesketh and Fleetwood (2006) examined the difficulty of developing theory in this field. However, the effect of their position is merely to argue the complexity of these relationships, not to demonstrate that the relationships do not exist.

At the core of this question is a series of judgements about whether, and to what extent, HR systems and practices support the organisation's 'value' creation process. This applies whether we are referring to 'economic' value, 'shareholder' value or 'public' value. Does work on organisation design, recruitment, talent and leadership development, performance management and communications support value creation? The experiential-based answer must be yes, as we know that if these are not present organisations cannot perform well. The work of Ulrich and Brockbank presents a complete set of data that indicates HR does add value, and that transformational HR creates more than transactional HR, though both must be delivered to enable the organisation to function.

The wider question is one of alignment and integration, and it also relates to the question of how these HR practices operate – but, more crucially, how and to what extent does the operation of these practices create understanding of the corporate strategy and the culture supportive of its integration in addition to equipping employees in key positions with the necessary skills and competencies and motivation/ ambition/commitment.

As we indicated in Chapter 4, there is evidence that there are links between high-performance HR systems and practices and performance. Returning to Ulrich and Smallwood (2003), these authors referred to a survey of 240 firms which showed that respondents saw clear links between strategic capabilities, such as:

- Speed to market.
- Talent acquisition.
- Capacity to learn.
- Innovation.
- Shared mind-set.
- Accountability.

Plus dimensions of company performance such as cash flow per employee, return in assets, market value and book value, and R&D investment as a proportion of sales income. Similar results have been shown by Pfeffer (1998) and Gratton (2000).

It is evident that some at least of the listed capabilities link directly to leader development activity. Thus talent acquisition, capability to learn, shared mindset and accountability all apply. For example, one of the obvious purposes of leader development is to take a group of people currently working in functional specialism (for example, engineering, marketing, client services, finance, operations and so on) and equip them with a shared language and understanding of all the relevant functional disciplines plus an overarching language – sometimes based on strategic management thinking but also feasibly based on the operating mode(s) of the organisation itself.

Certainly, there is now so much data that show a correlation between high-performing organisations and good leadership development from differing perspectives that even if a direct cause and effect cannot be proven beyond doubt, given the multitude of other factors there is a belief that there must be some reasonable cause and effect.

The development of an organisational leadership group must underpin the future world as well as the current one. Ulrich and Beatty (2001) link three sets of core workforce mindsets of 'operational excellence and cost of product leadership, innovation and customer intimacy' to typical behaviours. In turn, the behaviours range from an emphasis on teamwork, process and predictability to problem-solving, challenge and cross-functional work and creativity and, finally, to networking, boundary-spanning, collaboration and customer management. In Ulrich and Beatty's estimate, Federal Express, Dell and IKEA are good examples of the first; Sony, 3M, Microsoft and Burberry good examples of the second; and Four Seasons Hotels and Resorts an example of the third category.

10.13   Making leadership work across the organisation – is anything happening?

Reflecting on data and ideas from other parts of this book, and comments from others such as Ulrich and Brockbank, there appears to be a problem regarding the ability of organisations to develop leadership effectively. However this cannot really be for any lack of data or ideas on what needs to be done. A general review of studies and subsequent recommendations on leadership development from business schools, consultancies and research organisations undertaken by the present authors over the last ten years or so shows consistency of findings. People perform better at work:

- When they are happy.
- When they have the ability to use their skills, and to take decisions.
- For a boss who is capable and shows a genuine interest in them.
- When an organisation has a clear vision and values, and treats it staff well.
- When line managers have the skills to get the best work from people, develop them, and even inspire them.
- When organisations communicate well, value new ideas, obtain staff feedback.
- When staff are engaged in what they are doing.

Many of the reports state that if some of the above were to happen it would improve organisational performance. However, despite these findings being clearly stated and published a number of years ago, and the fact that the same issues are still being raised in current studies, this suggests that problems in leadership implementation still exist in a significant majority of organisations. This is supported by comments from other commentators, as we have seen. So, if organisations know what they need to do, why aren't they doing it?

Evidence from both research reports and the authors' personal experience suggests that in the intervening years not much has improved. Organisations have still not made any significant progress in ensuring that their employees are well managed and led to maximise their performance. This seems to be inexplicable, given the data that effective leadership development does improve organisational performance. Further additional data on staff engagement shows that engagement though good leadership can increase discretionary effort by up to 30 per cent. With all this evidence, why have organisations not moved on to improve leadership development significantly over the past 10 years or so?

This is not an insignificant discussion. What we are saying is that despite the evidence of the benefits of leadership, the presence of HR functions now focusing on transformational HR, statements from CEOs about the value of their staff, and clear examples of successful implementation in a few organisations there has not been a significant change in the spread of implementation to a significant percentage of organisations. Certainly, in general discussions in 2011 the authors found that some organisations who have invested significant amounts in leadership development over a number of years are starting to ask why there have not been significant performance improvements since the start of the initiatives.

The reason seems to be that there are a number of attitudes that appear to block progress in enabling organisations to perform to their real potential through leadership. These are:

1   *We have an HR strategy, so that covers it.* The assumption that having an HR strategy ensures that leadership will be effective at all levels of the organisation is false, as most HR strategies do not cover real leadership development at lower levels. In many cases, what is assumed to be an effective leadership strategy either is not an effective strategy in terms of what it is designed to deliver, and even if it is, the delivery often is not effective and therefore has little effect.

2   *Everything is running OK, so what's the problem?* The assumption that if the organisation is not in crisis it is therefore doing as well as it could be is false. Even improving engagement alone could add up to 30 per cent extra effort from perhaps 50 per cent of staff.

3   *It's nothing to do with me; or I didn't know it was my job.* Developing the leadership capability or performance is not my role – that is what HR does on development programmes. Again false, but very common, as there is often not sufficient clarity regarding the role of line managers and senior management in this area.

4   *It is all too complicated and it is not a priority – a 'nice to have' not a 'need to have'.* Getting line managers to develop their own performance and that of others is not complicated and must be a key priority. However, in many organisations it is said to be a priority but the evidence of day-to-day delivery contradicts that.

The real problem is that senior management still seem to believe many of these assumptions, so there are token gestures towards development, initiated by HR, mainly for high potentials and senior staff, but nothing really happens for the rest of the employees of the organisation. In addition, leadership development is still seen as an HR responsibility, not one for management. Interesting data from Roffey Park (2008) showed that 37 per cent of managers surveyed felt the general quality of leadership in their own organisations was poor or very poor. Even 38 per cent of those at board level said that leadership was not being developed at all levels, but worse. 73 per cent of junior managers, the customers in this case, said that leadership was not being developed at all levels, including theirs.

Clearly, from that, and from other data and experience, senior management, and indeed HR directors, must be assuming that implementation of leadership development is either taking place and is effective when it is not, or they are assuming that what is in place is what is required, when it is, in reality, not 'fit for purpose'. Either way, it is a lack of understanding of what is going on, or what should be going on. Symptomatic of failures in the HR function to either present a business case for leadership development, to set out an appropriate strategy for management to make it happen, to facilitate the delivery of it, or to measure its success. This has serious implications – poor leadership produces poorly performing staff, which produces poorly performing organisations.

The solution would appear to be to embed leadership development as a key part of corporate strategy, and not just a sub-component of HR strategy. This would increase the chance that the development of leadership is seen by senior and other management as a core part of the organisation's activities. Further, having a CEO who understands and sets an example confirms this message, but to do this support is needed from HR. Combined with clarity of role regarding what all the varied stakeholders are required to do to develop good leadership and HR function with the capability to facilitate and support delivery, then the chances of success are high.

10.14   Retention – keeping the assets you have developed

It is all very well spending vast amounts of money and other resources on developing leaders, but the organisation needs to get a return on investment and must prevent the leaders from being 'poached' by competitors until the organisation gets that return. There is often a misconception that offering individuals more money will make them stay, but the research data do not support this. Similar to performance, the key driver of retention is the individual's line manager. This confirms the need for leadership capability to be developed at all levels, and not just the top personnel in organisations.

This is confirmed by the Corporate Leadership Council's (2004c) Engagement Survey which showed the following top drivers of retention (note that everyone is the responsibility of the line manager):

- Manager cares about employees – 33.8%
- Manager puts right people in right roles at right time – 33.2%
- Manager accurately evaluates performance – 32.3%
- Effective career advice – 31.9%
- Quality of informal feedback – 31.6%
- Manager respects employees as individuals – 31.4%
- Manager demonstrates honesty and integrity – 31.2%
- Manager makes sacrifices for direct reports – 31.1%

- Manager provides necessary information for job – 30.7%
- Connection between job and organisational strategy – 30.3%

The highest remuneration-related driver was 14.4% satisfaction with total compensation.

Thus it is clear that the value chain for talent development must include effective efforts to retain and gain value from the talented people involved in order that both they and the organisation are benefiting. This is especially important for those selected as leaders of the future but applies to all employees. It should be noted that the impact on the organisation of the loss of a high performer can be as great as that of an identified high-potential future leader.

There are other factors in retention that relate to the wider organisation – in terms of whether the individual sees the organisation as a place he or she wants to be: in terms of vision, culture, career paths and advancement prospects. But the line manager is the key component.

10.15   The future

10.15.1   The challenges of complexity and change

The future will no doubt see those in leadership roles and pursuing the practice of leadership having to contend with ever more complex and fast-moving environments. It is this complexity and speed of change that make the leaders' roles more difficult, in particular at the strategic level. But this will apply to organisations as well as to their individual leaders, so they will have to ensure that those leaders are individually capable of dealing with the challenges they face, but that also as a group they have the strength of community that will withstand the negative stresses placed on it. This suggests that activities that have a positive effect on team collaboration will become increasingly important. It will be important in particular for organisations, where required, to find the optimum 'global/local' balance, driven by the need for increasing economies of scale but countered by the need for local differentiation in the local market.

10.15.2   Short-term perspectives

For the individual leader, and indeed most employees, the key question 'What should I be doing?' is followed by another: 'What am I rewarded (be it in the form of pay or promotion) for doing?' That is essentially what employees will think. These questions reflect the annual objectives employees have been set, which will, one hopes, be reflective of what the year's annual objectives are for their teams, their departments and the wider organisation. The problem is that this encourages employees not to think about anything outside that timescale as being important. At a stroke this means that many of the things we have said are important either to their own development as leaders or the development of leadership in the organisation, or indeed any long-term organisational strategy, will fall outside the objective setting and therefore be neglected. This is a classic problem in organisations that fail to become world class – the omission of effort towards the things that are not urgent but are important.

To address this objective setting, both for the organisation and for leaders, must have short, annual, and longer-term, perhaps two-year, objectives for both delivery and leadership development. This is very rare, but is a critical step that needs to be taken to enhance the chances of leadership development and organisational performance to reach anywhere near its full potential. At UBS in 2002 the leadership strategy that was developed had a three-year span, with annual milestones. In terms of real leadership and culture change this would be a realistic period in which to start to see significant results.

In addition, other trends will require changes to the organisational leadership development systems. These might be as detailed in the sections below.

10.15.3   Demographic challenges

In the UK in 2010, about 70 per cent of women and 75 per cent of men over 50 were in the workforce, and this is reflected in similar figures within Europe and the USA. Unless organisations retain older workers, shortages will be caused in terms of both numbers and skills as there are not enough young people to make up the shortfall. The peak of household disposable income occurs between the ages of 55 and 74. So older workers are critical to delivering customer service to the key customer group they reflect. Further, of those older workers, nearly two-thirds say they want to work on past retirement age.

Despite the fact that the majority of CEOs are over 50 across the globe, there seems to be an assumption that workers aged over 50 do not add as much benefit to organisations as younger workers. This is in direct conflict with the research showing that in fact older workers – represented by anyone aged over 50 – are often more flexible than younger ones, better with customers and can develop the skills of colleagues, which has the effect of increasing the performance of all. In addition, because of their valuable organisational experience, they play a key role in keeping the organisation running well day to day. Many have been through difficult experiences in their careers, which increases their determination to succeed and survive difficult economic conditions, as those experienced in recent years.

So, if older workers are less likely to give up on their organisation, why should some organisations give up on them? Performance and talent are not age related. There are young workers who can succeed, but according to the research, as a group, older workers have a higher percentage of the attitudes and skills that organisations need. Further, as they will become a more significant part of the workforce, and thus a potential leadership pool, organisations must take action to identify and develop leaders from this group. And on the other side, leaders who have older workers as subordinates must also adapt. So what should organisations be doing to realise this?

- Use potential identification across the organisation irrespective of age.
- Train leaders to leverage this group more effectively.
- Encourage older workers to develop themselves and others.
- Ensure older workers transfer intellectual capital before they retire.
- Balance the recruitment of new workers with the return of valued retirees.
- Ensure flexible and part-time working and lifelong strategy learning is in place.
- Senior leaders must set an example when dealing with older workers.
- The culture must change to encourage respect for and employment of older workers.

10.15.4   Remote leadership

With the development of technology and geographic expansion in teams it is likely that there will be a greater demand for the remote leadership of teams. In this situation, the inability of leaders to be physically present to motivate, develop and support team members will present a number of new challenges. Organisations will have to provide support and systems to enable leaders to provide a non-physical-presence style of leadership to enable teams to continue to perform well. This is not new, as many global organisations already operate on this principle in some areas but this is likely to increase with leaner leadership teams based on service or product delivery rather than function.

10.15.5   The challenge to implement

As was suggested earlier, the development of leadership, and in particular that for organisational rather individual benefit, has not advanced significantly over recent years. Thus the greatest challenge for the future is the same as that for the past – to take the principles of good leadership and implement them effectively across the organisation. This can only be undertaken in a partnership between HR, senior management, line management and individuals – both leaders and employees. However, it has to be initiated by someone and in most cases this has to be HR. But questions often remain regarding the relevance of what HR is proposing. Further, any actions must be underpinned by support from the CEO and the senior management team. HR function must undertake significant capability development to build credibility with the business and make the transition from delivering merely transactional HR to both transactional and transformational. This can be helped if HR takes significant steps to really understand the business and to service its needs, not just to force 'best practice' HR products on it.

The challenge is for the different components of the organisation's leadership group to come together, understand the business case for leadership development, align this to organisational strategy and critical deliverables, and then implement it throughout the organisation, top to bottom, to engage staff and align their extra effort with what really matters and at the same time identify and develop the leaders of the future. It sounds simple but in practice it isn't; however, even this simple and logical explanation of what organisations need to do would not be recognised by many at the top of organisations.

10.16   Summary

Leadership development must align to organisational needs as much if not more than individual needs. This is because organisations operate with teams and not just individuals. The leadership of the organisation must be aligned to the vision, values culture, strategy and current objectives via a system that also makes sure they have the right person in the right place at the right time.

Good leadership must be viewed as the foundation that underpins all activities undertaken as a 'need to have' and not merely a 'nice to have', as noted earlier. It must focus effort on what really matters – critical deliverables – in both the long and short term. Good leadership must be developed across the organisation at all levels, not just at the senior level, to maximise performance. To make this work, a pipeline (see Figure 10.3) or similar concept must be put in place. While initially this might focus on the more senior levels where the risks or ROI are higher, it must after time cascade down through the company. The organisation must identify key roles that need to be assured of leadership coverage. HR must take an initiating role at first, but then subsequently ensure that individuals, senior management and line managers take on their responsibilities for leadership development, and that these are clearly defined.

Further, an effective pipeline is delivered not only the by the initiatives that enable the data collection and demand/supply reconciliation but it must be supported by the whole panoply of leadership jigsaw components (see Figure 10.8). These create the culture and the environment for leadership to work by aligning other organisational activity to the pipeline, or the pipeline to those activities. Thus from the perspective of the organisation there is clear commonality of objectives between leadership initiatives and the organisation's vision, strategy and current objectives.

To identify future leaders there must be effective measurement of performance and potential based on a system of assessment that line managers operate effectively to produce accurate results. There must be a calculation of the balance between the availability of the line manager's time and the complexity of the tools in use, to ensure day-to-day relevance. Further, all staff should have the opportunity to be assessed on both their performance and potential on a regular basis.

Development must be delivered on a team as well as on an individual basis and focus on organisational deliverables – they must take into account all the different situations likely to face leaders and his/her team. The ability of teams to maintain their structural integrity through team spirit against the challenges the environment throws at them is vital. This can only be developed via teamwork and development.

As well as dealing with present challenges, development of leadership group performance must include the future needs of the organisation. Leadership is never static; it needs constant fine-tuning to keep up with the changing environment, the changing personnel and the changing needs of the organisation, that is why a leadership development system is never finished, it is only ever 'on the journey', as there is no such thing as perfect leadership in practice – we can always get better. If we ever think we have got leadership working perfectly in an organisation that is the day that things start to go seriously wrong.

Questions

1   What are the differences between the individuals' and organisations' objectives in leadership development?

2   What are the key elements in ensuring that the right person is in the right place at the right time?

3   What is the optimum balance between co-operation and competition for organisations' leaders on the same level?

4   Who is responsible for developing leadership in organisations?

5   Where would you start to implement the leadership pipeline in an organisation, and why?

6 How would you align a leadership pipeline to organisational needs?

7 Which is more important to measure – performance or potential? Who should assess it for an individual?

8 What would you define as a 'key' role for leadership planning purposes?

9 What domains of leadership are likely to be encountered in commercial organisations?

10 How does HR add the most value to organisations?

11 What are the roles of the CEO and senior management in the delivery of leadership development?

12 What is the role of line managers in the delivery of leadership development?

13 What is the role of HR in the delivery of leadership development?

11 Leadership through 'changing minds'

Ultimately this book has sought to examine what is special about the role and development of strategic leadership. Our concern has been to bring together a set of concepts to guide thinking and practice about how to develop senior leaders most effectively. All along, we have acknowledged that a focus solely on the behaviour of senior leaders, particularly in terms of relational behaviour, is insufficient for our purpose. We have argued that the way senior leaders conceive and make sense of their organisation and its context is just as important. If senior leaders make wrong decisions (for example, about which markets to exploit and how; which strategies and business models to implement; and how ambitious a strategic change programme the organisation can and should pursue) then the consequences can be long-lasting and profound for the destiny of the organisation over which they preside.

The objective of this final chapter is to bring together the various themes of the book by taking an explicitly ideas- and knowledge-based view of leadership. We shall further examine command, leadership and management, applying these concepts to the challenges faced in the real world, and the examination of the theoretical foundations on which they are built. We have emphasised uncertainty as an important determinant of leadership outcomes, and how 'changing minds' and social change are all part of effective leadership. We look at the organisation as a 'knowledge market', and show that leaders need to think about the impact of, and their roles in, significant and longer-term social change, given the uncertainty they may face. We discuss the problems around transferring the theory of good leadership successfully into the real organisational world.

11.1 Understanding leadership

Most scholars of leadership agree that leadership is a relational activity, both in theory and practice. But it does not follow that this relational component is the sole determinant of the success and failure of leaders. How leaders behave in relation to others in the short run is not the only success factor. Important though that may be, it is neither a necessary or sufficient condition for understanding leaders or their impact. At a senior level, while leaders must understand the impact they have on others in the short term, the longer-term impact of the assumptions and the decisions they make is likely to affect the organisation over many years. At a junior level, these assumptions and decisions will also have a long-term impact. Though not as significant in overall organisational terms as senior leaders, junior leaders do have a significant short-term impact on individual and team performance and thus will have some organisational impact. The long-term impacts of the entire middle and junior leadership groups are often ignored, but if they are not aligned with senior management in their leadership approach the impact can be confusion, wasted effort and reduced performance.

In any event, the decisions of all leaders have a significant impact on the personnel for whom they are responsible, and this impact can change performance, motivations, careers or even whole lives, for better or for worse. Neither we nor the leaders themselves must ever forget this, as with the power of leadership comes the responsibility to use that power wisely and not selfishly even in difficult circumstances.

Leadership in a modern organisation, by virtue of the complexity of the environment, is also a cognitive challenge. As we have learned from history, leadership is ultimately tested through decisions. Decision-making employs both ideas and information, combined with perception, preferences and sense-making. For example, decisions by leaders to enter particular markets, or to deploy particular business models, may have profound consequences long after they have vacated their roles. Further, the ideas they express, their judgements and the decisions they take based on their predictions regarding the way that customers and competitors may be behaving in the future can be the key to success or failure. The same applies to the cultures they drive; for example, GE after Jack Welch is still adhering in general terms to the culture and approach he developed many years before.

But it is also clear that short-term actions also have an impact in the long term – a leader who is more able to engage staff and encourage high levels of commitment in the short term will gain better input and support from their subordinates and therefore make better decisions. So good leadership creates a virtuous circle that feeds on itself and is likely to improve performance continuously.

It is clear that our judgement of leaders relates in reality to both the immediate impact they have with colleagues and others, and the longer-term organisational outcomes of the decisions and choices they make. Leaders are rightly measured by results they deliver in both the short and longer term. The road to longer-term corporate failure can be initiated by a set of seemingly sensible or good short-term decisions. This is well characterised by CEOs who maximise shareholder return and profits in the short term by reducing investment for the future to a minimum, thus making them appear successful for a few years but in fact creating significant dangers for the longer term because of investment for future growth, or even to deliver performance at current levels. Of course, by the time this is apparent, the CEO concerned will have departed with a significant bonus based on the short-term profits delivered.

11.2   Leadership from a problem-focused perspective

Grint (2005, 2008) has analysed the issue of authority in relation to the concepts of leadership and management – to use a common distinction, and command. He adds command partly because he writes both as a leadership theorist and a practitioner working at the UK Defence Leadership Academy, but also in his 2008 publication he uses an emerging analysis of leadership, management and command as the basis for examining the 1944 invasion of Europe by the Allied Forces on D-Day, 6 June 1944.

This still holds the record as the largest amphibious landing of all time, delivering nearly 200,000 troops over a 50-mile stretch of the French coast in a matter of hours, with nearly 5,000 ships and 200,000 naval personnel enabling the landing. It is interesting to consider whether the successful execution of such a vast and complex enterprise as D-Day could possibly have been successful without deploying the concept of command? But how does this fit with the decisions and actions of senior corporate leaders and the context within which they work? Could command play any part in the non-military world?

If the common perspective of most readers is that command is an authoritarian military approach, this would preclude it from being used in the corporate world. If, however, it is defined as the leader making rapid decisions without consultation because of the circumstances and expecting immediate action, then it is something that might often be required in the corporate world. It is also true that in some situations command may be used during the implementation of an action, but prior to that a consultation and analysis phase might have occurred – leadership and management making command effective. So, in some circumstances, command does have validity in the non-military organisation.

Grint's typology combines leadership, management and command with three problem types, namely tame, wicked and critical. Here he uses Rittell and Webber's (1973) typology of tame and wicked problems.

Tame problems may be complicated, but they are routine. There are well-established methodologies available, and executives are well practised in their application. *Wicked* problems are novel, with no obvious solution; there is no right or wrong answer. Wicked problems are characterised by uncertainty. Grint (2008) argues that 'wicked' problems are complex rather than complicated, and often intractable. 'Solutions' often cause other problems and there are no 'right' or 'wrong' answers, only more or less feasible ones. The key point here is uncertainty. In effect, 'wicked problems' are complex because they are both complicated and characterised by uncertainty. Tame problems are the province of management. Wicked problems give rise to the need for leadership because the key behaviour is to ask the right questions rather than to provide answers. Essentially a 'rush to judgement' is more likely miss one of the more feasible solutions. A collaborative process is needed. 'Tame' examples include planning the rail timetable, training the army or planning a heart operation, whereas 'wicked' examples might include developing a transport strategy for a nation, or an energy or a health strategy for a underdeveloped nation.

From Grint's view, command is the appropriate response to *critical* problems. His definition shows a critical problem as being one linked to a crisis (for example, a response to a train crash or major fire, a radioactive leak from a nuclear plant, a heart attack and so on). Here, a more authoritarian approach is needed and Grint defines command as being equivalent to authoritarian leadership. This is also mirrored in the proposed approach for such situations, from Vroom's 'decision tree' approach to decision-making (Vroom and Yetton, 1973) Because time may be of the essence, and such situations may well entail danger to life and limb, clearly leaders must act, and act fast. But in modern English the word authoritarian is loaded with negative meaning. Would people, when asked, perceive 'decisive' to be a positive term and 'authoritarian' a negative one? Many might.

The Heifetz (1994) model of 'adaptive leadership' is relevant here. Heifetz sees the origins of the model as being based on the search for solutions to deep-seated conflict, characterised by uncertainty where there is no clear basis for making progress. The focus of leadership in such circumstances is on creating a 'holding environment' within which 'space' is created to reframe questions and to move towards 'tough choices'. The key here is that in such circumstances long-held positions and preferences may need to be abandoned. That is not easy for anyone and takes time. This type of problem is covered later in the chapter with reference to the insurgency problems in Northern Ireland 1970–90.

In some situations the complexity of the environment and conflicting needs of key stakeholders means that there is no simple solution, or a single correct answer. Thus the concept of 'adaptive leadership' was developed, proposed by Heifetz (1994). The idea of adaptive leadership is exemplified by the title of his book: *Leadership Without Easy Answers*. Heifetz seeks to understand leadership in a particular context; that is, where the challenge is not merely one of an uncertain future but rather one in which key and powerful stakeholders are engaged in a deep-seated conflict and no obvious basis for reconciliation exists.

In Heifetz's formulation, leaders seek to engage those involved in any given situation in a process of facing up to tough choices and issues. The leader provides a 'holding environment' to allow this to happen. In effect, the leader creates a 'safe' environment within which stakeholders can explore issues and possibilities. The challenge for adaptive leadership relates to the often substantial gap that may be perceived to exist between the aspirations of different stakeholders, which might require responses well outside the repertoire and 'mindset' or 'mental maps' within which stakeholders currently operate.

Adaptive leadership is composed of processes to help narrow these gaps. It requires learning and compromise often of great significance to those involved. Adaptive leadership is seen as being based on the capability of the leader to create a 'safe' environment. Clearly, this will be based on the credibility and authority of the leader. Heifetz views authority as both a resource and a constraint on leadership, and that authority serves three purposes: namely direction, protection and order. The latter two are of particular relevance here. Built into the perception of authority is an assessment of the level of trust. Heifetz raises the obvious question. While people will trust a leader who delivers on the expectations they bring to the relationship, but how will they view a leader who challenges them and delivers messages they do not want to hear? Adaptive leadership involves a stance of working with and through stakeholders as a means of resolving the paradox of trust. Clearly, it involves learning, and just as obviously it involves learning that might be unwelcome and will certainly be uncomfortable.

Narrowing the 'expectations gap' involves working with stakeholders as they distinguish between what is essential and what is expendable. Central to this point is the concept of the experience of loss. Stakeholders giving way on issues deemed to be expendable represents a complex dynamic. Stakeholder group membership is diverse – both in people's knowledge and assessment of issues, and knowledge and engagement in the process of adaptive change. The salient point is that the situation to be resolved is deep-seated (for example, peace processes, civil rights, conflicts over issues such as nuclear power, the use of animals for experimentation, strategies for crime and violence, and much more). Accepting that long-held 'positions' are expendable implies loss, therefore not least potentially of identity, competence, and security and reputation.

Fundamentally, adaptive leadership views the people involved (in a problem situation) as the problem, so they are therefore the only source of a sustainable solution. On this basis, responsibility for problem-solving shifts to those stakeholders. Adaptive leadership is values-based because fundamentally it requires a reframing of the questions at issue. Ultimately, adaptive change is experimental and will generate avoidance and dissonance as well as change.

Often scholars working in the field of adaptive leadership note the importance of distinguishing authority and leadership. Authority is a resource but it might also represent a constraint on leadership when key stakeholders do not accept the authority of those in leadership positions. Holding a leadership position only conveys authority where legitimacy is accepted. Authority exists to provide direction for people's actions, protection (in given circumstances), and to establish and sustain order. The key question relative to legitimacy arises when those in leadership positions are unable to fulfil expectations of stakeholders and in addition raise issues, questions and challenges that conflict with those expectations.

Clearly such a situation will often arise in conflict situations – for example, Northern Ireland from the late 1960s to the recent past; or over issues relating to campaigns such as that for 'animal rights' where individuals are targeted. Such situations are not amenable to being treated as technical issues; they require stakeholders to learn. In particular, there is a real challenge involved in seeking to close the gap between aspirations and reality, which requires stakeholders to distinguish between what is essential, because it is of fundamental importance, from what could be expendable, but which will involve an experience of loss if conceded. In practice, adaptive work requires time. It is experimental and creates disequilibrium and avoidance behaviour. Adaptive work will lead to stakeholders needing to come to terms with loss, whether of identity, competence, security or reputation.

Adaptive leadership places specific demands on leaders. For example, how is it possible to work within a situation of disequilibrium? Is there a 'zone of disequilibrium wherein there is sufficient incentive for stakeholders to engage in productive reasoning and discourse'? Are there 'limits of tolerance' of loss which can be identified (Heifetz, 1994)? Whatever else this may require, 'reframing reality' is part of the process. This requires a willingness to take risks in discussions with stakeholders and the ability to find low-risk tests of ways forward. Ultimately, leaders need to engage with stakeholders in often very difficult conversations that set at issue their credibility in the situation at hand. Whatever else one can argue, it appears clear that adaptive leadership requires a systemic view to be taken of any conflict situation because only on that basis can a reframing of the situation be possible.

People often only accept that progress demands movement away from the status quo because it now incurs problems and costs, be they financial, social political or economic. In simple terms, the cost/benefit of the status quo is now negative rather than positive and this must be addressed. The emphasis in adaptive leadership includes ideas such as the 'zone of dis-equilibrium', 'limits to tolerance' and 'productive reasoning'. Overall, the task of the adaptive leader is to enable all involved to agree that the current situation is no longer viable and that change must occur, to develop a strategy for that change and then successfully implement it.

The association of command with authoritarian leadership or with crisis management is something that may be prevalent within non-military organisations. In the military command it is accepted as a means of delivering leadership and is not seen as inherently authoritarian. The non-military associate command with an old-style authoritarian military approach that is no longer practised. But command can provide a positive and effective approach to certain situations. Any situation requiring leaders to take decisions and responsibility because those around them are unable to do so requires command. Thus, where time pressure or limitations on knowledge among others mean that the leader is the only person who has the time or knowledge to make the decision, then command is the logical solution. This is again supported by the principles within Vroom and Yetton's decision tree (Vroom and Yetton, 1973) and to some degree the principles behind later models such as 'situational leadership' – after all is not 'telling' from Hersey and Blanchard (1988) effectively command?

For example, in the corporate world, the allocation of resources, or deciding on goals or market opportunities may well require command. Decisions to change strategy, mission or resource allocation significantly for any organisation will need command if time pressure applies. Command decisions will often involve subsequent collaborative working to implement, but are more likely to be characterised most effectively by the need to persuade different divisions or different organisations and agencies to work together quickly, especially in a crisis or where new tasks require novel forms of collaboration and/or new combinations. The BP Gulf of Mexico oil disaster of 2010 is a case in point – command was required at the outset to deal with the emergency, create a holding pattern to allow development of a strategy to deal with the problem, and then to implement it.

Grint (2008) argues that the problems leaders work on are socially constructed. Thus from his point of view the proper response in terms of leadership, management and command to achieve success is likely to be the most persuasive as viewed by those who have to deliver that success. To view command as being solely about 'forcing the answers on followers' is the point of departure that Grint adopted here. The Grint typology raises some important principles via the descriptions associated with each strategy:

- Leadership – to raise questions.
- Management – to organise process.
- Command – to provide answers.

Here we certainly agree that, in the operation of organisations, those in senior roles, if not those in any role with responsibility to get things done, have to embrace the three components listed above. Taking the view that 'command' is about making rapid decisions and giving clear direction at a time of complexity or crisis, this is much more than merely giving answers. The implication of providing answers is that this is in response to questions. In reality, however, the majority of command situations are not in response to questions but potentially where the leader is the only person who even knows the questions. In many respects it is more about providing clear direction towards achieving a solution.

If asked to say whether taking decisions under time pressure and giving clear direction was what leadership was about, then the majority of people in organisations would agree. Thus one could take the view that the command element is actually a sub-component of leadership and not a different thing – it could be seen as 'emergency' leadership, where the consultation, raising of questions and gaining of buy-in is not feasible because of a lack of time, or other circumstances. So, associated, at least implicitly, with the notion of command as being about providing answers is the notion that these are answers needed under the time pressure created either by an internal crisis or external factors, and where new combinations are needed.

To take a further example, a merger situation requires command. In the early stages someone has to decide on a range of matters which stakeholders positioned in the constituent parts of organisations about to be merged will view as being of paramount importance to their position in the new merged organisation. Neither leadership nor management is an appropriate response here. No process exists, because something new is being created. Stakeholders in particular divisions are unlikely to accept a long, slow process of leadership as defined by Grint, and in any event will know that the integrity of their own power, esteem and sense of self-worth are possibly under threat in the process. Some decisions are needed to establish the position even if, over time, these decisions might subsequently be changed through leadership processes.

Take, for example, the merger that created GlaxoSmithKline. The first CEO announced early in the merger process that the headquarters of the company would be in New York. He then retired and the newly appointed CEO quickly announced within days of his appointment that the HQ would be in Brentford, in west London. No doubt each discussed their plans with others before making the announcement. But the point we make here is that the decision process is command, because each CEO realised that an early decision was needed to resolve uncertainty for those involved, and that there would be many people affected by this decision.

It would therefore make practical sense to adjust the Grint typology by associating the word 'command' with decisive decision-making but leaving 'management' and 'leadership' as Grint presents them: the former is associated with rational procedure, the latter two with emergent thinking and social and emotional influence. However, we would note that the real issue here is how people change their minds. Following Gardner (2006), leaders' decisions must resonate for people to be persuaded to act in a new way. In command situations, decisions resonate because they are obviously needed from the perspective of those receiving them. In management situations they resonate because people understand the process. In leadership situations they resonate because people are being engaged as part of the process.

Following the Grint model we seek to relate leadership, management and command to the three problem types within which contexts are characterised in terms of levels of certainty and pressure, of time and/or competition, and what we might depict as decision-making preferences.

The role of command is to provide answers, that of management to set up processes and the role of leaders is to pose questions but perhaps also to ensure and facilitate the getting of answers. The formulation of problem type, context and solution is helpful in the model. Context embraces the level of uncertainty and the degree of pressures on leaders. The model seeks to posit a degree of fit between these two measures of context and the extent to which the leader solution ought to be based on collaborative approaches. But the reality is often more complex.

It is worth adding that media and other pressures may also impact the perceived validity of a leadership response. Thus the impact of various perceived failures in respect of the care of vulnerable children in the care of local government social care organisations in the UK in recent years has led to a public debate within which senior leaders in social care are often seen as the cause of the failures, which in truth are the consequence of a wider set of more fundamental causes with which those leaders grapple and tragically sometimes fail to handle.

Grint (2008) argues: 'These three forms of authority ... that is legitimate power ... Command, Management and Leadership are, in turn, another way of suggesting that the role of those responsible for decision-making is to find the appropriate Answer, Process and Question to address the problem respectively.' The crucial point he makes, however, goes beyond the idea that he seeks a fixed and immovable framework here. Rather, he seeks a way to enable us to make sense both of what decisions leaders take and how leaders talk about and how they depict those decisions. Thus as issues move or are perceived to move from being Wicked to Critical for example our view of any given decision may change – that is, the problem type determines our view of the validity of the answer.

In late April 2010 volcanic activity in Iceland gave rise to ash clouds blowing south over major aircraft routes and leading to the aviation authorities closing airspace. This led to thousands of people being delayed or stopped from travelling, and airlines and airports lost considerable revenue. This created a new situation. Initially, the issue was portrayed as being driven by safety considerations. Six days later, the media focus was upon people stranded far from home and running out of money. What may have initially appeared as a wicked problem came to be seen as critical. So, after six days of closed airspace it was announced that a meeting was taking place that evening and by 10.00 pm a decision to reopen airspace was announced. A British government minister appeared on TV arguing that what had changed over the six days was that new data were now available, that the operating rules governing flight operations in ash clouds had been 'tested to destruction' and a higher threshold could now be set. Anyone with any knowledge of how such operating rules are set knows that this cannot be a full account of how he decision was arrived at.

Did the wicked problem get recast as a critical problem in consequence of the pressures building, not least in the face of emerging evidence that different conclusions had been drawn elsewhere in Europe and at other times in the USA? If Germany was allowing some flights, and in consequence flights from Germany were flying in UK airspace 'over the ash clouds' could the UK's decision be maintained among these growing pressures. In the final analysis, the decision-makers were pressured into finding a credible way out of their initial position and into a changed one because the problem moved from wicked to critical.

Thus reworking Grint's typology if time pressure is added and 'the logic of the situation', essentially a concept derived from Mary Parker Follett (2003). In her view, situations requiring the intervention of senior managers had associated with them an inherent 'logic of the situations'. Not the 'one best way' of 'scientific management' as viewed by F. N. Taylor, Gilbreth and others (see Sofer, 1973, for a clear but critical summary of the ideas of scientific management), but nevertheless an inherent logic pointing the way to decisions. In truth, this is another way of describing 'precedent ordered decisions'. Namely, the principle that at any given point in time the choices available to anyone are substantially influenced by all prior choices or actions – the tendency to follow previous historical actions if possible rather than develop new ones.

An example illustrating this is the early attempts to introduce computerised phototypesetting of text in newspapers published in Fleet Street, the home of the UK printed media in London. This was considered by the senior management of various large-format newspapers (broadsheets) in the late 1960s but not implemented until much later. The reasons for this were portrayed as being a consequence of resistance from trade unions but the reality was different. Various newspapers had invested substantially in the previous generation of typesetting equipment – web offset printing – and this had to be used over a period of years to justify the outlay, thus new capital expenditure could not be justified. So the earlier decision to purchase offset equipment limited future choices unless significant competitive, cost or other pressures forced a 'paradigm shift' or 'transformational change'. This did not happen, so the implementation of the new technology was delayed until all value had been extracted from the old equipment.

Returning to Grint, at one point he observes that, of the 'strategies' employed by those in positions of authority, he considers 'leadership' as opposed to 'command' or 'management' is often not preferred because it implies that leaders do not have the answer, or that the leader's role is to make people face up to responsibility, which is often unpopular, or that it takes time or that it will need constant reinforcement. He notes 'command' might be preferred, because followers may prefer to be shown a simple 'answer' rather than themselves having to deal with uncertainty. This does occur in many day-to-day organisational situations where people prefer just be told what to do rather than to go to the effort of thinking about the problem. This may be simpler but should ring alarm bells in relation to staff engagement.

Just as is evident in a crisis, the need for action often requires 'command' in Grint's terminology. But there is a third case, where situations in which there are inherent dilemmas and contradictions mean that the people engaged have differing 'interests'. Leadership as formulated by Grint implies engagement, agreement, consensus and a shared sense of purpose. But not everyone involved be in possession of all the relevant information, or meet with all the others involved to reach agreement. In democratic practice we elect representatives to Parliament or assemblies, or delegates to conventions, to take decisions on our behalf. Thus for even simple, practical reasons there is an expectation that, for many decisions, others will decide and act on our behalf. This raises the point that, in real situations, many people may expect, and want leaders to command.

Are we really to believe that the employees alone in a global energy company can, or even wish to, make operational or even strategic decisions collectively? The argument here is that, in some decisions, leaders are expected to command and people readily accept that. That being the case, it seems false to argue that command is simply a matter of physical force and coercion. However, there is also a clear indication that, where appropriate, people want to be consulted; and that such consultation is an aid to effective decision-making, engagement and management of risk. This creates further dilemmas for leaders as to whether in some cases consultation is a prerequisite to command– that is, where time permits, relevant information is gathered, engagement obtained and action taken. Thus one could say that, in many cases, effective delivery is a combination of leadership to ask the questions and confront reality, management to organise process, and command to make it happen.

There are other questions about Grint's approach. For him, the issue is how leaders regard the decision situation in terms of uncertainty, but for us the issue is how both leaders and followers view the situation in terms of both uncertainty and the pressure for decision and action. In this sense, command may be deemed to be legitimate in a crisis, as all involved would readily accept, but also in situations where the pressure for decision and action is high, but not as high as in a crisis. In particular, senior leaders are often in situations that are not a crisis but which require them to command. This applies both outside uniformed services and outside crisis situations. Leadership and management as commonly defined (and Grint follows the traditional definition) are highly relevant to many but do not cover all the situations in which leaders find themselves. So Grint adds the idea of command, but by assuming that this is effectively a 'crisis only' tool he limits the concept more tightly than the reality of leadership in organisations suggests is actually the case

Typologies help only if they are robust and comprehensive. Thus this links to how 'command' capability is developed in leaders. Leadership development work, to be effective, must carry credibility with leaders, both current and potential. Thus it must employ concepts and practice that reflect leadership in the real world.

Typologies and theory provide a framework of concepts to aid understanding. Words and ideas serve the purpose of enabling us to reflect on practice and make better sense of it. Sumida (1997) discusses this in a book on, among other issues, the teaching of command. He quotes a Taoist saying, as follows:

> The purpose of a fish trap is to catch fish, and when the fish are caught, the trap is forgotten. The purpose of words is to convey ideas. When the ideas are grasped, the words are forgotten.

The study of command means that theory and words take us only so far, but it remains true that 'in war executive officers needed to be able to make decisions quickly in the face of considerable uncertainty caused by changing conditions, incomplete or even misleading information, and fear'. In these circumstances we find the realism of command with the dual features included in our reworking of the Grint model, namely the presence of significant pressure for decision and significant uncertainty. Pressure for decision is partly time pressure but it also derives from the actions of opponents and the need to galvanise those involved to face uncertainty and even fear. So it is in business and in the public sector, even if to a lesser degree that in some of the situations faced by the armed forces.

This question of degree has interesting implications for the development of leaders. One of the authors has been trained and subsequently presented at the Royal Military Academy, Sandhurst. The situations that graduates of the Academy– that is, British Army officers – may have to face sometimes would have significantly greater challenges and dangers than those experienced by leaders in commercial organisations. Thus the development of Army officers must be aimed at enabling them to operate effectively in the worst case scenario they are likely to meet. Based on this, the principle of the development of leadership capability must at least balance or exceed the impact of the worst possible situation the team is likely to encounter. This is critical. In other words, as stress, time pressure, resource issues and team dynamics all move to make the situation worse, to maintain the integrity of the team the skills and influence of the leader must be greater. If the situation cannot be balanced by the skills of the leader the team will be unable to function, and failure will occur. In simple terms, the leader's ability to keep the team together and operating effectively must always be greater than any situational pressures attempting to tear it apart or make it ineffective.

Thus the development of leaders must take into account not only generic capabilities but also factor in the worst case scenario that the leaders are likely to meet within their role requirements, and build the capability to lead effectively in those worst case scenarios. Having a surfeit of capability over and above the challenges of the situation gives leaders more 'bandwidth' to use the inspirational skills that are often required in tough situations where logic is not enough to address the emotional concerns of those involved.

In most cases there is a single 'best' answer to a problem faced by leaders, or at least a range of options that logical deduction will indicate. Sometimes, however, the issues, problems and dilemmas leaders face are insoluble, or at least appear that way for many years. An obvious example would be the issue of Northern Ireland during the period 1967 to 2007, in which more than 3,000 people were killed by insurgent and other actions. Essentially two communities existed in Northern Ireland, one that wanted to maintain its links to and be controlled by the UK, and the other that wanted independence from the UK and to be part of a united Ireland. Two seemingly opposite and irreconcilable positions, even within a democratic system with those supporting the UK link able numerically to outvote the significant minority that wanted the opposite. For many years this conflict, rooted deep in the history of Ireland, appeared to be intractable. Yet post-2007 a more optimistic scenario unfolded despite problems along the way.

Adaptive leadership as a leadership approach was brought forward as a means of resolving such intractable conflicts, together with the idea that built into current success is future failure, as the conditions created by an organisation to exploit a given set of conditions was overtaken by changes in the external conditions. The move to discussion from conflict was essentially driven by both groups coming to realise that there was no chance of success through violence, and that negotiation was the only real answer. Thus despite their perceived success in the courses that both sides had initially embarked on, the world had moved on, the paradigm had changed and so they had to change. This is a problem that is commonly experienced, and referred to often in this book. The following case study provides a good example.

Case study   **Tavistock**

Amy Fraher (2004) has produced a history of The Tavistock Institute of Human Relations (TIHR) originally based on The Tavistock Clinic in London. She traces the history of this organisation from its early work in group relations and the history of psychoanalysis, and through the application of these ideas in the Second World War. The Institute has a worldwide reputation for inter-disciplinary work and innovations in the field of group study.

She felt that writing the history presented a dilemma. One view was that the idea of group relations developed by Tavistock had, by 2004, begun to be overtaken by other changes in organisations and workplaces. Thus part of the history could be seen as a potential need to ask whether Tavistock could adapt to these changes. But she rejected that as too simplistic. TIHR was, and is, an ideas organisation – which inevitably faces periods of vitality and decay, of growth and decline, as part of a natural life cycle. Ideas organisations such as Tavistock experience intense conflicts, which put the organisations' survival at risk. Only if the members are able to set aside their own personal preferences and think about the organisation as a whole can this conflict spur innovation and renewal. So the alternative was to consider a cyclical model of growth and innovation, followed by inevitable conflict and decline, the origins of decline being built into the process of growth and innovation, and in the group and organisational relations that emerge during the period of growth. There is frequently a period of decline in organisations after a period of growth, but it is not inevitable if the organisations' leadership see the warning signs and act on them.

In practice, every 10 years or so in a period of growth, as new people were brought into the Institute as it expanded to meet the demands of growth, these new arrivals sought to differentiate themselves, in order to establish a position of credibility in the profession and prominence in the Institute. This subsequently led to the establishment of new groups and, in turn, to organisational fragmentation.

The underlying dynamic can be outlined easily enough. Ideas organisations are those designed to generate intellectual concepts and support learning, so any research institution may readily be characterised as such, indeed such teams and departments can be seen within commercial and public sector organisations as well. TIHR is one example, and the Institute of Advanced Study in Princeton, New Jersey, another. Most, if not all, think tanks, political or otherwise, and probably most consulting firms the world over share at least some features of an ideas organisation, as do universities, in particular those heavily engaged in research. Ideas organisations are characterised by innovation and thus become settings within which questioning of others' ideas and inter-group rivalries can create a dynamic that can eventually lead to inter-group rivalry and subsequent fragmentation. This is partly a consequence of the strong tendency of these organisations to innovate, and innovation inherently involves questioning the status quo or other ideas. In reality, individuals can become so attached to a set of ideas that they associate them with themselves, in particular if they were involved with the development. These are 'their' ideas, and it then becomes difficult to dissociate self from idea. If the idea is attacked, then so is the 'self'. In reality, this is also a common scenario and a significant challenge in commercial organisations where change is required, and moving people away from the status quo they were involved in creating is vital for success.

It is worth noting that the ideas, research, scholarship and professional practice undertaken by those associated with Tavistock were some of the most influential of their time in relation to applying social science to problems of organisation, organisation design and leadership. These include pioneering work on understanding group relations, a series of conferences on leadership, authority, organisation and related issues, work in officer selection in the Second World War, the idea of socio-technical systems, action learning, and studies of organisations as varied as coal mines, hospitals, and weaving in India. Of course, these various studies had precursors, and Tavistock staff worked with and within organisations on similar problems elsewhere in the world, notably in the USA. The fragmentation process that occurred, as set out above, was demonstrated by Tavistock people creating spin-off organisations to take forward their own work as it was undergoing challenge within TIHR itself. There were also a series of 'splits', in which key personalities came to the conclusion that they felt unable to work with each other.

Because ideas organisations are very open, with fluid boundaries, used to working in collaboration with other organisations and where secondments and attachments are common, it is possible that 'splits' are more easily resolved – but by continuing internal or external fragmentation. As new ideas take over, new leadership take up positions of influence, fragmentation results, and organisation change and related leadership changes also follow. This is also reflected in the corporate world, where senior leaders who sought but were not offered appointments as CEO or another senior role leave the business soon afterwards.

Central to understanding the conditions required for survival of an ideas organisation is the principle that cyclical fragmentation of such organisations is inevitable. These organisations are 'open systems' and, as such, are much more likely to be self-reflective, constantly evaluating their own views and strategies. They tend to respond best to leaders who inspire through ideas, and often this means charismatic leaders. Such leaders often play a key role in establishing, and then developing and sustaining, an innovative set of ideas around which the organisation grows. But they may also develop an almost 'cult-like' following that excludes people with different ideas from core and influential roles, thus depriving the organisation of the critical challenge and input it may need to prosper.

Source: Fraher (2004).

Case commentary

This case demonstrates the longitudinal nature of most decision-making. Here, decisions emerge as new circumstances interact with people's attachment to current ways of working. This theme is stronger here because of the intrinsic nature of the ideas organisations, which includes the idea and practice of 'professional autonomy'– that is, it is acceptable in principle to make statements that challenge the status quo, which is not often encouraged in the commercial world. Ideas organisations are viewed as 'open systems' and therefore experience cyclical fragmentation where specific, and often charismatic, leaders play important roles in the way the cycle plays out in practice.

In reality, in this situation, effective leaders are those who are able to formulate new ideas that attract revenue streams. In a sense this makes these organisations subject to something like a 'star system' of leadership, where other professional staff are highly dependent on the new revenue stream created by 'the star'. Thus, for a period of time, a 'star' leader may be more powerful in the ideas organisation than an appointed leader in more typically hierarchical organisations. But this professional autonomy comes with a cost, which is that of dependence on having leaders who are both intellectual and to some degree business stars in the particular academic or consultancy field. Such was the case with Tavistock at the time discussed. Much the same behaviour and cycles can be observed in political parties, hospitals, colleges, universities and other research organisations.

11.3   The 'disciplined' mind

The impact of ideas finds little explicit reference in various models of leadership considered earlier in the book (see Chapter 2). Yet when we examine leadership in practice it is difficult to ignore the ideas that leaders convey. While leadership development often focuses on changing behaviour, the evidence often suggests that we should also look at 'changing minds'. Gardner (2004, 2006) has done so and it is worth examining his views. This principle is reflective of what we see around us day to day – that change in behaviour is preceded by a change of mind to some degree. Whether this is reflective of a genuine desire to adopt the new, or a desire to be seen to adopt the new while in some ways preferring the old, a change has still occurred.

In his later book Gardner (2006) proposes that 'five minds' are necessary for human beings to master the challenges of a rapidly changing world. His purpose in doing so is nominative and idealistic: to create a set of value judgements. These are the five minds:

(i)   The *disciplined* mind. At least one discipline, whether academic or professional, has been mastered. Thus at least one way of thinking about the world is at least a part of it, with its language, mode of reasoning, thought–action sequences, routines, practices and so on has been understood. Gardner (2006) suggests that research indicates it takes at least six years to master a discipline.

(ii)   The *synthesising* mind takes ideas, concepts and data from different sources, makes sense of them and creates a new synthesis that makes sense to the synthesiser personally and to others. Always of value as more information becomes available, then this 'mind' becomes of even greater worth.

(iii) Using discipline and synthesis as a platform, the *creative* mind challenges accepted modes of thinking, raises question, perceives new ways of thinking, new options and possibilities. For this to be recognised, ultimately the new departures and innovations raised by the creative mind must quickly be recognised as being of value by what Gardner refers to as 'the knowledgeable consumer'. But are all creative ideas accepted? Perhaps here we refer to creative only in the sense that the idea comes to be accepted because of some need, whether practical and tangible or emotional, to be accepted, being met by the new departure. Only these departures are likely to be 'recorded' in any event.

(iv)   The *respectful* and the *ethical* minds notice and accept differences between individuals and groups, different cultures and organisation types.

(v)   In a complex and increasingly interdependent world this mind is central to the creation of trust and collaboration.

In line with Argyris (2004), the real issue is not the mind but rather that thought is the mainspring to action. Argyris notes that professionals of all kinds operate within certain constraints as they seek to formulate new approaches to deal with novel situations. In seeking to distinguish between single-loop and double-loop learning, he notes two critical behaviours – one individual and one organisational:

(i)   The life experience of most professionals through schooling, university and their early career is characterised by success, not failure. Because they have so rarely failed in anything they attempt, they have never learned how to learn from failure. When things go wrong for them they tend towards defensive behaviour, screening out criticism and seeking to place 'blame' on others. Ironically, their ability to learn diminishes just when they need it most. This is reflected in the fact that self awareness and the ability to learn from situations are two of the key capabilities of high-performing leaders. such people do not fall into this common trap.

(ii)   Commonly, organisations view learning as a motivational issue rather than one of facilitation. Create the correct structures of communication, reward, authority and accountability, and learning and development will follow. In other words, people can learn if they want to, if they do not it is because of a lack of motivation. Argyris argues that this approach fatally flawed. People learn through the way that they think, through cognitive rules or the reasoning they follow to design and implement actions. If these are limited by an organisation's approach, then so is learning. Thus as well as motivation being present, the organisation must facilitate learning proactively; motivation is not sufficient on its own.

The main difference between single-loop and double-loop learning lies in the willingness to challenge long-held assumptions rather than to adopt the 'bunker mentality' observed in point (i) in the list above. Argyris describes a behaviour he labels as 'skilled incompetence'. Here, the often high-level competence of a professional who has little experience of learning from failure and therefore tends to accept without question the cognitive rules of the profession in which he or she has been working brings its own form of constraint. This means that sometimes the professional is less able to engage in 'productive reasoning', defined here as the means of creating valid knowledge, informed choices and personal responsibility for decisions and actions. We can all recall situations where some professionals or other groups have exhibited 'groupthink' and not adopted new ways of working as a result of pre-existing professional assumptions of 'the way we do things properly in our profession'. Doctors, engineers, lawyers, IT and HR professionals all have 'professional' ways of working that are often used as a defensive approach to change, as indeed do individuals who, because of their seniority, have the ability to use past experience as their 'professional' view.

11.4 'Unlearning'

One interesting principle used within leadership development by some relates to the idea of 'unlearning'. While we discuss and debate leadership using words, concepts, models and theory, leadership is a set of actions, practices and behaviours embodied in particular individuals as they respond to a given situation. So we may seek to teach young executives leadership within an MBA programme, for example, by presenting the theories, models and frameworks set out above. Moreover, we may also seek to 'test' their understanding of the material by requiring them to demonstrate that they remember the theories, models and frameworks, or can describe verbally how they might apply them. But we learn leadership through practice, and leaders demonstrate their capabilities in the real world. They must thus convince, or not, those around them via practical demonstration and not through theoretical discussion and debate.

Interestingly, some who develop leadership within the corporate environment find that 'unlearning' is a key concept. This is because the level of leadership capability at first line manager level is not always high; organisations seem to prefer the apparent higher ROI, and risk the management benefits of developing the skills of more senior leaders. Thus junior leaders are left with a problem – how do they lead? No one has told them it is their first leadership role, so it is a guessing game. Trial and error mixed with a degree of copying the behaviour of successful more senior leaders is often their only apparent course of action. However, such copying assumes that the more successful senior leaders are in their roles as a result of their leadership capabilities. Often this is not the case, though – it is more likely to be their ability to make money or to fulfil a technical role. So copying, then, potentially leads the junior leader to adopt an approach that does not optimise performance of either him or her as a leader, or his/her team, but is merely reflective of more senior leaders who maybe good, but equally could be bad.

The dilemma for leadership development experts is that often junior and middle-level leaders arrive at senior level with self-developed established approaches that then have to be 'unlearned' to be replaced with the optimum approach. This is a key reason why all armed forces develop basic management and leadership capabilities as the very first step in a junior leader's career with the forces, enabling core capability, commonality of approach and language from the start. Were commercial organisations to adopt this strategy it would have significant benefits in terms of improved leader, individual, team and organisational performance at a relatively low cost. Instead, companies generally spend more money working with leaders later in their careers on unlearning and re-learning, and miss the ROI from the basic capability and value of common understanding that would have been delivered for a number of years prior to that had they taken the simple step of developing junior leaders.

All agree that leadership is relational. While leadership relates to position in most cases, leadership is real only in the sense that the leader is able to influence others to achieve. Thus any understanding of leadership must focus on the relations between leaders, followers, decision–action sequences and environments. We understand and measure leadership in terms of the decisions that leaders make and their influence, how and why they made those decisions and the consequences of them.

Case study | **The leadership of Hugh Dowding and the Battle of Britain, 1940**

The summer of 1940 saw Nazi Germany dominating continental Europe, having defeated France and forced the British army to evacuate France through Dunkirk. Following a brief lull, they then began preparations to invade Britain. Successful invasion required the command of the English Channel against the Royal Navy, and air supremacy command of the skies over the channel as a precursor.

The German air force significantly outnumbered the Royal Air Force (RAF). Hugh Dowding had been appointed Air Officer Commanding RAF Fighter Command in 1937. He had estimated that he would need 45 squadrons of modern fighters to defend Britain against air attack from the German air force – the Luftwaffe, which, after the fall of France, would be even closer, in Northern France, with increased capability. Prior to the fall of France, Dowding had been required to transfer squadrons to France to support the army as it withdrew. However, when he was finally placed under huge pressure to transfer more squadrons to France, both by the Air Minister and by the Prime Minister, Winston Churchill, he refused to do so. This was accepted, albeit some squadrons were required to fight over France from UK bases – and were therefore depleted in consequence.

Before being appointed to Air Officer Commanding RAF Fighter Command, he was Air Member (of the RAF Board) for Research and Development. In this role he supported the ongoing development of new fighter aircraft, but more important, was a major proponent of the use of radar and a significant person in the development of Fighter Command's command and control system.

Fighter Command was split regionally into groups, which were the principle players in the Battle of Britain. These were 11 Group, South of England (south of the River Thames) commanded by Air vice-marshal Park, and 12 Group (north of the Thames), commanded by Air vice-marshal Leigh-Mallory. These two officers held different views about the appropriate tactical doctrine to guide fighter operations against an attacking force.

Park sought to attack with one or two squadrons as quickly as possible. The early Luftwaffe attacks were on radar stations and fighter stations. Had the latter been destroyed, 11 Group would have had to withdraw further inland to place fighter stations out of effective bombing range, giving an advantage to the attacker and effectively conceding ground to them.

Leith-Mallory believed in the idea of a 'big wing'. The concept was that of forming multiple squadrons into a wing of sufficient size to give it local air superiority when it attacked. But his 'big wings' north of the Thames needed time to marshal themselves into an attacking formation. Park's view was that in the time it took to assemble the 'big wing' north of the Thames, the enemy would already be attacking 11 Group stations south of the river and then withdrawing. The doctrine agreed before the war was to attack enemy bombers before they reached their target. Park was clear that the early-warning methods, a combination of limited-range radar and observers, gave too little warning to enable the formation of 'big wings'.

Once information that an attack was starting came into the group command centre, Park and his sector colleagues found themselves constantly assessing likely enemy intentions and potential targets. Were any of the several enemy forces units going to combine into a large attack? Which directions of movement were feints? Were any of the reports of 'attacks' based on inaccurate reporting? Park's central point was that only when an attack had physically started on a target was that target definite. For the 'big wing' concept to be effective, the capability to asses intended targets accurately was essential as, failing that, a significant part of available RAF forces could be committed to going in the wrong direction and away the intended target. Moreover, Park was clear that Leigh-Mallory's wings claims were often exaggerated, and throughout remained of the view that the concept was not effective in terms of losses inflicted on the enemy.

Before the war Dowding had given Park and Leigh-Mallory tactical control of group operations at the 'local' level in the context of the need for Fighter Command to operate as an overall command, with the need to reinforce between the two groups as circumstances required. The air defence exercises of 1939 had shown that the procedures for responding to attacks where more than one group was involved were cumbersome. In addition, the Leigh-Mallory wing idea found support from some senior officers in the Air Ministry. As a result, Dowding created command and control arrangements between groups which, while delegating practical, day-to-day or operational control, left significant uncertainty as to the basis on which 11 Group south of the Thames might expect reinforcement from 12 Group to the north. The requirement for reinforcement would also only be likely to occur when 11 Group was under significant pressure, thus command arrangements would be working under pressure. Therefore, when Park requested reinforcements, the big wing controversy arose as Leigh-Mallory did not wish to compromise the effectiveness of his big wing by reducing its strength to reinforce. Dowding failed to intervene, thus leaving this significant problem unresolved.

According to at least one internal Air Ministry document, the official defensive doctrine was based on the view that, ideally, one would destroy attacking enemy bombers before they dropped their bombs. The key was to destroy enough of the enemy aircraft at any point in their operation such they would slowly be degraded until they were unable to mount further attacks. This appears to be a restatement of Leigh-Mallory's view, but the source of this document is uncertain. It seems also likely that it was Park's pragmatic view that in the time available it was not proving possible to deploy big wings at any point, even to attack the enemy force on its return flight. The operational and practical problem was that there was a clear 'dividing line' between these two concepts of operation: small, fast attacks as envisaged by Park, and Leigh-Mallory's 'big wing' in a situation where close co-ordination was required. The unresolved 'dividing line' restricted the effectiveness of Fighter Command as a united force.

This issue of the co-existence of differing concepts was not new. Even back in August 1939, a year before the major air conflict, Dowding had asked Park to rebut his big wing idea, so the controversy was recognised and was a source of debate long before the battle itself. There are clear arguments on both sides of the issue. The battle was reviewed at a meeting convened in the Air Ministry in November 1940, and one senior officer noted that 11 Group, south of the river and thus likely to be attacked first, did not want the support of 12 Group from north of the river other than on its own terms. Thus they, and the RAF as a whole, lost the opportunity of using 12 Group as an aggressive supporting force. As a result, by late August 1940, Park's southern squadrons were under significant pressure and experiencing losses that would rapidly become unsustainable. If this happened the RAF would lose command of the air over the UK, meaning that the UK could be invaded and therefore lose the war.

Throughout late August there were a series of written critiques by senior officers from Groups 11 and 12 on each other's performance. Dowding, in overall command, was sent copies of a series of messages, analyses and directives from Park on 28 August. It was clear that, even at this point, the controversy was ongoing and was a significant source of operational difficulty. Yet despite Dowding being in overall command of these two disagreeing subordinates who were damaging the effectiveness of his command, he still did not intervene.

On 7 September 1940, the focus of the German attack switched from bombing airfields to making direct attacks on London in an attempt to break the will of the civilian population. The enemy was able to reach and attack London, which gave renewed strength to 12 Group's view (also supported at the Air Ministry) of the value of the big wing. Attacks on London were more predictable, given the relatively small size of the potential target area and clearly there is a significantly larger warning available of an attack on an airfield or other targets much closer to the Channel coast that were within a shorter flying time of the Luftwaffe airfields in northern France.

On 8 October 1940, Dowding began a series of interchanges involving Leigh-Mallory and Dowding, which identified the pros and cons of each strategy but offered no decision. In addition, at this time a shift to night attacks was also under way, which led to further disagreement between Dowding and the Air Ministry to which he reported. To his credit Dowding's management of squadron rotation, to allow pilots to rest, and the training and supply of new pilots, had worked effectively. In general terms, Dowding had, under tremendous pressure, been effective at varying his approach according to changing circumstances. Despite this, he was removed from office on 25 November 1940. The controversy over the big wing concept continued and there is evidence that this continued to be among the reasons why the operations of 11 and 12 Group had room for improvement.

There is a parallel scenario from the First World War, again relating to changing strategies to match new environments, where the Royal Navy had been bitterly opposed to providing escorts for convoys of merchant ships crossing the Atlantic to the USA, which left them vulnerable to U-boat attack. It was the Navy view that hunter groups of warships should be formed to seek out and destroy the U-boats rather than using warships to protect convoys. However, it was only the use of convoys that was found to reduce the impact of U-boats. In the Second World War, however, the development of escort aircraft carriers, not available in the First World War, provided the means of attacking U-boats over wide areas of the sea. Available by 1943, these very successful hunter groups were deployed and took a 'seek and destroy' approach successful enough to force the withdrawal of U-boats from the Atlantic.

These examples demonstrate that changes in environment, technology or knowledge alter the leadership calculations around what is possible and optimal, thus what was previously not possible or valid is now seen to be so.

Sources: Ray (2000); Overy (2010).

Case commentary

If one considers this case in relation to the frameworks set out just before the case study, it can be concluded that Dowding succeeded brilliantly, adapting effectively to changes in situations, and his management of resources was sound, but his command capability was questionable. By not resolving the issues between Park and Leigh-Mallory, or taking a decision and imposing it, given the urgency and importance of the situation, he allowed controversy to continue, which had an impact on the over-all tactical performance of Fighter Command.

Looking at Gardner's typology regarding Dowding, we can see evidence of the disciplined mind, the synthesising mind and the creating mind through his work on new equipment, particularly radar, and on the evolution of the group-level fighter control system as clear indicators. The circumstances and the historical information available do not provide evidence on whether there were also elements of the 'respect-ful' or 'ethical' mind at work.

Looking at the Grint framework, Dowding appears again to have ranked posi-tively on leadership and management but to have failed on command. The 'logic of the situation' surely required command decisions to ensure more effective integration of 11 Group and 12 Group to deliver an integrated and effective defence. Having said this, the hindsight gained over the passage of time provides us very readily with apparently simple answers that Dowding, in such a pressured, complex, fast-moving and critical situation was unable to see.

Interestingly enough, the debate over fighter defence doctrine carried forward by senior officers was characterised by many of the features of an ideas organisation and the personal/emotional issues around them. Fraher (2004) observes that these may have impacted on the debate between the senior officers. Following Argyris (2004) we are left to conclude that Dowding's unwillingness to intervene made the reasoning being used by Park and Leigh-Mallory 'defensive'. Neither took on the features of 'productive reasoning' – it may well be that Park was right initially but when the focus of attack shifted to London, then Leigh-Mallory's view took on renewed credence. Yet Dowding left the issue unresolved until October or even later!

While Britain won the Battle of Britain, the issues noted in the case above are still debated today. Clearly, Dowding played his role as leader of Fighter Command with ability and courage. His refusing to bow to Winston Churchill's wishes represents one of the few examples of such refusal during the Second World War and contributed positively to the outcome. At the time, no one doubted the courage and foresight Dowding had shown. The issue of concern really related to what might be argued as a lack of command in not making two subordinates bury their differences and work more closely together. Perhaps, to Dowding, as he had delegated tactical control to his Group commanders, he felt that interfering would be seen as retracting that freedom and be counterproductive. We must also note that it could not have been easy to judge who was right between Park or Leigh Mallory; in fact, with the changing circumstances both could have been right at different times.

It was clear that, as a new concept, there were significant command and control problems associated with embracing the big wing strategy. The objective of the wing concept was clear enough – to manoeuvre a sufficient force of fighters into position to achieve local air superiority and therefore to gain prominence in the air fighting. This accords with the fundamental idea of concentration of forces and had to be an attractive and logical idea that conforms to a basic principle of military doctrine. But the operational delivery of this was not easy, nor was it always an effective approach if the enemy took the fast, small, local raiding party approach. Was Dowding of the view that the problems might be solved if he persevered with the concept? We shall never know, because, as often happens, fate intervened and the need for night-fighting capability overtook this issue.

11.5   Mobilising minds

It was argued earlier in the book that minds have to be changed before change can be truly effective in practice (see Chapter 6). Bryan and Joyce (2007) tackle the issues of complexity, the ideas organisation and performance together. They reported data on the world's top 150 companies, based on information from 1984 and from 2004. They used the size of the organisations' employee population as a proxy for internal complexity, and profit per employee as a measure of profitability.

For 1984, looking at the 150 largest companies, and using market capitalisation, they found a strong association between profit per employee and number of employees – the more employees, the lower the profit per employee. As the authors noted, this is what economists would predict, the increase in profit derived from economies of scale being eliminated by costs resulting from inefficiency. But by 2004 something had changed. Now the data were more mixed. There was a wider spread of data. Some companies appeared to have found organisational models which meant they were less affected by complexity issues.

They subsequently divided the companies into 'thinking-intensive' companies, Fraher's (2004) ideas organisations, and 'labour-intensive' companies. The data for the labour-intensive companies had not changed significantly between 1984 and 2004. In contrast, for the thinking-intensive companies, average profit per employee was higher, but the results showed much greater variation. Some companies appeared to outperform others significantly. Why, and how?

Was the answer related to the use of technology? Bryan and Joyce argued that the answer lies in the ability of some organisations to derive higher profit per employees by leveraging more value from the ideas of their people, develop better customer relationships, build their brand, and other 'intangible' assets. As Bryan and Joyce note:

The economic conditions of the 21st century are enabling some companies to create wealth by employing ever larger numbers of thinking-intensive workers who translate mind work into high-quality, high-return intangibles.

Their data also included a comparison of the top 30 companies' highest performers with the next 30 companies from the same sector. The data showed that the top 30 employed substantially more employees, and that the top 30 were achieving substantially higher profits per employee – in the order of 65 per cent more. Their conclusion was that these differences could not be related only to scale alone, or industry effects, but rather the ability of some companies to use organisation design, talent, leadership business models and other intangible assets to obtain a better overall performance from every employee.

Thus, if the company is better able to organise and motivate itself, it can become far more effective in capturing profitable opportunities. At times, certain organisations are able in some way to make all the elements 'gel' to create a performance culture and focus on key deliverables that sets them apart from competitors. For example Tesco, the UK supermarket chain, was better able to profit from retail growth between 2000 and 2009 than its competitors, and in banking UBS saw significant growth over and above its competition 2002–06.

Any organisation in reality, no matter what its size, should be trying to do the same thing – have motivated staff, headed by good leaders who align effort to key deliverables to enable optimum customer service. This is relatively easy for small organisations, but can create real problems for complex ones. With size comes complexity, and this complexity often creates ineffective communication and lack of clarity, which in turn builds confusion, lack of focus and diffusion of effort, ultimately leading to employee dissatisfaction. This is often to be blamed on the systems put into manage the complexity being more complex than necessary, or not being aligned with the desired organisational outcomes and in reality making the situation worse. Take this comment from a senior nurse in the British National Health Service in 2009 – 'I love my job but the system gets in the way.'

Thus the difficult-to-manage workforce structures, skills issues and reward systems, silo based structures, confusing matrix structures, and information and initiative overload all contribute to the lack of success. Bryan and Joyce argue for a flexible, evolutionary approach, in which leaders make decisions organised around a portfolio of initiatives. Balancing 'business as usual' with an experimental approach to the next initiative, and seeking always to test the risk associated with new initiatives. The organisation attempts to discover where and how to compete. This portfolio of initiatives mindset requires endless trade-offs between the short- versus long-term. The problem in the real world is that performance appraisal, upon which promotion and reward are commonly based, is inherently short-term and normally looks backwards not forward. This means that leaders tend to opt for the short-term success that wins the battle but which might over a number of years eventually lose the war.

In addition, leadership needs to be distributed; the creation of connections and knowledge markets within the organisation, building capability, game plans, working back from the optimum future organisation vision to the present organisation, identifying gaps, and plans to build 'line of sight' to the future organisation. To drive and monitor, and get round the short-term nature of delivery, Bryan and Joyce argue for role-specific performance evaluation based on grids, combining:

(i) *Individual performance measures* – such as financial performance, operations performance and the evaluation of individuals performance by the line manager, as compared to agreed expectation or objectives – to some degree the traditional appraisal process and focusing on the individual.

(ii) *Mutual performance measures* – such as knowledge-, network- and client relationship-building, communication and capability building across silos, and other things where people have to want to co-operate for mutual benefit. This would include progress on longer-term initiatives over a number of years.

These principles we have encountered before, but the crucial element here is to note the importance of mind power being used to enable leadership as a relational resource, whether that is operational, strategic or change leadership.

Bryan and Joyce consider the 'knowledge market place' to be a very important idea. Organisations use knowledge as a primary source of competitive advantage – 'we know more than our competitors' is a logical reason for customers to use their offerings. Knowing more means that one is likely to deliver a better service. All organisations may have roughly equal access to talent and to publicly available knowledge. However, Bryan and Joyce (2007) suggest that special value is associated with unique understanding about some specific body of knowledge that is of value to the organisation or its customers. For example, a company which thoroughly understands how to compete in China has a significant advantage over rivals who wish to do the same but do not have the same understanding. Those organisations that are able to capture and share knowledge across internal boundaries and silos are better positioned than those less able to do so. The important point here is not about technology. Many organisations have internal communication systems that lie idle: the reality is simple – if people do not want to exchange knowledge and ideas even if there is the technology available to do it easily, they will not do it; and if people *do* want to work together, even if there is no system set up, they will find a way. So it is essentially about capability to make new 'sense' of the data that lie in the minds of the people in the organisation and its clients and partners, and the willingness of those involved to share that insight across the organisation or among stakeholders.

Crucially, however, this new 'sense' may only be exploited to advantage if a series of effective choices made over a period of time have positioned the organisation appropriately – in simple terms, the right idea in the right place at the right time. History is littered with great ideas that were in the wrong place at the wrong time and had to wait to be 'rediscovered' in due course.

But if the time is right and those involved are ready to adopt the 'new', it will work. The idea of 'resonance' (see Chapter 6) applies here. Can we combine the resources and capabilities available to us to exploit new knowledge? Thus Dowding's system of 'command and control' depended on the development and exploitation of radar. Just having new ideas is not enough, as our discussion of the Tavistock case made clear. Many organisations appear to be driven to adopt change only as a means of reducing the threat of failure and collapse, or to deal with an external threat. Few seem genuinely to drive change on the basis of 'new ideas'. Going back to the case studies earlier in the book, the strategy of UBS (see Chapter 4) in 'Aligning the integrated firm' was an example of a change in environment creating the opportunity for new ideas and the development of those ideas across the organisation to create a new strategy, brand and culture enabling high performance that delivered significant bottom-line benefits.

It may be that leaders find it easier to argue the case for change by observing the possibility of threat, or warning of an impending crisis, or constructing a compelling vision of the future which convinces people that success is feasible and the threats avoidable – the 'change or die' speech – but at least part of that compelling vision should lie in a combination of new ideas and the ability to access the resources and capabilities to exploit them.

It is possible to consider these points from a perspective broader than an existing formally structured organisation. As Davis and Marquis (2005) argue, organisations are essentially networks of contracts among individuals which can form and re-form as opportunity arises or needs dictate. The modern organisation operates through networks of alliances. Much of any organisation's ability to exploit markets now is based on its positioning within networks of exchange. It is the constantly shifting networks of markets, resources, labour and so on that characterises the modern organisation, especially those operating on a global basis. Davis and Marquis observe that an attempt to understand the organisation requires us to comprehend three independent sets of mechanisms. These are, in turn, environmental (externally arising influences), cognitive (which operate through alterations of individual and collective perceptions) and relational (the connections among people, groups and interpersonal networks along with the capacity to re-form networks). They suggest that Campbell (2005) offers other mechanisms including framing (the use of metaphors and symbols that organise perceptions of issues and courses of action, linking problems and actions to prevailing conceptions of social and economic value), diffusion (the spread of ideas, structures and practices, often via networks), translation (the working of ideas to a local context or situation), bricolage (recombining elements to achieve new configurations) – we would use the word innovation, and strategic leadership (entrepreneurial activity). Gardner (2006) presents a similar set of mechanisms so it is reasonable to conclude that these together probably present as full a picture of the challenge to leaders that most are facing in the organisational world today.

While Davis and Marquis (2005) and others were concerned to identify mechanisms of social change, the better to understand how organisations need to create new combinations of partners to gain advantage. The question is how, through leadership, an organisation recognises and responds to the challenge that real advantage can only be achieved by moving to a new configuration. This means being able to move from 'status quo' to 'new world'. Thus the understanding of leadership entails looking at how leaders employ the mechanisms referred to above to find and enable the 'new world' to be reached as new opportunities arise. Thus analysing strategic leadership becomes a means of understanding how leaders seek new means of creating value and finding that 'new world'.

When we look at how leaders seek to resolve the problems they face it becomes clear that leadership is more than simply relational. Further, even with the relational aspect, the ideas we have reviewed show that the relational activity is not only internal to the organisation but also external. Clearly, the capacity to create new and effective relationships outside the organisation is also important. This is increasingly important with the management of stakeholders, markets, media and the public to develop the organisation's brand.

When we look at leadership, the importance of how effective leaders are as 'agents of change', and how they develop and deploy the mechanisms listed above are key to how effective leaders are in practice. This examination helps to develop leadership theory and practice to deal more effectively with the challenges leaders face in an increasingly complex, fast-moving and interrelated world that throws novel problems at them. Many of these are seemingly intractable: for example, the Northern Ireland social problems of the 1970s–1990s; and the impact on health care globally caused by the challenge created by increasing demands for services, and more complex and expensive treatments being developed versus decreasing resources driven by the demands for economic and financial rationalisation, whether stemming from pressure on state budgets in the current financial crisis or pressure from health insurers. We need to develop further the thinking and practice underpinning leadership and its development to enable leaders to solve, as best they are able, these increasingly complex challenges.

An important contribution of leaders is to focus attention on the future and gain acceptance of the fact that the existing organisational systems, structures, business model and boundaries may no longer serve as the best framework for competitive advantage or the creation of value. There is an even greater need to for leaders to be able to lead transformational change and use 'double loop' learning. Effective transformational change is not just about decentralising and or devolving decisions, or centralising and controlling, depending on an organisation's position in that cycle. This merely embeds the status quo in a different form. It does not change the minds of those involved, but may limit the focus of the organisation to the present and may create or strengthen the problem of organisational silos.

This is likely to create a false sense of security about where the organisation is at present, and where it is going. If we have completed a change, the logic is then we must be better off than we were before. Sadly there is a lot of bad change about that merely rearranges the deckchairs on the organisational Titanic, thus giving fleeting hope to the doomed. It is only change that really changes the course on which the organisation is set – breaking out of the status quo – that 'steers the ship away from the iceberg'. This, then, provides the organisational clarity about responsibility for the future performance needed if the change is to be sustained and ultimately be successful. Leadership is as much about handling an uncertain future as getting the present to go well – and spotting the corporate icebergs well before the organisation upon them.

It is unlikely that in the future the world will become simpler – it is more likely to become more complicated, in fact – but through approaches such as adaptive leadership, the development of ideas, networks and the expansion of leadership as a more flexible concept that includes a much wider spectrum of techniques, knowledge and actions than have been applied to it previously we may be able to deal with those challenges more effectively.

11.6   Summary

Dean Acheson held the post of US Secretary of State under President Harry Truman at the outbreak of what became known as the Cold War between the NATO powers and the Soviet Union and its allies at the time (the Warsaw Pact). He is often held to have been one of the most influential holders of the office. In his autobiography he argues:

> Our difficulty is that, as a nation of short-term pragmatists accustomed to dealing with the future only when it becomes the present, we find it hard to regard future trends as serious reality. We have not achieved the capacity to treat as real and urgent – as demanding action today-problems which appear in critical dimension only at some future date. Yet failure to develop this habit of mind is likely to prove fatal.

This is the core of the challenge faced by all leaders – be they military, national or corporate, not only to deal with the present world but also to prepare and guide those they lead into the new. It is the essence of the discussion of leadership throughout this book. We need better to understand and combine the development of personal leadership capability with operational and strategic leadership requirements. The relative importance of each varies according to where the leaders are within the hierarchy and the challenges they face. Yet understanding the pressures imposed by the likely situations the leaders will face, and thus the adoption and delivery of the optimum form of leadership for each, gives us a clear guide to the optimum development of the leaders' capabilities.

Our thinking about leadership must be set in the context within which it operates. Moreover, if operational delivery, strategic decision-making and enabling organisational change are a principal focus of what leaders do, then each is relevant to be examined and measured if we are to gauge the impact and contribution of leaders and leadership accurately. If leadership theory can help leaders to think on a deeper level about their own distinctive approach and personal capabilities, strengths and weaknesses for their present and future leadership roles, then it is more about the leader in relation to the organisation in the longer term. If organisations are seeking to enhance their market position through ideas, then the ability to re-configure, probably outside the modus operandi of the organisation, this becomes of paramount importance. Success requires that the two are achieved in tandem.

Viewed in a socioeconomic and organisational context, the impact of leaders over the longer term is important, but this longer-term impact is often neglected from the leaders' own consideration and often from theory. This links in particular to the way in which leaders constitute and deal with the issue of authority, their exercise of it, and how they derive and 'construct' the challenges they face from the situations in which they find themselves. Ultimately this is determined to a significant degree by the use of the knowledge leaders have as a resource to find answers. This links directly to the idea of the good leader as a constant learner. This relates not just to learning to improve current capability but also responsibility for the future, potentially rethinking how leadership in general and their own leadership in particular must develop and change.

Is our focus on command based on the narrow view that only senior leaders can provide answers? No, we would vehemently reject such a conclusion. Wherever or however answers are sought and found, the point about command is that senior leaders are expected to take the ultimate responsibility. By doing so they create the 'space' within which those who work for them can operate. Fundamentally the decision is partly one of 'timing' and 'resonance'. Does it make sense and is it achievable? If the senior leader is viewed as an 'agent of change', then, when looking at new strategy initiatives for the organisation, these are two fundamentally important decision criteria. We can see that in the Battle of Britain case in respect of the 'big wing'. The ultimate point was not that big wings were a flawed concept of air war, but rather that in the prevailing circumstances the idea was 'before its time'.

11.7   So what now?

As we look across the breadth of leadership and associated thought we are confronted by the inescapable fact that getting the answer right is never as simple as it first seems to be. There are always more factors impacting on the challenges we seek to address than we realise, or can take into consideration, and our actions, as well as having intended consequences, always have unintended ones. The complexity of the challenges we face confuse us and we often get it wrong; indeed, in many cases there maybe no right answer, just a least bad one. Why does this all happen? It is driven by the fact that leadership is about people and how they change over time, and how that affects teams, organisations and even societies. Despite all the logic we can muster, people still have an annoying habit, some might say, of being unpredictable, irrational, emotional and doing the unexpected. But this is both the joy and frustration of leadership and working with individuals, teams and organisations. This irrepressibility and unpredictability of the human mind is the reason why the human race develops over time.

Despite the best efforts of leadership theorists, there is no single answer to the question about what is a good leader, what leaders should do, and how they can do it. The best we can do is suggest you consider the ideas in this book, which we think explain what is happening and show the evidence for what works in the real world. That is what leadership is about at its core – getting things done and making a difference, not developing theories. The theories are just a means to enable better practical leadership, and the theorists must never lose sight of that. We hope that is what you have gained from reading this book – that the myriad of ideas set out here and the practical success stories will give you a better understanding of what may be happening in leadership and thus help you be a better leader, or help others achieve that goal.

To be a good leader, and a leader for good, and by so doing have a beneficial effect on the lives of others is a significant responsibility, opportunity and contribution to humanity, and if this book has helped you to be better at it then all of our work will have been worthwhile. If you hold or aspire to a senior leadership role then strategic leadership represents a body of ideas and practice with which you will engage. Becoming more effective as a strategic leader is an important goal, and generally requires that we change the way that leadership is thought about and practised in organisations. If reading this book has stimulated thought along these lines it will have served its purpose.

Questions

1   Are there different leadership styles that are more appropriate for different types of problems or challenges?

2   Is 'unlearning' vital to enable change?

3   How do you think it is best to change someone's mind and get them to do things differently?

4   How can an organisation best achieve this for all those within it?

5   Short-term focus or long-term vision? Which is better to concentrate on as a leader?

6   Of what significance is the 'what's in it for me?' question?

7   Should you need any further change initiatives in an organisation where good change management is embedded?

Bibliography

Adair, J. (1973) *Action-centred leadership*, New York: McGraw-Hill.

Adams, J. L. (1987) *Conceptual Blockbusting*, Harmondsworth: Penguin.

Adams, J., Hayes, J. and Hopson, B. (1976) *Transitions: Understanding and Managing Personal Change*, Oxford: Martin Robertson.

Adorno, T. W. *et al.* (1950) *The Authoritarian Personality*, New York: Harper & Row.

Alexander, L. D. (1988) 'Successfully implementing strategic decisions', *Long Range Planning*, 18 (3).

Alvesson, M. and Willmott, H. (1992) 'On the idea of emancipation in management and organization studies', *Academy of Management Review*, 17 (3): 432–64.

Amabile, T. M. (1983) *The Social Psychology of Creativity*, New York: Springer Verlag.

Amabile, T. M. (1988) 'Creativity to organizational innovation', in K. Gronhaug and G. Kaufman (eds), *Innovation: A Cross-Disciplinary Perspective*, Oslo: Norwegian University Press.

Ansoff, I. and McDonnell, E. (1990) *Implanting Strategic Management*, New York: Prentice Hall.

Antonakis, J., Cianciolo, A. T. and Sternberg, R. J. (2004) *The Nature of Leadership*, Thousand Oaks, CA: Sage.

Argyris, C. (1962) *Integrating the Individual and the Organization*, New York: Wiley.

Argyris, C. (1982) *Reasoning, Learning and Action*, San Francisco: Jossey-Bass.

Argyris, C. (1985) *Strategy, Change and Defensive Routines*, New York: Pitman.

Argyris, C. (1990) *Overcoming Organizational Defences*, Boston, MA: Allyn & Bacon.

Argyris, C. (2004) 'Double loop learning and organizational change', in J. Boonstra (ed.), *The Dynamics of Organizational Change and Learning*, London: Wiley.

Argyris, C. and Schön, D. (1974) *Theory in Practice: Increasing Professional Effectiveness*, San Francisco: Jossey-Bass.

Argyris, C. and Schön, D. (1978) *Organizational Learning: A Theory of Action Perspective*, Reading, MA: Addison-Wesley.

Ariely, D. (2009) 'Predictably Irrational: The Hidden Forces which shape our decisions', *Harvard Business Review* 87(8): 78–84.

Bachrach, P. and Baratz, M. (1963) 'Decisions and nondecisions: an analytical framework', *American Political Science Review*, 57: 532–42.

Badaracco, J. L. (1997) *Defining Moments: When managers must choose between Right and Right*, Boston, MA.: Harvard Business School Press.

Badaracco, J. L. (2006) *Questions of Character*, Boston, MA.: Harvard Business School Press.

Badaracco, J. L. and Ellsworth, R. R. (1989) *Leadership and the Quest for Integrity*, Boston, MA.: Harvard Business School Press.

Barnatt, C. (1995) *Cyber Business: Mindsets for a Wired Age*, New York: Wiley.

Barnett, C. (2002) *The Collapse of British Power*, London: Pan Books.

Barnett, J. H. and Wilstead, W. D. (1988) *Management: Concepts and Cases*, Boston, MA: PWS-Kent.

Barry, D. (1997) 'Telling changes: from narrative family therapy to organizational change and development', *Journal of Organizational Change Management*, 10 (1): 30–46.

Bartlett, C. A. and Ghoshal, S. (1989) *Managing Across Borders: The Transnational Solution*, Boston, MA: Harvard Business School Press.

Bass, B. M. (1985) *Leadership and performance beyond expectations*, New York: Free Press.

Bass, B. M. and Avolio, B. J. (eds) (1994) *Improving organizational effectiveness through transformational leadership*, Thousand Oaks, CA.: Sage.

Bate, P. (1994) *Strategies for Cultural Change*. Oxford: Butterworth-Heinemann.

Bate, P., Bevan, H. and Robert, G. (2004) *Toward a Million Change Agents: A Review of Social Movements Literature*, London: The Modernisation Agency, Department of Health.

Beckhard, R. and Pritchard, W. (1992) *Changing the Essence*, San Francisco: Jossey-Bass.

Beer, M. and Nohria, N. (eds) (2000) *Breaking the Code of Change*, Boston, MA: Harvard Business School Press.

Beer, M., Eisenstat, R. and Spector, B. (1988) *The Critical Path to Change*, Boston, MA: Harvard Business School Press.

Belbin, M. (2010) *Management Teams: Why They Succeed or Fail*, London: Butterworth-Heinemann.

Bennis, W. (1984) 'The four competencies of leadership', *Training and Development Journal*, 38: 15.

Bennis, W. and Nanus, B. (1985) *Leadership: The Strategies for Taking Charge*, New York: Harper & Row.

Berger, L. A. and Berger, D. R. (2010) *The Talent Management Handbook*, 2nd edn, New York: McGraw-Hill.

Bessant, J., Francis, D., Sandie, M., Kaplinsky, R. and Brown, S. (2001) 'Developing agility in SMEs', *International Journal of Technology Management*, 22 (1–3).

Bignell, A., Peters, G. and Pym, C. (1977) *Catastrophic Failures*, Milton Keynes: Open University Press.

Birchall, D. W. (1993) 'Information technology survey', Working paper, Henley Management College.

Bloisi, W., Cook, C. and Hunsaker, P. L. (2007) *Management and Organizational Behaviour*, New York: McGraw Hill.

Bobbitt, P. (2002) *The Shield of Achilles*, London: Allen Lane.

Bok, S. (1984) *Secrets*, New York: Random House.

Bones, C. (1994) *The Self-Reliant Manager*, Henley-on-Thames: Routledge.

Boonstra, J. (ed.) (2004) *The Dynamics of Organizational Change and Learning*, London: Wiley.

Boyatsis, R. (1982) *The Competent Manager: Model for Effective Performance*, New York: John Wiley.

Bowers, J. L. (1970) *Managing the Resource Allocation Process*, Boston, MA: Harvard University Press.

Brooke, M. (1984) *Centralization and Autonomy*, London: Holt, Rinehart & Winston.

Bruch, H. and Sattelberger, T. (2001) 'The turnaround at Lufthansa', *Journal of Change Management*, 1 (4): 344–65.

Bryman, A. (1983) 'Organization studies and the concept of rationality', *Journal of Management Studies*, October: 391–408.

Bryman, A. (1987) *Leadership*, London: Heinemann.

Bryan, L. L. and Joyce, L. I. (2007) *Mobilizing Minds*, New York: McGraw-Hill.

Buckingham, M. (2005) *Now, Discover Your Strengths*, London: Pocket Books.

Bullock, R. J. and Batten, D. (1985) 'It's just a phase we are going through: a review and synthesis of OD phase analysis', *Group and Organization Studies*, 10 (December): 383–412.

Bunker, B. B. and Alban, B. T. (1996) *Large Group Interventions: Engaging the Whole System for Rapid Change*, San Francisco: Jossey-Bass.

Burke, W. W. and Litwin, G. H. (1992) 'A causal model of organizational performance and change', *Journal of Management*, 18 (3): 528–34.

Burnes, B. (2004) *Managing Change*, 4th edn, Harlow: Prentice Hall.

Burns, J. M. (1978) *Leadership*, New York: Harper & Row.

Burns, T. and Stalker, G. M. (1961) *The Management of Innovation*, London: Tavistock.

Caluwe, L. de and Vermaak, H. (2004) 'Thinking about change in different colours', in J. Boonstra (ed.), *The Dynamics of Organizational Change and Learning*, London: Wiley.

Campbell, D. (2005) 'Globalization', in W. Mobley and J. Welden (eds), *Advances in Global Leadership*, Oxford: Elsevier.

Campbell, A., Whitehead, J. and Finkelstein, S. (2009) 'Why good leaders make bad decisions', *Harvard Business Review*, 87 (2): 60–7.

Cannon. T. (1996) *Corporate Social Responsibility*, Harlow: FT Prentice Hall.

Capra, F. (1986) 'The concept of paradigm and paradigm shift', *Revision*, 9: 11–12.

Capra, F. (1996) *The Web of Life*, New York: Anchor Books.

Carnall, C. A. (1976) *Diagnosis for Change*, Henley: The Management College.

Carnall, C. A. (1982) *The Evaluation of Work Organization Change*, Farnborough: Gower.

Carnall, C. A. (1986) 'Toward a theory for the evaluation of organisational change', *Human Relations*, 39: 745–66.

Carnall, C. A. (2004) 'Change architecture', in J. Boonstra (ed.), *The Psychological Management of Organization Change*, London: Wiley.

Carnall, C. A. (2007) *Managing Change in Organizations*, 5th edn, Harlow: Prentice Hall.

Casse, P. (1979) *Training for the Cross-Cultural Mind*, Washington, DC: Society for Intercultural Education.

Castells, M. (1996) *The Rise of the Network Society*, Oxford: Basil Blackwell.

Chandler, A. (1962) *Strategy and Structure: Chapters in the History of the American Industrial Enterprise*, Cambridge, MA: MIT Press.

Charan, R., Drotter, S. and Noel, J. (2001) *The Leadership Pipeline: How to build the leadership-powered company*, San Francisco: Jossey-Bass.

Chartered Institute of Personnel Development (2003) *Reorganizing for Success: CEOs' and HR Managers' Perceptions*, London: CIPD.

Checkland, P. (1986) *Systems Thinking, Systems Practice*, Chichester, UK: Wiley.

Checkland, P. and Howell, S. (1998) *Information, Systems and Information Systems*, Chichester: Wiley.

Checkland, P. and Scholtes, J. (1995) *Soft Systems Methodology in Action*, Chichester: Wiley.

Child, J. (1984) *Organization*, London: Harper & Row.

Clark, J. (1995) *Managing Innovation and Change*, London: Sage.

Clark, K. B. and Fujimoto, T. (1991) *Product Development Performance*, Boston, MA: Harvard Business School Press.

Clark, T. and Clegg, S. (1998) *Changing Paradigms*, London: Harper Business.

Collins, J. (2001) *Good to Great: Why Some Companies Make the Leap … and Others Don't*, New York: HarperCollins.

Collins, J. and Porras, R. (1996) *Built to Last: Successful Habits of Visionary Companies*, New York: Random House.

Conger, S. and Kanugo, F. (1998) *Charismatic Leadership in Organisations*, London: Sage Publications.

Cooper, G. (1981) *Psychology and Managers*, London: Macmillan.

Cooper, G. and Hingley, P. (1985) *The Change Makers*, London: Harper & Row.

Cope, M. (1996) 'The use of stage events to mobilise change', Paper presented at the Academy of Human Resource Development, Minneapolis, MN.

Corporate Leadership Council, (2003) 'Succession Management Survey'.

Corporate Leadership Council (2004b) 'Driving Employee Performance and Retention through engagement'.

Corporate Leadership Council (2004c) 'Employee Engagement Survey'.

Corporate Leadership Council (2004d) 'Engaging the workforce'.

Corporate Leadership Council, (2005) ' High Potential Management Survey'.

Corporate Leadership Council (2006) 'Managing for High Performance and Retention'.

Cuilla, J. B. (2007) *The Ethics of Leadership,* Belmont CA.: Thomson Learning.

Cummings, T. G. and Huse, E. F. (1989) *Organization Development and Change,* 4th edn, Eagan, MN: West.

D'Aveni, R. A. (1994) *Hyper-competition,* New York: Free Press.

Dalla Costa, J. (1995) *The Ethical Imperative:Why Moral Leadership is Good business,* Boston, MA.: Perseus Publishing.

Dalton, M. (1959) *Men Who Manage,* New York: Wiley.

Darwin, J., Johnson, P. and McAuley, J. (2002) *Developing Strategies for Change,* Harlow: Prentice Hall.

Davis, G. and Marquis, C. (2005) 'Prospects for organization Theory in the 21st Century', *Organization Science* 16(2): 332–43.

Dawson, P. (2003) *Organizational Change: A Processual Approach,* London: Routledge.

Deal, T. E. and Kennedy, A. A. (1982) *Corporate Cultures,* Reading, MA: Addison-Wesley.

de Geus, A.P. (1997) *The Living Company,* Boston, MA: Longview Publishing.

Deloitte (2007) 'Talent Management', London.

Dionne, S. D., Yammarino, F. J., Attwater, L. F. and Spangler, W. D. (2004) 'Transformational Leadership and Team Performance', *Journal of Organisational Change Management* 17(2): 177–93.

Dotlich, D. L., Cairo, P. C. and Rhinesmith, S. (2006) *Heart, Head and Guts: How the World's Best Companies Develop Complete Leaders,* San Francisco, CA: Jossey Bass.

Doz, Y. L. and Prahalad, C. K. (1991) 'Managing DMNCs: a search for a new paradigm', *Strategic Management Journal,* 12: 4.

Drucker, P. (1999) *Management Challenges for the 21st Century,* New York: Harper & Row.

Dubin, R. and Spray, S. L. (1964) 'Executive behaviour and interaction', *Industrial Relations,* 3: 99–108.

Dweck, C. (2008) *Mindset,* New York: Ballantine Books.

Eagly, A. H. and Carli, L. L. (2004) 'Women and men as leaders', in Antonakis, J., Cianciolo, A. T. and Sternberg, R. J. (eds), *The Nature of Leadership,* Thousand Oaks, CA: Sage.

Ellinor, L. and Gerrard, G. (1998) *Dialogue,* New York: Wiley.

Emery, F. and Trist, E. L. (1963) *Organisational Choice,* London: Tavistock.

Emery, M. (2004) 'Open systems theory: implications for development and learning', in J. Boonstra (ed.), *The Dynamics of Organizational Change and Learning,* London: Wiley.

Emery, M. and Purser, R. E. (1996) *The Search Conference,* San Francisco: Jossey-Bass.

Ernst, D. (1994) 'Inter-firm networks and market structure', BRIE Research Paper, University of California, Berkeley.

Felix, E. (2000) 'Creating radical change: producer choice at the BBC', *Journal of Change Management,* 1 (1): 5–21.

Ferdows, K., Lewis, M. and Machuca, J. (2004) 'Rapid-fire fulfillment', *Harvard Business Review,* 82 (11): 104–10.

Ferguson, N. (2007) *The War of the Worlds: History's Age of Hatred,* London: Penguin.

Fiedler, F. E. (1967) *A Theory of Leadership Effectiveness,* New York: McGraw-Hill.

Fleishmann, E. (1953) 'The description of supervisory behavior', *Journal of Applied Psychology,* 37(1): 1–6.

Forrester, J. W. (1969) *Industrial Dynamics,* New York: Wiley.

Foucault, M. (1970) *The Order of Things,* London: Tavistock.

Foucault, M. (1972) *The Archaeology of Knowledge,* London: Routledge.

Foucault, M. (1977) *Discipline and Punish: The Birth of the Prison,* New York: Pantheon Books.

Foucault, M. (1980) *Power/Knowledge,* Brighton: Harvester.

Foucault, M. (1986) *The History of Sexuality*, Harmondsworth: Penguin.

Fraher, A. (2004) *A History of Group Study and Psychodynamic Organizations*, London: Free Association Books.

French, J. R. P. and Raven, B. (1959) 'The bases of social power' in Cartwright, D. (ed.), *Studies in Social Power*, Ann Arbor, MI: University of Michigan Press

French, W. L. and Bell, C. H. (1995) *Organization Development*, 4th edn, Englewood Cliffs, NJ: Prentice Hall.

Friedman, M. (1972) *Studies on the Quantity Theory of Money*, Chicago: University of Chicago Press.

Fritz, R. (1996) *Corporate Tides*, San Francisco: Berrett-Koehler.

Fromm, E. (1944) *The Fear of Freedom*, London: Routledge.

Fukuyama, F. (1995) *Trust: The Social Virtues and the Creation of Prosperity*, London: Hamish Hamilton.

Furze, D. and Gale, C. (1996) *Interpreting Management*, London: International Thomson Business Press.

Galbraith, J. W. (1977) *Organizational Design*, Reading, MA: Addison-Wesley.

Gardner, H. (2004) *Changing Minds*, Boston, MA: Harvard Business School Press.

Gardner, H. (2006) *Five Minds to the Future,* Boston,MA: Harvard University Press.

Ghosal, C. (2002) 'Saving the business without losing the company', *Harvard Business Review*, 80 (1): 37–46.

Ghosal, S., Gratton, L. and Rogan, R. (2002) *The Transformation of BP*, London: London Business School.

Gilbert, M. (2005) *Continue to Pester, Nag and Bite: Churchill's War Leadership*, London: Pimlico.

Gilbert, X. and Strebel, P. (1989) 'From innovation to outpacing', *Business Quarterly*, Summer: 19–22.

Gitman, L. J. and McDaniel, C. (1983) *The Future of Business*, London: Thomson.

Godard, J. (2004) *Organisations*, London: Routledge.

Goffee, R. and Jones, G. (1996) 'What holds the modern company together?', *Harvard Business Review*, November–December.

Goffee, R. and Jones, G. (2002) *The Character of the Corporation*, London: Harper & Row 2nd edition.

Goffee, R. and Jones, G. (2005) 'Managing Authenticity: The Paradox of Great Leadership', *Harvard Business Review*, 83(12): 86–94.

Goleman, D., Boyatzis, R. and McKee, A. (2001) 'Primal leadership: the hidden driver of great performance', *Harvard Business Review*, 79 (11): 42–51.

Goleman, D., Boyatzis, R. and McKee, A. (2002) *The New Leaders*, London: Little, Brown.

Gordon, W. J. (1961) *Synectics*, London: Harper & Row.

Gouillart, F. J. and Kelly, J. N. (1995) *Transforming the Organization*, New York: McGraw-Hill.

Gould, M. and Campbell, A. (1987) *Strategies and Styles: The Role of the Centre in Managing Diversified Corporations*, Oxford: Basil Blackwell.

Gratton, L. (2000) *Living Strategy*, Harlow: Prentice Hall.

Gratton, L. (2007) *Hotspots: Why some companies buzz with energy and innovation*, Harlow: FT Prentice Hall.

Graen, G. (1995) *New Frontiers of Leadership,* New York: Information Age Publishing.

Gravenhorst, K. B. and in't Veld, R. (2004) 'Interactions in Organizational Change: Using Influence Tactics to Initiate Change', in Boonstra, J.J. (ed.), *Dynamics of Organizational Change and Learning*, Chichester: John Wiley.

Greenly, D. and Carnall, C. A. (2001) 'Workshops as a technique for strategic change', *Journal of Change Management*, 2 (1): 33–46.

Greiner, L. (1972) 'Evolution and revolutions as organizations grow', *Harvard Business Review*, July–August.

Grey, C., (2008) *A very short, fairly interesting and reasonably cheap book about studying organisations,* 2nd edn, London: Sage.

Grint, K. (2005) *Leadership: Limits and Possibilities,* Basingstoke: Palgrave Macmillan.

Grint, K. (2008) *Leadership, Management and Command: Rethinking D Day,* Basingstoke: Palgrave Macmillan.

Grundy, T. (1994) *Strategic Learning in Action,* London: McGraw-Hill.

Grunig, R. and Kuhn, R. (2001) *Process-based Strategic Planning,* Berlin: Springer.

Habermas, J. (1974) *Theory and Practice,* London: Heinemann.

Hackman, J. R. and Oldham, G. R. (1976) 'Motivation through the design of work', *Organizational Behaviour and Human Performance,* 3: 12–35.

Hall, R. (1980) *Organization,* New York: Wiley.

Hamel, G. (1996) 'Strategy as revolution', *Harvard Business Review,* July–August.

Hamel, G. and Prahalad, C. K. (1994) *Competing for the Future,* Boston, MA: Harvard Business School Press.

Hampden-Turner, C. (1996) *Charting the Corporate Mind,* London: Basil Blackwell.

Handfield, R. B. (1995) *Re-engineering for Time-based Competition,* London: Quorum Books.

Handy, C. (1983) *Taking Stock,* London: BBC.

Handy, C. (1984) *Organizations,* 2nd edn, Harmondsworth: Penguin.

Hannan, M. T. and Freeman, J. (1983) *Organizational Ecology,* Boston, MA: Harvard University Press.

Hansen, M. T. and van Oetinger, B. (2001) 'Introducing T-shaped managers: knowledge management's next generation', *Harvard Business Review,* 79 (3), March: 107–16.

Harre, R. (1984) *The Philosophies of Science,* Oxford University Press.

Hart, A. (1997) *Team Midwifery,* Brighton Health Care NHS Trust Research Report.

Haslam, S. A. (2004) *Psychology in Organisations,* London: Sage.

Hastings, C. (1993) *The New Organization,* London: McGraw-Hill.

Haxel, C. (2003) 'Foreword' in Mertins, K., Heisig, P. and Vorbeck, J. (eds), *Knowledge Management,* Berlin: Springer

Heifetz, R. (1994) *Leadership Without Easy Answers,* Boston, MA: Harvard University Press.

Hellreigel, D., Slocum, J. W. and Woodman, R. W. (1986) *Organizational Behaviour,* 4th edn, Eagan, MN: West.

Hersey, P. and Blanchard, K. (1988) *Organizational Behaviour,* New York: Prentice Hall.

Hersey, P., Blanchard, K. and Johnson, D. (2000) *Management of Organizational Behavior: Leading Human Resources,* 8th edn, Upper Saddle River, NJ: Prentice Hall.

Hesketh, A. and Fleetwood, S. (2006) *The Performance of HR: Toward a new Meta Theory* Cambridge: Cambridge University Press.

Hewitt (2005/7) 'Top Company for Leaders 2005/7'.

Hickson, D. J., Butler, R. J., Cray, D., Mallory, G. R. and Wilson, D. C. (1986) *Top Decisions,* Oxford: Basil Blackwell.

Higgs, M. (2003) 'How can we make sense of leadership in the 21st century?', *Leadership and Organizational Development Journal,* 24 (5): 27384.

Higgs, M. (2009) 'The good, the bad and the ugly: leadership and narcissism', *Journal of Change Management,* 9 (2): 165–78.

Higgs, M. and Dulewicz, V. (2003) Leadership: The long line, Henley Management College Paper, Henley-on-Thames, Oxon.

Higgs, M. and Rowland, D. (2001) 'Developing change leaders', *Journal of Change Management,* 2 (1): 47–66.

Higgs, M. and Rowland, D. (2005) 'All changes great and small: exploring approaches to change and its leadership', *Journal of Change Management,* 5 (2), June: 121–52.

Hofstede, G. (1968) *Culture's Consequences,* Harmondsworth: Penguin.

Hogan, R. (2003) Hogan Development Survey, Hogan Assessment Systems.

Hogan, R. and Hogan, J. (2001) 'Assessing leadership:A view from the dark side', *Journal of Assessment and Selection*, 9(1): 40–51.

Homer-Dixon, P. (2000) *Ingenuity*, New York: Alfred Knopf.

Hooper, A. and Potter, J. (2001) *Intelligent Leadership*, London, Random House.

Horne, J. H. and Lupton, T. (1965) 'The work activities of middle managers', *Journal of Management Studies*, 12: 14–33.

Hosmer, L. T. (1987) *The Ethics of Management*, Homeward, IL: Richard D. Irwin.

House, R. J. (1971) 'A Path-Goal theory of leadership', *Administrative Science Quarterly*, 16: 321–38.

House, R. J. (1996) 'Path-goal theory of leadership: Lessons, legacy and a reformulated theory', *Leadership Quarterly*, vol. 7(2): 32352.

Hunt, J. G. (1991) *Leadership: A new synthesis*, Newbury Park, CA: Sage.

Hurst, D. K. (1995) *Crisis and Renewal*, Cambridge, MA: Harvard Business School Press.

Itami, H. (1987) *Mobilizing Invisible Assets*, Cambridge, MA: Harvard University Press.

Jacobs, R. W. (1994) *Real Time Strategic Change*, San Francisco: Berrett-Koehler.

James, K. T., Mann, J. and Creasy, J. (2007) 'Leaders as Lead Learners', *Management Learning* vol. 38(1):79–94.

Jameson, B. J. (1984) 'The reception of politics into management development', Unpublished PhD thesis, Henley–Brunel University.

Janis, I. (1972) *Victims of Groupthink*, New York: Houghton Mifflin.

Janis, I. and Mann, F. (1976) *Decision-making*, New York: Free Press.

Janis, I. L. (1989) *Crucial Decisions*, New York: Free Press.

Jaques, E. (1952) *The Changing Culture of a Factory*, New York: Dryden Press.

Jaques, E. (1963) *Equitable Payment,* London: William Heineman

Johnson, G. (1987) *Strategic Change and the Management Process*, Oxford: Basil Blackwell.

Johnson, G. (1988) 'Rethinking incrementalism', *Strategic Management Journal*, 9 (1): 75–91.

Juch, B. (1983) *Personal Development*, Chichester, UK: Wiley.

Judson, A. (1990) *Making Strategy Happen*, London: Basil Blackwell.

Kanter, R. (1983) *The Change Masters*, London: George Allen & Unwin.

Kanter, R., Stein, B. A. and Jick, T. D. (1992)   *The Challenge of Organizational Change*, New York: The Free Press.

Kaplan, R. S. and Norton, D. P. (1996) *The Balanced Scorecard: Turning Strategy into Action*, Boston, MA: Harvard Business School Press.

Katzenbach, J. R. and Smith, D. K. (2005) *The Wisdom of Teams*, Boston, MA: Harvard Business School Press.

Kay, J. (1993) *Foundations of Corporate Success*, Oxford University Press.

Keeley, S. (1988) 'Managing change at ABF', Unpublished MBA dissertation, Henley–Brunel University.

Kelman, S. (2005) *Unleashing Change*, Washington, DC: The Brookings Institution Press.

Kets de Vries, M. F. R. (1980) *Organizational Paradoxes*, London: Tavistock.

Kets de Vries, M. F. R. (1993) *Leaders, Fools and Imposters: Essays on the Psychology of Leadership*, San Francisco: Jossey Bass.

Kets de Vries, M. F. R. and Miller, D. (1984) *The Neurotic Organization*, New York: Jossey-Bass.

Kingston, W. J. (1977) *Innovation*, London: John Calder.

Kirkpatrick, D. (1985) *How to Manage Change Effectively*, New York: Jossey-Bass.

Kirkpatrick, S. A. and Locke, E. A. (1991) 'Leadership: Do traits matter?' *Academy of Management Journal* 5:(1):48–60.

Kirton, M. J. (1988) 'Adaptors and innovators', in K. Grønhaug and J. Kaufman (eds), *Innovation: A Cross-Disciplinary Perspective*, Oslo: Norwegian University Press.

Kissinger, H. (1979) *The White House Years*, London: Weidenfeld & Nicolson.

Klein, G. (1998) *The Sources of Power*, Boston, MA: MIT Press.

Knights, D. and Morgan, G. (1991) 'Corporate strategy, organizations and subjectivity: a critique', *Organization Studies*, 12. (2): 251–73.

Kolb, D. A. (1984) *Experimental Learning*, Upper Saddle River, NJ: Prentice Hall.

Kotter, J. P. (1978) *Organizational Dynamics*, Reading, MA: Addison-Wesley.

Kotter, J. P. (1988) *The Leadership Factor*, New York: Free Press.

Kotter, J. P. (1990) *A Force for Change: How leadership differs from Management*, New York: The Free Press.

Kotter, J. P. (1996) *Leading Change*, Boston, MA: Harvard Business School Press.

Kotter, J. P. and Hesketh, J. L. (1992) *Corporate Culture and Performance*, New York: Free Press.

Kouzes, J. M. and Posner, B. Z. (1987) *The Leadership Challenge,* New York: Wiley.

Kouzes, J. M. and Posner, B. Z. (2009) 'Forethought: "To Lead, Create a Shared Vision"', *Harvard Business Review*, 87 (1): 20–1.

Kranz, G. (2000) *Failure is not an option,* New York: Berkley Books.

Landes, D. (1967) *Unbound Prometheus*, Cambridge University Press.

Lawler, E. E. (1978) *Motivation and the Work Organization*, Monterey, CA: Brooks Cole.

Lawler, E. E. and Bachrach, S. B. (1986) *Power and Politics in Organizations*, New York: Jossey-Bass.

Lawrence, P. R. and Dyer, D. (1983) *Renewing American Industry*, New York: Free Press.

Lawrence, P. R. and Lorsch, J. (1967) *Organization and Environment*, New York: Richard D. Irwin.

Lee, R. and Lawrence, P. (1985) *Organizational Behaviour: Politics at Work*, London: Hutchinson.

Lehrer, J. (2009) *The Decisive Moment*, Edinburgh: Canongate.

Leroy, F. and Ramansanto, B. (1997) 'The cognitive and behavioural elements of organizational learning in a merger', *Journal of Management Studies*, 34 (6): 871–94.

Lewin, K. (1948[1947]) 'Action research and minority problems', in G. W. Lewin and G. W. Allport (eds), (1948) *Resolving Social Conflict*, London: Harper & Row.

Liker, J. K. (2003) *The Toyota Way*, New York: McGraw-Hill.

Likert, R. (1961) *New Patterns of Management*, New York: McGraw-Hill.

Lindblom, C. (1959) 'The science of muddling through', *Public Administration Review*, 19 (Spring): 82–8.

Linley, A., Willars, J. and Buswas-Diener, R. (2010) *The Strengths Book*, Capp Press.

Linsky, M. and Heifetz, R. (2002) *Leadership on the Line,* Boston, MA: Harvard Business School Press.

Lipniack, J. and Stamps, J. (1994) *The Age of the Network*, New York: Wiley.

Loomis, C. (2006) 'The Tragedy of General Motors', *Fortune*, 20 February 2006.

Lorange, P. and Nelson, G. (1987) *Strategic Control*, San Francisco: West.

Lorenz, A. (1998) 'BP boss drives change through the pipeline', *The Sunday Times*, 26 April.

Lorsch, J. (1970) 'Introduction to the structural design of organizations', in P. R. Lawrence and J. Lorsch (eds), *Organizational Structure and Design*, New York: Irwin-Dorsey.

Lorsch, J. (1986) 'Managing culture: the invisible barrier to strategic change', *California Management Review*, 28 (2): 95–109.

Lukes, S. (1974) *Power: A Radical View*, London: Macmillan.

Lynch, R. (2000) *Corporate Strategy*, 2nd edn, Harlow: Prentice Hall.

Maccoby, M. (2004) *The Productive Narcissist: The Promise and Peril of Visionary Leadership*, New York: Broadway Books.

Macpherson, C. (1962) *The Political Theory of Possessive Individualism*, Oxford: Clarendon Press.

Mankins, M. C. and Steele, R. (2005) 'Turning great strategy into great performance', *Harvard Business Review*, 83 (7).

Mansfield, R. (1986) *Company Strategy and Organizational Design*, London: Croom Helm.

Mant, A. (1983) *Leaders We Deserve*, Oxford: Martin Robertson.

Manzoni, M. (2000) 'The Leadership Performance Puzzle', Paper presented to E-HR 2000 Conference, London, 25–28 September.

March, J.G. (1994) *Primer on Decision-Making: How Decisions are made,* New York: Free Press

March, J. G. and Olsen, J. P. (1976) *Ambiguity and Choice in Organizations,* Bergen: Universitetsforlaget.

March, J. G. and Simon, H. A. (1993) *Organizations,* New York: Wiley.Margerison, C.J. and McCann, D (1989) *Team Management: Practical New Approaches,* Bradford: Management Books Ltd.

Margerison, C. J. and McCann, T. (1989) *Team Management: Practical New Approaches,* New York: McGraw-Hill.

Markides, C. (2000) *All the Right Moves: A Guide to Crafting Breakthrough Strategy,* Boston, MA: Harvard Business School Press.

Martin, J. (1995) *The Great Transition,* New York: American Management Association.

Masuch, M. (1983) 'Vicious circles in organisations', *ASQ,* 30 (1): 46–62.

May, M. E. (2007) *The Elegant Solution: Toyota's Formula for Mastering Innovation,* London: Simon & Schuster.

McCall, D. Jr., Lombardo, M. and Morrison, A. (1988) *The Lessons of Experience: How successful executives develop on the job,* New York: Lexington Books.

McGrath, R. G. and MacMillan, I. C. (2000) *The Entrepreneurial Mindset,* Boston, MA: Harvard Business School Press.

McGregor, D. (1960) *The Human Side of Enterprise,* New York: McGraw-Hill.

Meadows, D. H. (1972) *Limits to Growth,* New York: Universe Publications.

Merkle, J. (1980) *Management and Ideology,* San Francisco: University of California Press.

Mertins, K., Heisig, P. and Vorbeck, J. (2003) 'Introduction' in Mertins, K., Heisig, P. and Vorbeck, J. *Knowledge Management,* Berlin: Springer.

Merton, R. K. (1940) 'Bureaucratic structure and personality', *Social Forces,* 18: 560–8.

Milborrow, G. (1993) 'Management development to the year 2000', Paper presented to the Management Development Conference, Henley Management College, Henley, UK, 20 October.

Miles, R. H. (2010) 'Accelerating corporate formations', *Harvard Business Review,* January/February: 69–75.

Miller, D. (1990) *The Icarus Paradox,* New York: HarperCollins.

Miller, D. and Kets de Vries, M. F. R. (1984) *The Neurotic Organization,* New York: Jossey-Bass.

Miller, D. and Kets de Vries, M. F. R. (n.d.) Unpublished communication – draft working paper.

Mintzberg, H. (1973) *The Nature of Managerial Work,* New York: Harper & Row.

Mintzberg, H. (1990) *The Strategy Process,* Harlow: Prentice Hall.

Mintzberg, H. (1994) *The Rise and Fall of Strategic Planning,* Englewood Cliffs, NJ: Prentice Hall.

Mirvis, P. H. and Marks, M. L. (1992) *Managing the Merger,* Englewood Cliffs, NJ: Prentice Hall.

Moss Kanter, R. (2001) *Evolve: Succeeding in the Digital Culture of Tomorrow,* Boston, MA: Harvard Business School Press.

Mulligan, M. (2009) 'Inditex chief tailors its strategy', *Financial Times,* 26 March.

Mumford, M.D., Zacarro, S.J., Harding, F.D., Jacobs, T.O. and Fleishmann, E.A. (2000) 'Leadership skills for a changing world: Solving complex social problems', *Leadership Quarterly,* 11(1):11–35.

Munch, B. (2001) 'Changing a culture of face time', *Harvard Business Review,* 79 (10): 125–32.

Muth, J. (2011) *Command Culture,* Denton, TX: University of Texas Press.

Myerson, D. E. (2001) 'Radical change, the quiet way', *Harvard Business Review,* 79 (9): 92–104.

Naisbitt, J. (1982) *Megatrends: Ten new directions transforming our lives,* Los Angeles: Warner Books.

Naisbitt, J. (1997) *Megatrends Asia,* New York: Simon Schuster.

Newmann, J. E., Holti, R. and Standing, H. (1995) *Changing Everything at Once,* London: Tavistock Institute.

Nohria, N. and Berkeley, J. (1995) 'The virtual organization', in C. Heckscher and A. Donnellon (eds), *The Post-Bureaucratic Organization,* Thousand Oaks, CA: Sage.

Nohria, N., Joyce, W. and Robertson, B. (2003) *What really works: The 4+2 formula for sustained business success,* New York: Harper Business.

Nonaka, N. and Takeuchi, H. (1995) *The Knowledge Creating Company,* Oxford: Oxford University Press.

Nonaka, N., Toyama, R. and Hirata T. (2008) *Managing Flow* Basingstoke: Palgrave Macmillan.

Norburn, D. (1988) 'The chief executive: a breed apart', *Strategic Management Journal,* 10: 1–15.

Norlton, G. (1998) 'Creating an opportunity for positive change', MBA dissertation, Henley.

Northouse, P. G. (2004) *Leadership: Theory and Practice,* London: Sage.

Ohmae, K. (1982) *The Mind of the Strategist,* New York: McGraw-Hill.

Orgland, M. Y. (1997) *Initiating, Managing and Sustaining Strategic Change,* London: Macmillan.

Ouchi, W. (1981) *Theory Z,* Reading, MA: Addison-Wesley.

Overy, R. (2010) *The Battle of Britain,* Harmondsworth: Penguin.

Padilla, A., Hogan, R. and Kaiser, R. B. (2007) 'The toxic triangle: destructive leaders, susceptible followers and conducive environments', *Leadership Quarterly,* 18 (3): 176–94.

Parker, M. (2000) *Organizational Culture and Identity,* London: Sage.

Parker Follett, M. ([1942]2003) *Dynamic Administration,* New York: Harper Brothers.

Parry-Jones, R. (1996) 'A vision for the future', *European Business Journal,* Summer: 47–55.

Pascale, R. (1990) *Managing on the Edge,* Harmondsworth: Penguin.

Peters, T. and Austin, N. (1985) *A Passion for Excellence,* New York: Random House.

Peters, T. and Waterman, R. H. (1982) *In Search of Excellence,* New York: Harper & Row.

Pettigrew, A. (1973) *The Politics of Organizational Decision-Making,* London: Tavistock.

Pettigrew, A. (1985) *The Awakening Giant: Continuity and Change in ICI,* Oxford: Basil Blackwell.

Pfeffer, J. (1981) *Power in Organizations,* New York: Pitman.

Pfeffer, J. (1998) *The Human Equation,* Boston, MA: Harvard Business School Press.

Piercy, N. F. (2004) *Market-Led Strategic Change,* 2nd edn, Oxford: Heinemann-Butterworth.

Piore, M. and Sable, C. (1984) *The Second Industrial Divide,* New York: Basic Books.

Porter, L. W. and Lawler, E. E. (1968) *Managerial Attitudes and Performance,* Homewood, IL: Richard Irwin.

Porter, M. (1985) *Competitive Advantage: Creating and Sustaining Superior Performance,* New York: Free Press.

Prahalad, C. K. and Hamel, G. (1990) 'The core competence of the corporation', *Harvard Business Review,* 68 (3): 79–91.

Pressman, J. L. and Wildavsky, A. (1973) *Implementation,* San Francisco: University of California Press.

Prokesch, S. (2009) 'How GE teaches teams to lead change', *Harvard Business Review,* 87 (1): 99–106.

Putnam, R. W. and Thomas, D. (1988) 'Organizational action map: pay and performance', in R. Putnam (ed.), 'Mapping organizational defense routines', Mimeo, Harvard Graduate School of Education.

Quinn, J. B. (1992) *The Intelligent Enterprise,* New York: Free Press.

Quinn, R. A. and Brockbank, W. (2006) 'The development of H R professionals at BAe Systems', *Human Resources Management Journal,* 45(3):77–94.

Quinn Mills, D. (1991) *The Cluster Organisation*, New York: Wiley.

Raphael, A. (1996) *The Ultimate Risk*, London: Bantam.

Rawls, J. (1999) *A Theory of Justice*, Cambridge, MA: Belknap Press.

Ray, J. (2000) *The Battle of Britain: Dowding and the First Victory*, London: Cassell Books.

Revans, R. (1972) *Hospitals, Communication, Choice and Change*, London: Tavistock.

Rickards, T. (1985) *Stimulating Innovation*, London: Frances Pinter.

Rieley, J. B. (2001) *Gaming the System*, Harlow: Financial Times/Prentice Hall.

Riffenburgh, B. (2004) *Nimrod*, London: Bloomsbury.

Rifkin, J. (1995) *The End of Work: The Decline of the Global Labor Force and the Dawn of the Post-Market Era*, New York: Putnam.

Rittel, H. W. J. and Webber, M. M., (1973) 'Dilemmas in a General Theory of Planning', *Policy Sciences* 4(2):155–69.

Roberto, M. (2013) *Why Great Leaders Don't Take Yes for an Answer*, Upper Saddle River, NJ: Pearson.

Roethlisberger, F. and Dickson, W. J. (1939) *Management and the Worker*, New York: Wiley.

Roffey Park (2008) *Generations and Leadership; Research report,* Horsham: Roffey Park Institute.

Rogan, M. (2002) *The Transformation of BP*, London: London Business School.

Rogers, E. M. (1986) *Diffusion of Innovations*, 1st edn, New York: Free Press.

Rose, M. (1975) *Industrial Behaviour: Theoretical Development since Taylor*, London: Allen Lane.

Rowland, D. and Higgs, M. (2008) *Sustaining Change: Leadership That Works*, Chichester, UK: Wiley.

Roy, D. (1954) 'Efficiency and the fox', in 'Formal intergroup relations in a piece-work machine shop', *American Journal of Sociology*, 60 (33): 255–66.

Rubinstein, M. F. and Furstenberg, I. R. (1999) *The Minding Organization*, New York: Wiley.

Schattschneider, E. E. (1960) *The Semisovereign People: A Realist's View of Democracy in America*, New York: Rinehart and Winston.

Schein, E. (1965) *Organizational Psychology*, New York: Prentice Hall.

Schein, E. (1996) *Organizational Culture and Leadership*, 3rd edn, San Francisco: Jossey-Bass.

Schwartz, H. and Davis, S. (1981) 'Matching corporate culture and business strategy', *Organizational Dynamics*, 10: 30–48.

Scholl, W. and Heisig, P. (2003) 'Delphi Study on the Future of Knowledge Management', in Mertins, K., Heisig, P. and Vorbeck, J. (eds), *Knowledge Management*, Berlin: Springer.

Scott, W. R. (1981) *Organizations: Rational, Natural and Open Systems*, New York: Prentice Hall.

Senge, P. (1990) *The Fifth Discipline*, London: Random House.

Simon, H. A. (1957) *Administrative Behaviour*, New York: Free Press.

Smale, G. (1998) *Managing Change Through Innovation*, London: The Stationery Office.

Snowden, D. J. and Boone, M. E. (2007) 'A Leaders framework for Decision-Making' *Harvard Business Review,* 85(10): 63–71.

Sofer, C. (1973) *Organizations in Theory and Practice*, London: Heinemann Education.

Spear, S. J. (2004) 'Learning to lead at Toyota', *Harvard Business Review*, 82 (5): 78–91.

Stacey, R. (1993) *Strategic Thinking and Organisational Dynamics*, Harlow: FT Prentice Hall.

Stacey, R. (1996) *Complexity and Creativity in Organizations*, San Francisco: Berrett-Koehler.

Stacey, R. (2003) *Strategic Management and Organisational Dynamics*, Harlow: Prentice Hall.

Stalk, G. and Hout, T. (1990) *Competing Against Time*, New York: Free Press.

Steare, R. (2008) *Ethicability: How to decide what's right and find the courage to stick to it,* London: Roger Steare Ltd.

Steers, R. M. and Porter, L. (1979) *Motivation and Work Behaviour*, New York: McGraw-Hill.

Stewart, R. (1977) *Managers and their Jobs*, London: Macmillan.

Stewart, R. (1982) *Choices for the Manager*, London: McGraw-Hill.

Stewart, T. and Stewart, J. R. (2001) *The Wealth of Knowledge*, New York: Crown Business.

Stewart, V. and Chadwick, V. (1987) *Changing Trains: Messages for Management from the Scot Rail Challenge*, Newton Abbot: David & Charles.

Stogdill, R. M. (1948) 'Personal factors associated with leadership: A survey of the literature', *Journal of Psychology*, 25(1): 35–71.

Stogdill, R. M. (1974) *Handbook of Leadership,* New York: Free Press.

Strauss, G. (1963) 'Tactics of lateral relationships: the purchasing agent', *Administrative Science Quarterly*, 7: 161–86.

Strauss, G. (1976) 'Organizational development', in R. Dubin (ed.), *Handbook of Work, Organization and Society*, New York: Rand McNally.

Strebel, P. (ed.) (2000) *Focused Energy*, Chichester, UK: Wiley.

Sucher, S. J. (2007) *The Moral Leader*, London: Routledge.

Sumida, J. T., (1997) *Professors of War: Inventing Strategy and Teaching Command*, Baltimore: John Hopkins University Press.

Sweet, T. and Heritage, V. (2000) 'How managers gain commitment to change', *Journal of Change Management*, 1 (2): 164–78.

Takeuchi, H., Osono, E. and Shimizu, N. (2008) 'The contradictions that drive Toyota's success', *Harvard Business Review*, 86 (6): 96–105.

Tannenbaum, A. and Schmidt, W. G. (1973) 'How to choose a leadership pattern', *Harvard Business Review*, 51(3):162–75.

Tapscott, D. and Caston, A. (1993) *Paradigm Shift: The New Promise of IT*, New York: McGraw-Hill.

Taylor, B. (1983) 'Turnaround – recovery and growth', *Journal of General Management*, 8 (2): 32–8.

Thornbury, J. (1999) 'KPMG: revitalising culture through values', *Business Strategy Review*, 10 (4): 1–15.

Tichy, N. and Sherman, S. (1995) *Control Your Destiny*, London: HarperCollins.

Tiplady, R. (2006) 'Zara: Taking the Lead in Fast-Fashion', *Business Week,* 4 April.

Tooze, A. (2007) *The Wages of Destruction*, London: Penguin Books.

Trist, E., Higgin, C., Murray, H. and Pollack, A. (1963) *Organizational Choice*, London: Tavistock.

Trompenaars, F. and Hampden-Turner, C. (2007) *Riding the Waves of Culture*, 2nd edn, London: Nicolas Brealey.

Tuckman, W. (1965) 'Development sequence in small groups', *Psychological Bulletin*, 63: 384–99.

Turner, B. (1986) 'Sociological aspects of organizational symbolism', *Organization Studies*, 7 (2): 101–17.

Ulrich, D. and Beatty, R. (2001) 'From Partners to Players: Extending the HR Playing Field', *Human Resources Management*, 40 (4): 293–307.

Ulrich, D. and Brockbank, W. (2005) *The HR Value Proposition*, Boston, MA: Harvard Business School Publishing.

Ulrich, D. and Brockbank, W. (2007) 'Building a Leadership Brand', *Harvard Business Review*, July–Aug.

Ulrich, D. and Smallwood, N. (2003) *How Leaders build Value*, New Jersey: John Wiley.

Van der Erve, M. (1994) *Evolution Management*, Oxford: Butterworth-Heinemann.

Vince, R. (1996) *Managing Change*, Bristol: Policy Press.

Vroom, V. (1964) *Work and Motivation*, New York: John Wiley.

Vroom, V. and Jago, A.G. (1988) *The new leadership*: *Managing participation in organizations*, Englewood Cliffs, NJ: Prentice Hall.

Vroom, V. and Yetton, P. W. (1973) *Leadership and Decision-Making*, Pittsburgh, PA: University of Pittsburgh Press.

Wall, T. D. and Wood, S. J. (2005) 'The impact of human resource and operational management practices on company productivity: a longitudinal study', *Personnel Psychology* 61 (3): 467–501.

Walton, R. E. (1985) 'From control to commitment: transforming work-force management in the USA', in K. Clark, R. H. Hayes and C. Lorenz (eds), *The Uneasy Alliance: Managing the Productivity–Technology Dilemma*, Boston, MA: Harvard Business School Publishing.

Watkin, J. W. N. (1970) 'Imperfect rationality', in R. Borger and F. Coffi (eds), *Explanation in the Behavioural Sciences*, Cambridge University Press.

Watson, G. H. (1993) *Strategic Bench-marking*, New York: Wiley.

Weick, K. E. (1979) *The Social Psychology of Organizing*, New York: Addison-Wesley.

Weick, K. E. (1995) *Sensemaking in Organizations*, Thousand Oaks, CA: Sage.

Welch, J. and Welch, S. (2009) *Winning: The Ultimate Business How To Book*, New York: Harper Collins.

Western, S. (2007) *Leadership: A Critical Text*, London: Sage.

Wheatley, M. J. (1992) *Leadership and the New Science*, San Francisco: Berrett-Koehler.

Wheatley, M. J. (1996) *A Simple Way*, San Francisco: Berrett-Koehler.

Whitehead, T. N. (1936) *Leadership in a Free Society*, London: Oxford University Press.

Whittington, R. (2001) *What Is Strategy – And Does It Matter?*, 2nd edn, London: Thomson Learning.

Wiener, M. J. (1981) *English Culture and the Decline of the Industrial Spirit, 1850–1980*, Harmondsworth: Penguin.

Wierdsma, A. (2004) 'Beyond Implementation: Co-creation in Change and Development', in Boonstra, J. J. (ed.), *Dynamics of Organizational Change and Learning*, Chichester: John Wiley.

Wilensky, H. (1967) *Organizational Intelligence*, New York: Basic Books.

Williamson, O. E. (1983) *Market and Hierarchies*, New York: Free Press.

Willmott, H. C. (1984) 'Images and Ideals of Managerial Work', *Journal of Management Studies*, 21 (3): 347–68.

Wills, G. (1991) *Lincoln at Gettysburg: The words that remade America*, New York: Simon & Schuster.

Wilson, D. C. (1992) *A Strategy for Change*, London: Routledge.

Wohlstetter, R. (1962) *Pearl Harbor: Warning and Decision*, Stanford, CA: Stanford University Press.

Womack, J. R. and Jones, D. T. (2003) *Lean Thinking* London: Simon & Schuster UK.

Woodward, H. and Buchholz, S. (1987) *Aftershock: Helping People Through Corporate Change* (ed. K. Hess), New York: Wiley.

Woodward, J. (1965) *Industrial Organization: Theory and Practice*, London: Oxford University Press.

Yukl, G. (2002) *Leadership in Organisations*, Harlow: Prentice-Hall.

Zinn, H. (1980) *A People's History of the United States*, London: Longman.

Index

Notes: **bold type** = extended discussion or term highlighted in text; f = figure; n = footnote; t = table.